Southern Living

Illustrated
Cookbook

Lillian Bertram Marshall

Library of Congress Catalog Number: 76-22383
ISBN: 0-8487-0419-3
Manufactured in the United States of America
First Printing 1976

Southern Living Illustrated Cookbook

Editors: Grace Hodges, Martha R. Fazio
Illustrations: Carol Middleton
Photographs: Taylor Lewis

This work is dedicated in loving memory to the late
Nina and Fred Peters,
who made me believe I could do it.

Contents

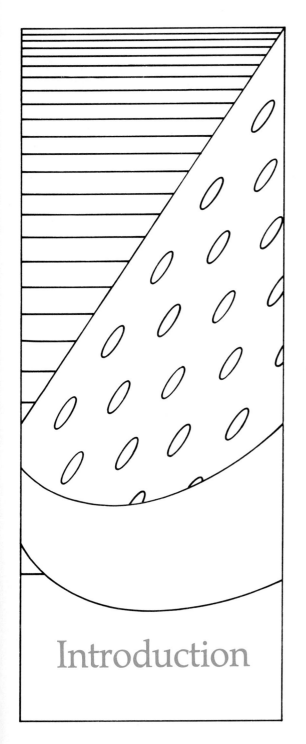

Introduction

If some remarkable time machine should deliver the fabled Auguste Escoffier back to earth at this moment and deposit him before a glossy push-button range, it is doubtful whether he could prepare his own breakfast. The facts of life have altered, and science, with achievements both marvelous and dubious, has given us things with which to work that were unknown a generation or two ago.

Escoffier died in 1935 at the age of 89. When he was in the busiest years of his professional life, the electric mixer was in the infancy of its development, and the blender had not arrived at all. Given the opportunity, would the good Auguste have embraced the convenience of culinary equipment as we know it and thus deprived subsequent missionaries of the classic French cuisine of the copper bowl-wire whisk syndrome? Interesting conjecture.

The bygone chef, his genius notwithstanding, could include green peas in his menus for only a few short weeks in springtime. We have a box of fresh frozen peas as close as the freezer section of our refrigerator. Our ovens have thermostats, and some of them clean themselves. Our refrigerators and freezers have freed us from daily forays to the green grocer's and the butcher's.

It is noteworthy that the new breed of French chef is beginning to pay attention to an older classic cuisine—that of the Chinese—finding beauty in its simple sauces and elegance in its presentation.

None of the foregoing is intended to downgrade the classic cooking of any country. After all, we are devoted to our own "classics," from New England clam chowder to Creole gumbo. And we are conscious of the fact that nearly all American "classics" are in some way put-togethers, or derivatives, or downright steals from other cuisines. With respect to food, we bow reverently to all points of the compass. We have gourmet groups and enormous collections of cookbooks to prove it.

This book is written for the aspiring cook only recently come to the discipline as well as for the accomplished cook who wants to refine his or her techniques. By aspiring cook, we mean not only the bride; we include the groom, the confirmed bachelor of any gender, and the middle-aged orphan.

"If you can read, you can cook." I quote myself a lot. What I mean to say is, "If you can read and have a consuming interest (no pun intended), you can make cooking an art. Without that spark, you can at least make cooking a craft."

An open-minded would-be cook may even find in these pages that elusive spark he needs to make his cooking an art, a reflection of his own personal attitude and life-style.

Our foundation material will tell you about ingredients and their functions. With how-to-do-it pictures, charts, and other practicalities, we hope to give you cooking lessons in your own kitchen.

You will learn how to read a recipe and find help on menu construction. You will find many of your cooking queries answered in a glossary of culinary terms as well as in question-and-answer sections following many chapters.

There is no mystery involved in cooking, no magic at all. Common sense, persistence, eagerness—these are the ingredients you must bring to this book. And there is one more quality you will need to make cooking your own recreational art form: a sense of humor. Without it you will remain a timorous amateur; with it you will become an intrepid swashbuckler at the range.

After you have worked for a while with the basic techniques, you will come to the instructions for boning a chicken breast. Face the possibility that the first couple you do may look like hash, and be cheerful as you leaf through for a Chinese stir-fry recipe instead of the Chicken Kiev you have had in mind. You will soon find it is possible to be dead serious as a cook and still have the time of your life in the kitchen.

One thing this book won't do for you is turn you into a "gourmet cook." The reason is that the word "gourmet" has lost its meaning through misuse. Cooks are like garage mechanics, C.P.A.s, or brain surgeons: some are better than others. Some are superb. Our goal is to make you one of the best cooks, to loosen up your thinking about food preparation, and to help you discover what cooking really is: fun, a creative outlet, an exciting indoor sport.

The
Total Kitchen

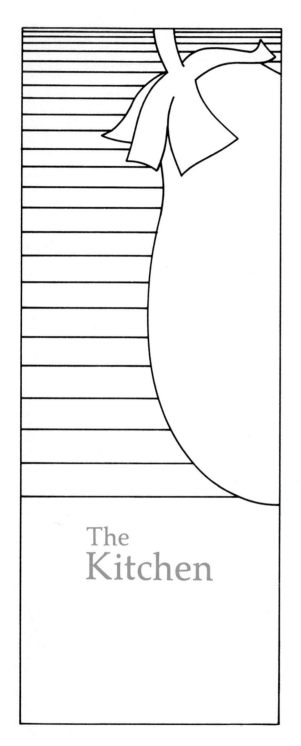

The
Kitchen

WELL-DESIGNED FLOOR PLANS

Modern builders recognize the fact that a well-planned kitchen can make or break the sale or rental of a housing unit. A kitchen may come in any size from the minimum "refrigerator-sink-range" type with a little counter space thrown in to the huge "eat-in" country style. But whether it is a makeshift or a dream come true, a kitchen has to have three main activity centers: a food preparation/clean-up center, a cooking center, and a food storage center.

The three basic centers are most ideally arranged in what is called the work triangle, a term that refers to the flow of work from one center to another. The most efficient work triangle allows the activity to progress in this sequence: from refrigeration, to food preparation/cleanup, to cooking, and back to cleanup. Allow room to move freely between centers. The total area of the triangle should be between 13 and 22 feet, with no one side of the triangle less than 4½ feet nor more than 7½ feet.

One hundred square feet of usable floor space is considered a minimum by professional kitchen planners, while more than 160 square feet can be not only unwieldy but also extremely tiring to the cook using it. If the kitchen contains more than 160 square feet, consider turning part of it into a separate playroom, dining or sitting room, or even a laundry room.

By all means, space permitting, plan a comfortable desk for telephoning, planning meals, and conducting household business. And here is something worth stealing for—a heavenly old-fashioned pantry. Out of the question? Find some wall space, either in the kitchen or adjoining laundry room; line it with shallow adjustable shelves, just deep enough to accommodate a box of oatmeal or large can of tomato juice, and cover the new pantry with folding louvered doors.

Common sense dictates that unless you are building or completely remodeling a kitchen, you must work within a premeasured space. But when remodeling it is sometimes possible to move a wall or readjust the existing space for a more workable plan. When starting from scratch you will have complete control over what goes into your kitchen, and you will want to organize the space around your family's activities. Consider the size of your family and your life-style: Is yours an eat-and-run family? How much and what kind of entertaining do you do? Do you like your kitchen to be a hospitable place where friends or family can sit and chat while you are preparing meals, or must you be alone in order to concentrate on food preparation? These are a few of the things you must remember while planning and shopping for your kitchen.

The photographs show the most popular and workable kitchen floor plans: the L shape, the U shape, and the corridor. Or, when space is at a premium, the one-wall kitchen can work for you beautifully, given sufficient counter and storage space.

THE THREE WORK AREAS

Refrigerator-Freezer Center

The refrigerator-freezer storage center is best placed nearest the outside entrance to the kitchen for convenience in unloading and storing groceries. There should be at least 15 inches of counter top next to the refrigerator, and the refrigerator door should open toward the counter. This is not difficult, as most manufacturers can supply refrigerators with doors hinged to open either to the left or right.

The refrigeration center is an excellent

An L-shaped kitchen allows flexibility in placing appliances and snack and storage areas. This is an excellent plan for large kitchens and kitchens used by more than one cook. Try not to break the L with doorways.

The U-shape kitchen is often used in connection with a family room or breakfast nook, with one arm serving as a room-dividing peninsula. This plan is excellent for use by one cook, and it may require more floor space than other floor plans; the aisle should be at least 4 feet wide.

A corridor kitchen is an excellent plan for long, narrow kitchens. An aisle at least 4 feet wide is recommended; if possible, one end of the kitchen should be closed off to prevent traffic through the work triangle.

The one-wall kitchen is used wherever space is limited, often in an open-plan arrangement, in a studio apartment, or a summer home. Care must be taken to provide adequate counter and storage space.

place beside which to locate your baking and mixing counter. Many cooks who enjoy baking build this counter lower than standard height for more comfortable kneading of bread and rolling of dough. I have a marble slab built flush with my mixing counter and find it invaluable not only for pastry and bread work but also for candy making.

This center is the logical place for an electric mixer, blender, mixing bowls, measuring equipment, baking pans, and baking supplies, such as sugar and flour. Built-in spice racks should go here instead of next to the range, where heat will hasten the destruction of the spices.

Food Preparation/Cleanup Center

The food preparation/clean-up center is considered the base of the kitchen's work-

ing triangle. This unit includes the sink, dishwasher, the food waste disposer, and that dandy newcomer to kitchen convenience, the trash compactor. Store in or near this center foods that do not need refrigeration (potatoes, onions, etc.), everyday dishes, glasses, and tableware, and of course, cleaning supplies.

If possible allow 30 inches of counter work space on each side of the sink. The dishwasher usually is located to the left of the sink, if it does not interfere with the opening of appliance doors. If you are right-handed, you will prefer the arrangement; if you are not, you will get used to it very quickly.

At the outset, if you cannot buy all the appliances you would like to have, reserve space for them by putting in cabinets large enough to be replaced by appliances. For example, you can replace a 15-inch wide cabinet with a trash compactor or a 24-inch wide cabinet with a built-in dishwasher.

Cooking Center

The cooking center contains the range, oven or ovens, and storage space for portable appliances. In organizing your cooking center try to allow 2 feet of counter work space on the side of the range that adjoins another activity center, and allow about 12 to 15 inches of heatproof counter on the other side. If you plan to build in separate ovens, make a heatproof counter space at least 15 inches wide beside them to receive hot pans and roasters.

The storage area around the cooking center should contain space for pots, pans, seasonings, and cooking utensils. Ideally, the cooking center is planned to be near the dining area. When space permits, a serving bar or counter may connect the cooking center with the dining space and be built to contain storage for linens, platters, and dry snack foods, such as cookies and crackers.

If at all possible, place your work triangle so that its effectiveness is not altered by regular traffic through the room. Four feet between parallel work surfaces is adequate, if the kitchen is a one-man type, but 54 to 64 inches should be allowed if two persons are likely to be cooking at the same time.

Once you have established your own best work pattern, try to isolate it, and keep the other activities connected with the kitchen outside that pattern. No matter how gregarious a cook you are, a tall guest leaning against the refrigerator when you need to reach in for the lettuce can be quite an obstacle, as can a child who suddenly must feed the family pet in front of the sink.

Space permitting (that phrase keeps intruding, because it is inevitably a factor in planning), an island, a freestanding table, or a monumental butcher's block can save you from kibitzers. If there is no room to place a physical barrier between you and "them," you can always paint or tape a yellow double line on the floor. That's a pretty widely understood and accepted sign that carries a playfully implicit message that "Trespassers will be prosecuted."

THE EXTRA AMENITIES

It sometimes happens in planning a kitchen, especially an extensive remodeling job or new installation, that one overlooks and fails to plan adequately for such important things as light, sound insulation, and ventilation. After the thrill of selecting appliances and decorating the kitchen to the hilt, such oversights can come as a shock.

Sound insulation

Sound insulation against noisy kitchen clatter is a help in keeping you cool-headed in the kitchen. Insulate against noise by using fabric curtains, paper or fabric on walls, and cushioned vinyl or carpet on the floor. Select appliances that run quietly, and have them properly installed by an expert. Install an acoustical tile ceiling.

Ventilation

Ventilation is one more important consideration in your kitchen planning. With more and more air conditioners in use, the open windows and the screen doors we once knew have given way to rooms or whole houses completely closed to the outdoor air. The kitchen range must be vented to the outside, unless it comes with a ventless hood containing activated charcoal or other smoke and odor-gathering material. Indoor grills must be vented to the outside, not only as a safety measure but also as a shield against smoke.

Lighting

Lighting in a kitchen should come from soft, overall general lighting, which can be accomplished by adequate incandescent or fluorescent fixtures, either ceiling mounted or suspended. The following is a good guide:

- Small kitchen (under 75 square feet)— incandescent, 150 watts; fluorescent, 60 watts
- Medium-size kitchen (75 to 120 square feet)—incandescent, 200 watts; fluorescent, 80 watts
- Large kitchen (over 120 square feet)— incandescent, 2 watts per square foot; fluorescent, 1 watt per square foot

These figures are for ceiling-mounted or suspended fixtures; double the number of fixtures when lighting is recessed. Plan extra illumination over the major work areas, such as the sink, range, food preparation center, and dining area.

The economy of fluorescent lighting is worth noting here; it will give three to four times more light per watt than incandescent lighting, and the fluorescent tubes burn much longer without needing to be replaced than do incandescent bulbs.

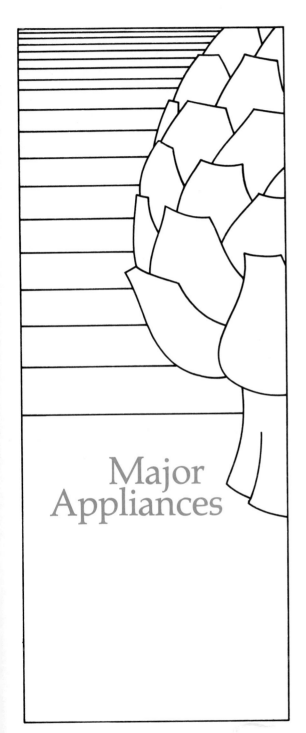

Major
Appliances

After your floor plan has been formulated, you are ready for the selection and installation of your major appliances. Let's separate the three major work areas again and consider how to supply them with efficient, good quality equipment.

REFRIGERATOR-FREEZERS

The thin wall insulation used in today's refrigerator-freezer combinations gives more usable storage per square foot of floor space than did the older models. The modern units are available with the freezer above or below the refrigerator. Separate doors for the freezer unit and the refrigerator are preferable in order to keep down loss of cold air from the freezer each time the refrigerator door is opened.

Budget and family size will govern your selection of cold storage equipment. You may choose manual-defrost, cycle-defrost, or no-frost models, which are priced according to the convenience they offer. Freezer capacity can range from a little over 1 cubic foot to around 9 cubic feet in the one-over-the-other combination. Again, convenience and price go hand-in-hand. The more you spend, the more amenities you will get.

The luxury line in the refrigerator-freezer is the side-by-side model. Separate vertical doors allow a stand-up approach to both sides, and some offer water, crushed ice, and ice cubes through dispensers on the outside of the freezer door. Some manufacturers offer models with connections so that an automatic ice maker can be installed at a later date.

A separate freezer is made to order for the large family needing to store big quantities of home-grown or purchased food. In addition to cutting down on grocery shopping trips and allowing you to take advantage of food sales, the space offered by the separate freezer makes it possible to cook double quantities of such foods as casseroles, desserts, and breads and to freeze the extra portions for later meals.

In shopping for a separate freezing unit, look for the no-frost feature, a safety light, which warns of breaks or failure in the power supply, and casters, which permit you to roll the monster out so the floor can be cleaned.

In buying a separate freezer you can select an upright or chest type. For convenience and accessibility, the upright model is better. But for truly immense storage space, the largest chest type may be your best buy.

FOOD PREPARATION/ CLEANUP CENTER

The sink

The sink you select can be of enamel over iron, which comes in colors to complement your overall color scheme. A one-bowl sink is sometimes considered sufficient, if you are to have a food waste disposer. But if space and budget allow it, a two-compartment sink is still better. At times you may want to soak a sticky pan in one side while preparing fruits or vegetables in the disposer side. The sight of food scraps and dirty dishes mixed together is an unpleasant one indeed; avoid it if you can.

Cleaning an enamel sink is simplicity itself. Use bleach on stains, and follow with hot suds to finish the cleaning. Avoid abrasive cleaners. Enamel is a form of glass and will get pits and scratches from skillets or other heavy cookware.

An alternative to enameled iron is the stainless steel sink. Again, select one or two bowls according to your space and use considerations. The utility of stainless steel is attested by its wide use in commercial installations. It is extremely durable and will not chip, as will enamel. While stain-

This kitchen counter top, made of high-pressure laminate for easier maintenance, is a single unit with the dishwasher built in. There is ample room on either side of the double sink for preparing food and for cleaning up after a meal.

less steel is not difficult to keep sanitary, it is hard to keep looking sparkling clean. Even water used to clean it leaves streaks, and to remove them requires an extra step. The cheapest way is to give the sink a good going over with a cloth or sponge wrung out in mild vinegar water.

Food waste disposer

The food waste disposer takes much of the dreaded mess out of after-meal cleanup. You may choose a batch-feed or continuous-feed model. This appliance is relatively inexpensive for the service it renders, since it gets rid of most of our insect-attracting, potentially odor-causing garbage.

Automatic dishwasher

The automatic dishwasher has taken the onus from dirty dishes. By all means select one with a "rinse and hold" feature, which enables you to collect dishes from several small meals and hold them until the machine is fully loaded. Since the dishwasher uses hotter water than the human hand can bear, dishes emerge in a more sanitary condition than if hand washed. Many families have actually found that the incidence of simple maladies, such as colds and sore throats, dropped noticeably after an automatic dishwasher was installed in the home.

If you haven't the space for a built-in dishwasher, choose the portable kind, which can be rolled to the sink for use and stored elsewhere when not needed. Some portable models can be built in later. If a dishwasher is not in your budget at all, at least earmark a 24-inch wide cabinet beside the sink to hold space for later installation.

Trash compactor

The introduction of the trash compactor struck a responsive chord in every man, woman, or child who has had to lug trash bags and cans. It occupies only 15 inches of space as a built-in unit. Some manufacturers offer a convertible model, which can go anywhere that has a three-wire, grounded 15-amp circuit. The compactor reduces trash, including bottles, to a quarter of its original volume and costs only cents a year to operate.

THE COOKING CENTER

The cooking center, for the sake of planning, can be divided into two units, surface cooking and baking. The separation of the two allows much more leeway in the arrangement of the kitchen. Several surface units can be installed in a counter or island, and two ovens can be built into a wall.

When trying to decide on cooking facilities, follow your own preferences, but do consider the costs of gas and electric power in your community.

Surface cooking units

Surface cooking units these days provide you with a wide range from which to choose. The newest of these is the ceramic cooktop, available in a freestanding range or in a built-in counter top unit. It has a surface as smooth and easy to clean as a plate. This cooktop neither heats up as rapidly nor (in most cases) reaches a temperature as high as do standard gas or electric burners. The pots and pans used on the ceramic cooktop must be perfectly flat on the bottom. If you opt for this model, you will have the opportunity to pitch out those old dented, round-bottom pots you have already kept too long.

Electric surface units now are available with "infinite heat" control knobs, replacing the old "high, medium, low" heat settings that offered no options in between.

Not all kitchens require tremendous space for cooking. This very compact cooking center features 3 built-in ovens and surface units installed in the countertop. An added feature is the wood insert in the drawer unit, which can be pulled out and used for serving.

The new control knobs allow the electric burner to be as finely tuned as its gas counterpart. A desirable luxury is a built-in gas or electric grill with ceramic briquettes and a powerful fan vented through an outside wall to carry away smoke and odors. Also, some models can be bought with a rotisserie attachment. If you are addicted to charcoal grilling but are not enough of an outdoorsman to indulge in it frequently, a built-in grill may make you happy. As you may know, the charcoal flavor of outdoor-grilled meats does not come from the charcoal at all, but rather, from smoke made by caramelized meat juices dripping on the hot charcoal. The same flavor results when the meat juices drop onto hot ceramic briquettes.

Baking units

Ovens are not just ovens anymore. Many new developments have made most of us guilty of harboring obsolete baking facilities. One of the most odious of kitchen chores has traditionally been the cleaning of the oven. No more. Many new ranges come equipped with a self-cleaning oven feature. You may choose one of two methods of cleaning, continuous clean or pyrolytic clean.

The principle on which the "continuous cleaning" oven is based is a porous, dark-colored ceramic oven lining. It is rough textured and low in abrasion resistance. The main difference in this oven lining and the standard old-fashioned porcelain enamel lining is that the "continuous clean" liner absorbs and masks spatters. This can be effective enough for those who seldom use their ovens for heavy cooking, such as roasts, casseroles, and fruit pies. These foods will deposit more spills than the liner can absorb. A buildup will eventually occur, which will have to be removed by hand cleaning.

Pyrolytic cleaning is automatically carried out at a temperature of almost 1,000° F. when you set the control knobs to "clean." Self-cleaning ovens are available in built-in units for wall or base cabinet installation or as integral parts of a free-standing range. In some of the two-oven range models the self-cleaning oven is the larger, bottom one, and the liners of the smaller, top oven can be removed and placed in the larger oven for cleaning.

Probably the most spectacular innovation in baking has been the introduction of the electronic, or microwave, oven. Not really new, it has been in use for decades and in recent years has become available for home installation. A microwave oven cooks with incredible speed; the microwaves penetrate the surface of the food and cause the molecules to vibrate against one another. This friction generates heat from within the food, as opposed to the standard oven heat that cooks food from the outside to the inside. A leg of lamb can go from the freezer to the microwave oven, defrost in minutes, then roast to mouth-watering perfection and take its place at the head of the table in less than an hour.

The electronic oven is available in a counter model or in combination with a regular-size self-cleaning oven. The latter is more expensive but allows the cook to operate the microwave while also setting the regular oven to brown food. The smaller counter model microwave at present does not do an appetizingly brown surface on roasts, though some brownness occurs from meat juices drying on the outside.

Within a few short years microwave cooking will be commonplace as the price becomes affordable for more people.

In conclusion, remember, when you are shopping for any major appliance, buy the highest quality you can afford, and buy from an established manufacturer who offers an iron-clad warranty and good repair service.

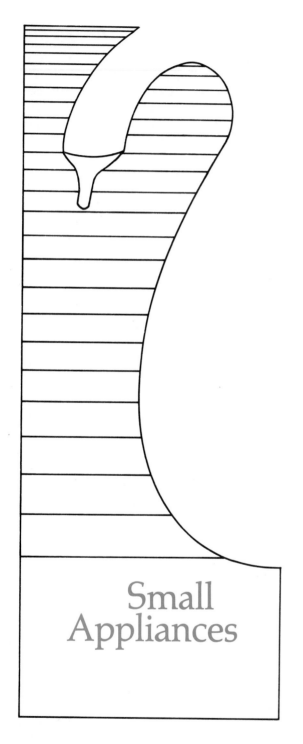

The world of small appliances is all too often a trap for the unwary. While there are a few that lend grace and ease to the day-to-day preparation of food, there are many that are of the "flash in the pan" variety. The latter are dedicated to the proposition that the cook in residence is to be separated from his or her money on the slimmest of "extra convenience" pretexts. Depending upon who is writing what you are reading, you are going to get fact mixed with some opinion; the following is my own mixture.

Of utmost importance and utility are these seven items: toaster; 8-cup coffeemaker; blender (a 2-speed will do just about anything a multibutton model will do and do it cheaper); counter model mixer (the heavy-duty ones with dough hooks are especially desirable if you're a bread baker and can afford the extra expense); waffle iron; food chopper-grinder (for sandwich spreads of cheese, etc., croquettes of all sorts, and for pickling time); electric knife.

Of secondary importance are hand-held mixer (you won't use it much after you get a counter model); electric skillet; can opener (I prefer a wall-mounted, manually operated model whose working parts are removable to go into the dishwasher or to be otherwise sanitized); party-size coffee percolator; rectangular food warmer for buffet serving (if you entertain very much).

Of tertiary importance (or Who needs it?) are deep-fat fryer, it can't do anything a heavy saucepan and spoon won't do; small toaster-oven, which won't pay its rent on the counter except perhaps for single and elderly folk whose needs are simple; luxury liner coffeemaker, which needs more than its share of counter space and for which the filters may not be so easy to find once the fad dies down; crock-, long-, or slow-cooking pot, which won't do anything an

Small Appliances

oven set at 200° won't do in the same time-span—and even the largest ones are too small for a large family; self-contained counter model rotisserie (where will you store it when not in use, and does your oven have a rotisserie attachment already?).

The items on this list simply duplicate facilities your kitchen probably already has. Laid end to end these small appliances would not only reduce your working counter space to zero but also pick your pocket of considerable money.

Always read and file carefully all "use and care" manuals you receive with any appliance, large or small. Pay attention to nonimmersible power units; they'll be useless after a good soaking. Take special care with nonstick-coated waffle irons, griddles, etc. A thorough wiping off after use is sufficient to keep them clean. A cloth wrung out in hot suds is the best appliance cosmetic you can find. Be sure to apply it soon after use before food particles dry on the surface.

Overleaf
When the first Saturday in May rolls around, and it's "Run for the Roses" time once again, serve your guests a hearty Derby Day Brunch: Kentucky Mint Juleps, Belgravia Court Appetizer, Bibb Lettuce Salad with Celery-seed French Dressing, Kentucky Derby Fried Country Ham, Shoepeg Pudding, Fresh-Cooked Asparagus with Unhollandaise Sauce, and Fresh Strawberries with Brandy-Caramel Sauce (see page 280).

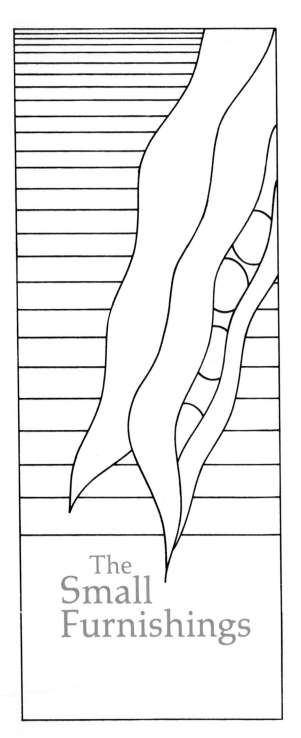

The Small Furnishings

Your kitchen is now in the happiest of states; each major element is in place. The large appliances you have selected are in your kitchen along with the best cabinetry you can afford. The counter space is adequate. You've done your homework and seen to it that your kitchen, tailored to you, is well ventilated, well lighted, and as well insulated against noise as you can make it. You have some of your small electrical appliances, and plan to add others as you find them necessary.

We now come to cookware and to those little things that make cooking an ease.

POTS AND PANS

Let's say you are going to a housewares department to make a selection of pots and pans that you hope will last for many years. First of all, take plenty of money with you; good cookware is not cheap. Conversely, cheap cookware is not good. You will lose money on it because foods will burn quickly in a lightweight metal pan, and low-cost enamelware will chip so quickly that it will soon be full of germ-collecting pockmarks.

Look at several different kinds of cookware. In making your selection, pick up and hold each piece. Examine it for good weight and balance as well as for well-fitting lids. See if handles are well and permanently attached. Sometimes there will be a sale on a multipiece set of cookware, making it difficult to resist. Remember that nothing is a bargain if you don't need it, and cookware is sold in sets not just to give you a break but to make sure each pan in the line has an equal chance of selling. It could well be that you need only half as many pans and that you could buy them in a higher quality material, given the same amount of money to spend.

Enameled iron

One of the most beautiful and expensive of the cookware materials is enameled iron. For all its wonderful, even distribution of heat, showy good looks, and the relative safety of carefree, long, slow cooking it offers, there are a few drawbacks; enameled iron is heavy to lift, especially when you get to the roasting pan or large casserole size; even the best enamel will chip in time, so it must be treated with care. Enameled iron is best cleaned with bleach because abrasive cleansers will tend to scratch the finish. It is, after all, glass.

Copper-clad stainless steel

The handsome line of stainless steel with copper-clad bottoms is fine quality merchandise, has a nice heft to it, distributes heat well, and lasts for a long while. But, whether you go in for tin-lined copper or copper-clad stainless steel, face it, you will have to polish it after almost every use to keep the finish looking great.

If you go in for copper, you have got a prize. Before you get into the quart-size bottles of commercial copper cleaner, you will want to know the copper cleaning method the colonists used and that works as well for us today: dip a cloth or sponge in vinegar; then dip it in table salt; rub the vessel until tarnish disappears; rinse and polish.

Nonstick-coated cookware

You will find several lines of nonstick-coated cookware, which are ever so tempting. Though the material has been improved in recent years, the finish requires extra precaution against scratching and marring as well as against dry heat damage. For the price and the trouble of upkeep, it seems of dubious utility in the long run. After all, how much effort does it really take to grease a cookie sheet lightly or to spray a pan on occasion with one of the lecithin nonstick products?

Stainless steel

Plain, thin, lightweight stainless steel has a penchant for making foods stick and burn, and so does thin aluminum. Heavy stainless steel is serviceable and good, especially when you get to the large stockpot sizes. Heavy or cast aluminum, which sometimes comes with a hammered finish, has a nice feel, but it also carries a few problems: acid foods, such as tomatoes, will pit and stain the finish; delicate foods, such as cream sauces and pie fillings, can pick up gray stains from the pan.

Stainless steel-aluminum

While neither stainless steel nor aluminum alone makes the most satisfactory cookware, there is a combination of the two that comes pretty close to the ideal. Such pots and pans are made of a good grade and weight of stainless steel for strength and durability and have aluminum-clad bottoms for even heat distribution. These are in the medium-price range, as good cookware goes, and require minimal care to keep their looks.

Tin-lined copper

Copperware lined with tin is usually imported and carries a price tag suitable for framing. It distributes heat evenly and is so lovable you will never part with it. Even years later when it needs retinning, you will canvass three states to find a tinsmith to repair it.

LITTLE THINGS MEAN A LOT

The little things do count. They count so much that one woman I know never

17

could make pastry because she couldn't get the shortening cut into the flour with two knives as directed by her cookbook. A dime-store pastry blender made a professional of her in about a week.

A bouquet of wooden spoons and other small, attractive implements may be usefully displayed in a bean pot near the stove top. Other handsome and utilitarian items, such as skillets, omelet pans, and muffin tins, may be hung on the wall as part of the kitchen decor. Below is our listing of the little things that make cooking more fun; these are arranged as either basics or desirables. Actually, they are all desirable, so make your own list of priorities.

	Useful Kitchen Utensils	
	Basics	*Desirables*
General purpose	Large wooden cutting board Knives 2-tine long-handled fork Soup ladle Timer (if your range doesn't have one) Pancake turner Spatula, flexible metal Can opener Rubber bowl scraper Potato masher Bottle opener Set of wooden cooking spoons Slotted spoon Wire whisks, 1 or more	1 or 2 small cutting boards reserved for onion, lemon, etc. Fruit juicer Grater-shredder, stainless steel Kitchen scale 6-inch sieve (can double as sifter) Rotary egg beater Colander, large enough for spaghetti Vegetable brush Kitchen shears Corkscrew Sandwich spreader, flexible metal Pepper mill Skimmer, long handle with shallow bowl for skimming off scum or fat Mouli grater for nuts
Baking-mixing center	Set of 4 measuring spoons (from ¼ teaspoon to 1 tablespoon) Set of 4 dry measuring cups (from ¼ to 1 cup) Set of liquid measures: 1 cup, 1 pint, 1 quart Set of cannisters Rolling pin Dough board or canvas Nest of 3 mixing bowls 2 range-to-table casseroles, in 1- and 2-quart sizes, with lids Biscuit cutter Roast meat thermometer	Pastry blender Two 6-hole muffin tins Two 9-inch layer cakepans 2 wire cake-cooling racks 9-inch square baking pan 1 or more 9-inch piepans (preferably glass) Bundt or tube cakepan, 9-inch Two 9- by 5-inch bread loaf pans (preferably glass) Roaster with rack and dome cover Jelly roll pan, 9 by 13 inches Soufflé dish A 9-inch springform pan (for cheesecake and other desserts that cannot be inverted
Range top	2 saucepans with lids, 1- and 3-quart sizes 2 cast-iron skillets, small (7- or 8-inch) and large (10-inch or larger) Whistling teakettle Double boiler with lid, 2-quart size, designed so each unit can be used as saucepan 6- or 8-quart kettle with lid for soups, chili, spaghetti Cast-iron Dutch oven	French fryer with basket Collapsible, metal steam basket Spatter shield Deep-fat thermometer Candy thermometer (also used in jelly making) Crêpe pan Heat diffuser for use over surface units; sometimes eliminates need for double boiler

The job of food preparation is made easier by these general purpose utensils: (left to right) colander, vegetable brush, pepper mill, rotary beater, Mouli grater, large-size strainer, kitchen shears, corkscrew, sandwich spreader, and large cooking spoon.

Proper baking and mixing utensils will help the cook produce perfect baked goods. Shown here are pastry blender, large cookie sheet, a pair of 6-cup muffin tins, and a pair of 9-inch round cakepans.

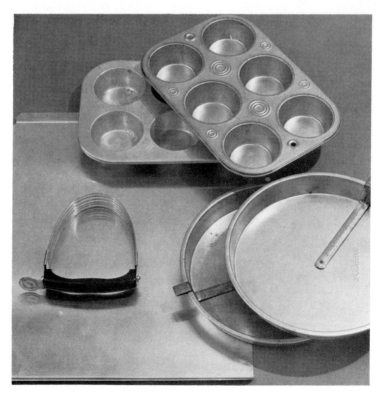

To prepare even the simplest meals, every cook should have these basic, general purpose utensils: (left to right) wire whisk, slotted spoon, egg turner, metal spatula, bottle opener (above), can opener, potato masher, set of wooden spoons in 4 sizes, and rubber spatula.

Accurate measurement of ingredients is one of the keys to successful baking. The necessary equipment for measuring includes graduated liquid measuring cups (glass), graduated dry measuring cups, and a set of measuring spoons.

The baking-mixing center should be supplied with storage containers for staple products as well as mixing equipment and cookware. Pictured here are a set of canisters, a graduated set of mixing bowls, covered casseroles, a rolling pin and canvas dough cloth, and a 2-tined fork.

Although it is possible to make do with a few basic cooking utensils, the aspiring cook will want to add these as his cooking repertoire increases: covered roasting pan with rack, meat thermometer, grater, juicer, springform pan, jelly roll pan, small cutting board, 9- x 5-inch glass bread pan, 9-inch glass piepan, 9-inch square cakepan, and a pair of cake cooling racks.

Rangetop cooking provides the backbone of many meals. These basic utensils allow the cook to prepare almost any rangetop dish: soup kettle/steamer, perforated inner basket, covered Dutch oven, 2 heavy saucepans with lids, whistling teakettle, 2 cast-iron skillets, and a double boiler.

While they are not absolutely essential, these utensils combined with the rangetop basics provide maximum rangetop flexibility: French fry pan with fitted basket, deep-fat thermometer, spatter shield, collapsible steam basket, and an asbestos heat diffuser.

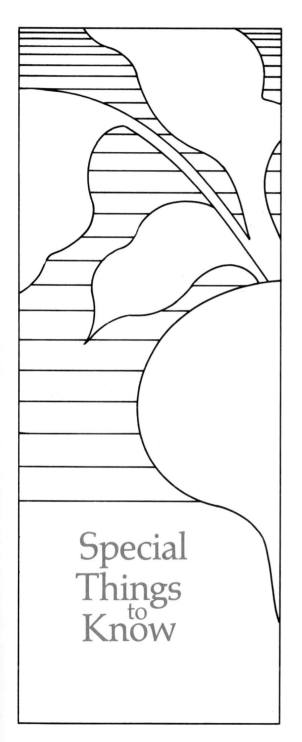

Cutting boards, ironware, and knives deserve special consideration, both in their selection and in their care. Here are some guidelines to bear in mind.

CUTTING BOARDS

First of all, your main board should be large enough (approximately 12 x 18 inches) to accommodate the chopping of a quantity of vegetables without scattering bits on the counter. In addition to your large board, you should have one or two small wooden boards reserved especially for the slicing or mincing of onion and garlic.

We always think first of the good, old-fashioned wooden board, full of nicks and dents. (Especially fortunate is the flea marketeer who turns up an old butcher's block.) The wooden board has a warm, homey feel and looks divine on the counter or hanging on the wall by a leather thong. But keeping it clean could be one of your main sanitation problems in the kitchen.

Never use your wooden board to cut up or bone raw meat without scrubbing it down with hot suds and rinsing it well afterward. Dry it in the sun as often as possible. Once a week, sluice it down with a weak bleach solution, and use a scrub brush to get at the germs in the pores and cracks in the wood; follow with suds and a thorough rinsing. Bleach helps eliminate residual odors from onions and garlic.

Failure to sanitize a wooden board can result in cross-contamination; deteriorating meat juices will do bad things to the next batch of food you chop. A butcher's block poses special problems: obviously you can't drag it out in the sunshine for drying. Suds and rinse the block after each use, and after each raw or cooked meat operation, a bleach solution should be used, followed by suds and a rinse.

Special Things to Know

There are some good alternatives to wooden cutting-board material: polyethylene, hard rubber, and acrylic. The warmth of wood may be missed, but sanitation is no problem with the new materials. Look for them in a restaurant supply house or in a kitchen specialty shop.

Polyethylene does not dull knives, but in time it does show marks and scratches. It should stand up well under normal home use for many years. The hard rubber board will dull your blades but not be scratched by them and will last indefinitely. A little less than an inch thick, the polyethylene and hard-rubber boards are made in colors ranging from creamy white to beige and bear a slight resemblance to marble. Clear acrylic is quite thin and can lie almost invisibly on your counter top.

IRONWARE

Properly seasoned and cared for, the old iron skillet is the original nonstick cookware. New ironware usually comes labeled "preseasoned." Still it is not a bad idea to work on it a little bit, just to make sure. Everything I have ever read about seasoning iron has said to coat it with unsalted vegetable shortening or oil, then heat it. Invariably the piece ended up with a coat of sticky varnish-like material that could not be removed. Here is where I part company with those experts. I recommend that you rub your new skillet, Dutch oven, or other ironware with a bacon rind, or, working with both hands, rub it very sparingly with bacon drippings both inside and out. Wipe off excess with paper towels, and bake it in a 250° F. oven overnight. Your new ironware should then be ready to use.

The penny pincher's best source of ironware is the flea market, where people frequently discard pieces with thick buildups of burned grease. Snap up a bargain. Just make sure the piece isn't warped, and don't worry about paint or rust or grease deposits. Now, if you have a self-cleaning oven (the pyrolytic kind, not the continuous clean type) or if you know someone who does, you are ready to go to work on your bargain.

Put the filthy-looking piece into the oven, and let it run through an oven-cleaning cycle. When the cycle has finished, you will have a piece of iron that is absolutely clean, down to the bare metal. Wash away the ashes and rust particles in hot suds, using a stiff brush. Rinse and dry.

To season the piece of ironware, use the bacon rind- or drippings-baking method. After it has baked overnight, examine the surface. If there is a smear too much grease in one spot or a little rust showing, sandpaper it off.

Now repeat the light greasing process, and return it to the oven. Iron is very porous, and to prevent rusting, it needs two thin applications of fat. Either bake it overnight again at 250° F. or, if you can do without it, leave the piece in the oven for a week, letting it bake and cool repeatedly as you carry on your normal baking operations. My ironware collection is my pride and joy and stands proof to this seasoning method.

With care, iron skillets and other utensils will keep their seasonings for many years. Never overheat an empty skillet, which will burn off the seasoning. Always wash a skillet immediately after emptying it of food. If there are browned particles stuck to it, pour in an inch of water, cover, and bring to a boil; let cool a few minutes before cleaning.

Protect the sink when you are washing ironware or any heavy pan. The best wash is simply hot running water and a plastic scrub ball; no detergent is necessary. Dry well, and hang or store. You may want to put it into a warm oven to finish drying, but make sure there is not enough heat to burn off the seasoning. The ironware should feel neither greasy nor bone dry to the touch.

KNIVES

Knives, which are of good quality and are sharp, are an absolute necessity in every kitchen. They are being treated separately from the food preparation lists, because they require extra care in selection and maintenance.

Blades may be made of carbon steel or stainless steel. Carbon takes and keeps an edge longer; stainless is easier to keep clean. The choice is yours. Buy the very best quality you can afford.

In better knives, the metal of the blade runs the full length of the handle, and several brads run through the handle to keep the knife together. You will need a steel to help you keep your blades in good condition. Your cutlery dealer will show you how to use it. Every year or so, bundle up your knives, and take them to be professionally sharpened.

Never keep your knives loose in a drawer. In addition to the danger of accidents, there is the fact that the edges will be ruined by rubbing against each other. Magnetic wall racks are available, as are wooden ones. The most unusual and attractive knife holder I have seen is made of a driftwood plank three feet long with a two-inch wide leather strap nailed neatly along the length of it. The nails are spaced to accommodate blades from the narrowest paring knife at the left end to the heroic, French chef's knife at the right end.

Every cook will give you his or her knife preferences, so here are mine: If I am to be marooned on the proverbial desert

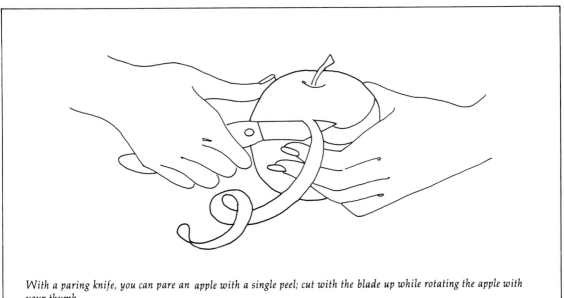

With a paring knife, you can pare an apple with a single peel; cut with the blade up while rotating the apple with your thumb.

island, with plenty of provender of course, let me have my heavy, French chef's knife, my 5-inch utility knife, and my concave-bladed boning knife; I'll send for the rest.

You might want to build your set of knives in this more conventional order: paring knife, 4-inch blade; utility knife, 5-inch blade; butcher knife, 8- or 9-inch blade; boning knife, 5- or 6-inch straight or concave narrow blade; heavy, French chef's knife, 10-inch triangular blade; bread knife, 8-inch blade with serrated edge; and ham- or roast-slicing knife, straight 11- or 12-inch blade.

SPECIAL CARE ITEMS

There are some good kitchen items that will be damaged by an automatic dishwasher, so it is best to wash them quickly after use by hand, and then put them away.

- Woodenware of all kinds. Salad bowls, cutting boards, and wooden spoons will dry out, become brittle, and crack from the heat of the drying cycle.
- Plastic or rubberware. These materials will be damaged by the drying cycle. Unless your dishwasher has a rinse-and-hold cycle (which is usually sufficient to clean these items completely), wash by hand.
- Anything that will rust. Kitchen knives are best washed under hot, running water, then dried, and put away immediately after each use. Skillets and other ironware will not only lose their seasoning to detergent wash, but will also impart rust stains to items stored next to them.
- Hollow-handled sterling or plated silver knives. Detergent and dry heat will destroy the cement between the blade and handle.
- Any sterling flatware with an antiqued finish. The characteristic oxidation in the pattern will be washed away.

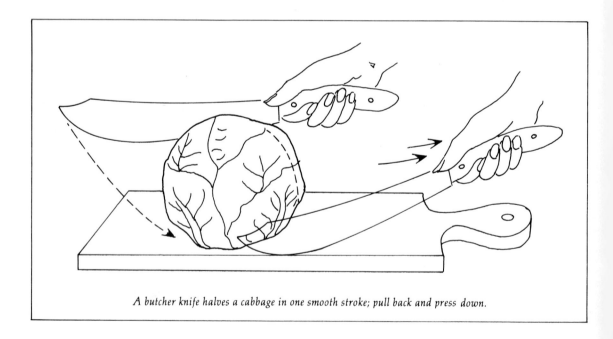

A butcher knife halves a cabbage in one smooth stroke; pull back and press down.

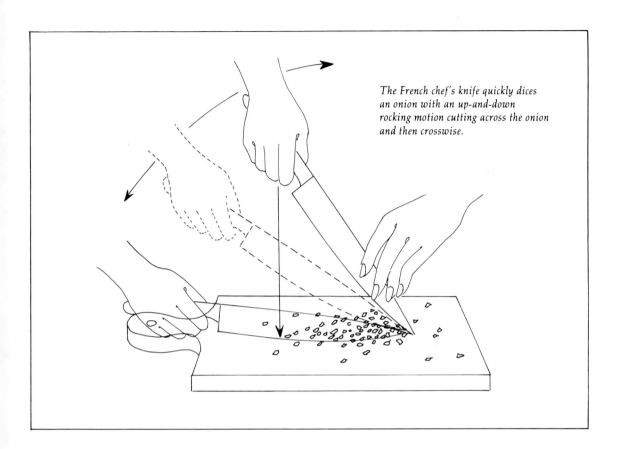

The French chef's knife quickly dices an onion with an up-and-down rocking motion cutting across the onion and then crosswise.

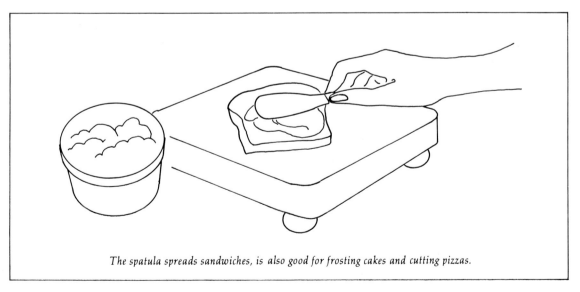

The spatula spreads sandwiches, is also good for frosting cakes and cutting pizzas.

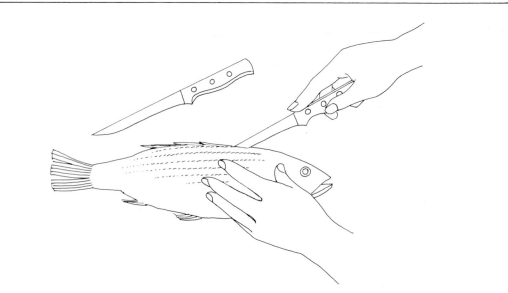

The boning knife, used for cutting and fileting, is one of the most useful of all blades. Keep it razor sharp, as all knives should be. In addition to fileting fish, you will find that, with practice, you can bone out legs of lamb or chicken breasts and thighs and make new dishes from them. Remember always to bear the blade against bone, and use short, scraping motions when boning meat.

The carving knife is for meat with bones. Knife slices with an easy, sweeping stroke while the carving fork anchors the meat.

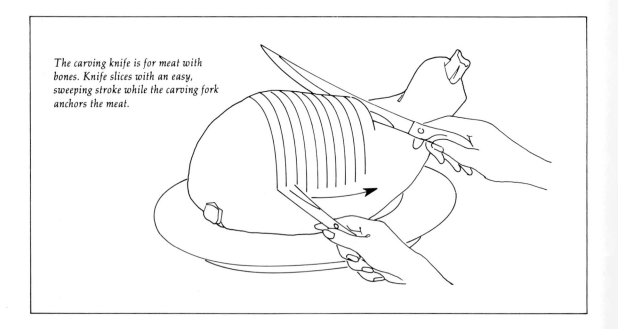

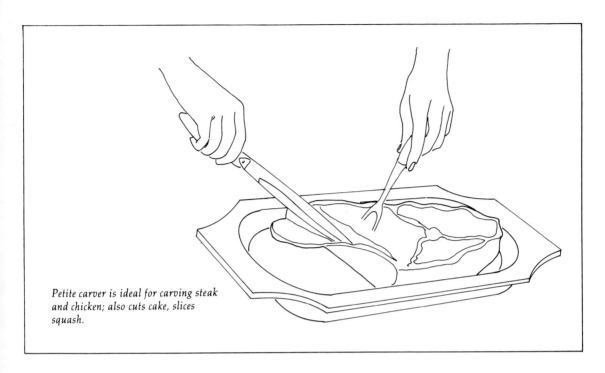

Petite carver is ideal for carving steak and chicken; also cuts cake, slices squash.

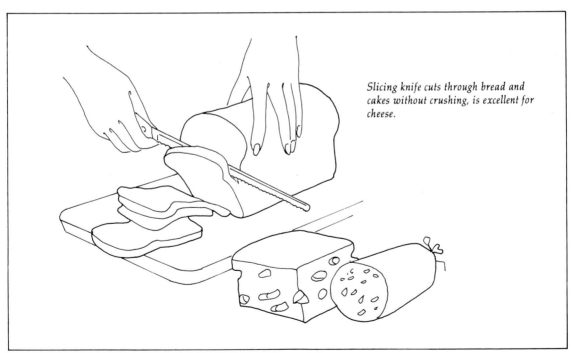

Slicing knife cuts through bread and cakes without crushing, is excellent for cheese.

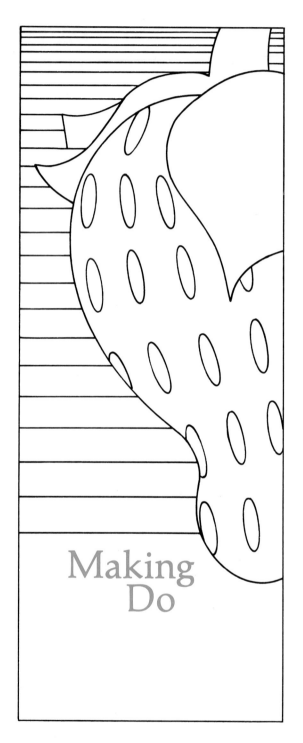

Making Do

Many young married couples and millions of singles have set up housekeeping with little more than a skillet, a saucepan, and a long-handled spoon. Bridal showers have been the traditional sources of fringe benefits, those extras that make cooking a simpler and smoother operation. Of course, if money is no object, you can tour housewares departments, hardware stores, and discount houses and quickly come up with a complete line of utensils and appliances.

While there are no substitutes for standard measuring spoons and cups, there are a few tricks to know for making do when you don't have the equipment you would like to have.

- No rolling pin? The most obvious substitute is a smooth bottle. But you can go to a lumber dealer and buy a 1- or 2-inch dowel that is 12 or 14 inches long, and you may never even want a rolling pin. Or, saw a length off an old broom or mop handle, and sand off all the paint.
- No double boiler? Use a saucepan over a larger pan of boiling or simmering water, with the top pan touching the water or not, according to the recipe directions.
- No muffin tins? Buy paper cupcake pan liners, and place them close together in a cakepan or skillet. The muffins won't be perfectly round.
- No flour sifter? Just use a sieve, and stir the dry ingredients gently through it with a wooden spoon.
- No pastry blender? The generally recommended method of blending shortening into flour without a pastry blender is to cut the shortening into the pastry flour using two table knives. However, to me this is a totally unsatisfactory method. A better approach is to chill the shortening thoroughly, and

then work it into the flour with the fingertips, working quickly lest the warmth from your hands melt the shortening and ruin the flakiness.

- No bread board or canvas? A clean counter top or table top dusted with flour will serve. An even better method (since I prefer to work with a canvas) is a clean tea towel with flour rubbed into it. You can fold and place it in a plastic bag between uses.

- No pepper mill? Freshly ground pepper is a must in cooking. The recipes in this book assume freshly ground pepper. Put peppercorns into a heavy cup, and proceed to break them up, as coarsely or as finely as you like, with the handle of a wooden spoon.

- No springform pan? This takes a bit of doing, but it works: Select a cakepan of the diameter and capacity called for in the recipe. Cut a piece of heavy cardboard ¼ inch smaller than the inside bottom. Cover the cardboard smoothly with aluminum foil, folding the cut edges flatly underneath. Now, tear two lengths of foil about 8 inches longer than the pan's diameter, and fold them so they are about 2 inches wide. Lay them in an X shape across the bottom of the pan, so that you have about 3 inches of foil standing above the pan sides. Put in the false bottom, pressing down tightly, and then spray with a nonstick product. When your food has baked and cooled, run a spatula around the edges of the pan to loosen the cake and lift it out by the four "handles." (Four hands are better than two at this point.) Lift the cake, false bottom and all, onto a serving plate, and carefully pull out the aluminum strips.

- No steam basket? If you have a metal colander and a covered kettle large enough to hold it, there will be no problem. Just put water into the kettle, but not enough to touch the colander. Put the food into the colander, cover, and steam away. Otherwise, invert a cakepan in the kettle, place food in a bowl or handleless pan, and set it on the inverted pan. Add ½ inch of water to the bottom of the kettle, cover, and steam. This method is slower, but it works. We include this because, while a little slower than boiling, steaming is the best way to cook many soft vegetables for vitamin and color retention.

- No French fryer? All you need is a heavy saucepan, a slotted spoon, and extreme caution. After the cooking oil has reached the proper temperature as given in the recipe, use the slotted spoon, not your hands, to place food in the hot oil. When food is done, lift it out with the same spoon, and place it on paper towels to drain.

- No crêpe pan? Just use your 6- or 7-inch skillet. The crêpes will taste exactly the same as if they had been made in the "proper" pan.

- No soufflé dish? Any straight-sided, ovenproof baking dish will serve, so long as the capacity matches that called for in the recipe. To measure capacity of any cooking container or salad mold to see if it is the right size for a given recipe, do the obvious: Fill the container in question with cupfuls of water, counting as you go.

- No biscuit cutter? I have lost so many biscuit cutters over the years, I stopped counting. I now have a whole nest of cutters ranging from tomato paste cans to tuna cans. Just punch a hole in the closed end of the can so the air can escape when you cut into the dough.

How
to
Shop
for
Food

THE SHOPPING LIST

To enter a supermarket without a shopping list is to enter a battle of wits unarmed, It is not by accident that stores place their temptations up front where you will trip over them; they have paid good money for market researchers to tell them how to position things for impulse buying. Grocery shopping, then, begins with a list, a tight list, not to be abandoned when you enter that garden of eating, the supermarket. One shopping trip a week should be enough, if you have sufficient refrigerator-freezer storage space in your home.

Build your list by keeping a sheet of paper in a prominent place in the kitchen, and write down each item you run out of and must replace. Add to it, before you go to the store, a week's worth of main-dish dinner materials, bearing in mind that protein does not come from beef alone. Include fish, poultry, eggs, cheese, and organ meats, such as liver, in addition to lean muscle cuts of pork and lamb.

Shopping for your family's protein requirements need not bankrupt you. Do some reading: newspapers and magazines are good sources of information as are government pamphlets. Also, see Appendix I for a book list. Learn to serve combinations of vegetable proteins once or twice a week to replace those expensive meat cuts. Learn how to combine vegetable and grain protein, such as dried beans with corn bread, and red beans with rice. Learn about soy products and how to use them: one part textured vegetable protein to three parts ground beef, for example, will stretch your ground beef dollar when used for meat loaf, chili, and burgers. Learn the joy of "beefing" up your homebaked breads by the addition of milk solids and soy granules.

It has never seemed necessary to me to plan a week's menus in advance; I like to be looser than that in my meal planning. Therefore, on your list should be seven entrées for seven dinners. Include two fruits and three vegetables per day. Salad ingredients, heavy on the deep green leafy ones, and yellow vegetables, such as carrots, sweet potatoes, and squash, are musts for every shopping trip.

Buy fresh fruits and vegetables that are in season for economy's sake. Be a label reader. For example, there are federal standards for orange juice, so don't be misled by ads offering a good buy on something that may contain as little as 10 percent real orange juice at the price you would pay for the real thing.

Read the newspaper ads for special sales. Clip money-saving coupons, and use only ones for which you have a need; otherwise, the coupon is an expense rather than a saving. Returnable bottles are an economy measure as well as a sound ecological practice. And somewhere along the line, we must decide how much we are willing to pay to have someone else do our peeling, grating, stirring, mixing, etc. Next time you are in a market, price a chunk of cheddar; then find a comparably weighted package of the same cheese, grated. The price per pound will be almost double for the grated. People will slice your sandwich meats for you too, for a price.

CONSUMER COMMON SENSE

The following list suggests a few things you can do, as a consumer, to stay on top of the food shopping situation:

- Expect freshness in the food you buy. The advent of open dating has given us a simple way to know if a product is fresh. Read those dates. On a dairy shelf you may find 10 days difference in the dates on cottage cheese cartons. Select the latest date. If you find outdated food offered for sale, complain to the store manager. Then check later to see if action has been taken.
- Buy only what you can store and use in a reasonable length of time.
- When you get home, open packages of fresh food to check for offensive odors or other signs of staleness, regardless of the date stamped on the package. If you find obvious signs of spoilage, make an effort to return the package to the store manager in person.
- Read labels for special storage suggestions. It makes no sense at all to put a canned ham on the pantry shelf when the label reads, "refrigerate."
- Use perishable products within 1 or 2 days. You may hold them longer if experience has shown that the products keep unusually well.
- Remember to rotate your stored foods. Place oldest cans up front in your pantry and oldest frozen foods at the front of your freezer.

If you shop regularly at the same supermarket, you will save time by making up your list according to the store's layout. Then, once you are in the store, put on your mental blinders, and stick to your list.

MEAT

It is important to think in terms of price per serving, not price per pound. Envision that big bargain beef chunk minus the bone and fat, and rethink the price as opposed to a boneless round roast. (Neither is a model of tenderness; they will both need moist cooking.) But try to estimate the lean servings you will get for each dollar. In boneless cuts, you will need only one-third of a pound or less, per adult serving. This ration can go up to about a pound or more per serving when you purchase spareribs, short ribs, lamb shanks, or whole turkey.

Beef and Lamb

Look for the purple, shield-shaped grading stamp on beef in your grocer's counter, but don't be surprised if the cut you choose is unmarked. Since the official USDA shield is stamped on the outside fat which covers the beef carcass, it is often removed when the excess fat is trimmed from the meat. In addition, inspection to see that beef meets federal standards for fitness for human consumption is mandatory, but the law does not require that beef be graded. It is up to the packer to choose whether his beef will be graded or not, and the packer must pay the cost of having the USDA grader examine and grade his meat.

Under present regulations, the carcasses which are graded must be graded according to both quality and yield. Because it indicates the amount of edible meat on the carcass, the yield grade can help you get more for your money: the lower the yield grade number, the more edible meat and the less fat and bone. This requirement is primarily helpful to those who may buy a quarter, half, or whole carcass for the freezer or freezer locker; those who buy individual cuts can see the edible meat on each cut. In respect to quality of beef, however, their are eight grades:

- *U.S. Prime* is the highest grade alotted a carcass. Prime beef is abundantly marbled with fat, which makes it flavorful and tender, and because of its thick fat cover, it is most suitable for the natural aging process. Since Prime beef is available in such limited quantity, most of it goes to top-quality restaurants and specialty or gourmet

meat stores. Very little prime meat is found in retail food stores.

- *U.S. Choice* is the most popular grade of beef in today's supermarkets and is also served in many restaurants. Slightly leaner than Prime, Choice beef can still be aged moderately, and it yields a tender, juicy morsel on the plate.
- *U.S. Good* follows Choice in grading designation, and *U.S. Standard* falls below Good on the scale. These designations normally indicate leaner beef that is less juicy and tender than Choice, but its milder flavor is an excellent contribution to stews and ground beef meatballs or hamburgers.
- *U.S. Utility, Cutter, and Canner* grades are not often found in supermarkets. Instead, these grades are sold to processors to be used in processed foods such as sausage and cold cuts.

Unlike beef, lamb is almost never tough. Look for the inspection stamp and the packaging date on the label. Lamb does not keep as well as beef, which is aged somewhat even before it is sold. Again, think price per serving, compared with price per pound.

Pork

The modern lean-trimmed pork is mild in flavor, high in nutritive value, and comparable in caloric value to other meats.

Until recent years it was recommended that pork always be cooked to well done because of fear of trichinosis. Today, however, the recommended temperature is 170° F., high enough to kill trichinae, but not high enough to destroy the palatability of the meat.

Pork is usually ungraded, but look for meat that is fine grained, firm, and has white fat — all signs of high-quality pork.

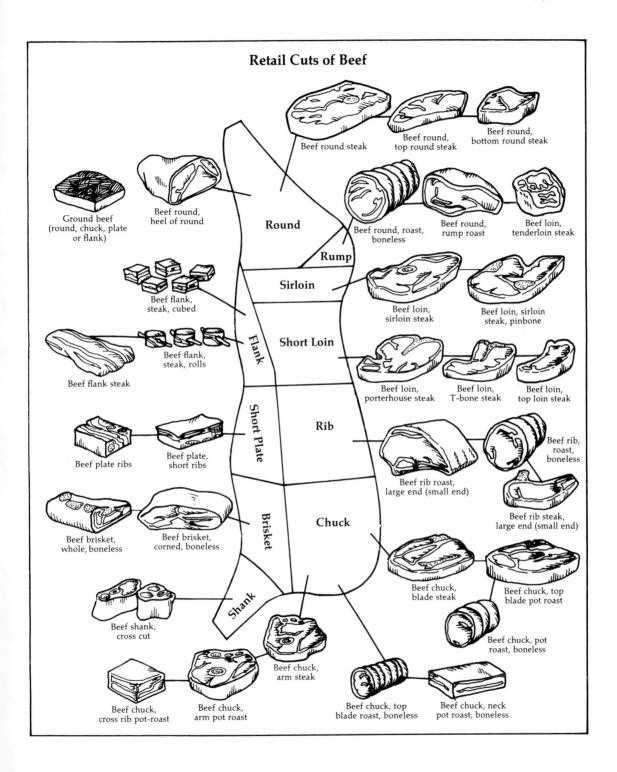

Retail Cuts of Beef

Beef round steak

Beef round, top round steak

Beef round, bottom round steak

Beef round, heel of round

Ground beef (round, chuck, plate or flank)

Round

Beef round, roast, boneless

Beef round, rump roast

Beef loin, tenderloin steak

Rump

Sirloin

Beef flank, steak, cubed

Beef loin, sirloin steak

Beef loin, sirloin steak, pinbone

Flank

Short Loin

Beef flank, steak, rolls

Beef flank steak

Beef loin, porterhouse steak

Beef loin, T-bone steak

Beef loin, top loin steak

Short Plate

Rib

Beef plate ribs

Beef plate, short ribs

Beef rib, roast, boneless

Beef rib roast, large end (small end)

Brisket

Chuck

Beef rib steak, large end (small end)

Beef brisket, whole, boneless

Beef brisket, corned, boneless

Beef chuck, blade steak

Beef chuck, top blade pot roast

Shank

Beef shank, cross cut

Beef chuck, arm steak

Beef chuck, pot roast, boneless

Beef chuck, cross rib pot-roast

Beef chuck, arm pot roast

Beef chuck, top blade roast, boneless

Beef chuck, neck pot roast, boneless

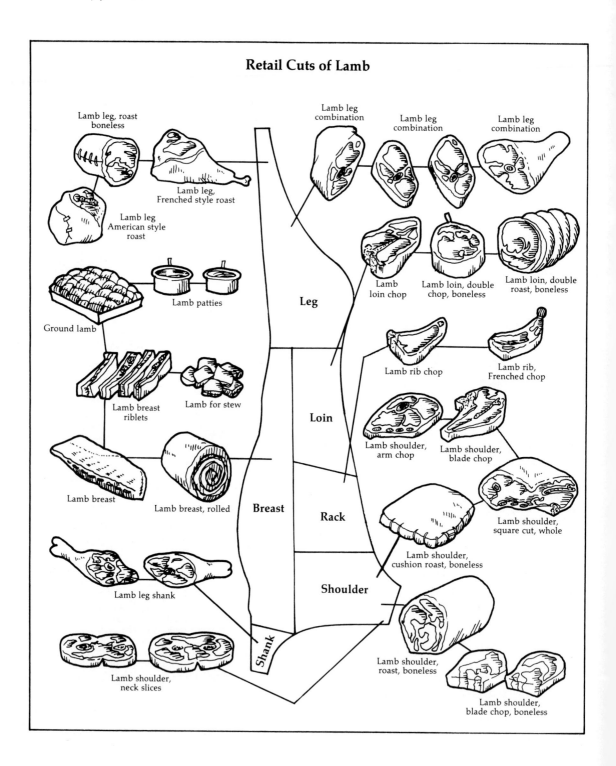

Retail Cuts of Lamb

Lamb leg, roast boneless

Lamb leg, Frenched style roast

Lamb leg American style roast

Lamb patties

Ground lamb

Lamb breast riblets

Lamb for stew

Lamb breast

Lamb breast, rolled

Lamb leg shank

Lamb shoulder, neck slices

Lamb leg combination

Lamb leg combination

Lamb leg combination

Lamb leg combination

Lamb loin chop

Lamb loin, double chop, boneless

Lamb loin, double roast, boneless

Lamb rib chop

Lamb rib, Frenched chop

Lamb shoulder, arm chop

Lamb shoulder, blade chop

Lamb shoulder, square cut, whole

Lamb shoulder, cushion roast, boneless

Lamb shoulder, roast, boneless

Lamb shoulder, blade chop, boneless

Leg

Loin

Rack

Breast

Shoulder

Shank

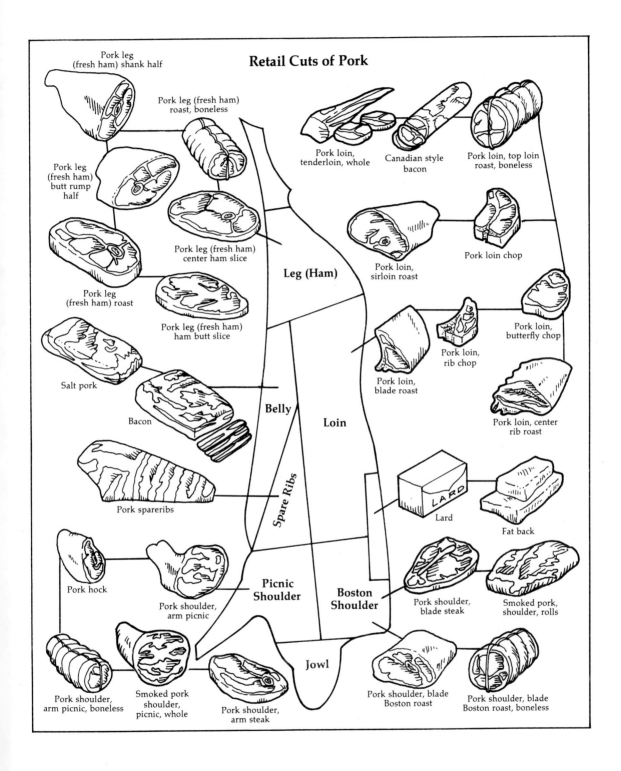

Retail Cuts of Pork

Pork leg (fresh ham) shank half

Pork leg (fresh ham) roast, boneless

Pork leg (fresh ham) butt rump half

Pork leg (fresh ham) center ham slice

Pork leg (fresh ham) roast

Pork leg (fresh ham) ham butt slice

Leg (Ham)

Salt pork

Bacon

Belly

Spare Ribs

Pork spareribs

Pork hock

Pork shoulder, arm picnic

Picnic Shoulder

Pork shoulder, arm picnic, boneless

Smoked pork shoulder, picnic, whole

Pork shoulder, arm steak

Jowl

Boston Shoulder

Pork loin, tenderloin, whole

Canadian style bacon

Pork loin, top loin roast, boneless

Pork loin, sirloin roast

Pork loin chop

Pork loin, butterfly chop

Pork loin, blade roast

Pork loin, rib chop

Pork loin, center rib roast

Loin

LARD

Lard

Fat back

Pork shoulder, blade steak

Smoked pork, shoulder, rolls

Pork shoulder, blade Boston roast

Pork shoulder, blade Boston roast, boneless

POULTRY

Poultry selection brings to mind the old cooking school admonition to "look for bright eyes and soft feet." The federal inspector, if the bird came across a state line, has already looked at those, and you will never see them unless you know a chicken farmer. An inspection stamp is a good guide, letting you know that certain standards of sanitation have been met. Look for a soft breast bone, and for pale, moist skin free of hairs and bruises on the whole bird. You will save money on every pound of chicken you buy, if you buy it whole and disjoint it yourself.

Chicken

Chickens are called broilers if they weigh 2½ pounds or less, and fryers if they weigh 2½ to 3½ pounds. Roasting chickens weigh 3½ to 5 pounds and are excellent for baking and for long, slow rotisserie cooking. The capon (castrated male bird) can weigh up to 8 pounds and makes a fine special occasion roast. Old chickens, too tough for any other purpose, can still bring character and flavor to the stock pot.

Turkey

Turkeys, thanks to modern processing, shipping techniques, and freezer storage, are available year round. Still the mechanics of those shipping-and-freezing devices are not infallible. It is impossible to know whether something potentially dangerous has occurred between the processor and your market basket. The truck refrigeration system or the freezing compartment in the store may have failed, allowing food to warm up, then quietly be refrozen. For this reason, it is unwise to buy a prestuffed frozen turkey under any circumstance.

To select a high quality whole turkey, choose one that is well fleshed with well-distributed fat and unblemished skin. The larger birds are frequently a better buy than the smaller ones (cheaper per pound), and the butcher will probably saw the frozen turkey in half so that you can cook part and store the remainder in your freezer for later use. Too, the bigger bird generally has more meat in proportion to bone, which gives you a greater value.

Fryer or roaster turkeys weigh 4 to 5 pounds, are ready to cook, and have delicate flavor and tender meat. Other young turkeys, from 6 to 24 pounds, may be labeled young hen, young tom, or young turkey. The flavor of these larger turkeys is more fully developed. Producers are now marketing halves or quarters of turkeys, which fill a need for those needing lesser amounts of meat or those having a preference for white or dark meat. If the turkey is not labeled young or (sometimes) yearling, assume that the bird is an old one and ready for the stewing kettle, to be made into salad, or used in other recipes calling for cooked meat.

"Ready-to-cook" birds have been bled, eviscerated, and divested of head, feet, and oil sac. "Dressed" birds have been bled, and picked, but that is all; the rest is up to you. Turkeys that have been federally inspected or federal-state inspected will bear the shield-shaped stamp "U.S. Grade A, B, or C."

Hen or tom turkey — which to buy? The hen is likely to be a little breastier, at least it costs more; but the difference in flavor is not discernible except to the select and imaginative few. In contemplating the purchase of a whole turkey, allow ¾ to 1 pound per person. Turkey breast, in terms of edible meat, is cheaper per serving than whole turkey and is your best buy, unless a member of your family is a card-carrying drumstick lover.

Of the so-called "turkey roasts" there is little good to say. Somewhere in the process of being boned and squeezed into a loaf, the meat, dark and white alike, has given up its flavor. Over-handled or over-processed, call it what you will, foods so treated are best left where they are, be they stuffed turkeys, turkey roasts, or TV dinners.

FISH AND SEAFOOD

Fish and seafood come to us fresh, frozen, or canned. Those fortunate enough to live near salt water can feast on seafood at will, and all they need to know is their favorite varieties and how to tell a fresh fish from an oldie. Fresh fish will have bright eyes, which are clear and bulging. The gills will be red-pink and not slimy, while the scales will be tight, bright, and shiny. Firm and elastic flesh and fresh odor are other signs of freshness.

Here are some common ways in which fish are marketed:
- Whole or round fish are sold just as they come from the water and must have their entrails removed, along with their scales, before cooking. Remove head, tail, and fins, except on small skillet-sized fish to be fried or on a very large one to be poached or baked whole.
- Drawn fish have had the internal organs and scales removed. Prepare such fish for cooking just as you would whole or round fish.
- Dressed or pan-dressed fish have had the internal organs and scales removed. Usually head, tail, and fins have also been removed.
- Steaks are cross-section slices of the larger, dressed fish. Ready to cook, they have only a cross section of backbone left in.
- Filets are the meaty sides of the fish, cut away lengthwise from the backbone. Practically boneless, they are ready to be cooked.
- Sticks are pieces of fish cut from frozen blocks of filets; usually each stick weighs about an ounce.

In purchasing fresh fish, think price per serving; whole fish may be cheaper per pound, but there is a lot of waste.

Shellfish
Clams

Ever since the Indians invited the Pilgrims to their first clambake, Americans have regarded clams, along with apple pie and hot dogs, as indigenous to our shores. Hard currency in those days was made from clam shells, which were polished, pierced, and pieced into wampum.

East Coast clams, taken in commercial quantities, are of three varieties: Quahog (hard shell), which comes in the small-size littleneck, medium-size cherrystone, and the large-size chowder clam; steamer (soft shell); and surf clam (also called sea clam or skimmer).

Clams are available even to inlanders thanks to modern freezing and canning techniques. But if you are in a position to buy fresh clams, count on 3 dozen shell clams or a quart of shucked hard-shell clams for every 6 persons. About 16 cherrystones or 3 dozen littlenecks, fresh, will yield one cup of meat. It will take two 8-ounce cans, drained, to make a cupful of clams.

Fresh shell clams must be purchased alive, then used as soon as possible. An open shell or a neck that does not recoil when touched is indication that the clam is dead, and it shouldn't be bought. Allow a quart of steamer clams per person when planning your purchase. If live clams must be held for a little while, refrigerate, and avoid sudden temperature changes.

To remove sand, cover clams with clean sea water or fresh water with cornmeal or salt added. Let stand 20 to 30 minutes. Repeat the process with a change of water, if this seems necessary. Then scrub away any residual sand, if the clams are to be cooked in their shells.

Crab

Although some varieties of crab are native to our shores — from Cape Cod, off Florida and California, to the Aleutians, in sizes from the bite-size hermit to the Alaskan King Crab — the heart of the crab industry is around the Delaware and Chesapeake Bays.

There are several varieties of crab:
- Blue crab comes mainly from the Chesapeake and Delaware Bays and ranges south through the Tidewater area.
- Soft-shell crab is found in the same areas as the blue crab and is nothing more than the blue crab caught between shells (discarding his old shell in order to grow a larger, more comfortable one). The soft-shell crab can be bought and is widely available.
- Rock crab is a favorite of New Englanders and Californians alike.
- Stone crab is a regional delicacy of Florida with its overdeveloped lobsterish claws of superlative flavor.
- Jubilee crab is a mysterious fellow who turns up in the Mobile (Alabama) Bay and is the cause of wild rejoicing and feasting when he makes his unscheduled appearance.
- Dungeness crab, also called Pacific or market crab, is a West Coast native and is probably the best buy of all. The meaty, smooth-shelled crab is taken from November through August and may weigh up to 3½ pounds.
- Alaskan king crab is a monster, weighing up to 20 pounds and sometimes measuring 6 feet from claw to claw. Much of the frozen crabmeat we buy is of this variety.

Lobster

Although the most popular size range is from 1 to 3 pounds, purchased whole, either freshly cooked or live, the lobster grades are as follows: chicken, up to 1 pound; quarters, up to 1¼ pounds; large, from 1½ to 2¼ pounds; and jumbo, over 2½ pounds. (A 2½-pound lobster will yield about 2 cups of meat.)

Look for a lively one of blackish or blue green color; all lobster turns red when cooked. Lobster is at peak season from May through December in the Northeast and from October to March on the West Coast. Cook lobster the day of purchase. If you must hold one overnight, keep him in a cool place but never in the coldest part of the refrigerator. If he succumbs in the night, it is still safe to go ahead and cook him immediately in the morning.

To test for freshness in a live lobster, see if the tail snaps back into a curve when you straighten it. If he has been in the holding tank too long, he'll be sluggish because lobsters fast in captivity.

Mussels

Greatly underestimated and underused in this country, the mussel is a favorite delicacy in other parts of the world. Unshelled, fresh mussels run approximately 16 to 20 per pound. Our East Coast mussels are blue black; their West Coast counterparts sport brownish shells. The meat is tastier during the nonspawning season (the same is true for oysters), which means that they are better in winter. West Coast mussels can be dangerous from May through October due to an ocean plankton, which may or may not give a reddish tinge to the feeding waters of the mussels, clams, and oysters there. The waters are monitored by health agencies.

One possible reason Americans don't take too readily to mussels is the inordinate time and effort it takes to clean them. Wear rubber gloves, arm yourself with a strong knife to scrape off the barnacles, scrub the shells with a wire brush, and change the water as often as you can dump and refill. Using all your strength, tear off the "beard" (byssus), which is the mussel's traveling and attaching mechanism.

Buy mussels live. They can be held a short while under refrigeration. When taken from the refrigerator, mussels will open their shells a little because of the temperature change. Snap their shells closed, and if they do not reopen slowly, discard them, as they have died overnight. Occasionally you will find a particularly heavy shell, which could mean it is filled only with mud and debris.

Oysters

Within that homely shell, the oyster holds one of nature's most complete foods. With a form of protein almost 100 percent usable by the body, the oyster is also especially rich in copper, iron, and iodine.

Up until about 1900, the East Coast oyster beds were believed to be inexhaustible. But overharvesting, pollution, natural disasters, and predators reduced the annual harvest drastically. The federal government, allied with the conservation groups and the oystermen themselves, has brought back the oyster harvest, not to its earlier richness,

but to a definite uptrend as shown in the annual gains made by the industry.

In buying oysters in the shell, plan on six large oysters per person served on the half shell. A pint of shucked oysters, either select or standard size, should serve six. Select oysters are generally preferred for frying, and standard, for stews, casseroles, or stuffing.

Shell oysters should be bought live and should remain alive for a month, if stored, deep shell down, unopened, and dry, in the coldest part of the refrigerator until near serving time. A shell gaping open indicates a dead oyster. Shucked oysters will remain fresh for three days, refrigerated. Frozen oysters should be used as soon as thawed, and no oyster should have any odor except an utterly fresh one. The deep shells may be kept after use. When washed they can be reused with oysters purchased fresh in bulk, already opened. Do not wash shells in an automatic dishwasher; shell flakes will clog the drain.

The old injunction about eating oysters only during months with an *R* in them stems from a fact of oyster life; during the summer, the oyster spawns, and its meat tends to be thin and watery. In New York state, the taking of oysters is prohibited from May through August, as a conservation measure, to let the life cycle proceed undisturbed.

Scallops

In the United States only two varieties of scallop are commercially valuable. The Eastern shores, from Nova Scotia to South Carolina, abound in the large sea scallop, which is harvested the year round. The muscle, or eye, sometimes measures 2 inches across, and it is the only part that is marketed. The beautiful scallop shell, up to 8 inches wide, so useful around the kitchen for baking and serving, is usually dumped overboard when the scallop is shucked at sea. Smaller and more expensive is the bay scallop, which comes from inshore waters from New England to the Gulf of Mexico. Sweet and delicate in flavor, the bay scallop is usually not much more than half an inch across, with a 4-inch shell.

The little bay scallops may run as many as 40 to the pound and are available from September through March, fresh. Frozen, of course, they are available the year round. Sea scallops run about 18 to the pound and are always in season. They account for about three-fourths of the total scallops marketed.

Shrimp

Before flash freezing and refrigerated transportation, shrimp was chiefly a southern dish, with New Orleans being the proprietary center of shrimpdom. Now 90 percent of our shrimp are marketed frozen (heads off). Increasingly popular are the ready-to-cook, shelled and cleaned, flash-frozen shrimp, packed in bags of a pound or two, which permit the cook to use any amount and keep the rest frozen for the next use.

The number of shrimp you buy depends on how you plan to use them and on the size of the shrimp. Shrimp are marketed by the size or count: jumbo-size come 8 to 15 per pound; medium-size shrimp will run 16 to 20 per pound; small shrimp will run 21 or more to the pound; and the tiny, pink Pacific shrimp can run as high as 180 per pound, with a delicacy of flavor which vies with that of a species taken off Greenland and prized by the Danes, who use some 50 of them for one of their marvelous open-face sandwiches.

Raw shrimp are called green shrimp.

Among the most perishable of foods, shrimp with a hint of ammonia odor or slippery feel are not fresh. Fresh shrimp should be cooked within a day or two of purchase; after cooking they will keep refrigerated for a few days. If you buy frozen, cooked shrimp, expect to keep them in your freezer no longer than six weeks. If you buy frozen raw shrimp, however, they will keep in your freezer up to six months.

Langouste

Langouste is the French name for rock lobster, and langoustine is the name given to the smaller European spiny lobster. In the United States the crayfish found along the coasts of California and Florida resembles this spiny lobster. The rock lobster has no claws, but its meaty tail is a delicacy. Most of the rock lobster tails consumed in this country are imported from South Africa, Brazil, Australia, and New Zealand.

VEGETABLES AND FRUITS

From a nutritional standpoint, fresh fruits and vegetables are better than frozen ones, which have lost some of their vitamins and minerals, and better still than canned ones, which have given up even more. Dried fruits, such as raisins, figs, etc., retain their natural sugars, and dried beans and legumes are good sources of protein and carbohydrates. All are useful in the diet, and when fresh things are difficult to obtain, happy is the cook with a well-stocked freezer and pantry.

As a matter of economy, buy vegetables and fruits when they are in season in your locality. Transportation costs of produce shipped great distances are passed along to the consumer.

The freshness of produce is more easily

judged than the freshness of meats. Wilt and bruising are obvious flaws. Head lettuce and cabbage that have had parts trimmed from them are visibly unfresh. Avoid all fruits and vegetables with soft spots; they show the onset of decay.

Look for good color and medium size in vegetables. Those that have grown overlarge will have developed pithy centers, as in radishes and turnips, or large, seedy centers, as in cucumbers and summer squash, or hard cores, as in parsnips and carrots. Old eggplants are likely to be pithy, tough, and strong in flavor.

Look for citrus fruits with thin, smooth skins. Citrus can have a greenish color when ripe, so color is often added by the grower to give it eye appeal. Remember, too, when using any fruit, to wash it well, even if you are going to peel it, because of possible residues of pesticides. A lemon or orange, from which the zest is to be grated and used, should be scrubbed thoroughly. American lemons sold in France are labeled "rind unfit for human consumption" because of our use of dyes and pesticides.

Melon selection is a bit more problematical. A cantaloupe should have a fine allover "netting" with no green color showing through. Pick up the melon in both hands; it should have a heavy feel for its size. Smell it; the fragrance is definitely fruity when ripe. Finally, press the stem end (the place where it was severed from the vine) with your two thumbs. It should yield to the touch, but not be soft. Reject any melon with a soft, dented spot, which may indicate overripeness or decay.

A honeydew melon should be smooth and symmetrical and have a pale, yellowish green color and heavy feel. It could have a whitish spot where it has lain on the ground; examine it and reject it if the spot has begun to soften. Again, the stem end should yield to gentle pressure.

A watermelon, if the dealer will not cut a plug out of it to show you the color, must be selected on the basis of faith and sound. A ripe melon will give back a dull "thunk" sound when struck with the middle finger propelled by the thumb, indicating development of high water content. Underripe, it will sound like any other large, solid vegetable, such as a cucumber. Test the stem end; it should give somewhat when pressed. A ripe melon is proportionately heavier for its size than a green one because of the water content.

Once you have filled your market basket and checked out of the store, go straight home to put away your perishable foods. The dry cleaner, if you have forgotton him earlier, can wait until tomorrow. Proper food storage cannot be overemphasized, and it is the topic of discussion of the following chapter.

Overleaf
A light and lovely Summertime Luncheon for 6 or 8 includes Strawberry Frappé, Pumpernickel Strata, Vegetable Garnish, and Demitasse Mousse (see page 262).

Food
Storage

Considering the emphasis we place on shopping for the freshest of everything, it must seem paradoxical when you are advised to shop only once a week. How can we eat fresh food on the sixth day after shopping? The answer has to do with getting to know the fresh life of foods and learning how to store them to retain it.

VEGETABLES

Take into account that some foods stay fresh longer than others. Let's take vegetables first. Plan to use your asparagus, peas, fresh corn, spinach, and mustard greens within the first 2 days after purchase.

Longer lived are the following vegetables; use them the third and fourth days: cauliflower, collards, kale, Swiss chard, okra, watercress, and ripe tomatoes.

Save these vegetables for the last of the week: beets, broccoli, cucumbers, eggplant, endive, green peppers, green onions, and summer squash.

Here are some that won't give you any problems; they keep their freshness well over a week with proper storage: winter squash, artichokes, cabbage, carrots, celery, dry onions, and potatoes.

When you buy tomatoes, buy a range of ripeness, from barely pink to red ripe. Put the pink ones on the window sill to ripen while you enjoy the ripe ones. The same good sense prevails in buying avocados. Buy a range from green to ripe, eat the ripe ones first, while the rest come to perfection at room temperature. Once they have ripened, refrigerate, and use tomatoes and avocados as though you had just brought them home from the store.

Vegetable juices
M. F. K. Fisher, my favorite food writer of all time, tells in her classically useful

and funny book, *How To Cook a Wolf*, how to save the good juices in which vegetables have been cooked. She was quite sure the only suitable container was an empty gin bottle. The vitamin-laden liquids went into that refrigerated bottle and came out frequently to be doused into soups or drunk hot or cold as a picker-upper. The book was written in 1942 during World War II to illustrate food economy and would serve as well today.

Mrs. Fisher would certainly subscribe to my "soup collection," and you might like to try it: Keep a one- or two-quart plastic container with a tight-fitting lid in the door shelf of your freezer to receive tiny leftovers. A spoonful of anything from the liquid drained from steamed vegetables to mashed potatoes, macaroni and cheese, corn, tomatoes, peas, beans, and bits of meat all add interest to a soup mix. When the carton is filled, all you need to add is a good broth, and you will have a fine vitamin-filled vegetable soup.

If you plan to do large-scale home freezing, by all means order *Home and Garden Booklet #10*, Office of Information, U.S.D.A., Washington, DC 20250.

FRUITS, BERRIES, MELONS

Again, it is a matter of planning and timing the consumption of these fresh foods. Use berries, ripe peaches, bananas, and apricots within the first day or two. Buy peaches ripe; they do not ripen successfully when picked green.

Keep your grapes, nectarines, pears, plums, less ripe apricots, and rhubarb 3 to 5 days. Bananas do ripen successfully at home and may be bought underripe for use later in the week. Store bananas at room temperature; refrigerate the remaining fruits.

Citrus fruits, apples, and melons will hold, refrigerated, for a week.

MEATS

With meats, use the same sort of judgement in storage. Decide which meats you will use the first and second days. Store them in the meat drawer of your refrigerator. Chicken, pork, fish, liver (and other variety meats, including cold cuts), and ground meats are especially perishable and potential troublemakers. Beef (loosen the wrapping so it can "breathe") may be refrigerated up to five days. Meats, except beef, not to be used within two days must be overwrapped and frozen. You can see it is basic to plan the order in which you intend to use the meats you buy.

Leftovers must be treated with extreme respect. If you are not going to use them within one or two days, wrap them properly, and freeze them. Leftover stuffed poultry poses a hazard so great that I no longer stuff poultry at all; I bake bird and dressing separately. If you do bake stuffed poultry, then *as soon as the meal is over*, remove the stuffing, and remove meat from bones. Boil the bones, if you want them for soup stock, immediately. If you are not going to use any of these poultry and dressing leftovers within two days, freeze them.

FOOD POISONS

The reason for over-caution in the storage of fresh and leftover foods is that the aerobic (meaning it grows in air) bacteria salmonella lurks just around the corner waiting for us to get careless. It accounts for nearly all food poisoning on picnics (chicken salad, potato salad, etc.), in school lunchrooms, and in the home. So for safety's sake, mind your meats, and care for your carbohydrates. Salmonella does not attack lactose or sucrose, so you may feel reassured to know that the mold that forms sometimes on syrups is harmless, needing only to be removed before the syrup is used.

The other and even more dangerous food poison is botulism. It is anaerobic (meaning it grows without air, in a vacuum). It can grow only in canned foods, commercial or home-canned. Never buy or even open a tin of food with bulging ends or a dark line of leakage down the seam. Home-canned foods must be discarded *without tasting* if the lid is swollen or if liquid is oozing out from under the lid.

It is because of fear of botulism that home canning of low-acid foods must be done in a pressure canner. The boiling water-bath method of canning can reach only 212°F., while a temperature in excess of 400°F. is required to kill the botulinus toxin.

Additional safety precautions

- Never refreeze a food that has accidentally thawed. You may cook it; then refreeze.
- Sprouts on potatoes and on the leaves of rhubarb contain chemicals that will cause illness; *never eat them.*
- Chopping boards, utensils, and knives used in the preparation of raw meats must be thoroughly sanitized before being used on any other food. If you carve your roast chicken or other meat on the board on which you prepared it earlier without an intervening thorough cleaning, you are asking for trouble. The stale, raw meat juices can contaminate the cooked food.
- Always drive straight home after grocery shopping. A hot day, a delay of an hour or more, and you'll be left with wilted lettuce with lowered vitamin content, thawed frozen foods which certainly should not be refrozen, and thawed orange juice with its vitamin C in a nosedive. If delay is unavoidable, and you know it in advance, toss a cooler chest into the car to help insulate your cold foods.

In addition to the storage of foods mentioned in the chart, there are a few that deserve special discussion: the refrigeration and freezing of milk and cream, processed dairy products, butter, and the freezing of eggs.

Some Useful Definitions

Refrigerator Storage
Normal temperature between +2°C. and +8°C. (36°F. and 45°F.). In summer or when refrigerator is heavily filled, temperature should be set colder, because refrigeration losses are greater.

Freezer Compartment in Refrigerator
Temperature about −18°C. (0°F.) for short-term storage of frozen foods, meat products, and frozen desserts.

Freezer Storage
Temperature preferably −23°C. (−10°F.) but not over −18°C (0°F.). For long-term storage of frozen meats, fruits, vegetables, and baked goods, and for home freezing.

Cool Storage
Store in refrigerator or cool cellar.

Protected from Light
Store in dark place such as tightly closed cabinet, or wrap in aluminum foil.

Dry Storage
Store in dry place without extreme temperature changes.

Perishable Foods Storage Chart			
Food	*Storage Time*	*Food*	*Storage Time*
Fruits		Cabbage, cauliflower, and snap beans	Store as above. Use cabbage within 1 to 2 weeks, other vegetables in 3 to 5 days.
Apples	Store mellow apples, uncovered, in refrigerator. Unripe or hard apples are best held unwrapped at coolest room temperature possible until ready to eat. Use ripe apples within one week.	Carrots, beets, parsnips, radishes, and turnips	Remove tops and store, covered, in refrigerator. Use within 1 to 2 weeks.
Apricots, avocados, grapes, nectarines, pears, peaches, plums, and rhubarb	When ripe, store these fruits uncovered in refrigerator. Use or preserve within 3 to 5 days. When unripe, allow to ripen in open air at room temperature. Keep out of sun.	Green peas and limas	Leave in pods and store in refrigerator. Use within 1 to 2 days.
		Lettuce	Wash thoroughly, dry and store in crisper or plastic bags. Use within 1 to 2 days.
Bananas	Store unwrapped at room temperature. Keep out of sun.	Onions	Store mature onions at room temperature or slightly cooler in loosely woven open-mesh containers. Stored this way, onions keep several months. They sprout and decay at high temperature and in high humidity. Keep green onions cold and moist in plastic bags in refrigerator. Use within 2 to 3 days.
Berries and cherries	Keep whole, uncovered and unwashed in refrigerator until ready to use (washing and stemming before refrigerating results in loss of food value and more rapid spoilage). Use or preserve within 1 to 2 days.		
Citrus fruits and melons	Best stored unwrapped (remove plastic bags even if perforated) at coolest room temperature possible. Use within a week. Short-term holding in refrigerator is not harmful to quality, but if citrus fruits are held too long at too low a temperature, the skin becomes pitted and the flesh discolors.	Potatoes	Store in dark, well-ventilated place at cool room temperature. Light causes greening which lowers eating quality. High temperatures hasten sprouting and shriveling. Use within 1 week .
		Spinach, kale, collards, chard; beet, turnip, and mustard greens	Wash thoroughly in lukewarm, then cold, water. Lift out as grit settles to bottom of pan. Drain well and store in crisper or plastic bags. Use within 1 to 2 days.
Vegetables			
Sort vegetables before storing. Discard any that are bruised or soft or that show evidence of decay or worm injury. The vegetable crisper in your refrigerator performs better if at least two thirds full. If it's less full than this, vegetables will keep better if put in plastic bags before being stored in crisper.		Sweet corn	Store, unhusked and uncovered, in refrigerator. Use within 1 to 2 days.
Asparagus	Discard tough part of stalks. Store as above. Use within 1 to 2 days.		

Perishable Foods Storage Chart (Continued)

Food	Storage Time	Food	Storage Time
Sweet potatoes, hard-rind squashes, and rutabagas	Store at room temperature. These will keep several months at 60° F. but only 1 week at higher temperature.	**Fats and Oils**	
		Fat drippings and margarine	Store same as for butter.
Tomatoes	Store ripe tomatoes uncovered in refrigerator. Use within a week.	Cooking and salad oils	Keep small quantities at room temperature and use before flavor changes. For long storage, keep oils in refrigerator. Some oils may cloud and solidify. This is not harmful. If warmed to room temperature, oils will become clear and liquid again.
Meat, Poultry and Fish			
Cold cuts	Store in original wrapping in refrigerator. Use within 3 to 5 days.		
Cured and smoked meats	Store ham, frankfurters, bacon, bologna, and smoked sausage in original wrapping in refrigerator. Uncooked cured pork can be stored longer than fresh pork, but the fat will become rancid if stored too long. Bacon should be eaten within 1 week, a half ham or ham slices in 3 to 5 days, a whole ham within 1 week.	Hydrogenated shortenings and lard	Most firm vegetable shortenings and lard have been stabilized by hydrogenation or antioxidants. These can be stored at room temperature. Lard that is not stabilized should be refrigerated. Keep covered.
		Mayonnaise and other salad dressings	Keep all homemade salad dressings in refrigerator. All bottled dressings, especially mayonnaise, should be refrigerated after opening.
Seafood, poultry, meat roasts, chops, and steaks	Remove poultry from original wrapping and store, loosely covered, in coldest part of refrigerator or in special meat compartment. Meats can be held 1 to 2 days in original wrapping. For longer storage, unwrap and cover loosely. Use poultry and seafood within 1 to 2 days. Roasts, chops, and steaks can be held 3 to 5 days.	**Miscellaneous**	
		Honey and syrups	Store at room temperature until opened. After opening, honey and syrups are better protected from mold if refrigerated. If crystals form in refrigerated honey, dissolve by putting container in hot water.
Ground and mechanically tenderized meats	Store in coldest part of refrigerator. Use within 1 to 2 days.		
		Jellies, jams, preserves, catsup, and chili sauce	After opening, store, covered, in refrigerator.
Variety meats: liver, kidneys, brains, and poultry giblets	Store in coldest part of refrigerator. Use within 1 to 2 days. Before storing poultry giblets, remove from separate bag, rewrap, and refrigerate.	Nuts	Store in airtight containers in refrigerator or freezer to delay rancidity.
		Peanut butter	After opening, store in refrigerator. Remove from refrigerator shortly before using to allow peanut butter to soften.

Perishable Foods Storage Chart (Continued)			
Food	*Storage Time*	*Food*	*Storage Time*
Leftover cooked meats and meat dishes, stuffing gravy, and broth	Cool meats and meat dishes quickly (container can be placed in cold water), cover and refrigerate promptly. Remove leftover stuffing from poultry, cool at once and store in refrigerator. Cover gravy and broth, and refrigerate at once. Use all the above within 1 to 2 days, or package and freeze.	Cheese spreads and cheese foods	After containers of these foods have been opened, cover and store in refrigerator.
		Hard cheeses: Cheddar, Parmesan, and Swiss	Keep in refrigerator, tightly wrapped. Use original wrappings when possible. Hard cheeses will keep several months.
Eggs	Store promptly in refrigerator. Eggs lose their mild flavor quickly at room temperature. Use within 1 week. Cover leftover yolks with cold water and store, covered, in refrigerator. Egg whites should also be stored, covered, in refrigerator. Us both within 1 to 2 days.	Soft cheeses: cottage, cream, Brie, Camembert, etc.	Store tightly covered. Use cottage cheese within 3 to 5 days, others within 2 weeks.
		Butter	Store tightly wrapped or covered, in refrigerator. Use within 2 weeks. Don't let butter stand at room temperature; heat and light hasten rancidity.

DAIRY PRODUCTS

Milk and cream

In the refrigerator a temperature of about 40°F. is necessary to protect the freshness of dairy products. These pasteurized foods can be kept in a palatable condition up to two weeks, in some cases, but because of variation in refrigerator temperatures, it is recommended that they be used within four or five days. Always close the container to keep the product from picking up odors and flavors from other foods.

Freezer storage of milk and cream is not recommended except as an alternative to losing it to spoilage, if long storage is necessary. Milk that has been frozen and thawed will show flaky deposits of protein on the glass. While these deposits do not affect the nutritional value, the appearance is different from that of fresh milk.

Milk or cream that has been frozen should be thawed slowly overnight in the refrigerator. Or immerse the container in cold water for several hours. Rapid thawing tends to increase separation of fats and other solids, making it difficult or impossible to remix. Heavy whipping cream, frozen and thawed, will neither whip smoothly nor have good volume. However, freshly whipped cream may be frozen to good advantage. Place individual portions to be used for garnish on a waxed paper-lined cookie sheet. Freeze; then carefully package, seal, and store.

Processed dairy products

Refrigerate yogurt, sour cream, and buttermilk exactly as you do any other fresh milk product. For maximum flavor, use within 4 or 5 days. Longer storage results in stronger acid flavor but does not affect the value for use in cooking.

Cottage cheese and cream cheese are stored in a similar manner and must be kept tightly closed to prevent their picking up other food odors. For utmost enjoyment of the delicate flavors, use these cheeses soon after purchase.

Because of the adverse effect of freezing on the smoothness and texture of cultured products, freezing is not recommended. Creamed cottage cheese will be mushy upon thawing, but uncreamed (dry) cottage cheese and cream cheese can be frozen, well sealed, then thawed slowly in the refrigerator. These do lose some of their nice texture but are usable.

Butter

A temperature of 40°F., the same as for other dairy products, is the correct one at which to store butter. It should be kept closed, in its original wrapping. Salted butter will keep fresh for several weeks, but unsalted butter is more delicate, since it has no salt to act as a preservative, and should be held for a limited time lest rancidity overtake it. Two or 3 weeks is long enough, depending on how long it was in the store before you bought it, to expect it to stay fresh.

Butter freezes well and will hold from 6 to 9 months at 0° to –10°F. To freeze, overwrap the original packaging with air-and vaporproof material, wrapping each pound separately. Butter is one of the things to look for at sale prices since it can be stored so successfully.

EGGS

Eggs may be frozen, but bear in mind that freezing does not improve the quality of eggs; they do lose some of their freshness. Freezing should be used only as an alternative to losing the egg.

Whole eggs should be beaten lightly, enough to mix yolk and white, with either a teaspoon of salt or a tablespoon of sugar per cup, depending on how you intend to use them. Freeze in ice-cube trays; then transfer them to freezer bags, put the date on the label, and freeze.

Egg yolks may be frozen. Beat them, adding a teaspoon of water per yolk. Freeze them all together in a glass freezer jar, stating date and number of yolks on the label, or freeze singly in ice-cube trays, transferring them to freezer bags when frozen. When thawed, they may be used in any recipe calling for egg yolks.

To freeze egg whites stir just enough to break them up, then freeze all together in a glass freezer jar or singly in ice-cube trays, transferring them to freezer bags when frozen.

Stocking
the
Pantry

The pantry shelf, thoughtfully stocked and maintained, can help you have a smooth-running kitchen and avoid such difficulties as when unexpected visitors drop in and it happens to be mealtime; or when you want to have that nice neighbor in for lunch, but nothing is ready to serve. A pantry should be well stocked, but should not contain anything that is useless because of old age due to overbuying on some bargain. About two months' worth of unopened shelf-stable food, kept replenished, is about what you need.

Remember to rotate your stock; put the oldest can of sardines on top of the new ones, older cans of soup in front of the new additions, and so on. When you are down to one of an item, put it on your automatic, ever-ready grocery list for replacement.

PANTRY STAPLES

Here are a few staples for the pantry shelf:

Cans, Jars, and Bottles

Vegetables, several kinds	Tomato catsup
Fruits, several kinds	Soups, a variety
Sardines	Extra cream soups for casseroles
Deviled ham	Mushrooms
Tuna fish	Tomato puree
Vienna sausage	Tomato sauce
Dried chipped beef	Pickles, olives
Jelly, jam, preserves	Party nuts
Tomato and vegetable juices	Corn syrups, dark and light
Evaporated milk	Molasses
Beef stew	Honey

Dry Packages

Soda crackers	Dry milk solids
Party crackers	Spaghetti, macaroni, noodles
Potato flakes (emergency use only)	Beans
Long grain rice	Split peas, lentils
Instant rice (emergency use only)	Raisins, prunes
	Oatmeal, grits, barley

Tapioca
Brown and powdered
  sugars
Extra can of coffee
Tea bags
Cake and brownie
  mixes
Ready-to-eat high
  protein cereal

Soft drinks and mixers
  such as soda, tonic
  water, etc.
Plain gelatin
Flavored gelatin desserts
Pudding mixes
Cocoa

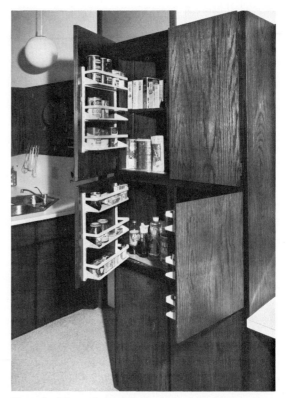

This list presupposes that your flour, corn-meal, salt, sugar, vanilla, baking soda, and spices are stored conveniently around your baking-mixing center.

Please notice "emergency use only" in the potato flakes and instant rice listings. They are patently inferior to freshly cooked potatoes and regular rice; nevertheless, there are times when even the purists among us must use them.

It is gratifying to find quickly an appetizing tray of snacks can materialize from the pantry shelf to go with a spur-of-the-moment invitation to "drop in for a drink." Nuts, party crackers, sardines, Vienna sausages, and deviled ham, with or without a cheese or two from the refrigerator, garnished with pickles and olives, can make sudden guests feel as though you expected them all along.

If you don't have the luxury of a large old-fashioned pantry, look around your own kitchen, and try to find some space for a modern-day minipantry. In this kitchen, cabinets and the backs of their doors were outfitted and turned into handy, adequate storage space.

How
to
See
Right
Through
a
Recipe

We will begin with the most transparent of all recipes.

RECIPE 1: HOW TO BOIL WATER QUICKLY

1 kettle with lid
Water to half-fill kettle

Pour hot tap water into kettle; place on high heat, and cover with lid. Water will come to a boil much more quickly with a cover than without one. Would you believe some people don't know that? But you do; you are now cooking, and you are ready for Recipe 2.

RECIPE 2: SOMETHING GOOD ON TOAST FOR 2

1 (11-ounce) can condensed cream of
    cheddar cheese soup, undiluted
1 (2½-ounce) jar sliced dried beef
4 slices bread

Open soup can and beef jar. Place soup in small, heavy-bottomed saucepan. Heat over low heat, stirring, until it is hot and smooth. Turn beef out on cutting board; it will be in a tight roll. Cut across roll 3 or 4 times with sharp knife. Add meat to soup. Stir over low heat while you process bread in toaster. Place toast on two warm plates, and spoon cheese-beef mixture over it. Easy, right? Saw right through it, didn't you?

Now let's read through Recipe 3. This one is harder and you may not want to make it until tomorrow, but we will use it because it is delicious, and it incorporates several techniques you will learn from the illustrations in this book.

RECIPE 3: APRICOT CHARLOTTE

2 envelopes unflavored gelatin
1 cup milk
1 cup apricot nectar or ¾ cup apricot
**   nectar plus ¼ cup apricot- or**
**   orange-flavored liqueur**
¾ cup sugar, divided
2 egg whites
**   Pinch (about ⅛ teaspoon) salt**
2 cups whipping cream
10 to 12 ladyfingers, split

Soften gelatin in cold milk. Heat the nectar or combination nectar-liqueur to boiling point; add ¼ cup sugar; then stir it into the softened gelatin, stirring until gelatin is completely dissolved. Chill until slightly thickened. Meanwhile, beat the egg whites with the salt until soft peaks form, and add the remaining sugar slowly, beating until stiff and glossy. Fold into gelatin mixture. Whip 1½ cups of the cream, and fold into the gelatin mixture. Arrange the split ladyfingers in 8 glass dessert dishes. Spoon gelatin mixture into the dishes, and chill until set. At serving time, whip remaining cream, and garnish each serving. Yield: 8 servings.

Read the recipe and instructions carefully. Then have a little talk with yourself: What must I get from the store? I have gelatin, etc. I'll need apricot nectar, whipping cream, etc. A small saucepan will do for the gelatin softening and will also contain the nectar and the sugar. First operation is to get that gelatin mixture mixed and cooling.

My electric mixer has a small bowl and a large one. The small one will hold egg whites, and the large one will do for the cream. I must have the egg whites at room temperature, but the cream has to be ice cold. Just to make sure, I will put the cream

into the bowl and refrigerate them both until I am ready.

Liqueur? I don't like alcohol. Oh yes, alcohol dissipates at 170°F., and the liqueur will not do anything except emphasize the apricot flavor. When that first mixture thickens, I will stir a spoonful of beaten egg whites into it to loosen it; then I will pour the gelatin mixture over the egg whites instead of the other way around because it is easier to get egg whites folded up off the bottom than it is the sticky jelled part. And I will pour that mixture over the whipped cream and fold it up all together in the largest bowl.

Why must I whip the cream in two separate operations? No reason at all; I know I can whip all of it and save enough out for garnish by putting it in a bowl lined with cheesecloth. That will drain off the whey, and the garnish will be ready at dessert time, so I won't have to keep my guests waiting for dessert while I whip the topping.

But I don't have 8 matching glass dessert dishes. I will use that lovely glass bowl Aunt Maude left me and serve the charlotte right from that onto chilled, flat dessert plates.

Sound silly? Of course it does. But soon you will think through a recipe in a flash, even to remembering to cover those 2 egg yolks with water for tomorrow's scrambled eggs and being glad you bought the large can of apricot nectar, because it makes a wonderful change from orange juice in the morning.

You will tailor your preparation to the equipment you have. If you have no electric mixer and do have a hand-held rotary beater, use it. As with any other beater, it is all right to rinse and dry it after beating the egg whites and before whipping the cream. But if it were the other way around, with fatty material being beaten first, as in "cream the butter and sugar" or "whip the cream" before the egg whites, you would have to wash the beaters with detergent. Egg whites will not whip to a full volume if there is a trace of fat about the bowl or the beater, remember?

In a little while you will see straight through a recipe. In principle, you will know an envelope of gelatin jells a pint of liquid, but jells more of whipped material, such as egg whites and cream.

You can single out that can of apricot nectar and liqueur as the flavor ingredient.

Do you like coffee flavor? Then substitute hot coffee and coffee-flavored liqueur, and add chocolate for mocha, keeping proportions the same. If you like orange flavoring, thaw frozen orange juice, and pour about ⅓ cup into a measuring cup; then add water to the ¾-cup line and orange liqueur, such as Grand Marnier, Curaçao, or Triple Sec, to the 1-cup line.

The possibilities are endless. Then you will have your own "Signature Charlotte." You will find other ideas for "signature" recipes later in the recipe section.

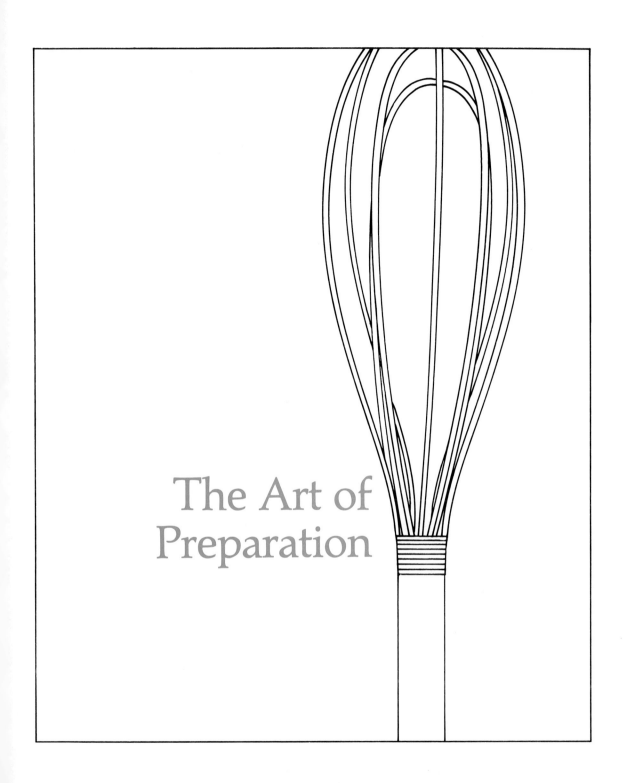

The Art of
Preparation

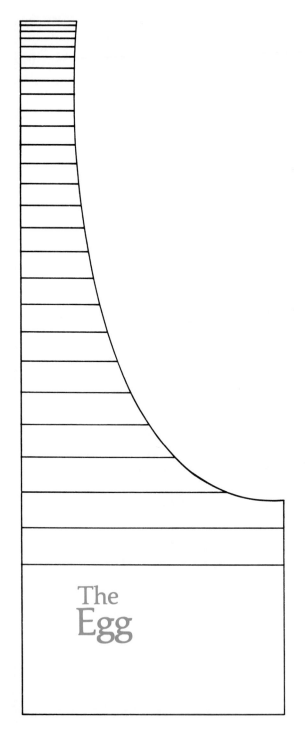

The
Egg

Few cooking teachers would quarrel with the traditional view of the egg as one of nature's most perfect and versatile foods. It comes double-wrapped in membrane and outer shell. In a pinch, it can serve as its own cooking utensil, and its beauty is as appreciable as its function.

People who make and sell packaging have, in recent years, taken a critical look at nature's egg container and considered taking it out of its shell, which they believe is too fragile and porous, and putting it into one of those marvelous plastic tetragons they use to pack servings of nondairy "coffee whitener" or "baked potato sauce" that one sometimes gets in restaurants.

So far, so good; the egg still comes in its shell. One reason it does may be that egg producers, after candling and washing the eggs, spray them with a fine oily mist to reseal the pores and render them less susceptible to surrounding odors. On the subject of shells, let's lay the matter of brown-shell egg versus white-shell egg to rest: there is no difference in the egg, superstition notwithstanding. (Certain hen breeds produce brown-shell eggs.)

COOKING WITH EGGS

The beginning cook will do well to master the egg early. First, consider the functions it performs in cooking:

- It thickens, as in sauces, puddings, cream fillings, soft and baked custards.
- It leavens, as in sponge cakes, butter cakes, quick breads, soufflés, and puffy omelets.
- It coats for breading, as in croquettes, meats, and other fried or baked foods.
- It binds, as in meat loaves, croquettes, and casseroles.
- It emulsifies, as in mayonnaise, salad dressings, and cream puffs.

- It clarifies, as in boiled coffee or soup stock.
- It retards crystallization, as in cake icings and candies.
- It is a browning agent when brushed on breads before baking.
- It is a fine edible glue for making seeds stick to bread loaves.

Chemically, the egg is very important in the human diet. Among its blessings we find fat, complete protein, iron, and vitamins A, B, and D. The egg combines well with milk, most cheeses, and meats. It stands alone as breakfast fare and, hard cooked, it can be the central ingredient in many delicious meatless main dishes.

The term "hard-cooked egg," as used in this book, is the same thing you may think of as "hard boiled." Our reason for calling it so is that eggs should never be allowed to come to a full boil at all. They should barely simmer. If you have had the experience of shelling a really hard-boiled egg, you may have seen the white tough and rubbery and the yolk with a green stain covering it. If you simmer eggs gently, this will not happen. Egg protein, like other protein, becomes more solid as it is heated. Hard boiling causes loss of flavor, and lowers the digestibility of the egg. Gentle heat is the rule for egg cookery, whether fried, scrambled, poached, soft, or hard cooked.

Nowadays, only a farmer has farm-fresh eggs. The rest of us rely on egg factories in which the chicken has never touched ground zero. But we are still in charge of selecting and storing the egg we use. Egg sizes range from pullet eggs, which weigh only about a pound per dozen, to extra large, which weigh about 27 or 28 ounces per dozen.

When a recipe in this book calls for an egg, we assume a Grade A large egg (24 ounces per dozen). In some circumstances, Grade B eggs may be a good buy for cooking or baking on a large scale, but stick to Grade A for poaching or frying sunnyside up.

BUYING AND STORING

How does one judge the freshness of an egg? Outer appearance can tell you just so much; look over them closely before you buy. No cracked ones, of course; cracks let in odors and bacteria. The egg should have a "bloom" of protective coating, either nature's own or the processor's mist, to seal pores, and the shell will have a fairly slick feel. We must rely on the processor to quick-cool the eggs and get them to the store in refrigerated trucks. The grocer must keep them properly refrigerated in the store.

An egg, properly handled and stored, should keep about ten days. It is not necessarily bad after this time, but you may wish to test it, if it has been held longer than usual. Place the egg in a pan of enough cool water to cover; if it lies flat, it is fresh. If one end tilts upward, go ahead and use it, but if the egg stands on end, throw it away.

After storage, the egg undergoes some change in its properties; the yolk may lose some of its thickening power, while the white may increase in leavening power.

Always store eggs near the bottom of the refrigerator, which is the coldest part, and don't wash them until you are ready to use them or the protective coating will be removed. Never mind the cunning wire baskets for displaying eggs as kitchen decor, you can get imperishable glass eggs for that purpose.

That is the storage story, but at cooking time, switch your thinking. Most hotel and restaurant chefs will take the eggs to be used that day out of refrigeration in the morning. Whites beat to greater volume at room temperature. Plastic bowls should not be used for beating egg whites, as some fat could be on the surface from previous use despite apparent cleanliness. Use a copper bowl and whisk, if you have them, or a stainless steel or glass bowl. When separating eggs, if any bit of yolk gets into the white, remove it with a piece of shell; yolk is fat and will prevent the whites from beating fully.

DRIED EGG SOLIDS

Dried egg solids are eggs from which 90 percent (or more) of the water has been removed. They can be purchased as whole eggs, egg yolk, or egg white and are packaged under strict U.S.D.A. regulations. For home use, they are packaged in 5- and 8-ounce containers. Eight ounces of dried whole egg solids equal 16 large eggs; 8 ounces of dried egg yolk solids equal 27 egg yolks; 8 ounces of dried egg white solids equal 50 egg whites.

Storage

Dried egg solids must be stored in a dry, cool place, preferably in the refrigerator. In any case, they must be refrigerated, once the package is opened, in an airtight container. They will keep sweet and mild in flavor for about a year when stored under these conditions.

Dried egg solids can replace fresh eggs in many recipes. But occasionally the possibility of contamination exists, so it is best to use them in dishes that are to be thoroughly cooked. Some processors maintain more rigid controls against bacteriological contamination than others. Again, read the label to make sure the product is

Measuring Ingredients

A widowed friend who had to turn to cooking in middle age took me to task over and over again for giving him recipes calling for a "small onion" or a "large potato." "That means nothing to me," he said. "I want to know exactly what you mean by a small onion." He forced me to think, bless him. I am now able to say what I mean by a small onion. There may be someone else interested (or amused) by these funny measurements based on water displacement.

Small, medium, and large onion size can be determined, loosely, thus: Put a cupful of water into a 2-cup, glass measuring pitcher. A small onion will displace about ¼ cup of water, a medium-size onion about ⅓ cup, and a large one, ½ cup or more. Potatoes, small, medium-size, and large, will displace ⅓, ⅔, and 1 cup water, respectively. Of course when any solid food is chopped, it measures more, owing to the air surrounding the pieces. Usually the measurement is not all that critical; but if it is, the recipe will specify spoons or cups. In other measurements, please note the following:

- We assume mayonnaise, not salad dressing, when recipe calls for mayonnaise.
- We assume Grade A large when an egg is called for.
- For a cup of flour, spoon flour lightly into a dry-measuring cup and level off with a straightedge. In most recipes it is not necessary to sift, as most flour now comes presifted. If it is necessary to sift (usually to blend dry ingredients), the recipe will say so.
- To measure a teaspoon, tablespoon, or fraction of either (dry), fill, and level with straightedge.
- A pinch is the amount of dry ingredient (salt, sugar, etc.) that can be picked up between the thumb and forefinger from an open container. It will vary, of course, with the size of the cook's hand.
- A dash (dry) is the shake of a container with perforated top such as a salt or spice shaker, or (liquid) a bottle with a hole in the top such as hot sauce or Worcestershire sauce. Again, if it is critical, measurement will be stated as "about 3 drops" or "¼ teaspoon."

safe for uncooked or slightly cooked dishes. If the label does not specifically say the product is safe for these uses, then use the dried egg solids only for dishes to be thoroughly cooked or to make noodles that are to be boiled for at least 12 minutes.

Reconstituting

When reconstituting dried egg solids, take from the package only enough for the dish you are making. Sift the egg solids; then measure, leveling with a straightedge. Put lukewarm water in a bowl; sprinkle the dried egg over the water, and stir to moisten the egg. Beat until smooth, scraping down the sides of the bowl with a spatula.

Substituting

Substitute dried egg solids in any recipe calling for fresh eggs in dishes to be thoroughly cooked. Sometimes it is easier, as in cake baking, to add the dried solids to the other dry ingredients, and then add the correct amount of water with the other liquids.

THE EGG: QUESTIONS AND ANSWERS

Q: What are those stringy white pieces in egg whites?

A: Normal components, called the chalazae; they will whip with the rest and go unnoticed. In custard making, they are strained out before cooking. Actually a prominent chalaza indicates a high-quality egg.

Q: What are blood spots?

A: One egg in a hundred will have a blood spot on the yolk for one of several reasons: breed, feed, and condition of the hen causing rupture of a blood vessel on the yolk. Most of these eggs are removed during grading. If the egg seems otherwise fresh, remove the spot with a spoon, and use it.

Q: What size bowl should I use for beating egg whites?

A: The bowl size depends on the purpose and number of the egg whites in question

Dried Egg Solids Chart

If a recipe calls for—	You may use—	
	Dried egg product, sifted	Lukewarm water
Whole eggs:[1]		
1.	2½ tablespoons	2½ tablespoons
6.	1 cup	1 cup
Egg yolks:		
1.	2 tablespoons	2 teaspoons
6.	¾ cup	¼ cup
Egg whites:		
1.	2 teaspoons	2 tablespoons
6.	¼ cup	¾ cup

[1]Large eggs weighing 24 ounces per dozen.

and whether other ingredients are to be folded in. Rule of thumb: Whole eggs will about double in volume, egg yolks alone will double, whites alone will triple. If beating only one yolk, one white, or one whole egg, use the smallest bowl that will accommodate the beaters, or beat by hand.

Q: Sometimes my egg whites won't beat to proper volume. Why?

A: One of several reasons: There may have been some fat, such as a bit of egg yolk, accidentally put into the whites, or the bowl or beaters may be slightly greasy; the whites could have been too cool (they must be at room temperature); the whites may have been too fresh (older egg whites beat to better volume).

Q: Can I beat egg whites ahead of time so they will be ready to fold into a mixture later?

A: No. Beat them just before adding. Held over, they tend to separate, becoming dry on top with a collection of water on the bottom.

Q: What is the best way to add egg yolks to a hot mixture?

A: You don't. The hot mixture is added very slowly to the beaten yolks while stirring vigorously until almost half the hot mixture is blended into the yolk. This slowly cooks the yolks, after which the yolk mixture is stirred back into the remaining hot mixture. Yolk added to a hot mixture will cook into lumps.

Q: What can I do with yolks leftover from angel cake or meringues?

A: Place them in a cup, cover with cold water, and refrigerate. Use them (drain off the water first) to augment custard, mayonnaise, rich pastry, breads, and shortcakes, or add them to the morning "scrambles."

Q: What do I do with leftover whites?

A: Use them in angel cakes, white cakes, meringues, and soufflés. Either white or

yolk, beaten with a little water, makes a fine "wash" on the tops of bread loaves to make a fine crust, and serves to "glue" on seeds of any kind you wish to put on top of your loaves.

Q: How do I clean tarnish and hardened yolk from utensils?

A: Egg yolk oxidizes silverware and must be cleaned off with silver polish. Pans or plates should be soaked in *cold* water to remove egg residue; hot water hardens the egg, and makes it more difficult to remove.

Q: Why are my hard-cooked eggs sometimes tough?

A: They are probably cooked too fast at too high temperature. With few exceptions (omelets, for example), eggs should be cooked slowly.

Q: Can a slightly cracked egg be hard cooked in the shell?

A: Yes, if you add a few drops of vinegar or lemon juice to the water, the egg should remain intact.

Q: How can I keep the shells from cracking when hard-cooking them?

A: Eggs should be at room temperature before cooking. You may remove them from the refrigerator and temper them: Place them in a pan, and cover them with warm tap water; let stand for about 15 minutes, and occasionally shake the pan gently. (It is also helpful to pierce the large end with a needle.) Bring to boiling (not bubbling) point. Reduce heat, and cook slowly for 15 minutes.

Q: Why are some hard-cooked eggs so difficult to shell?

A: A very fresh egg is usually harder to shell. Drain off the hot water, and replace it with cold, cracking each egg as you do so. Let stand a few minutes. Then peel. Sometimes holding the egg under cold running water helps. Take off shell and membrane at the same time.

Q: Why do my scrambled eggs seem hard and dry when I serve them when they seemed to be nice and moist just from the pan?

A: Eggs continue to cook with their own heat after they are removed from the stove. Take them up moments before they reach the degree of doneness you desire. Serve them on warm (not hot) plates immediately.

Q: What is a coddled egg?

A: This is an egg that has been gently lowered into boiling water. The pan is then immediately taken off the heat and covered. Let stand 6 minutes for a soft, 8 minutes for a firm egg.

Q: What is a shirred egg?

A: It is baked. The French call it *en cocotte* for the individual ramekin in which it is baked. Butter a custard cup or ramekin, break the egg into it, and add a teaspoonful of milk or cream and a bit of salt. Bake at 350°F. just long enough for the white to set. Remember the egg will continue to cook after it comes from the oven, so be careful not to overbake.

Q: What makes a soufflé fall?

A: Soufflés fall for several reasons. 1) Egg whites should be beaten until they are firm but not dry, then carefully folded into the base mixture. 2) Possibly not enough egg whites were used; it takes 1 or 2 more whites than yolks. 3) Too rapid cooking. A soufflé is made to fall, actually, but one hopes it makes it to the table and the serving spoon before it happens.

Q: What is a soufflé omelet?

A: One in which the eggs are separated, the whites beaten stiff, then folded into the yolk mixture.

Q: Why do my pie meringues sometimes fall?

A: One or more of these faults may have occurred: egg whites too cold when beaten; sugar imperfectly dissolves, always use superfine sugar; too little egg white, always use at least 3 whites per pie.

Q: Why do I sometimes get little beads of caramelized sugar on top of my pie meringue?

A: Perhaps you used too much sugar, which has not been completely dissolved. The excess caramelizes on the surface. Two tablespoons per egg white is plenty; many good cooks use slightly less. (I happen to love those sugar beads.)

Q: Why does my pie meringue shrink away from the edge of the pie?

A: The meringue was not spread all the way to the edge of the crust. Be careful to seal the meringue to the crust. Always cool a meringue pie slowly, away from drafts.

Q: How can I keep the meringue from tearing when I cut and serve my pie?

A: Use a wet knife blade.

Q: Are egg shells good for anything?

A: Indeed they are. Water in which eggs have been boiled is good for houseplants, and finely crushed shells are a valuable addition to the soil around outdoor plants because of their lime content.

Q: There seem to be so many food preparations called by the name "meringue" that I get confused. What are they, and how do they differ?

A: Meringues are an interesting family of foods. Depending on the additions you make to egg whites, you can have a beautiful pie topping, crisp meringue shells, egg kisses, or a poached soft meringue to float on a custard. The Italian meringue, which bakers use to top their pies, is a cousin of divinity candy in that it is made by beating cooked sugar syrup into beaten egg whites. The main difference between Italian meringue and divinity is the temperature to which the syrup is cooked. Italian meringue, used as a pie topping, may be browned slightly under the broiler.

Separating an Egg

Eggs separate more easily when cold, but must be allowed to attain room temperature after separating, before they are used in a recipe.

1 Have ready two bowls, one for whites, one for yolks. Strike egg sharply against rounded edge of bowl, making a horizontal crack in the shell almost an inch wide.

2 Push both thumb tips into the opening, and gently pull egg apart, tilting the egg so the yolk stays in one half of the shell while white drops into waiting bowl. The jagged shell edge cuts the white so it can fall away.

3 Carefully roll yolk to other half of shell, letting more white drop into bowl.

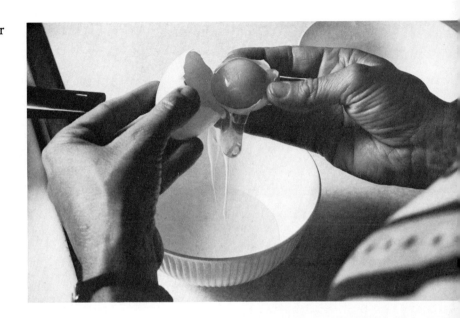

4 It may be necessary to roll the yolk back and forth between halves of shell 3 or 4 times. If a bit of white still clings, discard empty half of shell, and use a free finger to press white against edge of shell to complete separation.

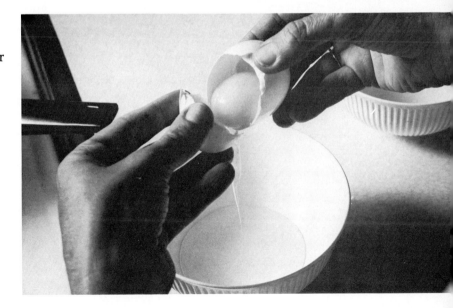

Making an Omelet

3 eggs
1 tablespoon cooking oil or clarified
   butter
Salt and pepper to taste
Filling

Fillings
- Herb Omelet: Add 1 teaspoon fresh,
  minced herbs or ¼ teaspoon dried
  herbs to omelet before cooking. Some
  possibilities are chervil, basil, celery

1 Have ready 3 eggs at room temperature,
an omelet pan measuring about 7 inches
across top and 5 inches across bottom (or
a plain cast iron 6-inch skillet), a fork,
and a tablespoon cooking oil or clarified
butter. (Plain butter will brown before it
becomes hot enough.) Beat eggs with wire
whisk until creamy, not foamy. Add no
salt or milk which toughens egg. You
may use a tablespoon water per egg,
though purists insist on only egg; no
more.

2 Add oil or clarified butter to pan, and
rotate pan to coat well. If nonstick skillet
or nonstick spray is used, use the oil or
butter anyway for flavor.

seeds, chives, parsley, or combinations.
- Meat Omelet: Fold ½ cup finely chopped cooked meat, fish, or poultry into eggs before cooking.

- Filled and Sauced Omelet: Add finely chopped meat to a can of cream of mushroom, cream of chicken, or cream of celery soup; heat. Spoon about ¼ of the mixture over omelet

3 As soon as a few drops of water dance and evaporate when flicked into pan, it is ready for the eggs. Pour beaten eggs all at once into pan. Keep heat on medium.

4 Hold handle of pan with left hand, and tilt or shake pan back and forth as you lift edges of egg with fork, allowing liquid egg to run underneath the cooked part.

(Continued)

just before rolling it out of the pan; then pour remaining sauce over the top.

• Cheese Omelet: You may add 3 tablespoons of your favorite cheese, grated, to beaten egg before cooking, or wait, and sprinkle it over top of omelet just before rolling it onto the plate. Use additional shredded cheese on top for garnish.

5 Let pan sit on heat for a moment to brown bottom only slightly. Remove from heat while top is still moist and creamy. Add salt and pepper and Filling (½ cup for a 3-egg omelet) desired. Shake pan to make sure omelet is loose. Start with the edge nearest handle and, with fork, fold or roll about ⅓ of the omelet toward center of pan.

6 Tilt pan sharply over warm plate, and make another push with fork to roll omelet onto plate. It may be rolled, with both edges underneath, or it may be simply folded, depending on how you handle it. Yield: 1 or (with Filling) 2 servings.

Poaching an Egg

Note: Alternate method for poaching eggs is to cook them in commercially sold egg poaching cups (see *Eggs Benedict*).

1 Break egg into a small dish or cup.

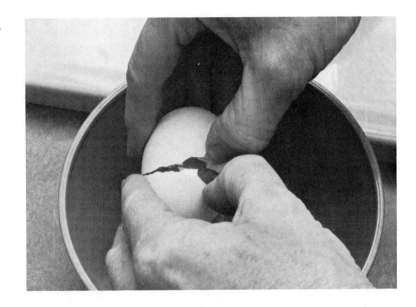

2 Bring water to simmering in a shallow pan. Add a few drops of vinegar. Then, just before sliding egg into water, stir water to form a little "whirlpool."

(Continued)

3 Quickly slip egg from dish into center of water that is still in motion from stirring. This helps keep the egg rounded instead of allowing it to spread.

4 When egg has reached desired degree of doneness, lift it carefully from the water with a slotted egg turner. Hold for a moment to drain.

5 Trim ragged edges, if desired, hold egg turner on paper towel for further draining.

6 Have toast, cut into bite-size pieces, ready on a warm plate, if desired. Slide egg onto the toast, using knife to position it.

Overleaf
The morning meal is easily transformed into an "occasion" with a breakfast or brunch of Cheese Blintzes Topped with Sour Cream, Crisp Bacon Curls, and Bloody Marys (see page 270).

Blender Hollandaise Sauce

6 whole eggs or 3 yolks
1 stick (½ cup) butter
2 tablespoons lemon juice
¼ teaspoon salt
    Dash white or black pepper

1 Put (room temperature) eggs into blender jar. Meanwhile, melt butter on lowest heat; it should be hot but not browned.

2 Add lemon juice to blender jar.

Note: You may flavor Hollandaise slightly
with garlic or onion by adding a sliver to
the original egg-lemon juice mixture
before blending.

3 Add salt to blender jar.

4 Add pepper; cover, and turn blender on
and off once.

(Continued)

5 Turn motor on high, remove cover, and pour hot butter in a steady stream into egg mixture. Turn motor off; you will find the sauce emulsified and ready for use. You may keep it warm for a while by setting jar in a pan of warm water, or you may refrigerate, and reheat when needed, over hot water. If sauce thickens too much in storing, reblend it, adding 1 or 2 tablespoons hot water to restore consistency.

6 Perfectly smooth and velvety Hollandaise is delicious poured over any hot vegetable and elegant over Eggs Benedict. Yield: about 1 cup.

Eggs Benedict

Blender Hollandaise Sauce
2 English muffins
Butter or margarine, softened
4 slices Canadian bacon, cooked
4 poached eggs

1 Assemble materials and make Blender Hollandaise.

2 Split English muffins; spread cut sides with butter, and toast under broiler. Cook Canadian bacon to desired doneness.

(Continued)

79

3 Break eggs into custard cups, and slip into buttered egg-poacher cups. Cover, and steam 3 to 5 minutes or until whites are solid and yolks are of desired doneness. Or poach in water (see *Poaching an Egg*).

4 Place a slice of Canadian bacon on each muffin half, and top with a poached egg. Spoon Blender Hollandaise Sauce over egg. Yield: 4 servings.

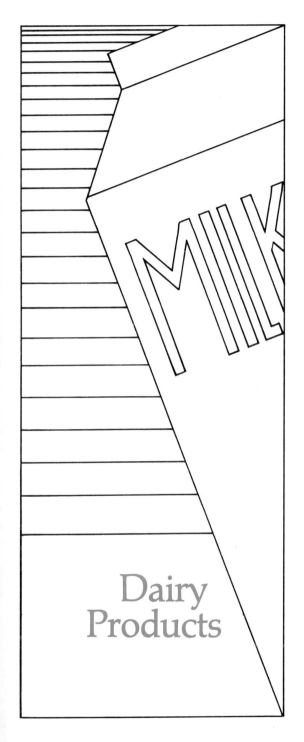

Dairy
Products

Of the four basic food groups, the dairy group is the single most dependable source of calcium. Milk and milk products come in many forms: ice cream, cheese, processed milks, sweet and sour creams, yogurt, etc. Intelligent use of a variety of dairy products lends excitement to the diet and assures not only a steady calcium supply but also a perfect protein source, because milk contains all the amino acids.

There are over 100 food elements in milk including riboflavin (vitamin B_2), phosphorus, thiamin (vitamin B_1), niacin, and vitamin A. The latter is one of the chief benefits of milk, for it helps the body fight infection and night blindness and aids in keeping the skin clear and smooth.

Since the vitamin A content is in the fat part of milk and is removed in the skimming process, skim milk or low-fat milk will have the vitamin A replaced by artificial means; vitamin D is added at the same time.

NONFROZEN PRODUCTS

There are standard terms used for the varied forms in which milk is marketed:

- Whole milk contains 3 to 5 percent fat on the average; exact standards are set by the individual states. Nonfat milk solids comprise an average of 8 percent of whole milk and are the source of the proteins, minerals, and most of the milk vitamins other than A. Most whole milk is pasteurized, homogenized, and fortified with Vitamin D.
- Low-Fat, or 2 percent, milk contains 1.75 to 2 percent fat. Usually fortified by adding nonfat milk solids plus vitamins A and D.
- Skim milk, almost completely fat free, is usually fortified with nonfat milk solids and vitamins A and D.

- Chocolate milk is whole milk with chocolate flavor added.
- Chocolate drink is skim or partially skimmed milk with chocolate flavor added.
- Cultured buttermilk is made from fresh fluid skim milk artificially soured and thickened by the addition of a bacteria culture. Sometimes bits of butter are added to augment flavor.
- Evaporated milk is whole milk that has been reduced to half its original volume by a vacuum process. The concentrate is homogenized and fortified with vitamin D, and then canned, sealed, and sterilized.
- Sweetened condensed milk comes from fresh whole milk to which sugar has been added; then 60 percent of the water content is removed under vacuum. The resulting concentrate is cooled, canned, and sealed.
- Instant nonfat dry milk is a water-soluble dry product made by extracting water and milkfat from pasteurized fresh milk. Sometimes fortified with vitamins A and D. Read the label for this information.
- Half-and-half is a mixture of milk and cream averaging 11 percent butterfat.
- Cream may be packed under pressure in an aerosol container that whips the cream as it comes from the can. Such cream may contain sugar, stabilizer, and emulsifier. Read label to see if the cream is real or a non-dairy product.
- Dairy sour cream (also called salad cream, Hampshire cream, Devonshire cream, or cream dressing) is light (about 18 percent) cream pasteurized, homogenized, and blended with a lactic acid culture to produce a custardlike consistency and a tangy flavor.
- Sour half-and-half is a product comparable to sour cream but containing only 10 to 12 percent butterfat. May be used instead of sour cream.
- Imitation sour cream is similar to the natural product, but vegetable oil has replaced the butterfat. Skim milk and/or cereal proteins sometimes are added.
- Imitation half-and-half is similar to the natural product, but vegetable oil has replaced the butterfat. Sometimes skim milk and/or cereal proteins are added.
- Yogurt is a thick custardlike, tangy-flavored product made of fresh milk whose butterfat has been reduced to an average of 2 to 3½ percent. After pasteurization and cooling, nonfat milk solids, a lactic acid culture, and stabilizers are added. Yogurt is available plain or in many flavors including fresh fruit.
- Cottage cheese (also called Dutch cheese or Schmierkäse) is the solid form of milk. An unripened or semi-cheese, it is the curd of pasteurized skim milk or reconstituted nonfat dry milk, coagulated by the addition of a lactic acid-producing bacteria. Rennet may be added to assist the formation of curds, which separate from the whey, or liquid part, of milk.
- Creamed cottage cheese contains a dressing of pasteurized fresh cream or cream mixed with milk and/or skim milk. The product is 4 percent butterfat by weight and contains not more than 80 percent moisture.
- Baker's cheese (also called pot cheese or hoop cheese) is a skim milk product similar to dry cottage cheese but finer grained and slightly more acid in flavor. It is soft like a cream cheese without the fat. Sometimes it is pressed into brick or loaf form.

- Farm cheese (also called farmer's or pressed cheese) is a white, dry, cottage cheese pressed into a cake form and wrapped in parchment paper. The flavor is that of milk, and it should slice without crumbling.
- Large-curd cottage cheese is a sweet curd, creamed cottage cheese made with controlled acidity.
- Small-curd cottage cheese is a product with small, firm curds, close to the cottage cheese formerly made in the home and called Schmierkäse.
- Dry cottage cheese (uncreamed or plain) is the salted, drained curd without added cream. It contains almost no fat and comes in large or small curd.
- Butter is the solid fat part of milk, which is made from sweet, pasteurized cream that has been separated from the lighter liquid and churned to produce solid lumps of butter. The butter is further worked to remove moisture and is formed and wrapped for marketing. Butter may be purchased salted or unsalted.
- Whipped butter has had air and/or liquid beaten into it. It cannot be used to replace regular butter in recipes; it is made to be used as a spread.

FROZEN PRODUCTS

- Ice cream is a dessert made of milk and cream, sweetening, stabilizing agents, sometimes eggs, and various flavorings. The butterfat content may range from 10 percent to 16 percent and caloric content from 875 to 1,000 per pound. Commercial ice cream will seldom approach the upper levels stated here.
- Ice milk is a dessert made of milk, some cream, sweetening, stabilizers, and flavorings. The butterfat content ranges from 2 percent to 8 percent and there are approximately 689 calories per pound.
- Sherbet is a frozen mixture of sugar, milk solids, stabilizers, food acid, and water. Fruit juices and extracts are used for flavoring. Butterfat content ranges from 1 percent to 5 percent and calories, about 600 per pound.

DAIRY PRODUCTS: QUESTIONS AND ANSWERS

Q: Why does cream whip easily sometimes and with difficulty at others?

A: The cream may be too fresh; it should be two or three days old to whip to greatest volume. Or, you may not have chilled your cream, bowl, and beaters sufficiently.

Q: Why does cream turn to butter when whipped too long?

A: Whipping cream has to be watched closely. There is a point at which the fat solidifies, and you find yourself churning butter instead of whipping cream.

Q: What can I do if the cream starts to turn toward the butter stage?

A: If it hasn't turned completely, serve lumpy whipped cream. If it has separated, whip it some more, and use it as butter. Work the liquid out by turning butter into a bowl of ice water and squeezing the water through it. Drain water off and work in ½ teaspoon salt per cup.

Q: When preparing butter for browning food, how can I tell when the temperature is right?

A: Butter foams when it melts. There is a point at which the foam diminishes before the butter browns. Add the food before the butter browns.

Q: Can margarine always be substituted for butter?

A: Yes, although butter adds flavor that margarine cannot to certain foods. A compromise is to use half butter and half margarine. Exception: margarine is better in some candy recipes because of its lecithin content. Always use margarine when specified.

Q: How can I soften butter without melting it?

A: Cut it up and place it in a warmed bowl. Let it stand, covered, for a few minutes, then stir it. Usually it is soft enough if kept in the butter compartment of your refrigerator.

Q: Why can't I use whipped butter in recipes?

A: Whipped butter is softened for spreading by having air and/or liquid beaten into it. Recipes calling for butter require solid fat.

Q: What is clarified butter?

A: Butter that has been melted and chilled. The solid is then lifted away from the liquid, and discarded. Clarification heightens the smoke point of butter. Clarified butter will stay fresh in the refrigerator for at least 2 months, much longer than regular butter.

Q: Why do recipes call for clarified butter?

A: It has a higher smoke point than regular butter and is better for sautéing.

Q: Some people refer to evaporated milk as "cream." Can I use it when cream is called for in a recipe?

A: No. Evaporated milk is milk and is used, diluted, to replace fresh milk in recipes. True, it will whip, if chilled almost to the freezing point, but it has a "dead" flavor. Use it whipped only if you are going to use plenty of flavoring to cover the taste of it. Never substitute evaporated milk in candy recipes; it will curdle almost every time.

Q: Why is my homemade ice cream grainy in texture?

A: For several reasons: Too much salt in the ice mixture will cause too rapid freezing and a grainy texture. The container may have been too full; it should never be filled more than ⅔ full. Making your own ice cream is one instance in which evaporated milk may be substituted for about ⅓ of the cream called for in a recipe. The addition of evaporated milk seems to produce a smoother finished product.

Whipping Cream

Note: If whipped cream must be held much longer than half an hour, prepare a bowl with a double thickness of cheesecloth fastened over it with a rubber band. Cheesecloth should reach down to within about an inch of bottom of bowl. Pour in whipped cream, and refrigerate. Whey will drain through cloth, and whipped cream will remain firm on top of cloth.

To freeze whipped cream, line a cookie

1 Equipment needed for whipping cream is minimal: electric or rotary beater, sifter or small strainer for the powdered sugar, and measuring spoons for sugar and vanilla. Note that a deep bowl is used; in early stage of whipping, cream tends to splash.

2 Note softness of cream, whipped until it barely shows form. Cream at this stage is called Chantilly cream, and it will "drape" down around the sides of the food it garnishes. Sift in the sugar, and stir or fold it in.

(Continued)

sheet with waxed paper. With spoon, drop garnish-size dollops of whipped cream on paper. Freeze. When frozen, transfer to plastic bag, and place in a protected place in freezer so dollops will not be mashed. To use for garnish, place dollop of frozen cream on top of dessert; cream will be thawed by the time it reaches the table.

3 Measure and add vanilla, folding or stirring it into cream.

4 To make whipped cream that will stand up and hold its shape as garnish, continue to beat after addition of sugar and vanilla until desired stiffness is obtained. *Caution:* Do not overbeat or cream will separate into solid butter and water.

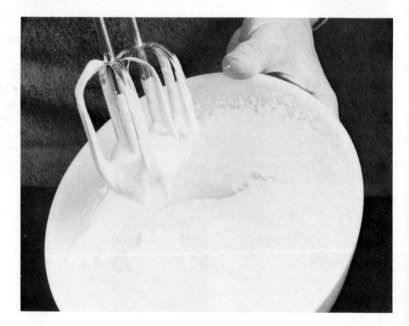

Making Cream Puffs (Pâté à Choux)

½ cup butter or margarine
1 cup water
 Pinch salt
1 cup flour
4 eggs

1 Cream puffs and éclairs belong to the same family of hollow, crisp breadstuffs as do Yorkshire pudding and popovers. To make them, combine butter with water in a heavy saucepan. Cook, stirring with wooden spoon, until butter is melted. Add salt. Add flour at once, stirring hard.

2 Cook, and stir over medium heat until mixture leaves sides of pan and collects in a ball around spoon. Remove from heat.

(Continued)

Note: For éclairs use the same basic recipe given for Cream Puffs, and form dough (a pastry bag is nice but not necessary) into rectangles ¾ inch wide by 3 to 4 inches long. Bake as for cream puffs, then gash along side to fill with whipped cream or pastry cream, flavored to taste. Top with a chocolate glaze.

3 Using either wooden spoon (shown) or electric mixer, beat in eggs, one at a time, beating hard after each addition until smooth and glossy. Continue to beat until mixture will hold peak when spoon is lifted.

4 Recipe makes 12 large, dessert puffs or 2 to 3 dozen tiny party puffs depending on the size spoon you use; pick up portions of dough, and deposit on greased cookie sheet. Leave 2 inches between large puffs, 1 inch between tiny ones, for spreading.

5 To make puffs crustier, sprinkle them lightly with water just before baking. If you happen to keep an atomizer of water for your houseplants, using it works beautifully. Bake large puffs for 10 minutes at 400°, reduce heat to 350°, and bake about 25 minutes longer or until firm on outside and lightly browned. Bake tiny puffs 10 minutes at 400°, reduce heat to 350°, and bake about 10 minutes longer.

6 Crisp, hollow puffs hot from the oven are ready to be cooled on racks. When cool, split crosswise, not quite through. Pull out filaments of soft dough, and fill as desired.
Yield: 12 large puffs or 2 to 3 dozen tiny puffs.

Whipping Butter

Note: Whipped butter is not intended for use in recipes; use it only as a spread. Used in this way, it costs less and contains fewer calories per serving than regular butter.

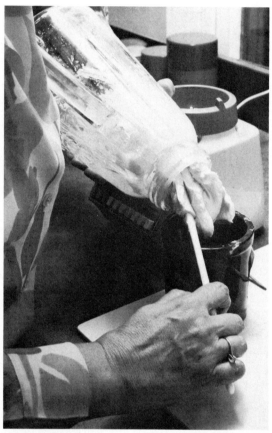

1 Have ready butter at room temperature and one-fourth as much ice water as butter (or ½ cup water to a pound of butter); this is how much water the butter can safely absorb without risk of separating. Place butter in blender; blend a few seconds. Without stopping motor, add ice water in a thin trickle.

2 With rubber spatula, scrape whipped butter from blender jar into storage container.

3 Whipped butter should be stored in crock or other jar with a tight-fitting lid.

4 Alternate method for making whipped butter is to beat it with an electric mixer, which works fine, although the blender is quicker.

Nondairy
Fats
and
Oils

ANIMAL FATS

- Bacon fat (drippings) is a by-product of the bacon cooked at breakfast, which can be kept to be used as seasoning. If the container is large and the fat infrequently used, the can should be kept refrigerated to keep it from becoming rancid. Other drippings, as from beef, lamb, etc., may be saved in separate containers to be used for cooking that particular meat next time.
- Chicken fat (schmaltz) is most used by Jewish cooks for reasons of dietary laws. It is as fine for seasoning as are bacon drippings.
- Lard is fat rendered from the fatty tissues of pork. It may be smooth or slightly grainy, depending on the processing. Most of the lard sold is steam rendered at a high temperature, then refined to remove any dark color and strong flavor. Most home-rendered lard is kettle-cooked and strained through cloth.
- Suet is the fat from beef. It may be rendered and used as shortening. While it accounts for very little of the shortening consumed at home, it is used a great deal in commercial frying. Ground suet is an essential ingredient in mincemeat and plum puddings for the Christmas holidays. It is also an excellent bird food, as birds like it uncooked.
- Salt pork (fat back) is the salt-cured flank or side of the hog. It is highly regarded, especially in the South, as seasoning for vegetables. Blanched and cubed small, it is a valuable addition to other dishes such as stews and seafood chowders.
- Hog jowl (jowl bacon) is the cheek of the hog, cured by salt alone or salt and

smoke, and used for seasoning. Actually, either salt pork or jowl bacon can be a delicious breakfast bacon. Sliced thin, blanched, and floured, it is then fried slowly until it is crisp, and drained on paper towels.

VEGETABLE FATS

Hydrogenated all-vegetable shortening

Hydrogenated all-vegetable shortenings are vegetable oils that have been purified, bleached, then solidified by the addition of hydrogen. The most common bases for hydrogenated shortening are cottonseed and soybean oils, but varying amounts of other oils such as corn and peanut are sometimes used. The oil thus hydrogenated becomes a "fat," which remains solid at room temperature. The product is then deodorized by steam under vacuum and high temperatures to produce bland flavor.

The final step in the manufacture is called "plasticizing." This process consists of rapid chilling and whipping to put air into the shortening, which gives it the characteristic smoothness. It is then packaged. Nearly all of the all-vegetable hydrogenated shortenings sold contain small quantities of mono- and diglyceride fats to improve baking performance.

Oleomargarine

Oleomargarine may contain only vegetable oil, or it may be a combination of vegetable and animal fat. The label must state the kind of fat or fats used.

Vegetable margarine

Vegetable or nut margarine is emulsified, refined oil with cultured milk added. It is processed by crystallizing and kneading by machine to produce a butterlike consistency. Legally, margarine must contain 80 percent fat. Salt is optional. Most margarine is enriched with vitamins to make it nutritionally competitive with butter.

Liquid lecithin

Liquid lecithin is an oily derivative of soybeans. It is an excellent material for coating pans so that foods will not stick. Commercial aerosol cans of lecithin are available, of course, for use on cookie sheets and other pans. But a far cheaper version may be purchased at health food stores, in liquid form, which looks terribly unattractive and has a slight odor that disappears during baking or cooking. This is not a food product as such, but a very useful one for a nonstick coating. It is excellent for the fat-free diet when you must not grease pans, and makes the cleanup after cooking much easier.

VEGETABLE OILS

Vegetable oils are the liquid fats most commonly used in this country. They are made from the seeds or fruits of plants by one of two methods: squeezing out the oil under pressure (expelling), or by dissolving it out with an organic solvent that is later evaporated (solvent extraction.) The raw oils are then refined, bleached, and deodorized before packaging. Oils most commonly used are made from olives, peanuts, corn, soybeans, cottonseed, and sunflower seed.

NONDAIRY FATS AND OILS: QUESTIONS AND ANSWERS

Q: How can I tell without a thermometer when my deep-frying oil has reached the proper temperature?

A: Drop a 1-inch cube of bread into the hot fat. At about 350° F., the bread will brown in 1 minute; at about 375° F., in 40 seconds; at about 385° F., in 20 seconds. Or sprinkle a pinch of flour into the fat. If the flour is promptly "seized" and browned, the fat is ready—at least it is hot; to whatever degree one never knows. May I ask a question? Why not buy a thermometer? They don't cost much, and if you do much deep frying, you need accuracy.

Q: What is shortening?

A: Any animal or vegetable fat or oil used in cooking.

Q: Can oil used for deep frying be reused?

A: Yes, unless it has taken on too heavy an odor from a food such as onion. Drop a thinly sliced unpeeled potato into the oil, then slowly heat the oil. The potato will absorb most food odor. Strain through cloth fastened over a coffee tin, and store for reuse. Delicately flavored foods should be cooked in fresh oil.

Q: Why do some recipes call for a combination of butter and oil for sautéing?

A: Cooking oil has a higher smoke point than butter. Sautéing can be carried out at a higher temperature than with butter alone and still have a nice buttery flavor.

Q: What is meant by the "smoke point"?

A: The point during the heating of a fat at which it starts to smoke is the smoke point. It is just short of burning and imparts a smoky, bad-tasting flavor to food cooked in it at that temperature.

Q: How can I clarify bacon drippings?

A: Use a saucepan with twice the capacity of the bacon fat and water: Combine 1 part water with 3 parts bacon fat and bring to a boil, stirring. Pour into a coffee tin, cool, and refrigerate. The impurities will be carried to the bottom with the water. When fat has solidified, either cut the clear fat into quarters, and remove to another container, or cut a triangular hole in the bottom of the tin with a tin-can opener, and drain the water off. If you use the latter method, you'll need to put an extra plastic coffee can lid on the bottom. Keep refrigerated. Would it surprise you to learn that clarified bacon drippings help to make delicious crust for apple pie?

Q: Should all fats and oils be kept refrigerated?

A: Hydrogenated vegetable shortening does not need refrigeration. Some hydrogenated lard will keep on the shelf. (Read the label.) With oils, it depends on how frequently you use them. Olive oil will solidify in the refrigerator, but if you don't use it often, refrigerate it. It takes only a few minutes under warm tap water to liquify.

Q: Which is the best vegetable oil to use for a low-cholesterol diet?

A: Safflower oil is best, as it contains the highest percentage of polyunsaturated fats. Olive oil is at the other end of the spectrum with the lowest polyunsaturated fat content.

Q: What are cracklings?

A: Cracklings are the crisp residue of fat and rind left after lard has been extracted. Excellent chopped and added to cornbread.

Q: How can I render chicken fat?

A: Use only the fat; no meat or bones. Cut up fat, and put it either into the top of a double boiler over boiling water or into a pan in the oven set at 250° F. When it has melted, strain through cloth and refrigerate. Rendered poultry fat tends to have a low smoke point, so it is well to use it in combination with cooking oil.

Q: Is there a difference between cooking and salad oils?

A: Yes. Oils to be used for salad are more highly refined by heat treatment and filtering to remove the high melting portions of the oil; this process permits the remainder to remain clear when refrigerated.

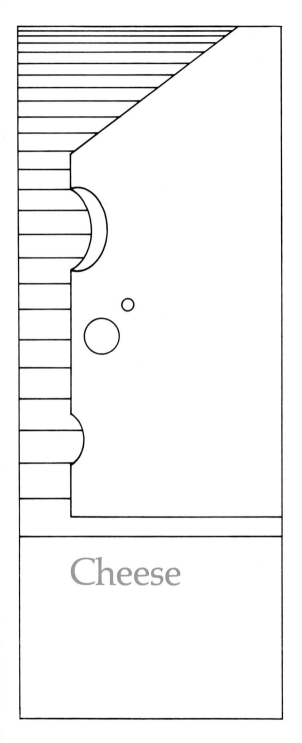

Cheese

Cheese is not only an excellent source of protein but also combines well with other foods. A "meatless" meal with cheese can be as nutritious and satisfying as one featuring meat. However, the subject of cheese is not a simple one. There are enough books on cheese to constitute a fine library for the would-be specialist. And upon the student who achieves a complete mastery of all aspects of cheese, a Bachelor of Science degree should be conferred.

The run-of-the-mill consumer of cheeses (and that includes most of us) is not a discriminating one. He regards the word "cheese" as merely a generic term for a sort of solid dairy product. The fact is that there are many fine cheeses, lots of mediocre ones, and some "cheeses" hardly deserving of the label.

NATURAL VS. PROCESSED CHEESES

There is, first of all, confusion about the difference between natural cheese and "pasteurized process" cheese.

To put it in the simplest terms, natural cheese is made from the milk of cows, goats, ewes, or, in some parts of the world, camels. (Mozzarella, the famous Italian cheese, was originally made from buffalo's milk.)

Processed cheese is made from cheese. In this country, major cheese processors buy natural cheeses from many small and large producers. Then the manufacturers grind two or more kinds of cheese and melt, pasteurize, emulsify, and blend them into a homogeneous mass.

Processed cheeses are sticky to the palate and low in flavor. Yet they have their uses in cooking, as they will take more heat without breaking down than will natural cheese. They are useful for hurry-up lunchbox stuffing, and they are a boon for those involved in institutional feeding, as for hospitals and schools. We all use them, but it is important to know one difference. They are not as high in food value as are natural cheeses.

The next step in the degradation of cheese came with the development of "pasteurized process cheese food," which by legal definition can contain only 51 percent natural cheese by volume. Most of the remaining 49 percent of its bulk is, of course, water.

Still another step down in food value are the "process cheese spreads," which have enough artificial stabilizers added to give them a cheese-like texture and appearance and make us forget they may contain up to 80 percent water; yes, legally. Use these products if you wish, but take time to realize how much these meltable, squeezable, spreadable wonders are running up your water bill!

Still in the testing stage, but coming soon, is a completely artificial cheese made of soybeans. This is to be an honest product, not pretending to be "cheese." And it should be welcomed by all of us and recognized for the sensible and useful product it is, vegetable protein (for which a large part of the world is starving).

SELECTING CHEESE

The cheese chart in this chapter will guide you in selecting cheeses for specific needs. Not all those listed are to be found on your grocer's shelves, but there are fine shops specializing in cheese in the large towns and cities of every state.

CHEESE: QUESTIONS AND ANSWERS

Q: What should the cheese label tell me?
A: In the case of a natural cheese, the name will appear most prominently: Cheddar, Swiss (Emmenthal, if it came from Switzerland), Blue (Roquefort, if it came from France), and so on.

Pasteurized process cheese will be labeled as such along with the variety or varieties of cheese used, as in "Pasteurized Swiss and American Cheese." "Pasteurized Process Cheese Food" will be so stated on its label, along with the other contents, such as milk solids, moisture content, stabilizers, etc., and are listed in order of proportion used, ranging from most to least. If the first ingredient listed is "water" as in some "Pasteurized Process Cheese Foods," water is the predominant ingredient, and the "cheese" is a bad buy.

Q: What are the major types of cheese?
A: There are at least six major families of cheese, each containing subgroups:

• Unripened cheeses include the soft ones such as cottage, farmer's, cream, and neufchâtel. They are high in water content and are eaten fresh. A firm unripened cheese like mozzarella has a lower moisture content and may be kept several months. When purchased, unripened cheese has a fresh milk odor.

• Soft ripened cheeses are the "smelly" ones such as Camembert, Limburger, Liederkranz, and Brie. The ripening begins on the outside and progresses to the center. The particular mold or bacteria on the surface of a soft cheese helps to bring out the characteristic flavor, body, and texture. To select, if packaging permits, press center to see that it is soft. If not, open it when you get home, and if the center hasn't ripened, leave it at room temperature for a day or two before serving. Store, after opening, in a screw-top, glass jar. Brie, known as "the queen of cheeses,"

Get To Know Cheese		
Type	*Color, Texture, Flavor*	*Use*
Cheddar	Semihard cheese nearly white to yellow in color. Mild to sharp in flavor depending upon aging. From firm to crumbly texture.	Appetizers, sandwiches, salads, in cooked foods, desserts.
Cheddar Type Colby Monterey or Jack	Mild in flavor. In texture, somewhat softer body than Cheddar.	Generally used for sandwiches and appetizers.
Pasteurized Process Cheese Cheese Foods Cheese Spreads Cold Pack Cheese Food or Club Cheese	Blend of natural cheeses which have been shredded, mixed. Semisoft; smooth texture. Spreads easily, melts quickly.	Appetizers, sandwiches, salads, in cooked foods, desserts.
Gouda and Edam	Red wax outer surface; yellow interior. Semisoft to firm. Nutlike flavor.	Appetizers, salads, in cooked foods, desserts.
Camembert	Smooth creamy yellow with edible white crust. Soft, surface-ripened. Mild to pungent flavor.	With crackers or fruits for appetizers or desserts.
Muenster	Creamy white, semisoft with tiny holes. Mild to mellow flavor.	Appetizers, sandwiches, salads.
Brick	Creamy yellow; semisoft with small holes. Mild to sharp flavor.	Appetizers, sandwiches, salads, desserts.
Swiss	Light yellow, large holes. Firm. Nutlike sweet flavor.	Appetizers, sandwiches, salads, in cooked foods.
Blue	Blue-veined, crumbly. Semisoft to firm. Sharp salty flavor.	Appetizers, salads, salad dressings, in cooked foods, desserts.
Gorgonzola	Blue green-veined. Semisoft to firm. Sharp, salty flavor. Less moisture than Blue.	Appetizers, salads, salad dressings, in cooked foods, desserts.
Provolone	Light yellow, semihard, smooth and somewhat plastic. Mellow to sharp, smoky flavor.	Appetizers, sandwiches, in cooked foods, desserts.
Parmesan Romano	Yellow white. Hard, granular. Sharp piquant flavor.	Grated in soups, breads, on spaghetti, in cooked foods.
Mozzarella Scamorze	Unripened semisoft cheese. White stretchy cheese —when served hot it becomes chewy. Varying moisture content. Sometimes designated for pizza. Delicate, mild flavor.	Sliced, in cooked foods, on pizza, sandwiches.

is the most subtle in flavor and delicate in keeping quality. It comes in rounds, has a powdery surface, and is usually packed in straw-lined boxes. It should be bought in a quantity to be consumed at once. A runny center in Brie indicates overripeness.

- Semisoft ripened cheeses ripen both from the center and the outer edge. Examples are Bel Paese, Port-du-Salut, and Muenster. Wrapped airtight, they will keep for weeks in the refrigerator.
- Firm ripened cheeses have bacterial culture throughout to aid the ripening. They have a longer curing time and therefore a lower moisture content. A few examples are Cheddar, Edam, Provolone, Swiss, Gouda, and Colby.
- Very hard ripened cheeses undergo a slow, long rate of curing which results in low moisture, high salt content. Some examples are Parmesan, Romano, and Sap Sago. Properly wrapped, in a screw-top container, they will keep for months.
- Vein-mold ripened cheeses are developed with a mold culture, usually blue, which permeates the entire cheese in streaks. In order of decreasing firmness, they include the English Stilton, Danish Blue, French Roquefort, and the Italian Gorgonzola, which has green mottling instead of blue.

Q: Can cheese be frozen?

A: Never resort to freezing except as an alternative to losing cheese. If you must freeze it, wrap cheese tightly in air- and vaporproof freezer wrap and in blocks no larger than half a pound for rapid freezing. Thaw in refrigerator in its wrapping. You must expect some deterioration in the cheese's texture; it will be pebbly to mealy.

Q: Does repeated change in temperature damage cheese?

A: Yes. If you have a large chunk or round of cheese, cut a piece only as large as you think will be consumed on that occasion. To slow drying of the remaining cut edge, place plastic wrap tightly against it, wrap cheese, and return it immediately to the refrigerator. Repeated room-to-refrigerator changes will result in drying and overripening.

Q: How is cheese stored to keep fresh as long as possible?

A: The unripened cheeses are refrigerated and used within several days. All other cheeses, unless you have a cellar of 50° to 55° in temperature, should also be refrigerated. Cheeses kept at room temperature will soon become overripe.

Q: If a cheese gets hard and dry before it can be used, must I throw it away?

A: No. Use it, grated, in salads and casseroles.

Q: How can I keep a crumbly cheese, such as Roquefort, from drying out?

A: Smooth the cut surface with a wet knife, or pick up a lump of soft butter and, using your hands, gently coat the entire surface. Wrap tightly in plastic.

Q: If cheese shows mold on the surface, is it spoiled?

A: Not necessarily. If mold is only on the surface, simply trim it off, and use cheese. However, if mold has spread through the body of the cheese, discard it.

Q: At what temperature should cheese be served?

A: Authorities will always say to serve cheese at room temperature. Allow a soft cheese to stand unrefrigerated about 20 minutes before serving, a hard cheese for up to an hour. If you are to serve one of the soft ripened cheeses, such as Camembert, and it is not yet quite ripe in the center, give if half a day at room temperature. Exception: If you like to eat your cheese cold, do so, and let the experts talk to themselves.

Q: What kind of server is best for cheese?

A: A wooden board of appropriate size is best. There are marble cheese servers available, but one suspects they are a by-product of the marble sellers' larger items. Cheese cutters come in a variety of shapes, sizes, and sharpnesses. A silver butter knife is nice for a small soft cheese.

Q: How should cheese be cut?

A: Be guided by the original shape of the cheese. Cut out a wedge from a wheel, a thick slice from a loaf-shaped cheese. Present a flat, round cheese, such as Brie, whole so guests may cut wedges as desired. Cylindrical cheese is cut crosswise like a sausage. A cheese ball may be cut (by the guests) in wedges or the ball may be cut in half and presented on the board, cut sides down.

Q: Is the rind of a soft cheese left on for serving?

A: Yes, and it is eaten along with the cheese.

Q: Should wax wrappings be removed?

A: Ordinarily, yes. However, since some of the wax coverings are so attractive, a neat edge or band of color left on (black wax on sharp Cheddar or red on Gouda) makes a nice presentation on a party cheese board. Otherwise, all wrappings should be removed for serving.

Q: Should butter be served with cheese?

A: Many people enjoy butter with cheese. Butter should be unsalted, so as not to detract from the cheese flavor. A delicious cheese spread can be made, using 1 part unsalted butter to 3 parts of a veined cheese. Serve with unsalted crackers, such as English water biscuits.

Q: How much cheese should be allowed per person?

A: It depends on what place the cheese

has in your overall plan. More than 2 ounces per person served with crackers and drinks before dinner will cut down on your guests' enjoyment of the meal. Two ounces also fills a fine sandwich. Two ounces, perhaps 3, if the meal is to be light, accompanied by fruit, is a splendid dessert.

Q: What about other cheese rinds?

A: Before serving, trim away previously cut edges if they seem dry. Trim the rind from only the size piece which you expect to be eaten.

Q: Is there a difference between cream cheese and neufchâtel?

A: They are both soft, unripened cheeses and may be used interchangeably; neufchâtel is lower in calories.

Q: Should cheese for a party be cut ahead of time?

A: No. Slices will dry out. It is part of the fun for guests to help themselves at the cheese board.

Q: I'd like to serve cheese and fruit for dessert on occasion but am uncertain about which cheese goes with which fruit.

A: Here is a list for guidance, but your rule should be to serve the combination you yourself like best:

Cheese	Fruit
Blue	Apples, pears
Brick	Apples, apricots, cherries, grapes, melon, peaches, pears
Camembert	Apples, peaches, pears, plums
Cheddar	Apples, cherries, melon, pears
Edam, Gouda	Apples, grapes, oranges, pineapple
Liederkranz	Apples, grapes, pears
Muenster	Apples, cantaloupe, cherries, grapes, melon
Swiss	Apples, apricots, grapes, melon, oranges, peaches, tangerines
Provolone	Pears
Brie	Peaches, cherries, plums, pears

Q: Is it all right to grate a firm cheese, such as Cheddar or Swiss, before storing it?

A: This is not recommended as some flavor loss will occur. For the same reason, buying cheese that has already been grated makes no sense. (It is also more expensive.)

Cooking with cheese

Q: What causes cheese to become stringy and ball up when cooked?

A: Heat. Cheese separates at about 150°F. A starch or stabilizer in the recipe will help prevent separation. If cheese is to be melted alone, use a double boiler with hot, not boiling, water underneath. Stir gently with a wooden spoon.

Q: How can I melt cheese quickly and easily?

A: Grate it first. Note, cheese is easier to grate when it is cold, and therefore hard, than when it becomes soft at room temperature. Once grated, cheese melts more evenly over hot water.

Q: Is there any way to get around the cheese-melting problem?

A: Whenever possible, mix the grated cheese with a warm sauce before combining it with the other ingredients. Soufflés and cheese-flavored cream sauces are made in this manner. A casserole of macaroni and cheese will be smoother if you use a hot cream sauce base and melt the cheese in it before combining.

Q: If a cheese mixture begins to curdle, what can be done?

A: Remove it from heat quickly, and beat vigorously with a wire whisk or electric mixer, adding one teaspoon of cornstarch mixed with 2 teaspoons cold water per cup of cheese. Try again, stirring over hot water, and give the cornstarch a chance to cook and smooth the mixture. It will be usable but not as smooth as it should have been.

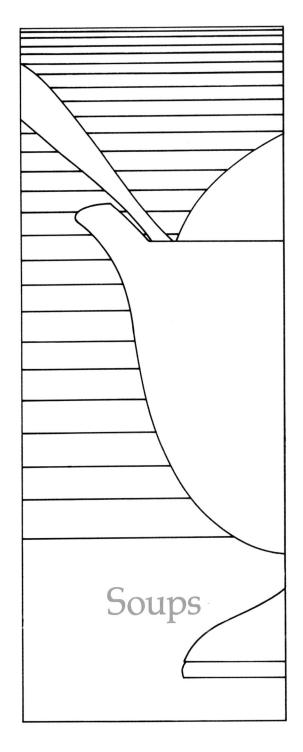

Soups

SOUPS: QUESTIONS AND ANSWERS

Q: What are the basic types of soups?

A: There are four, including the dessert soups:

- Clear soups are made from broth in which soup bones are slowly boiled to extract their flavor. The flavor may be enhanced by the addition of vegetables. The broth is then clarified. Some clear soups are made of the broth from vegetables alone.

- Cream soups are usually based on a flavorful broth, thickened by the addition of selected, pureed vegetables and a little flour if necessary. Many, such as pumpkin, vichyssoise, and cucumber are delicious served cold as well as hot.

- Thick soups come in great variety, including chili, vegetable, gumbo, and chowder. Most are suitable for main-dish serving.

- Fruit soups, Scandinavian in origin, are a refreshing dessert after a heavy meal. They are made with crushed fruit, preferably fresh, and a thickener, such as tapioca or cornstarch. A touch of an appropriate wine adds verve to fruit soups.

Q: What is stock?

A: The liquid obtained from boiling meat, bones, poultry, fish, or vegetables.

Q: How is stock clarified for use as clear soup?

A: First, strain out the solid matter, and replace the pot of liquid over heat. Separate an egg, reserving the yolk for another use. Beat the white slightly, and add it, along with the crushed egg shell, to the boiling broth. Boil hard for one minute. Line a colander or other strainer with a damp cloth, and place it over a clean container to receive the clarified liquid; then pour the broth through it.

Q: Why do some broths jell naturally while others do not?

A: The jelling of a broth depends on the gelatin content of the bones used. Veal bones are especially rich in gelatin. If you wish to congeal a broth that is too thin, reduce it by boiling. After it is reduced by one third, place a small quantity on a saucer in the refrigerator; if it does not congeal, continue boiling until it will do so.

Q: What is bisque?

A: This is a cream soup usually based on seafood, named for the creamy white color of once-fired pottery.

Q: How does Manhattan clam chowder differ from New England chowder?

A: Manhattan chowder contains tomato, the New England-style chowder does not; it is made with milk and cream.

Q: Must I be strict about following recipes for the French bouillabaise or its Italian counterpart, cioppino?

A: Not at all. Both these delicious soups originated in their respective coastal regions as a way of using whatever sea creatures were caught that day. Make them with any combination of seafoods obtainable.

Q: What is borsch, or is it borscht?

A: Both spellings are correct for this Ukrainian peasant soup. The central ingredient is beets; other ingredients vary widely. Sour cream is the garnish of choice for borscht.

Q: In making vegetable soup, are all the vegetables added at the same time?

A: No. First add the vegetables that take longest to cook, such as carrots, and green beans. Put in potatoes and/or pasta, corn, celery, onion, and okra when the first vegetables are partially done. Tomatoes and cooked, canned, or frozen vegetables

should be added only half an hour before the soup is done. Alternative: Shred or chop the hard vegetables; cut the softer ones into larger chunks.

Q: Is it possible to overcook vegetable soup?

A: Indeed it is. The soup kettle simmering all day is mostly nostalgic emotion. Vegetables should hold their shape and never be cooked to the point of mushiness. The meat stock base should be prepared first, and the vegetables added in sequence, as outlined in the previous paragraph.

Q: How can I remove an excess of grease from my soup or chili?

A: The very best way (and especially important for persons on a fat-free diet) is to prepare the base the day before the finished product is wanted. For chili, cook the ground beef and onions until meat loses its color. Then "flush" (douse it to cause the grease to rise) it with boiling water, barely enough to cover it. Stir well. Cool quickly, and refrigerate overnight. In the morning all the fat can be lifted off the top, the remaining ingredients added, and the cooking completed.

In making vegetable soup, make your meat stock; then strain out the bones and meat. Cool, and refrigerate the liquid overnight or several hours, and lift off the fat. Any meat should be picked from the bones and refrigerated separately and returned to the soup for the final cooking.

Here are some other stop-gap methods that will cut the fat down but not out: Skim fat from the top with a skimmer or shallow ladle. Or drop a pan of ice cubes into the soup, fat will cling to them; but skim them out quickly, or they will dilute the soup. Slices of bread or paper toweling may be laid on top of the soup to absorb some fat, then lifted off.

A better method, if you cannot start your

soup the day before, is to strain out the solids, placing the liquid in a tall, narrow container; then, use a bulb baster to lift the fat from the top. Finally, reunite liquid and solids.

Q: Can homemade soup be frozen?

A: Yes, though it is best, if possible, to remove potatoes because they get mushy when frozen. Mashed potatoes or dried potato flakes are a better form of potato to use, if you plan to freeze; they not only serve to thicken a soup nicely but are unaffected by freezing.

Q: How can I add flavor and interest to commercially canned soups?

A: Any canned soup is better if you use broth instead of the water called for. If you have no homemade broth in storage, dissolve a chicken or beef bouillon cube, as appropriate, in the water you add.

Sometimes mixing two varieties will give you a new soup. Tomato and pea soups, combined and mixed with milk; cream of asparagus and celery or mushroom, mixed with milk or broth.

Experiment with flavorings of your own: a pinch of sage or thyme in vegetable-beef soup, sherry in black bean, or chicken-rice with a dash of curry and enough real cream to reach the taste buds.

Q: Which soups should I keep on the shelf to be used as ingredients in other foods?

A: Most of the cream soups will stand you in good stead as substitutes for the more time consuming thick sauces called for in some recipes. Many casseroles use cream soup as flavor agent and binder. You can even make a delicious short-cut asparagus soufflé based on canned cream of asparagus soup. (See *Your Signature Soufflé*.)

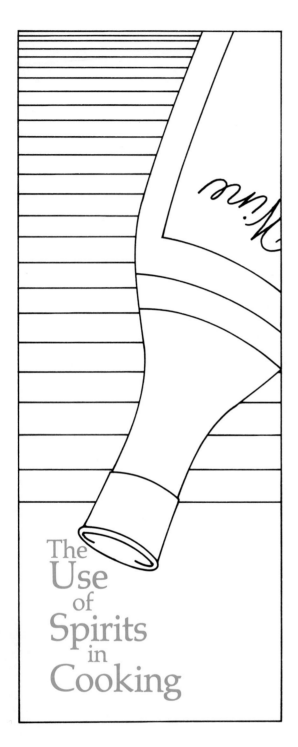

The
Use
of
Spirits
in
Cooking

Good cooks the world over have been cooking with wines and kindred spirits for centuries, a practice that needs no defense. You will find reference to wine in food in Homer's writings on early Greek civilization. Yet many of us remain hesitant about experimenting with wine cookery or about adding beer, bourbon, cognac, and other liquors to our food.

If the thought of alcohol in the cook pot troubles you, rest easy. Alcohol dissipates when the mixture reaches 170° F., 42° short of the boiling point of water at sea level. When the alcohol goes, most of the calories go too. This holds true with every alcoholic beverage from beer to brandy. What is left after cooking is an ineffable taste and aroma that can give a dish the dash that nothing else can impart.

Under no circumstances should one purchase bottles labeled "cooking wine." They contain salt and other additives, which only detract from the finished product. Buy table-grade wines and spirits for your cooking.

If you do not serve wine in your home, you might still consider keeping a medium-priced bottle of white and a bottle of red for cooking; dry vermouth is a good all-purpose white, and a dry burgundy will serve when red wine is required.

CHOOSING A WINE

The wine chart will help you decide which wines go with which foods, although you have the final word. If it suits your fancy to use a dry white with roast beef, then follow your tastes.

MEAT

Experimentation with wine cookery can open up new frontiers to the busy cook who must necessarily make use of convenience foods. Frozen chicken à la king is no pedestrian dish to be offered with an apologetic, "I didn't have time to make anything else," when enlivened with a goodly dash of white wine. Cream soups, likewise, are emboldened when each serving carries with it the bouquet of wine; sherry added to black bean soup is a special treat.

Try combining tomato and pea soups, using a half cup of sauterne in place of part of the liquid called for. A can of beef stew

can almost achieve Boeuf Bourguignon status, given a splash of burgundy as it heats.

Wine can bring out the full flavor of meat without injecting itself into the consciousness; try basting roast beef with burgundy, leg of lamb with a dry white, or brush a tender steak with a dry red as it broils.

In a marinade, spirits act as a tenderizer in the same way that vinegar or lemon juice does. If you suspect that the steak you have bought is less than tender, try something

Use Wine in Cooking

	Foods	Amount	Wine*
Soups	Cream Soups	1 tsp. per serving	Sauterne or Sherry
	Meat and Vegetable Soups	1 tsp. per serving	Burgundy
	Mock Turtle Soup	1 tsp. per serving	Sherry
Sauces	Cream Sauce and Variations	1 tbsp. per cup	Sherry or Rhine Wine
	Brown Sauce and Variations	1 tbsp. per cup	Burgundy
	Tomato Sauce	1 tbsp. per cup	Sherry or Burgundy
	Cheese Sauce	1 tbsp. per cup	Sherry or Chablis
	Dessert Sauces	1 tbsp. per cup	Port
Meats	Pot Roast — Beef	¼ cup per lb.	Burgundy
	Lamb and Veal	¼ cup per lb.	Burgundy or Rhine Wine
	Gravy for Roasts	2 tbsps. per cup	Burgundy
	Stew — Beef	¼ cup per lb.	Burgundy
	Stew — Lamb and Veal	¼ cup per lb.	Chablis
	Ham, Baked — Whole	2 cups (for basting)	Port or Muscatel
	Liver, Braised	¼ cup per lb.	Burgundy
	Kidneys, Braised	¼ cup per lb.	Sherry or Burgundy
	Tongue, Boiled	½ cup per lb.	Burgundy
Fish	Broiled, Baked, or Poached	½ cup per lb.	Chablis
Poultry and Game	Chicken, Broiled or Sauteed	¼ cup per lb.	Sauterne
	Gravy for Roast or Fried Chicken and Turkey	2 tbsps. per cup	Burgundy or Sherry
	Chicken, Fricasse	¼ cup per lb.	Sauterne
	Duck, Roast — Wild or Tame	¼ cup per lb.	Burgundy
	Venison, Roast, Pot Roast or Stew	¼ cup per lb.	Burgundy
	Pheasant, Roast or Sauteed	¼ cup per lb.	Burgundy or Sherry
Fruit	Cups and Compotes	1 tbsp. per serving	Port, Muscatel, Sherry, Rose, Sauterne or Sauternes, or Burgundy

*Appetizer, dessert, and table wines listed are only recommendations. Should you wish to experiment, wines in any similar category may be used.

surprising and delicious: marinate it for several hours in equal parts gin and soy sauce with perhaps a tablespoonful of brown sugar added.

For those who are convinced that food should be interesting and varied, there is always the challenge to make a good dish better. Often a new seasoning will make an exciting change for the better, and wine is one of the seasonings to employ. For example, if a recipe calls for diluting tomato sauce with water, use wine instead. A recipe that calls for a cup of boullion can be greatly enhanced if half the boullion is replaced by wine or even beer.

Fresh roast of pork will gain new flavor dimensions if you will pour a can of beer, a cupful of white wine, or even half a cup of bourbon over it before it goes into the oven. Roast it, uncovered, and as the liquid evaporates, the meat will be permeated with the flavorful vapor. Not overpowering, never calling attention to itself, the spirit gives a hint of mystery. Gravy made from the drippings is equally splendid.

CHEESE

Cheese and wine have a natural affinity; a cupful of cheese sauce becomes extraordinary with the addition of a tablespoonful of white wine. Try wine as a flavor boost in Welsh rabbit or as an ingredient replacing part of the liquid next time you make a cheese soufflé.

DESSERT

In dessert cookery, wine plays a stellar role. The classic zabaglione is probably the winiest, consisting as it does of Marsala beaten with sugar and egg yolks over hot water until it is thickened. Pears poached in red wine make a fabulous dessert, espe-cially if you add sugar to the wine after the pears are removed, and reduce the liquid to make a sauce.

SPIRITS IN UNCOOKED PREPARATIONS

To this point, the discussion has centered on foods that are cooked in wine, i.e., the alcohol is evaporated out by the heat of the cooking process. There are myriad ways in which to use spirits in uncooked preparations. Here are just a few:

- Marinate fruits for an appetizer or dessert compote in your favorite liqueur. Kirsch and curaçao are especially good with fruit
- Add a dash of sweet wine to whipped cream to be used as a dessert topping.
- Douse freshly baked apples with port just before serving.
- Soak ladyfingers for charlotte russe in sherry.
- Drizzle crème de menthe over chocolate ice cream.
- There are several superb gelatin molds containing wine. (See recipe section.)
  On this point, it is good to know that alcohol weakens gelatin a little, so reduce the other liquid by 2 or 3 tablespoons per pint.

Flaming desserts
We have all looked on with admiration when the restaurant lights go dim, and the waiter or maître d'hotel comes out with a creation flambé. Yet there is nothing esoteric about the operation, nothing we can't reproduce at home with spectacular results.

Liquor or brandy for flaming must be high in alcohol content, at least 80 proof. It is of utmost importance to have everything in readiness for the presentation. The liquor must be warmed so measure it a few minutes ahead of time into a small sauce pan or butter melter, and set it in a container of warm water. Warming releases the alcohol vapors, so do not let it stay too long—just until it is barely warm. You want those vapors to flame when the time comes.

Be sure you have checked the recipe beforehand and have the necessary ingredients at hand, including a trivet to protect the table top or (preferably) a side table or buffet, in view of your audience; a potholder to protect your hands, and a supply of long matches, just in case the first couple get doused and fail to ignite the liquor.

With the dish to be flamed installed on the trivet, sprinkle a bit of salt or sugar over it, as appropriate to the food, then pour on a little of the warmed liquor. This preliminary dash of liquor will act as a torch to make sure the flame materializes. Now, standing well back from the dish, strike a long match, and set fire to the vapors over the warm liquor in the little pot. Don't dip the match into the liquid; it will just go out. Pour the flaming liquor over the food.

Using the potholder, move the dish gently to aid combustion, spooning the liquid over the food until the flame goes out. Serve immediately.

Place a double emphasis on safety when you flame a dish; this caution includes keeping long hair, tablecloths, bouffant sleeves, and even the potholder, a safe distance from the flame.

Overleaf
An elegant dinner party featuring Pork Shoulder in Bourbon Sauce is sure to bring plaudits to the accomplished cook: Pork Shoulder in Bourbon Sauce, Pure Green Salad, Creamed New Potatoes with Peas, Jelled Coffee with Pour Custard (see page 274).

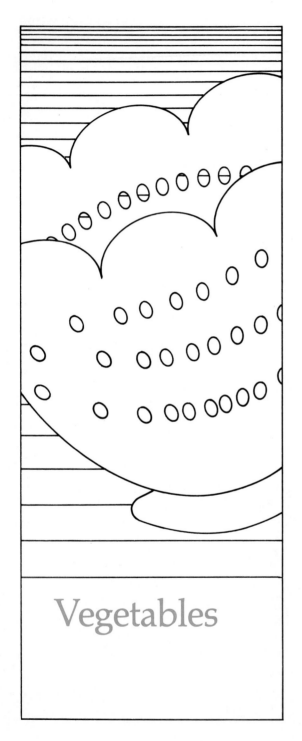

Vegetables

SALAD GREENS

Know your salad greens so you can put color, flavor, texture, and interest into your salads.

Since fresh, crisp greens are essential for success in salad making, select the best quality available. Remove any wilted leaves; wash greens well in tepid water. Handle greens gently as they bruise easily. Drain greens after washing; pat dry with paper towels. Store cleaned greens in refrigerator in a crisper or plastic bag. When preparing salad, tear, rather than cut, greens into bite-size pieces.

For both taste and eye appeal, a combination of several greens makes an interesting salad:

- Boston lettuce has a head slightly softer, lighter, and less crisp than iceberg. Outer leaves are dark green and inner ones are light yellow. Velvety leaves have a delicate flavor and are easily separated.
- Leaf lettuce has pale green, delicate leaves which grow loosely from a small slender stalk. These ruffled leaves are crisp in texture and sweet in flavor.
- Chinese Cabbage has a firm, tapering stalk (about 14 to 16 inches long) which forms a compact head that looks like romaine and has characteristics similar to romaine and cabbage. The tightly closed broad leaves are crisp; the color is pale green to white.
- Iceberg is the most popular lettuce. Its firm crisp-textured head has green leaves on the outside with a pale green core. Curly leaves overlap slightly but can be separated into cups for various salads.
- Chicory has a large, bunchy head of tightly curled and lacy dark green outer leaves with yellowish white leaves at

core. Center leaves are milder in flavor than the slightly bitter outer leaves.

- Romaine has rather coarse, crisp leaves with heavy ribs which form an elon-

gated head. The dark green outer leaves shade to lighter leaves at the root end. The inner leaves are particularly tender and flavorful.

Boston lettuce

Leaf lettuce

Chicory or Curly endive

Iceberg lettuce

Romaine

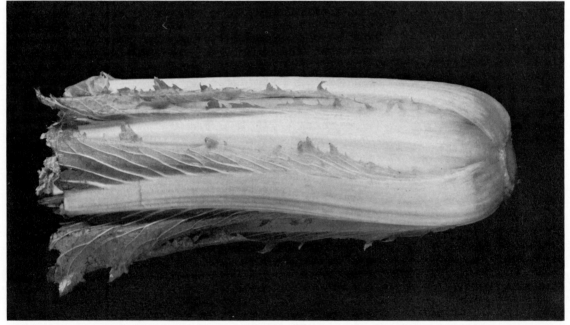

Chinese cabbage

Steaming Asparagus

Note: Alternate method of steaming asparagus: Lacking a steam basket, tie washed asparagus in bundles with string. Stand bundles upright in an old-fashioned percolator or in bottom of double boiler.

If tips protrude above percolator, wrap tips with foil, pressing foil against sides of percolator. If using a double boiler, use the top pan, upside down, for a lid. With either utensil, pour about 3 inches of boiling water

1 Wash asparagus well, with special attention to the tips. A forceful spray of water is most helpful in removing the sandy, gritty particles hidden in the little buds.

2 Find the point near the end of the stalk at which it becomes brittle; then snap it off. Woody stalk ends are tough but serve well for making cream soup when cooked and put through a ricer to remove the stringy part.

(Continued)

113

around bottom of stalks; steam will cook the tender tops.

3 Put washed tips in a steam basket; place basket in a pan containing enough water to come almost up to the bottom of the basket.

4 Cover, and steam until vegetable is tender, not one minute longer. Salt to taste may be added after the onset of cooking. New peas and corn are also good candidates for steaming.

Preparing Southern-Style Green Beans

Beans such as snap beans or "bunch" beans have no strings.

1 Snap off ends of beans, and break into 1- or 2-inch pieces. If working with string beans, as you break off an end, use the end piece to act as a "zipper" to remove string the length of the bean; the other end, broken, will do the same for the other side of the pod. Break up string beans after strings have been removed.

2 Wash beans thoroughly under cold running water.

(Continued)

3 Cut off a chunk of salt pork; about ¼ pound will season 2 to 3 pounds of green beans. Cut pork down to, but not through, the skin in 3 or 4 places. When cut this way, the seasoning permeates the beans better than when the meat is left in one piece.

4 Push salt pork down into the beans. Add water up to within an inch of top of beans. Bring to boiling, cover with lid, and reduce heat to low. Simmer until beans are almost tender. Add salt as necessary. Continue to cook with the lid askew to allow steam to escape, until beans have "cooked down," as Southerners call it, meaning that most of the liquid has evaporated. Tender young snap beans may take only 2 hours; mature pole beans, 4 to 5 hours.

Preparing Fresh Beets

Fresh beets should be well shaped, firm, and smooth; small- to medium-size beets are generally the most tender.

1 Cut off leaves, leaving 1 inch of tops on beets. Leave roots on.

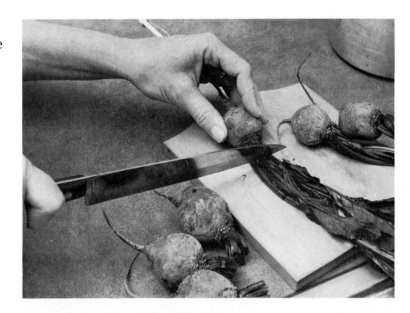

2 Wash beets thoroughly in cold water.

(Continued)

3 Place beets in steamer. Put half an inch of water in pan, and place steamer over, not touching, water. Cover. Cook until tender. Size will dictate cooking time; test with sharp fork.

4 Skins will slip right off as soon as they are cool enough to handle. Beets are now ready to use in any recipe, including pickling.

Cooking Fresh Cauliflower

To steam (not shown): Place in steam basket, and place basket in kettle containing enough boiling water to reach not quite up to vegetable. Cover, and cook until tender, approximately 15 to 20 minutes for a 2-pound head.

1 Cut stem end away, but keep the tender leaves nearest the head of cauliflower.

2 Wash thoroughly by sloshing up and down in cold water. Change water, add a tablespoon salt, and let cauliflower stand in it 10 minutes.

(Continued)

Note: To help retain whiteness, use milk instead of water in the simmering kettle or 1 tablespoon lemon juice in the water used under steam basket.

3 To cook as shown: Fold a clean kitchen towel in fourths lengthwise, and place in kettle before adding cauliflower. Tuck towel ends down a bit at sides so they will not interfere with lid, but where they will be reachable when you need them to lift the cauliflower out whole. Pour in 1 inch boiling water. Put on lid, slightly ajar, and simmer about 15 minutes, or until tender. Lift out with towel ends, protecting hands with pot holders. Drain, and place on serving plate.

4 Cauliflower can be served topped with a sauce of Blender Hollandaise and a sprinkling of paprika.

Preparing Fresh Corn on the Cob

If you own a large steamer, cooking corn is one of the best ways to use it. With boiling water underneath, water does not touch corn at all, leaving more of the nutrients intact. (Steaming adds a couple of minutes to cooking time.)

1 Fresh corn on the cob needs only to be husked, the silk pulled off, then brushed with a stiff vegetable brush to remove the silk along the corn rows.

2 After brushing away all possible silk, break off tip end. Drop into a kettle containing enough boiling water to cover. Boil 4 to 6 minutes, depending on maturity. Do not salt until halfway through cooking. Add a pinch of sugar to the water as well.

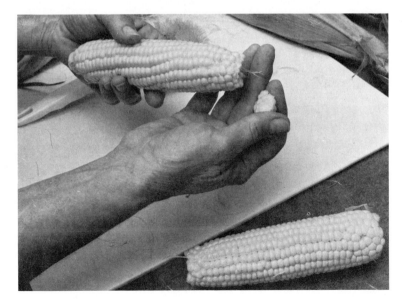

Preparing Fresh Peas

Steaming is an even better method for fresh peas, as water never touches them. Or try the French method: Line pan with a large lettuce leaf, add peas, and cover with a second leaf. Add ¼ cup water, put on lid, and simmer about 30 minutes. Discard lettuce, and serve peas in warmed bowl, tossed with salt to taste and butter.

1 Shell tender young peas just before cooking. Place in colander, and wash under cold running water. A pound of unshelled peas will serve two people.

2 Bring ¼ inch of water to boil in saucepan. Add peas and cook, partly covered, on low heat until tender. Salt to taste midway through cooking. Never use baking soda for color retention; it destroys nutrients. Cooking will require 20 to 30 minutes, depending on maturity. If not too much water is used in the beginning, it should be practically cooked away by the time the peas are tender.

Puree of Spinach

Note: Other cooked-vegetable purees are prepared in the same manner.

1 Break off stalks of tender young spinach leaves. Wash in several changes of water by lifting spinach out of water, then replacing it with fresh water. Place in saucepan with only the water clinging to the leaves from the final rinse. Cover, and cook over low heat until quite tender.

2 When spinach is cooked, drain through colander, pressing to remove as much moisture as possible.

(Continued)

123

3 Put spinach into blender, and whirl to puree.

4 Remove pureed spinach from blender jar, and measure amount needed for the recipe with which you are working, such as cream soups, soufflés, etc.

Preparing Stuffed Potatoes

Choose from smooth potatoes of the baking type. Scrub potatoes thoroughly and dry. If you like a crunchy crust, bake without any coating or covering. If you like the skin soft, rub with shortening or cover with aluminum foil. Bake at 425° for 40 to 60 minutes, depending on size.

1 As soon as hot, freshly baked potatoes can be handled, cut in half lengthwise, and, with a spoon, scoop out meat into mixing bowl; leave shells intact.

2 Add butter to taste first, while potatoes are hottest.

(Continued)

125

3 Add salt and pepper to taste and a little milk; start beating.

4 Beat, using medium to high speed of mixer, adding more milk as necessary for a smooth, finely textured mixture. Use other seasonings as desired; chives are good or grated cheese.

5 Spoon whipped, seasoned potatoes back into skins, heaping mixture in center.

6 Place stuffed potatoes on baking pan. Top with grated cheese, as shown, or with Mornay Sauce. Place in 400° oven for 10 to 15 minutes until thoroughly hot and lightly browned.

Preparing Globe Artichokes

To serve stuffed, cut out the prickly "choke" just above base. Stuff with salad of shrimp, chicken, or lobster.

1 Wash artichokes by plunging up and down in cold water.

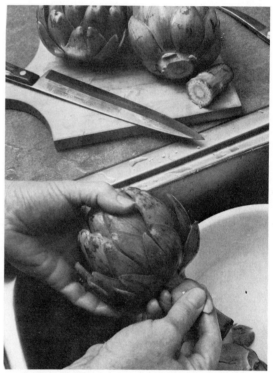

2 Cut off stem end, and pull off loose bottom leaves.

3 With scissors, trim away about ¼ of each outer leaf; then slice about ½ inch from top of each artichoke.

4 Place artichokes in kettle with about an inch of water, as shown, and simmer, covered, until tender, about 30 minutes, depending on age and freshness. Or place, tops down, in steam basket; place over boiling water, and cook, covered, about 45 minutes, depending on age and freshness. In either method, the addition of a few celery leaves, a slice of lemon, and a bay leaf to the water will add to flavor. Once cooked, they are ready to be served hot with melted butter or cold with seasoned mayonnaise.

Preparing French-Fried Onion Rings

3 or 4 large Spanish or Bermuda onions
2 to 3 cups buttermilk or ice water
1 egg, beaten
1 teaspoon salt

1½ teaspoons baking powder
⅔ cup water
1 cup all-purpose flour
1 tablespoon salad oil

1 Select mild, sweet onions (Spanish or Bermuda). Peel, and cut into slices ⅜ inch thick.

2 Pour buttermilk into a shallow pan. Separate onion slices into rings, and soak in buttermilk for 30 minutes.

1 teaspoon lemon juice
¼ teaspoon cayenne pepper
  Salad oil

3 Prepare batter by combining remaining ingredients except oil. Remove onions rings from buttermilk, and dip into batter.

4 Fry onion rings in oil heated to 375°. Allow to cook until golden brown. When onion rings are brown, remove from oil, and drain on absorbent paper.

Cutting Up Vegetables

These techniques are illustrated with a potato; the same methods pertain to any firm vegetable.

1 To slice, place peeled vegetable on cutting board. With French chef's knife, make straight down cuts to board for thickness desired.

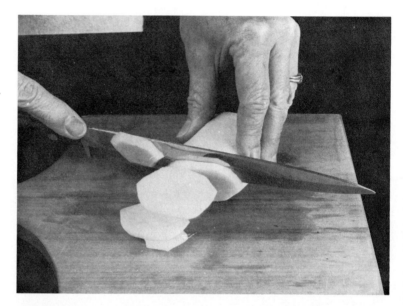

2 The vegetable may be squared off in order to make further cuts perfectly uniform although this is not really necessary and is slightly wasteful unless you intend to use trimmings in another dish, or if looks matter a lot.

3 Slice the squared-off potato preparatory to cutting for French fries or for dicing.

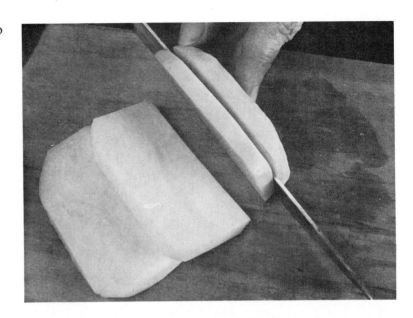

4 Here French fries are shown being cut one slice at a time. Actually, you would want to stack the potato slices, and cut down through the whole stack at one time.

(Continued)

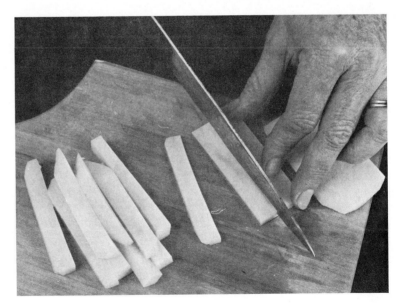

5 Cubing or dicing. Cut across precut strips, making more or less uniform cubes.

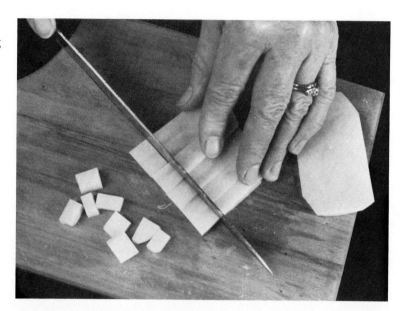

6 Julienne strips are small as matchsticks. They are made by first cutting slices much thinner than for French fries, then cutting across slices to make uniformly thin sticks.

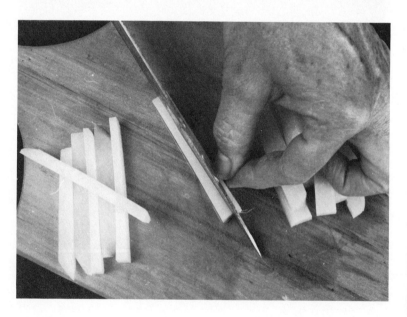

Using a Wok: Start with Sukiyaki

1 pound sirloin steak
1 cup sliced celery
½ pound fresh sliced mushrooms or 1
    (8-ounce) can sliced mushrooms,
    drained

¼ cup peanut oil or salad oil
2 medium-size onions, diagonally sliced
½ head Chinese or celery cabbage,
    diagonally cut into ½-inch slices

1 With a cleaver, diagonally cut meat into thin strips. Meat will slice easier if partially frozen before slicing.

2 Place celery on cutting board; using the cleaver, cut stalk on the bias into ½-inch strips.

(Continued)

1 (10- to 12-ounce) can bamboo shoots,
    drained
2 (6-ounce) cans water chestnuts,
    drained and thinly sliced

8 scallions, cut into narrow strips
½ cup chicken broth or 1 chicken
    bouillon cube dissolved in ½ cup
    hot water

3 With the cleaver, cut fresh mushrooms
through stem and crown into thin
T-shape slices.

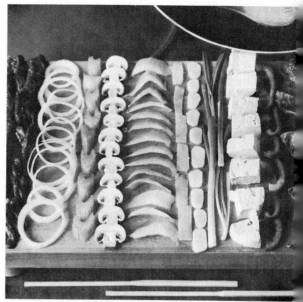

4 To prepare sukiyaki, arrange all sliced
food on tray in sequence it will be added
to the hot oil (as listed in ingredients).
Pour oil into wok or skillet; heat at 375°
for 4 minutes.

Note: Precise timing on stir-frying
should be followed so vegetables will be
cooked until tender but slightly
undercooked. They will be crisp in texture
and bright and translucent in color.
Spinach or other greens will merely be
somewhat wilted after stir-frying.

½ cup bean curd, cut into ½-inch cubes
1 green pepper, thinly sliced into strips
1 tablespoon firmly packed brown sugar
1 teaspoon salt

½ cup soy sauce
3 cups fresh spinach, torn into large
    pieces
Cooked brown rice

5 To stir-fry sukiyaki, place meat in hot oil, and stir-fry for 2 minutes; push meat up sides of wok. Add onion, and stir-fry for 2 minutes; push onion up sides of wok. Continue same procedure and cooking time for celery, mushrooms, and Chinese cabbage, adding more oil, if needed. Combine bamboo shoots, water chestnuts, scallions, and chicken broth; add to wok, stir once, cook for 2 minutes, and push up sides. Add bean curd, green pepper, brown sugar, salt, and soy sauce; stir once, and cook for 30 seconds. Do not push up sides of wok. Sprinkle spinach over all ingredients in wok, cover, and simmer for 2 minutes.

6 Reduce heat to warm for serving and serve immediately over cooked brown rice. Yield: 6 to 8 servings.

Overleaf
When you and your guests must make an 8 p.m. meeting or concert, serve this make-ahead Mexican buffet, and let everyone help himself: Upside-Down Tacos, Avocado Salad, Margaritas, and Chocolate-Covered Ice Cream Sticks (see page 276).

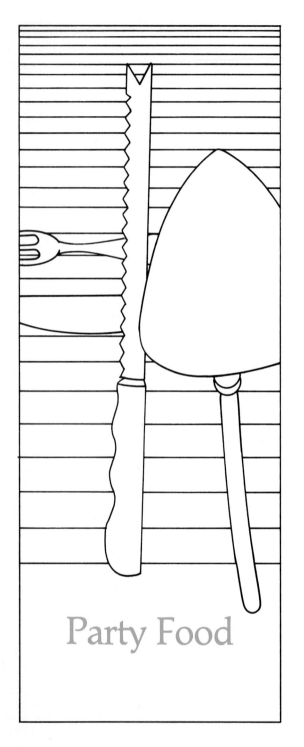

Party Food

Since there are so many different kinds of parties from casual bridge get-togethers to gregarious cocktail parties, to formal receptions, there are necessarily all sorts of party foods appropriate to each occasion. Appetizers are a type of party food we often use when dinner must be a little late to allow time for guests to assemble. Often accompanied by an aperitif, appetizers should be light and served in small quantities; they are supposed to tease the palate, not blunt it.

Most parties, of course, call for more substantial offerings, and often such foods can be geared to the party's theme or decoration. A party at the beach, for example, might star Party Seafood Mold, Shrimp Spread, and Tuna Dip supported by an assortment of crackers, raw vegetables, and something for those with a sweet tooth.

Since most parties are not complete without an assortment of foods, at least some of the dishes must be prepared well ahead of time. If, perhaps, you are planning a watermelon basket filled with fresh fruit as the centerpiece (which will require last-minute preparation), choose the remainder of the foods from those that can be made in advance: Cheese balls are even better if stored for a few days to allow the flavors to meld; marinated vegetables must be chilled, preferably overnight, before serving; and meatballs can be frozen, then thawed and heated just before serving.

In planning party foods, let yourself go, enjoy the fun of planning and preparing them. Be cautious in two respects, however: Try to present a variety of colors and textures to give the display a vibrant, festive air; and present a balance of tastes so that each guest will see something that appeals to him. You may adore highly seasoned foods, but offer something bland and something sweet for those who do not.

Speaking of Parties

Cover sandwiches with waxed paper and a damp towel to keep them fresh until serving time.

1 A sandwich does not always have to be flat. Rolled sandwiches are fun for a party. Trim crusts, and roll bread slices flat with rolling pin. Spread with just a bit of soft herb-flavored butter (for holding in refrigerator) or mayonnaise (for serving at once). Filling can be asparagus, cooked or canned and drained, sticks of cheese or ham. Roll up, and secure with wooden picks.

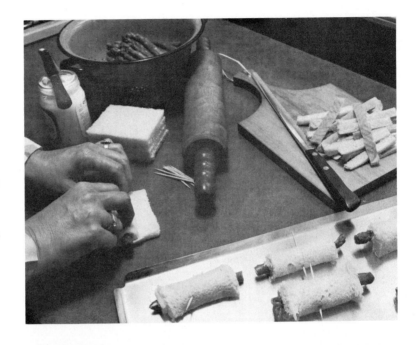

2 A hearty hot sandwich is mighty comforting at times. This one is party rye bread slices topped with thin slices of mild Bermuda or Spanish red onion. A dollop of mayonnaise is swirled on top, then a dash of cayenne or seasoned salt. Run them under the broiler for a few moments; the mayonnaise will puff and brown slightly. Serve at once.

(Continued)

3 There's more than one way to cut a sandwich, as you can see. Triangles, squares, or fingers can vary a sandwich tray or add interest to a salad luncheon. To hold sandwiches a few hours, use herb-flavored butter as spread to keep bread from getting soggy.

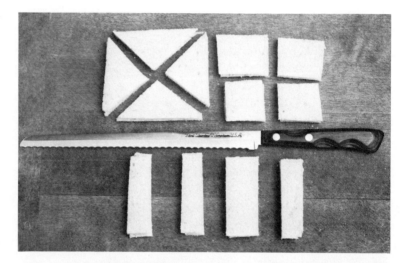

4 You can ignore all the foregoing suggestions, and spread a colorful, luxurious meal-on-a-tray or "Dutch lunch" for any time of day, from lunchtime to evening after-theater get-togethers. Just go to your friendly neighborhood deli, and buy the goodies: cheese, meats, good Kosher dills, and some interesting breads. Deviled eggs add a pleasant sight and taste, and don't forget the hot mustard. Fruit included on the tray is ready to do the honors as dessert.

Fresh Vegetable Marinade

1 bunch small carrots
¼ cup vinegar
¼ cup olive oil or salad oil
1 small clove garlic, pressed
¾ teaspoon seasoned salt

¼ teaspoon salt
¼ teaspoon dried dill weed
   Dash freshly ground pepper
   Pinch oregano, crushed
½ teaspoon dried parsley flakes

Pare and cut fresh carrots into 2-inch lengths. Steam or cook until tender in a minimum of water. Drain, and place in jar. If canned carrots are used, drain off liquid, and leave carrots in jar. Blend remaining ingredients, and pour over carrots. Cover tightly. Allow to ripen overnight or all day in refrigerator, turning jar over from time to time. Drain, and serve with other freshly cooked vegetables on an appetizer tray with Norfolk Party Dip. Yield: About ½ cup.

Note: Marinade is also good for other freshly cooked vegetables.

This is the kind of appetizer tray that can replace the salad on a dinner menu.

Norfolk Party Dip

1 (8-ounce) package cream or
    Neufchâtel cheese, softened
½ cup mayonnaise or sour cream
1 teaspoon chopped parsley
1 (4½-ounce) can deviled ham

Hot pepper sauce, to taste

Place all ingredients in blender, and blend thoroughly. (The consistency is that used for dip.) Yield: about 1⅓ cups.

For a spread (heavier consistency) use only ⅓ cup mayonnaise or sour cream.

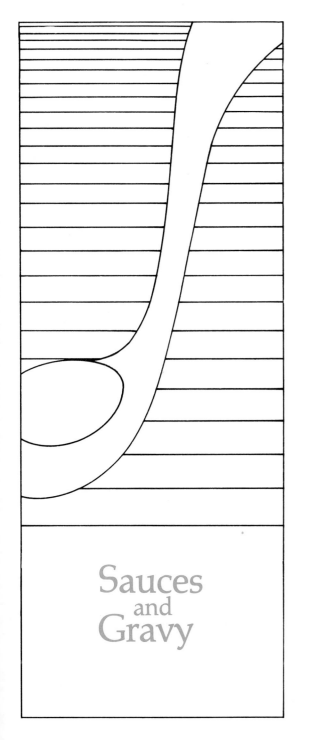

Sauces and Gravy

BASIC WHITE SAUCE

White sauce (Béchamel) is the simplest and most basic of sauces. The necessities are simple and few. Basic to the sauce is a properly made roux: a mixture of butter and flour cooked together before the addition of liquid. Use a heavy (not aluminum) saucepan. A wire whisk is the best implement for stirring up a smooth sauce, but a wooden spoon will do.

Some cooks keep on hand a small container of "instant blending" flour just for sauces and gravies. It does seem to work a bit more easily than plain flour. The flour-butter mixture should be stirred and cooked over low heat before liquid is added. If the flour is not cooked first to release the starch, which is the thickening agent, you could end up with a thin, floury tasting sauce. White sauce is usually made in one of three thicknesses, light, medium, or heavy, depending on the use to be made of it.

Light white sauce is the thickness used for creaming vegetables and is the foundation for other sauces. Some other sauces based on light white sauce are Mornay, cheese, Florentine (spinach added), and a white wine sauce for fish.

Velouté sauce is made exactly like white sauce except that chicken or veal stock is used instead of milk. Velouté, in turn becomes the foundation for Aurore Sauce (flavored with tomato puree), Soubise (white onion sauce), and Supreme (flavored with mushrooms and cream), to mention a few.

LIGHT WHITE SAUCE
   1 tablespoon butter or margarine
   1 tablespoon all-purpose flour
   1 cup warm milk
     Salt and pepper

MEDIUM WHITE SAUCE
   2 tablespoons butter or margarine
   2 tablespoons all-purpose flour
   1 cup warm milk
     Salt and pepper

1 The necessary ingredients and implements for making Basic White Sauce are salt and pepper, milk, butter, flour, measuring spoons, saucepan, and wooden spoon.

2 Put butter into small, heavy saucepan. Melt over low heat.

HEAVY WHITE SAUCE
3 tablespoons butter or margarine
3 tablespoons all-purpose flour
1 cup warm milk
   Salt and pepper

3 Add flour to melted butter.

4 Stir and cook over low heat for 3 or 4 minutes to cook flour and release the starch, which is the thickening power. This cooked mixture is your roux.

(Continued)

147

5 Add milk gradually, stirring constantly with whisk or wooden spoon. (It helps, until you get the hang of it, to warm the milk first, pull the roux off the heat, and beat in the milk. It is less likely to lump. Cook, stirring, over low heat about 6 to 8 minutes or until thickened. If lumps form, keep stirring and beating until sauce is smooth.

6 Season with salt and pepper. Yield: about 1 cup.

Degreasing Stock

Use the stock instead of water when cooking vegetables or making soup.

1 When you don't have time to refrigerate stock for fat to rise and solidify on top, use a bulb baster. Insert tip into hot liquid fat at top, and lift out into bowl. Or, if there is a large proportion of fat to stock, you can reverse first procedure, using bulb baster suction to pull stock out from under fat, leaving only the fat in the jar when finished.

2 When degreasing is finished, all possible fat has been lifted off stock.

(Continued)

3 The best way of degreasing stock is to refrigerate it for several hours or overnight so fat can come to top and solidify.

4 Holding back solid fat with fork, pour liquid stock out from underneath into another container. This method of chilling the fat is especially worthy of the attention of persons who are on a low fat diet.

Mornay Sauce

2 tablespoons Parmesan cheese
2 tablespoons Swiss or Gruyère cheese
1 egg yolk
2 tablespoons whipping cream

1 cup Light White Sauce
1 tablespoon finely minced onion or
   shallot
Salt and pepper to taste

1 To make Mornay sauce, which is based on Light White Sauce, you will need salt and pepper, whipping cream, white sauce, egg yolk, Parmesan and Swiss cheeses, onion or shallot, a grater, wire whisk, and measuring spoons.

2 Grate Parmesan and Swiss cheese; reserve.

(Continued)

Mornay Sauce is useful in casseroles, used instead of the plain white sauce on which it is based. It is also delicious with fish or vegetables. If the dish containing Mornay is to be browned in oven or broiler, you may wish to use a little extra cheese on top, although it contains enough cheese to brown nicely without the addition.

3 Beat egg yolk with whipping cream; reserve.

4 Combine White Sauce with finely minced onion or shallot in small heavy saucepan. Cook over very low heat, stirring constantly, 4 or 5 minutes until onion is tender.

5 Gradually stir about ¼ of the sauce into the egg-cream mixture.

6 Stir egg mixture back into sauce in pan. Cook on low heat just until hot.

(Continued)

7 Use wire whisk to blend cheese into sauce. A wooden spoon may be used if whisk is not available. Remove from heat when melted.

8 Taste sauce; add salt and pepper. Yield: about 1¼ cups.

Making Southern Cream Gravy

A Southern cook will cast a practiced eye on the fat remaining in the skillet after the meat has been cooked and removed, then pour off some fat if it is too much.

The beginner will need to do some measuring until gravy-making becomes an automatic, second nature accomplishment.

1 Pour fat into a cup.

2 Decide how many cups of gravy you want. Then measure back into the skillet 2½ tablespoons fat per cup gravy desired. Then measure into the fat 2 tablespoons flour per cup gravy desired. Stir, and cook fat and flour over low heat, scraping browned particles loose from skillet, for 4 to 5 minutes or until you are sure the flour is cooked.

(Continued)

155

3 Gradually add liquid, which can be all milk, or half milk and half water (use 1 cup liquid per 2½ tablespoons fat and 2 tablespoons flour). Stir rapidly to prevent lumping. Turn heat up to medium, and boil, stirring, for 4 or 5 minutes or until thickened.

4 Season with salt and pepper to taste. A few drops of commercial browning liquid will improve the eye appeal of a pale gravy and is one of the best "cosmetics" to keep on your kitchen shelf.

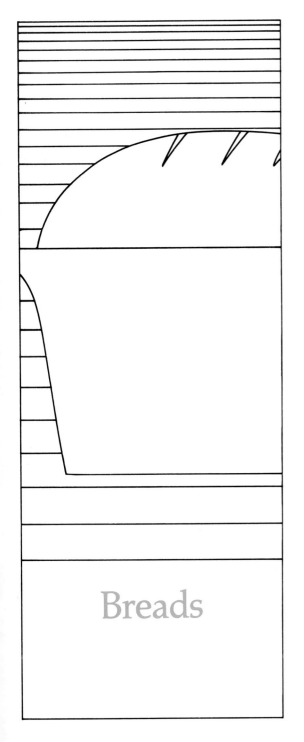

Breads

Freshly baked bread slathered with butter ... what could taste better? And, indeed, bread making has had a renaissance of popularity in recent years due in part, no doubt, to the fact that no manufacturer has yet been able to package the warm fragrance of fresh bread which itself is a product sufficient to make the job worthwhile. In addition, bread baked at home can be made with unbleached and whole grain flours that are richer in vitamins and minerals than their refined, bleached counterparts which are used most often in commercially produced breads.

Bread is not difficult to make. In fact, bread making doesn't take great skill; it just takes some practice by the cook and plenty of time for the yeast to work and make the bread rise.

The only other trick for baking perfect bread is the kneading, which insures that the bread will have the proper texture and height. Kneading is best learned through practice. After several sessions of bread making, you will have learned to recognize the feel and texture of a properly kneaded dough. To insure perfect bread until then, simply knead the dough a moment or two longer than the recipe calls for. It is difficult to overknead bread dough, but insufficiently kneaded dough will not rise and will not have proper texture.

Rolls are made from essentially the same sort of dough as bread; but instead of shaping the kneaded dough into loaves, shape it into rolls according to your preference.

For the cook who decides to make bread but who doesn't have time for the kneading and rising, there are quick breads which do not require yeast. Such breads take less time to mix than a cake batter and require no rising before baking. Corn bread, biscuits, and gingerbread are all deliciously simple quick breads.

Making Baking Powder Biscuits

2 cups all-purpose flour
1 tablespoon baking powder
1 teaspoon salt
¼ cup shortening
⅔ to ¾ cup milk

Note: To make drop biscuits, increase milk to 1 cup, then drop dough from spoon onto lightly greased cookie sheet or into muffin cups. Drop biscuits are fluffy inside, rough outside.

1 Experienced Southern cooks are known for the airy flakiness of their biscuits. Sometimes they use buttermilk and soda; other times, sweet milk and baking powder. Here is the classic baking powder biscuit; make it by the book a few times, and soon you will be able to make it almost with your eyes closed. Spoon flour into dry-measuring cup, and level with straightedge. Pour into sifter.

2 Baking powder is the leavening agent; it makes quick breads rise. Make sure your baking powder is fresh. To check freshness, put a teaspoonful into half a cup of hot water. If it is fresh, the mixture will foam enthusiastically. If it doesn't, pitch it out and buy a new can. Again level measurement with straightedge.

158

3 Salt makes biscuits taste good; measure it into the sifter with other dry ingredients. Then sift all together into mixing bowl.

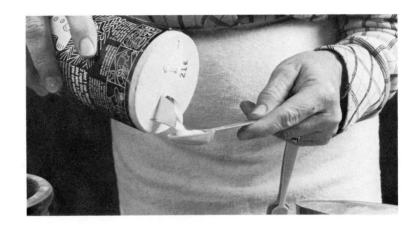

4 Next comes the solid shortening. Lard once was the shortening of choice, and it still makes fine biscuits, although we now generally use hydrogenated shortening. There are two ways to measure shortening. It can be packed into a measuring cup with rubber spatula and leveled off (as shown), or using the water displacement method, cold water can be put into a cup so that the required amount of shortening, when added, will bring the water to the 1-cup line. Drain off water, and add shortening to dry ingredients. *(Continued)*

5 With a pastry blender, cut shortening into dry mixture. Many experienced cooks "rub" the shortening in with their fingers, which works fine. The pastry blender is just a little less messy. When this step is finished, mixture should have the texture of coarse cornmeal.

6 The milk goes in last. Here again, the exact measurement may differ because of varying dryness of flours. Feel free to use more or less milk than the recipe calls for. What you are looking for is a soft dough with just the right amount of milk to make it handle well without being sticky.

7 Add the milk gradually, stirring with a wooden spoon, until the dough forms around the spoon in a soft mass. Turn dough out onto floured surface. Knead dough a few turns, only enough to smooth it. Biscuit dough, unlike yeast dough, should be handled very little.

8 Roll out dough with floured rolling pin to ½-inch thickness. Dip biscuit cutter into flour, and cut biscuits close together, turning the cutter a quarter turn to free each biscuit. Place biscuits close together in lightly greased baking pan, and bake at 425° for 12 to 15 minutes. Yield: about 18 (1¾-inch) biscuits.

Shaping Dinner Rolls

1 cup milk
¼ cup sugar
1 teaspoon salt
¼ cup margarine
2 packages dry yeast

½ cup very warm water
2 eggs, beaten
    About 5¼ cups all-purpose flour
    Melted butter

Scald milk; stir in sugar, salt, and margarine. Cool to lukewarm.

Soften yeast in very warm water. Add milk

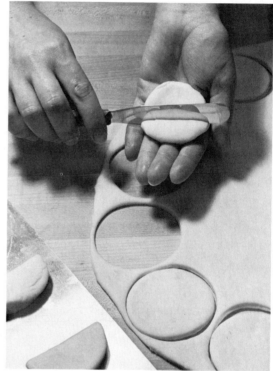

1 Crescents: Roll dough into a circle about 10 inches in diameter and ¼ inch thick. Cut into 12 wedges, and brush with melted butter. Roll each wedge tightly, beginning at wide end. Use a drop of cold water to seal points. Place on greased baking sheets with point underneath. Curve into crescent shape.

2 Parker House: Roll dough into a 12-inch circle ¼-inch thick. Cut into 2½-inch rounds with a biscuit cutter. With dull edge of knife, make a crease just off center on each round. Brush with butter. Fold over so top overlaps slightly; press edges together. Place on greased baking sheets or ¼ inch apart in a greased 9-inch pan.

162

mixture, eggs, and 2 cups flour; beat until smooth. Add enough remaining flour to make a soft dough.

Turn dough out on a lightly floured surface; knead about 8 to 10 minutes or until smooth and elastic. Place in a greased bowl, turning to grease top. Cover, and let rise in a warm place until doubled in bulk (about 30 minutes). Punch down.

Turn dough out on a lightly floured surface, and shape. Cover; let rise in a warm place until doubled in bulk (about 30 minutes). Brush with melted butter. Bake at 400° about 10 to 15 minutes. Yield: 2½ to 4 dozen rolls, depending on shape.

3 Fan Tans: Roll dough into a 13- x 9-inch rectangle about ⅛ inch thick. Brush with melted butter. Cut crosswise into 6 strips 1½ inches wide. Stack strips evenly on top of each other. Cut into pieces about 1 inch wide. Place, cut side down, in greased muffin cups.

4 Cloverleaf: Shape dough into ¾-inch balls. Place 3 balls in each greased muffin cup.

Overleaf
An Al Fresco Luncheon to serve 12 features those elegant but easy-to-make French pancakes, crêpes: Curried Seafood Crêpes topped with Cheese Sauce, Green Goddess Salad, and Black Walnut Carrot Cake (see page 278).

Baking Gingerbread Men

1 (14½-ounce) package gingerbread mix
⅓ cup warm water
   Raisins
   Decorator candies
   Decorator icing

1 Combine gingerbread mix and water in a bowl; stir until well blended. Chill dough 1 to 2 hours.

2 Work with half of dough at a time; roll ¼ to ⅛ inch thick on a lightly floured surface.

3 Cut dough with a gingerbread man cutter. Shape unused pieces of dough into a ball; roll, and cut again.

4 Place gingerbread men on ungreased cookie sheets. Press raisins into dough to make eyes and nose; trim as desired with decorator candies. Bake at 375° for 8 to 10 minutes. Cool on cookie sheets 1 minute. Remove cookies from cookie sheets to cool completely. Trim as desired with decorator icing. Yield: about 2 dozen.

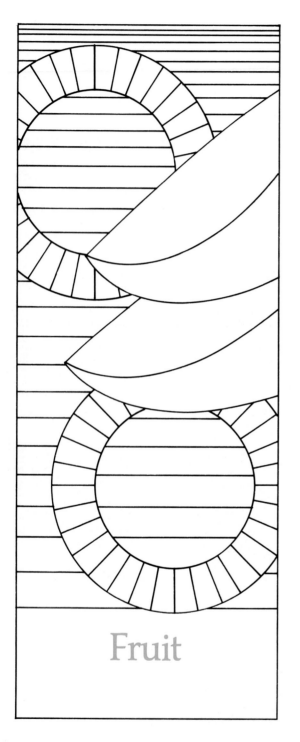

Fruit

Fruits provide many of the vitamins that are mainstays of health, and although modern packaging techniques have made seasonal fruit available year round, fresh fruits are even more vitamin rich. The variety of fruits offers something for every taste from the luscious sweetness of cherries and berries to the sharp tartness of pineapple and grapefruit; textures, too, vary from the mouth-watering juiciness of citrus fruit to the velvet firmness of melons.

It is likely that fruit constitutes the most versatile food group; for fruits work well alone as well as in combination with other fruits, vegetables, and meats. In addition, fruits are not limited to one particular role; for example, try a cold fruit soup for an unusual appetizer, or halve seedless green grapes into a chicken salad lunch to complement the chicken flavor. Alone or with a wedge of cheese, fruit provides a delicious and satisfying snack for a school lunchbox or a pick-me-up for the dieter. Meat dishes, too, are highlighted by a sidedish of fruit, from the popular antipasta combination of prosciutto and melon to elegant glazed ham with raisin sauce or broiled pineapple rings to the simple cold weather favorite, sausage with potato pancakes and stewed apples.

The domain of fruit has always included dessert: fresh, ripe fruit peeled at the table, poached pears or peaches with a cookie, perhaps, or engineered into exotic poire Hélène or peach Melba. Fruit compotes such as the classic macédoine provide a light refreshing finale, especially when splashed with the accent of your favorite liqueur. And, of course, fruit is unsurpassed in the traditional American apple pie.

Fruit can play almost any role in a meal. This fact together with the visual beauty of fruit, its delicious taste, vitamin content, and easy preparation make fresh fruit one of the best buys in the marketplace.

Sectioning Citrus Fruit

With practice, you can segment a whole bag of grapefruit or oranges in a few minutes, and keep them ready to eat, in tightly closed jars in refrigerator. You will find this method easier and less wasteful than serving the traditional half-grapefruit.

1 Cut slice from top or bottom to determine depth of skin to be peeled away.

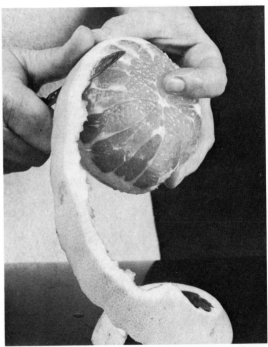

2 Peel fruit at a depth that will remove both peel and white membrane with the same cut.

(Continued)

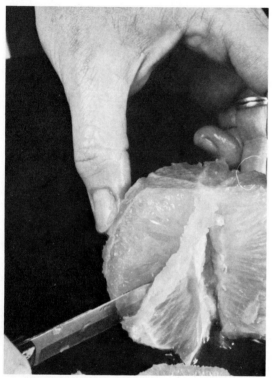

3 With sharp blade, cut downward at side of membrane that separates sections.

4 To remove segment, make another downward cut at side of next membrane, as shown. Or simply reverse knife blade, cutting upward, and bringing blade out against the membrane of adjoining segment. When sections are all out, squeeze juice from what is left of the fruit, and reserve.

Trimming Fresh Pineapple

This method probably wastes less fruit and juice than other ways you may have used.

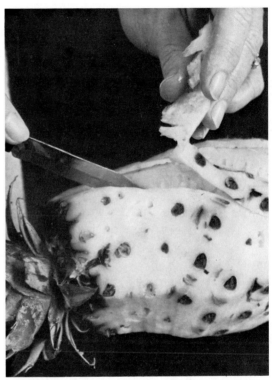

1 Holding pineapple by the leaves with one hand, peel fruit from top to bottom with sharp knife.

2 You will see that the "eyes" are arranged in neat spirals the length of the fruit. With fruit lying on cutting board, slant paring knife, and make a ½-inch deep cut under a spiral row of the eyes. Slant knife in the opposite direction, and cut down the other side of the same row of eyes so that the entire strip can be lifted off.

(Continued)

171

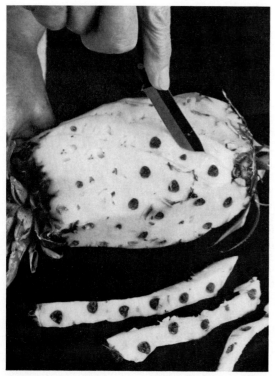

3 Continue cutting until all eyes are removed.

4 All eyes removed, the pineapple is now ready to have the top and bottom cut away. You may cut it into rounds, then cut core from each slice, or you may cut it into wedges, and remove core from each wedge with 1 straight cut of the knife.

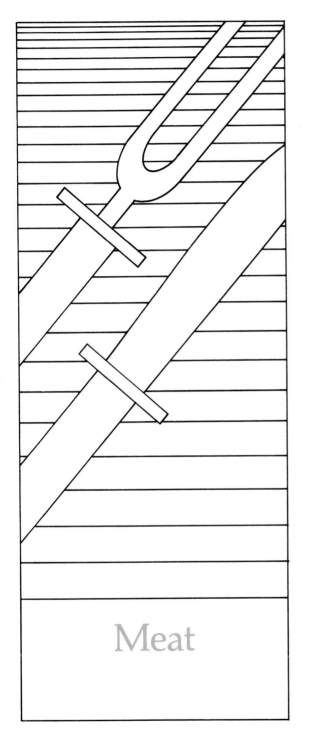

Meat

Whether it be a platter of spicy barbecued spareribs at a Fourth of July picnic or an imposing glazed ham crowning the Christmas dinner, the meat course is most often the *pièce de résistance* of the American table. Since most large cuts of beef, pork, and lamb are baked or roasted, it is important for the cook to learn to use a meat roasting thermometer. The thermometer should be inserted well into the thickest portion of the prepared meat, but it should not rest in fat or right against the bone. The meat is then placed in the oven at the oven temperature called for by the recipe. When the thermometer registers the internal temperature given in the recipe, the meat is done. Clearly, with the help of a meat thermometer, baking or roasting meat becomes fairly simple. In fact, carving the cooked meat no doubt flusters more cooks than the cooking itself. Of course no host or hostess wants the ham to fly off its platter and across the room at the first touch of the knife; on the other hand, a platter of meat sliced in the kitchen is not half as imposing or attractive as an uncut well-glazed ham commanding the table. Thus, this chapter includes not only meat preparation techniques, but also illustrations and diagrams for carving a variety of meats.

Not all meat cuts are appropriate for baking or roasting; instead, many are better prepared with moist heat by braising or stewing. Such cuts have less fat than roasting cuts and are thereby less tender. Consequently, such cuts are somewhat cheaper than the more tender ones. Nevertheless, these less expensive cuts can be just as tasty if you use a little imagination in the preparation. The illustrated example in this chapter is Beef Roll-ups, more elegantly known as Paupiettes, guaranteed to please the palate and impress your guests or family with your culinary expertise.

Beef Roll-ups (Paupiettes) for 4

4 (5- to 6-ounce) slices beef round
1 cup commercially prepared seasoned
    stuffing mix
1 rib celery, minced
1 small onion, minced

Boiling water
1 tablespoon cornstarch
1 (4-ounce) can mushroom pieces with
    liquid

1 Have beef slices ready.
Place each slice between
sheets of waxed paper, and
flatten by pounding with
meat mallet or half a brick
wrapped in foil. (The same
method of flattening is
used for veal or chicken.)

2 Spread meat with a mixture
of seasoned stuffing mix,
celery, onion, and enough
boiling water barely to
moisten.

3 Roll meat, enclosing stuffing, and secure with wooden picks. Place, seam side down, in baking pan or Dutch oven; add ½ cup water to pan, and bake at 325° for 1½ hours, or until tender.

4 Remove meat rolls to warmed serving dish. Measure pan juices, and add water to make 1 cup. Blend in cornstarch, and return to pan. Add mushroom pieces with their liquid, and cook, stirring, until transparent and thickened. Spoon some gravy over beef rolls, and pass remainder in a gravy boat. Yield: 4 servings.

Preparing Oven-Barbecued Spareribs

Allow about 1 pound, bought weight,
spareribs per person.

1 Separate (or ask your
butcher to separate)
spareribs into serving-size
pieces by cutting between
bones. Place in grooved
pan, as shown, or on rack in
baking pan; season with
salt and pepper to taste.

2 Cover spareribs with thinly
sliced onion and lemon.
Sear in 400° oven for 30
minutes. They will begin to
brown, and fat will melt.
Drain off fat.

3 Pour commercial or homemade barbecue sauce over spareribs. Reduce oven heat to 325°, and bake an hour or more until meat is completely tender.

4 Baste with additional barbecue sauce once or twice during baking time.

Carving Basics

Properly carved servings appeal to the eye as well as the economy—a well-carved cut of meat gives extra mileage to the servings.

1 Place roast on platter with rib bones up.

2 Insert fork between ribs, and slice between bones.

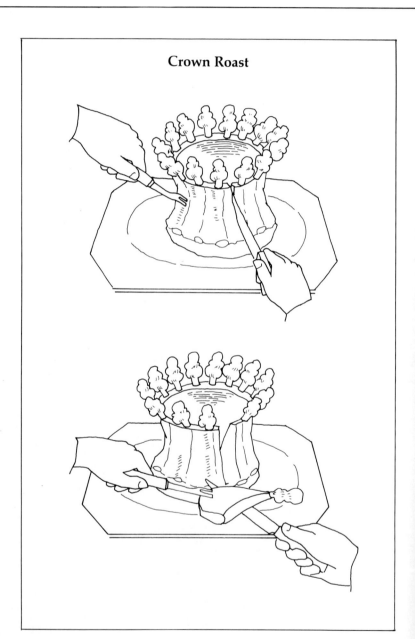

Crown Roast

3 Have the butcher free the backbone from the ribs. Leave backbone in place for roasting but remove before carving roast. Place the roast on the platter so the smaller end is toward the carver's right. Insert the fork, tines downward, into the heavy part of the meat between the ribs.

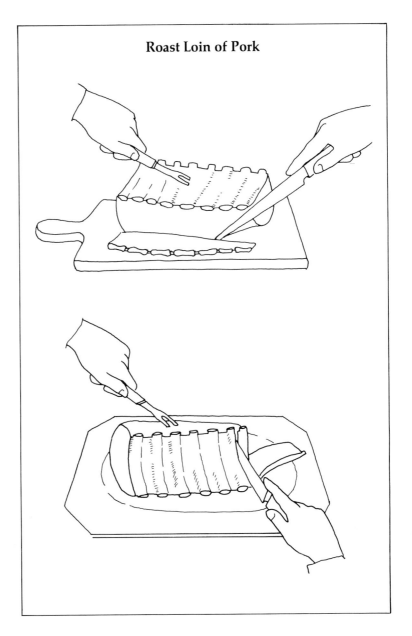

Roast Loin of Pork

4 Beginning at the right, cut down between each rib bone, allowing one chop per person.

1 Place on platter with flat side up. Insert the fork with tines downward about halfway down the roast. Slice meat from right to left in ¼-inch slices. Remove string and skewers as the meat is sliced.

2 Transfer meat to platter, using knife to lift and fork to stabilize slice.

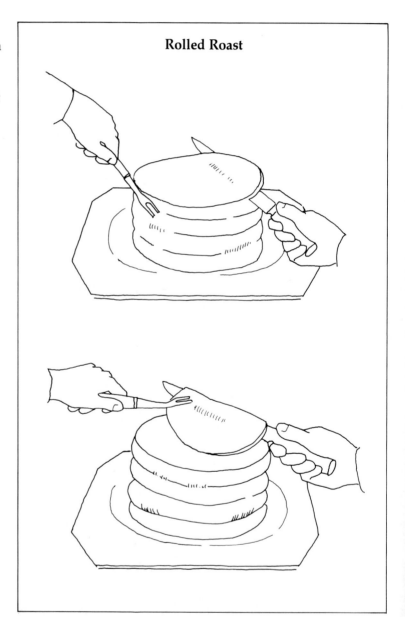

Rolled Roast

1 If possible, remove bones before bringing to table. Separate the various sections by running the knife tip around the connective tissues and natural dividing lines.

2 Turn the first section on its side to bring the grain of the meat (emphasized in drawings) parallel with the platter.

3 Cutting vertically, make ¼-inch slices across the grain. Slice remaining section the same way.

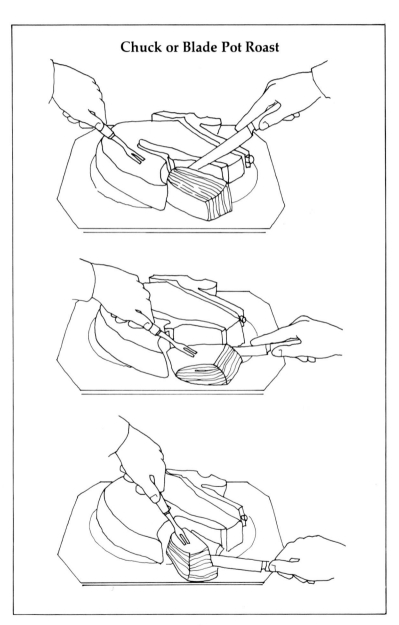

Chuck or Blade Pot Roast

Glazing a Baked Ham

One of the simplest and best-tasting glazes is made of equal parts of prepared mustard and brown sugar, thinned with a little water.

1 After baking ham, by using directions on ham package or on meat chart, remove skin, and cut off excess fat. Leave ⅓-inch fat covering.

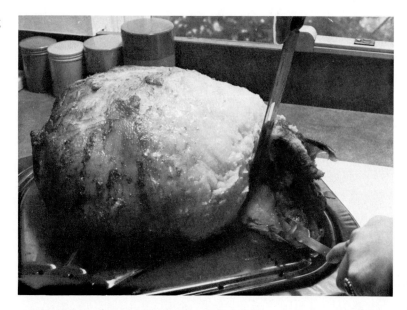

2 With sharp blade, score fat in a pattern of squares or diamonds, making cuts ¼ inch deep.

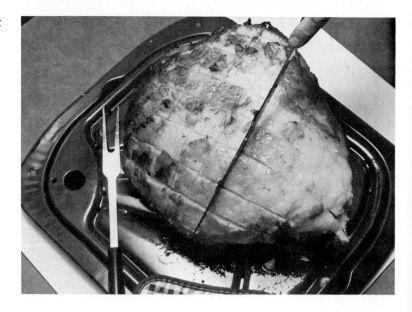

3 Push sharp ends of whole cloves into intersections of cuts to define pattern.

4 Brush glaze over ham. Return to oven (325° to 350°) for about 30 minutes until surface is browned and shiny.

Carving a Ham

Note: A cold, baked country ham is carved in the same way, except that the slices are cut paper-thin. Leg of lamb is carved in exactly the same way.

1 For carving, you will want to start with the meatier side up. This means that the shank end will point upward when ready to carve. Therefore, you will want to carve a few slices from the bottom side first, in order to give it a flat bottom. This helps ham to stay in position while you carve.

2 Having leveled the bottom, turn ham over, with shank end pointing upward. First, cut a wedge, as shown, from shank end. This gives you a starting point for beginning to slice.

3 Holding ham in position with fork, start slicing straight down to bone from the open cut you made by removing the wedge of meat.

4 After cutting as many slices as the occasion warrants, bring blade underneath slices, bearing against the bone. This severs all the slices at one time.

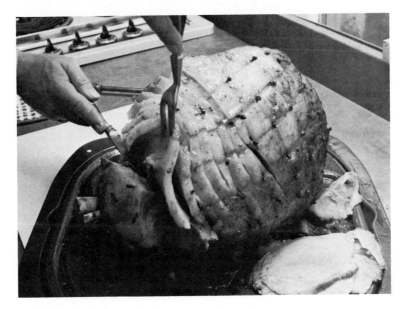

Preparing a Standing Rib Roast

An optional step, but a delicious lift for *au jus* gravy, is a covering of sliced tomato, onion, and celery tops.

Roasting is a dry heat method of cooking, so roast uncovered, or apply a tent of foil to keep vegetables from overbrowning.

1 Trim extra fat from roast, if necessary. This will help at the end of roasting time when you must remove excess drippings to make sauce.

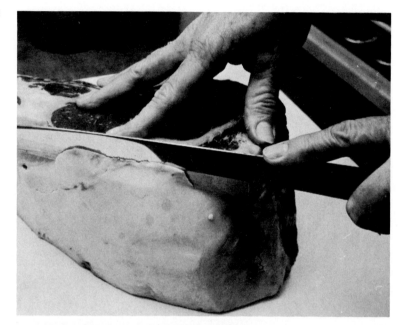

2 Placed fat side up, standing rib roast forms its own rack; other cuts for dry roasting require a rack in the bottom of roasting pan. Use a rack or channeled roasting pan, and place rib roast in a lying down position, as shown; sprinkle with salt on all sides.

3 Shake or grind pepper to taste, rubbing it well into meat.

4 Consult timetable for roasting beef of the size you have; a meat thermometer, inserted so tip is at center of meat, not touching fat or bone, is the surest way of getting exactly the degree of doneness you want.

Remove meat from oven when thermometer registers about 5° less than final reading desired, since meat continues to cook for several minutes after removal from heat. Place meat on warm platter to finish cooking and to firm up for carving. It should wait, kept warm, 15 to 20 minutes. *(Continued)*

5 Remove excess fat by pouring all liquid into heat-proof glass measuring cup, and standing cup in ice water; fat will rise. Spoon it off, and return meat juices to pan. An alternate method to remove fat is to tip pan so juices accumulate in one corner. Use spoon or bulb baster to take fat off. Then deglaze pan by adding ⅓ (or more) cup water, beef stock, or dry red wine (shown). Cook, stirring, about 5 minutes to dislodge the brown particles adhering to pan. Serve with roast.

Carving a Rib Roast

The carving knife and fork are placed at the right side. After carving they may be laid together on the platter, or one may be placed at each end of the platter.

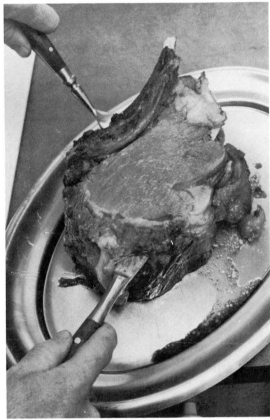

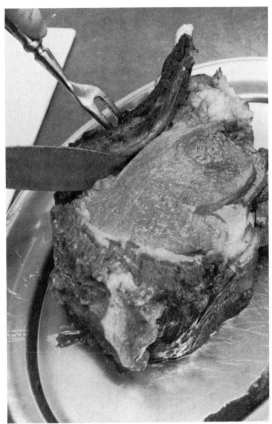

1 Insert fork firmly between ribs at midpoint of roast, as shown. With sharp carving knife, cut slices all the way to the bone. Do not remove slices; continue to slice until you have as many servings as you need, or until you reach the bottom third of meat.

2 Blade bearing against bone, remove entire rib bone section. This automatically frees the slices you have made.

(Continued)

3 To serve, lift slice on knife blade, supporting with fork from the top.

4 Serve *au jus*.

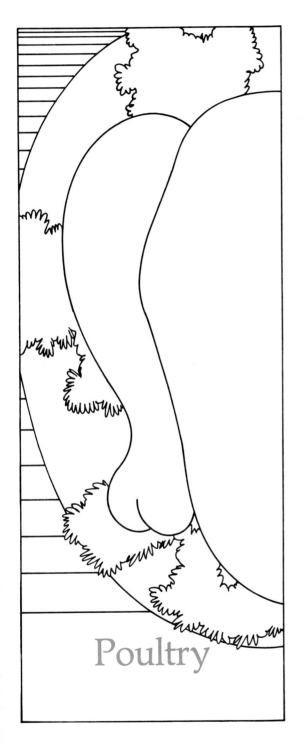

Poultry

Poultry is one dish you can count on to be a favorite with family and guests. Its popularity is quite understandable since poultry can come to the table in an endless variety of dishes. In addition, poultry is recognized by nutritionists as an important source of protein: rich in essential amino acids which are needed to build and maintain the body's muscles, tissues, and cells. Moreover, no meat is lower in fat content than poultry — a 3-ounce serving of a skinless broiled chicken breast has only 115 calories — thus it is quite useful for people who must count calories. Keep in mind, of course, that cooking oils and sauces will increase the calories.

Because poultry is short fibered, it is easy to digest. And digestibility is an important consideration in selecting food for children, older people, and those who have digestive problems.

Thanks to its delicate flavor, poultry takes naturally to many seasonings and cooking methods. Since it teams well with fruits and vegetables, it can be dressed up for company occasions without extravagant expenditures of time or money. Such versatility makes poultry one of the best food buys.

Some recipes require chicken or turkey pieces, others require chicken breasts or boned chicken breasts; still others instruct that the chicken be cooked whole and then carved. Your butcher can perform these operations for you, but his expertise is expensive. The solution, obviously, is to learn to carry out these three techniques yourself. Just follow the step-by-step instructions and illustrations in this chapter, and you'll soon be disjointing poultry, boning breasts, and carving well-cooked entrées with aplomb.

Trussing a Chicken

With a few materials at hand, you are ready to truss a chicken in such a way that no stuffing will fall out, and the bird will hold its shape during roasting.

1 You will need metal skewers or aluminum nails from the hardware store and some clean string.

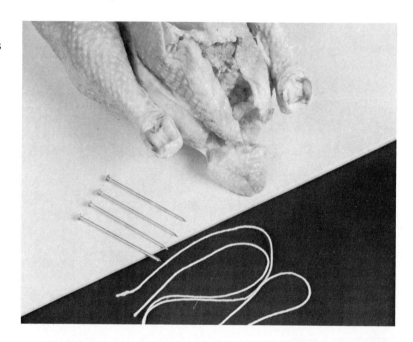

2 Tucking the tail piece inside the chicken is optional. Insert aluminum nails in one side and out the other side of the opening. Four nails will suffice, usually, for a chicken; a turkey will take a few more.

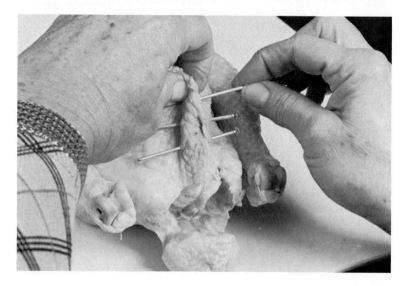

3 Now as though lacing up a big shoe, center the string over the top nail, cross string, go around the next nail, cross string, and so on, tying securely at the bottom. You may wish to tie the legs together by including them in the second or third cross-and-tie-motion.

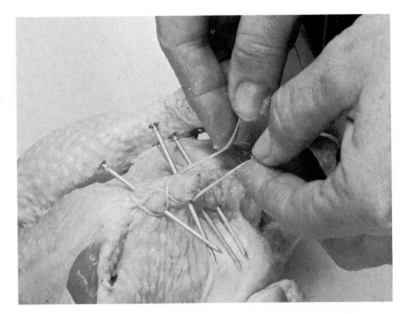

4 Fold the wing tips underneath shoulders of the bird, place in roasting pan, and proceed with the recipe you are following.

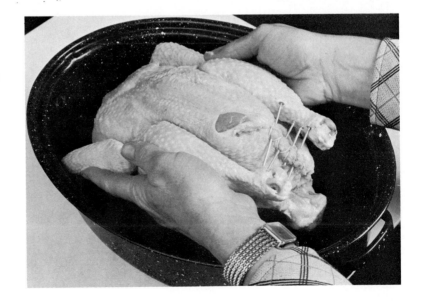

Carving Roast Chicken

After removing meat or fowl from the oven, allow it to "set" a few minutes to make the carving easier.

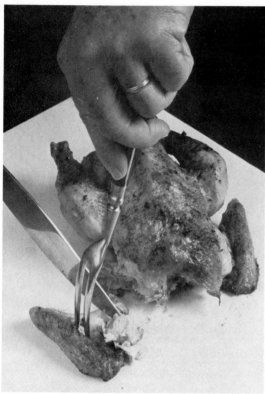

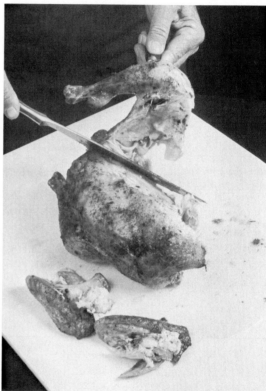

1 With neck end of chicken facing away from you, find joint where wing joins body; sever with carving knife. Repeat with other wing.

2 Lifting thigh-drumstick away from body of chicken with fork, find the joint that joins thigh bone to body; sever joint with knife. Repeat with other side.

194

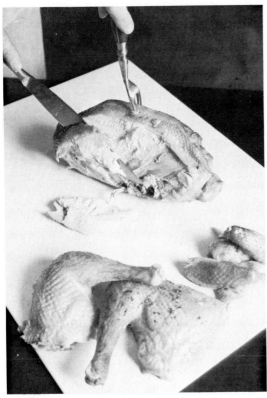

3 Hold body firmly with fork, and slice breast meat as thinly as possible until all meat is cut from one side. Turn bird around, and slice other half of breast meat.

4 Sever drumstick from thigh at joint. Arrange chicken on warm platter. Spoon stuffing, if any, onto platter with meat. Garnish as desired, with parsley or watercress.

Overleaf
A liberal sprinkling of tangy paprika will make Chicken and Dumplings a favorite with your dinner guests: Chicken Paprika, Hungarian Dumplings, Sliced Tomatoes with Herbed Mayonnaise, Baked Summer Squash, and Minted Pineapple Cup (see page 256).

Disjointing a Chicken

You may wish to make three serving pieces of breast, especially if it is a large bird. Here are two methods (not shown):

1. To get the old-fashioned "pulley bone," grasp whole breast tightly so that the top point of breastbone is clearly defined. Insert knife blade just in front of the top breastbone, and cut, following and bearing against curved bones, which are behind knife blade. Make cut to shoulders.

1 There are two good reasons for taking time to learn how to disjoint a chicken (note the word "disjoint" as opposed to "cut up"): "Cut-up" chicken is what you usually get at the market because the meat man does not have the time for careful disjointing. He breaks down a chicken by chopping through bone and meat, so you find slivers of bone in the oddest places; that's reason number one. The other is that whole chickens are cheaper. To address the task you will need a whole chicken and a razor-sharp knife.

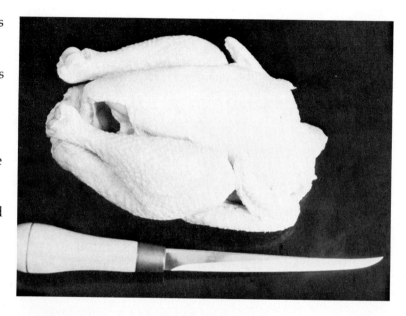

2 The wings come off first: Find the joint by moving the wing to find where it naturally joins the body. Then hold the wing out from the body, and bring your knife up through the shoulder joint and, with a circular motion, across the cartilage that holds wing to body. Repeat with other wing.

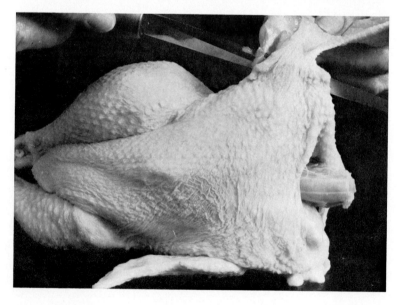

With hands, break shoulder joints, and finish by cutting apart with knife. Cut remaining breast apart as described above.

2. To make three pieces of breast, French style, lay whole breast on cutting board, skin side up. Cut off bottom third of breast with a cleaver, if you have one. Or place the blade of a heavy, French chef's knife at desired cutting point, and give the top of the blade a heavy blow downward

3 Legs come off next: Pull leg away from body and make a circular cut through skin on underside. Then, grasping chicken with both hands, bend leg away from body to expose joint, and exert force to snap (you'll hear it) the joint.

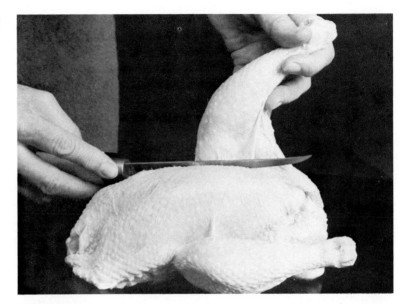

4 Cut through exposed cartilage and top skin.

(Continued)

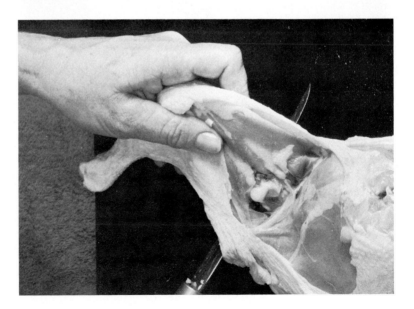

with the fist. It may take two or three blows, depending on the force you can give it. Then separate remaining breast into halves.

5 Separate leg from thigh: This cut is easily found by flexing the knee joint. Holding the whole piece in a folded position, bring knife upward until it touches solid joint. Unfold, and snap apart at joint. After you hear it "snap," complete cutting cartilage and skin that hold leg to thigh.

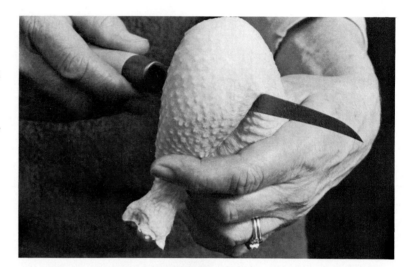

6 With your hand, find the natural separation between back and breast of chicken; you can actually put your fingers through the holes left by removal of wings. This is where you insert your blade, and make a complete cut toward tail end. This cut leaves back and breast attached only at shoulders. Grasp back and breast with hands, and use force to snap joint at shoulders. Use knife to sever shoulder cartilage and skin.

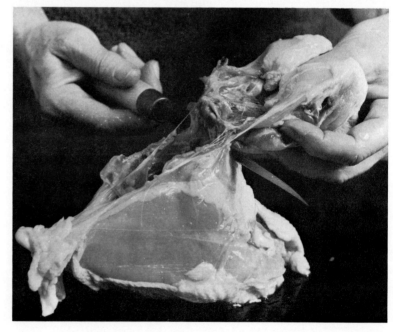

7 Separate breast into serving pieces. Method shown makes two pieces. The breastbone is the only bone in the chicken that must be broken. You can avoid even this one break if you choose to bone it out. Grasp breast firmly with both hands, and fold it backward with enough force to break breastbone. Then, with knife, finish by cutting through to end of breast. You may cut out the larger of the broken breastbone pieces, or leave all bone in, as desired.

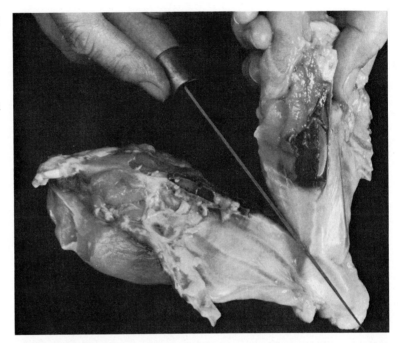

8 The job completed, 8 serving pieces are ready for your recipe, and the bony parts and other extras (on right) are ready for the stock pot.

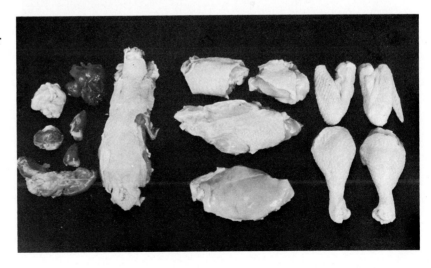

Frying Chicken

Persons on low-fat diets should skin chicken first and fry meat in safflower oil.

1 Disjoint chicken, wash, and dry. Into a heavy paper bag, put about ½ cup flour, 2 teaspoons salt, and 2 teaspoons paprika.

2 Add several shakes or grinds of black pepper; then shake bag to blend seasoned flour. There should be enough flour to coat chicken and to make gravy.

3 Starting with the heavier pieces, drop chicken, a few pieces at a time, into seasoned flour, and shake bag to coat well. Have ready a large skillet with ½ inch fat, hot enough to sizzle when chicken goes in. Reserve and measure remaining seasoned flour.

4 When all chicken is in and sizzling well, cover, and reduce heat to medium-low. Heat set too low will allow fat to penetrate chicken; you should be able to hear a faint frying sound the entire cooking time. Turn chicken when brown on one side, using tongs, and try to turn each piece only once. Timing will range from 20 minutes per side for a small chicken to 25 to 30 minutes per side for a very large fryer; you want to be sure there is no redness at the bone. For crisp chicken, remove cover after it is done, and cook 5 minutes or more, until moisture has evaporated. For "smothered," uncrisp chicken, drain off fat into measuring cup when chicken is done; add 3 to 4 tablespoons water, cover, and steam about 10 additional minutes.

Boning Chicken Breasts

Breasts are the meatiest part of the chicken; they are all white meat and usually weigh 12 to 15 ounces each.

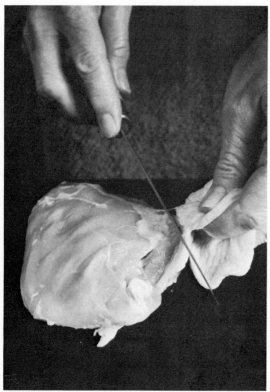

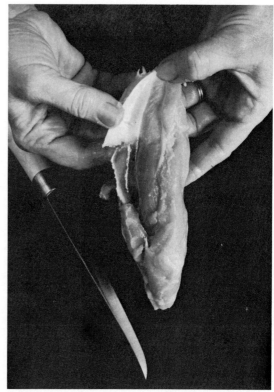

1 You may wish to start by removing the skin of the chicken breast. If you like it, leave it on; for a low-fat diet, remove it. The skin practically slips off by itself; just pull it as far as it will go; then sever the skin from the meat with boning knife.

2 Place piece on cutting board. The center breast bone will still be on one half or the other, whether you buy chicken breast already halved or halve it yourself. Center bone, like the skin, can be almost completely pulled off with the hands. Help it along with the knife where it is attached to the meat at the gristle end near breast tip.

3 Grasp rib side firmly with the left hand, and use short scraping (not slicing) motions with the front end of the knife blade. Bear blade against bone at all times, not cutting into meat, and slice meat away from bone.

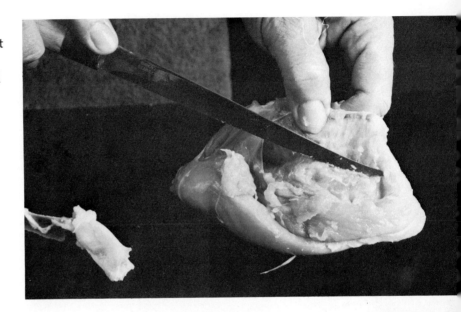

4 Then sever meat from bone at both ends.

(Continued)

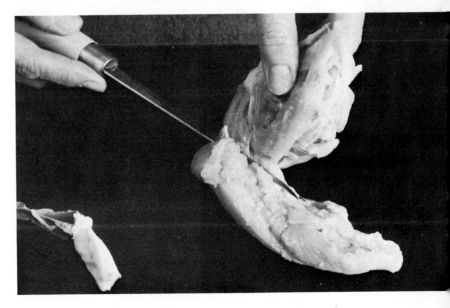

5 Note the cut side of the meat has not been mangled by the knife. Bones may go into your freezer bag with other chicken bones to be used for a pot of stock.

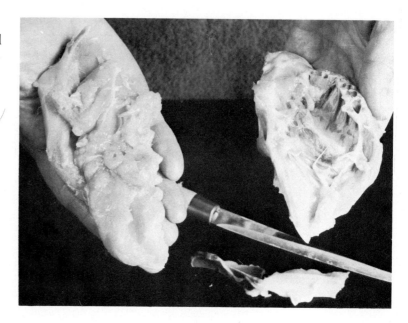

Preparing Chicken Kiev

1 cup butter, softened
2 tablespoons chopped parsley
1 teaspoon rosemary
¾ teaspoon salt
⅛ teaspoon pepper

6 whole chicken breasts, split, boned,
   and skinned
¾ cup all-purpose flour
3 eggs, well beaten
1½ to 2 cups bread crumbs
   Salad oil

1 Combine butter and seasonings in a small bowl; blend thoroughly. Shape butter mixture into 2 sticks, and put in freezer about 45 minutes.

2 Flatten chicken breasts with a meat mallet or a foil-wrapped brick. Cut each stick of butter mixture into 6 pats. Place a pat in center of each half of chicken breast. Fold sides and ends of chicken over butter; secure with toothpick.

(Continued)

207

3 Dredge each piece of chicken in flour, dip in egg, and coat with bread crumbs. Refrigerate about 1 hour.

4 Fry chicken in oil heated to 350°. Cook 5 minutes on each side or until browned, turning with tongs. Place in warm oven until all chicken is fried. Yield: 12 servings.

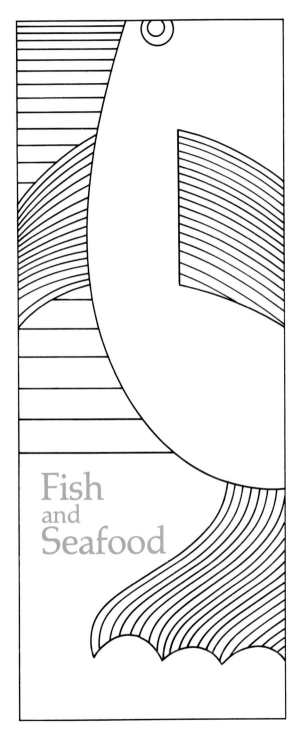

Fish
and
Seafood

Those who have an amateur angler in the family are probably quite familiar with the fun and good eating offered by a fish fry — the unforgettable taste of just-fried, freshly caught fish, a generous helping of coleslaw, and a basket full of crisp-crunchy hush puppies.

Inland, fish and seafood are very popular as evidenced by the many thriving seafood restaurants at a distance from the coast. And although few landlubbers have had the opportunity to learn the proper procedures for preparing fish and other seafoods, those who have never seen a shrimp or oyster in its habitat can now try a hand at their preparation, thanks to modern, fast-freezing methods which insure seafood availability.

Moreover, seafood provides an excellent change of pace from heavy meat dishes, and, while high in protein, it is low in fat. Fish also works well with heavier foods; a truly formal dinner has both a fish and meat course. This compatibility with other foods makes seafood particularly good for use as appetizers.

In coastal areas, especially, the availability of seafood prompts clambakes, shrimp and crab boils, and oyster roasts. At these casual affairs most of the actual cleaning of the seafood is done on the spot; for more formal occasions the fish or seafood must be prepared ahead of time. Thus, this chapter includes illustrated, step-by-step instructions for fileting a fish, opening fresh oysters, and peeling and deveining shrimp.

Fileting a Fish

Reserve skeleton and skin and use to
prepare fish stock.

1 Start with a fish that has
already been scaled and
eviscerated. (If filets are to
be skinned, you do not
need to scale fish.) Using a
very sharp knife, run blade
along both sides of back
ridge so the top (dorsal) fin
will be left with the
skeleton.

2 Cut down behind gills on
both sides of fish until you
hit the backbone; do not
cut through it. Also run
blade across tail end where
meat joins tail fin, until you
strike bone.

3 With the blade flat and bearing against bone, slice into the cut behind gill and, with short slicing motions, separate meat from bone. Lift filet with the other hand and continue cutting against bone until the tail cut is reached. Lift off filet. Turn fish, and repeat.

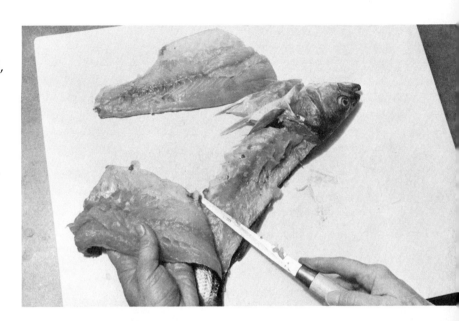

4 To remove skin, place filet skin side down. With tail end to your left and holding skin down firmly with left hand as you work, cut meat away from skin. Knife should bear against skin throughout the cut.

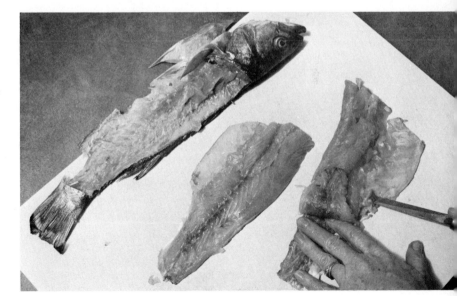

Opening Fresh Oysters

Note: Let no one tell you shucking oysters is easy, at least at first. Should desperation overtake you, pop oysters into a 400° oven for 5 minutes; that will make them more amenable to opening. Empty them from baking sheet into ice water and proceed with shucking.

1 A special oyster knife is necessary for prying open oysters.

2 Scrub oyster in shell with stiff brush under cold, running water. Hold oyster, deep shell down, over a strainer placed over a bowl. Holding oyster knife as shown, insert blade into hinge of shell; pry, turning knife, to force hinge loose. Continue to pry and lift all around edges of shell.

3 Pull shells apart, and finish cutting through the tough muscle. Do not allow muscle to be torn off in pulling shell apart; you want it to come out with whole oyster.

4 Oyster shell is now separated with oyster lying on deep shell. Run knife around oyster to loosen it completely, and let it drop into strainer. When all oysters are opened and in the strainer, pick up each one and examine it for bits of shell before dropping it into strained liquor in bowl. Fresh oysters will hold for up to 3 days in their own liquor, covered, in refrigerator.

Peeling and Deveining Shrimp

You may shell shrimp before or after cooking.

If you wish to shell the shrimp before cooking, add the shells to the water too; this makes a more flavorful court bouillon.

1 To cook, bring to boiling a quart of water per pound of shrimp. For each quart water, add a slice onion, a slice lemon, a bay leaf, and a few celery leaves. When water boils, drop in shrimp. When water returns to boiling point, reduce heat, and barely simmer 5 minutes. Tiny shrimp will take only 2 to 3 minutes, frozen or large shrimp, 7 or 8 minutes. Drain immediately. Begin shelling by pulling away the leggy underside. This effectively unzips the shell.

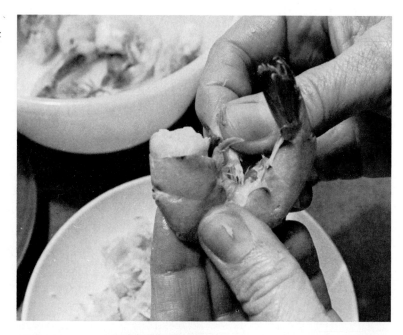

2 Remove the loosened body shell.

3 Remove shell from tail. Sometimes, if shrimp is to be served cold with sauce, the tail shell is left on to serve as a "handle."

4 The black vein runs down the outside curve. Devein shrimp by using a pointed knife, a wooden pick, or a small skewer.

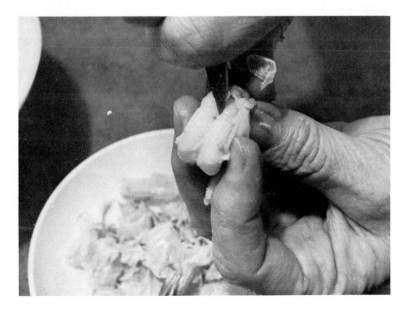

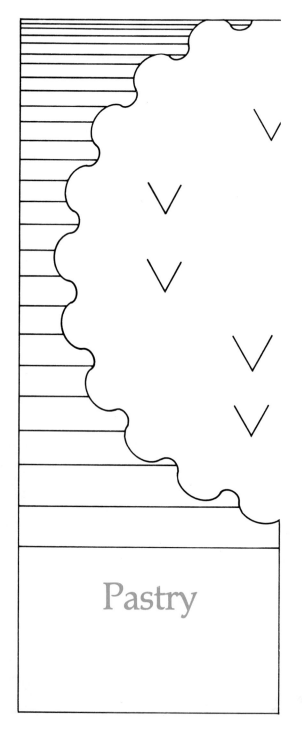

Pies are year-round desserts: summer provides its seasonal bounty of peaches and cherries to go into them, autumn provides apple and pumpkin favorites, winter glories in rich pecan and mincemeat, among others, and spring offers the ever-popular berries—blackberries, blueberries, and strawberries. In addition to fruit pies, there are rich sweet concoctions, such as Blackbottom Pie, on one end of the spectrum all the way down the line through sweet potato pie to the meat pies, such as chicken or shepherd's pie, on the other extreme.

Most dessert pies are about 9 inches in diameter, but sizes can vary to a small, fluted, individual tart or an even smaller appetizer size to the little half-moon shaped pasty. The fillings vary, but pies must have some sort of pastry or crust. Most easily made are cracker crumb crusts. Simply crush enough crackers to cover the piepan with a generous layer of crumbs, add enough melted butter to bind the crumbs, and add sugar to taste. Then, pour the mixture into the piepan and press it into an even layer covering the bottom and sides of the pan. Refrigerate the crumb shell until you are ready to fill it. However, there is nothing esoteric about making pie pastry notwithstanding all the "Don't overhandle its" and "Don't put too much water ins" you hear about it. Pastry, even more than yeast bread or biscuits depends on "feel."

Pastry is one endeavor in which practice makes perfect. Do not be disappointed if the first pie shell isn't pretty. If it tears, wet the edges, and press together. A great deal of tearing probably means that next time you need to use more water in the dough. Meanwhile use pastry trimmings and water as glue to patch the holes and smooth the rough spots. Your second effort will look nicer, the third even better, and from there it is downhill all the way.

Making Pie Pastry for a Two-Crust Pie

2 cups flour
1 teaspoon salt
⅔ cup shortening
4 to 6 tablespoons ice water

Note: Use trimmings from first crust (keep them flat, don't wad them up) along with remaining dough for second crust. To enlarge recipe, use 1 part shortening to 3 parts flour.

1 In addition to ingredients, assemble the tools of the trade before beginning: measuring utensils, rolling pin, pastry blender, pastry canvas or other floured surface, knife or kitchen shears for trimming edges and readied piepan or pans.

2 Begin with the flour, spooning it loosely into measuring cup, then leveling with straightedge. Use a sifter (although most flour now comes presifted) because it is the best way of combining salt uniformly with flour.

(Continued)

217

It is those particles of shortening which, when they melt in baking, keep separate the layers of flour to make flakes.

The reasoning behind the words "toss lightly" or "handle, but quickly" is this:

You don't want those bits of shortening to soften or melt. Your hot little hands will do just that, if you are not careful, and there goes your flakiness.

Many experts recommend chilling the

3 Measure the salt into the flour.

4 Measure cold shortening and add it to flour. Here is where judgement starts to enter the picture.

pastry at this point. I maintain that it should be rolled immediately while it is still malleable. Chilling hardens the shortening, making it harder to roll. But if you have followed directions, using cold ingredients and mixing quickly with as little hand touching as possible, your shortening bits will hold up and the flakes remain intact.

5 With pastry blender, cut shortening into flour. If you like your pastry to break apart in large, flat flakes, cut shortening in until it is the size of tiny peas, no smaller. But if you prefer pastry with meltaway, crumbly tenderness, keep going with the blender until the mixture is homogeneously cornmeallike in consistency.

6 The addition of ice water is the next judgement you must make. Do not be afraid of too much water. Just add it gradually, dribbling it with a spoon here and there; don't just pour it in the middle. "Toss lightly" with a fork, dribbling water where the dry parts are, then working those lumps into one main mass.

(Continued)

7 You may prefer to use your hands, but toss quickly, until the mass will barely hold together, uniformly dampened, not the least bit sticky to the touch, and with no dry crumbs left in the bowl.

8 Here is exactly how the ready-to-roll pastry should look. Pulled into halves, this dough may be used for either a 2-crust pie or two single pie shells.

Preparing a One-Crust Pie Shell

Note: Oven heats given are for metal piepans. If glass ones are used, reduce the heat by about 10°.

A technique worth knowing about is called "blind baking." Crust is prepared and pricked full of holes with fork, brushed with slightly beaten egg white, and baked 5 minutes at 425°. This crust is used for custard or other fillings most likely to soak into the crust.

1   Sprinkle rolling surface of your choice with flour. Pick up dough for one crust, and form it into a round. Press it on the floured surface, then turn it over, floured side up. With floured rolling pin center outward in all directions, trying to keep dough round. If a sticky place develops, sprinkle a little flour on the afflicted spot.

2   After pastry is rolled to an even thickness of about ⅛ inch, place piepan upside down over it, and measuring, if necessary, cut a circle large enough to fit pan with ½ inch extra to overhang edge of piepan.

(Continued)

If pastry is to be baked alone, as for a cream filling to be added later, prick it all over, even fluted edges, with floured tip of fork. To keep the crust from bubbling during baking, fit a sheet of foil into bottom and up sides of crust. Pour a pound of dry rice or beans (kept for the purpose) into the foil and bake. Empty pie shell should be baked at 450° for 10 to 12 minutes, or until lightly browned.

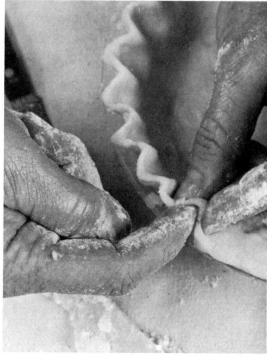

3 Pick up circle of dough by folding it loosely in half; then lift it carefully, and center it in the pan. Unfold. Never stretch pastry in pan. Indeed, it should be fitted in loosely, even slightly wrinkled. If you do this, you will not have the unpleasant surprise of finding your crust shrunk halfway down the inside of the pan when it is baked.

4 Fold the ½-inch extension of dough under, even with edge of piepan. If you have enough moisture in the dough, you will have no trouble fluting the edge, as shown. If dough is too crumbly to flute, simply flatten folded edge, and press edge all around with floured fork tines. (Remember to use a bit more water next time. A fluted crust will hold a little more filling than a flat-edged one.)

Assembling a Two-Crust Pie

Sometimes a fruit pie will overflow, so it is well to place the pie on a cookie sheet to catch drippings and minimize necessary oven cleaning. A cookie sheet is also easier to remove from oven than a hot piepan alone.

1 Roll out crust slightly larger than piepan. Fit loosely into pan; then trim edges of pastry even with pan edge.

2 Add cool pie filling to prepared shell.

(Continued)

3 Brush top edge of crust with water; this acts as a glue that holds the top and bottom crusts together.

4 Roll top crust large enough to cover pie to outer edge of bottom crust. Cut slits in an attractive pattern to allow steam to escape. Without these vents in top crust, steam will break sealed edges. Place top crust loosely over pie. If crust is stretched, it will pull away from its bond with bottom crust during baking.

5 Crimp sealed edges as shown, or simply flatten with floured tines of fork. Place on cookie sheet, and bake a fruit pie 10 minutes at 425° to set crust and start browning before reducing heat to 350° and proceeding with recipe. If using glass pie plate, reduce heat by 10° in both phases of baking.

Overleaf
Be you 5 or 50, your birthday couldn't be any more fun than when celebrated with homemade Coconut Cake and Fresh Lemon Ice Cream (see page 283).

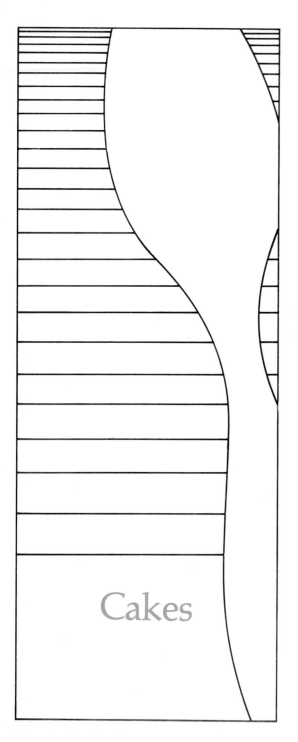

Cakes

All of us use cake mixes from time to time, and they do have their desirable features. But they only save you money if you bake cakes so seldom that the staples you need for them would spoil between bakings. Some cake mixes will stay fresh for up to 2 years, but to make this possible, they contain some additives you might not want to eat.

Not only are mixes more expensive, they won't save you all that much time. Consider this timing for putting a cake together from scratch: 3 to 5 minutes for creaming the butter and sugar together, 2 minutes for beating in the eggs or yolks, 2 more minutes for adding the flour and liquid, another minute if you're to fold in the beaten egg white; the total time is only 10 minutes from a standing start. Of course, you will have made advance preparation just as you would for a "mix" cake: oven temperature set, all ingredients at room temperature, pans greased and floured. (Pans for angel and sponge cakes are never greased.) You will save time if you plan in advance.

On the theory that it is better to know some why's and wherefore's in advance than to forge ahead with a recipe and wonder what went wrong afterward, let us start with some positive thinking.

In my earlier years as a food writer, I continually used the expression "Combine butter with sugar, and cream until . . . ." The phone would ring with unnerving regularity: "How much cream?" I try to find other ways of saying it, but "cream" is the right word for putting the sugar into the butter. The mixture will look like heavy, thick cream when it is ready for the next step. I believe that if you read over these check points before beginning your cake-baking career, you will have answered your own "what went wrong" questions in advance.

MIXING

All ingredients for the cake should be at 70° to 72° room temperature. Eggs, if they are to be used separated, should be separated when cold, then allowed to warm.

Avoid overbeating. Cream the softened butter a bit before adding the sugar. The creaming process that combines butter with sugar should not take more than 3 minutes at medium-low speed, 5 at the outside. Overbeating can cause butter to separate, making it difficult or impossible to combine for a well-textured cake. Other consequences of overbeating at all stages of mixing are dense (too fine) texture and smaller volume.

Eggs are usually added one at a time, beating to blend, using fairly high speed of electric mixer. It should not take more than 2 minutes, even for several eggs. Scrape batter down from sides of bowl with rubber spatula while beating. If necessary, stop motor a moment to scrape down sides.

Flour, with whatever other dry ingredients mixed in, is usually added in 3 parts; the liquid, in 2 parts, beginning and ending with flour. If cake flour is called for and you want to substitute plain, measure, level, remove 2 tablespoons, and sift 2 or 3 times.

Egg whites should be added at last possible moment before cake goes into oven. Check oven temperature before starting to beat the whites. Make sure beaters and bowl are entirely free from grease. As soon as egg whites are folded into batter, put the cake into the oven. Egg whites play an important role in leavening; you don't want to lose the air beaten into them.

PAN TYPES

Metal pans are assumed in most cake recipes. If you are using ovenproof glass pans, reduce baking temperature by 25°.

Use pan size specified. Batter should fill pan ½ to ⅔ full, except for tube or bundt pans, which may be filled ¾ full. Pans that are too large will result in uneven browning and coarse texture. Pans that are too small may run over in the oven or sink (fall) in cooling. If your pans are too small to hold the batter to the level suggested above, make a few cupcakes from the remainder. After batter is in pans, use rubber spatula to push batter into corners and up sides, making center lower. This makes for even rising.

BAKING

For butter cake layers, the oven rack should be positioned in the center of the oven. Bake only 2 layers at a time, on the same shelf, with space between and around them for air to circulate. They will rise unevenly if overcrowded. If you must bake a third layer at the same time, position oven racks just above and below center of oven. Place 2 pans on top shelf and the third pan below, staggered, so it is not directly underneath either top pan.

Angel and sponge cakes, tortes and soufflés should bake on rack placed below center of oven. Never open oven door on sponge cakes until minimum baking time is up.

Tests for Doneness

When done, layers will shrink slightly away from pan sides. A wooden pick or cake wire inserted in center will come out clean. A small dent made with the finger will disappear from a fully baked cake. But there is an exception to the latter rule: chocolate and other rich cakes may keep the depression even when fully baked. Use the other tests to be sure.

REMOVING CAKE FROM PAN

Plain cakes should cool in pans set on racks for 5 minutes before being turned out on racks, rich cakes 10 to 15 minutes. After specified pan cooling time, run knife around edges, and invert rack over cake; turn over and out. Then place a second rack over cake, and turn it right side up to finish cooling. (Top crust will stick to rack and tear if left to cool upside down.) Angel and sponge cakes are cooled completely, upside down, in their pans. If the pan has no "legs" to support it up off the counter, turn cake-pan over with the tube part over the neck of a heavy bottle, letting it hang until cool. To remove run knife blade carefully around sides and tube, using a careful up and down motion, to loosen edges of cake from pan.

OVEN THERMOSTATS

If, in spite of following all the foregoing instruction, you should have a couple of flops in a row, suspect your oven. All oven thermostats should be checked once a year for accuracy. You can easily do this yourself with a dependable oven thermometer. If oven proves to be several degrees off, either compensate or call the utility company or a repairman to reset it. Some ranges come with instructions for resetting the oven thermostat yourself.

FREEZING CAKES

All cakes may be successfully frozen. There is difference of opinion as to whether it is preferable to freeze cakes frosted or unfrosted. Butter frostings freeze better than egg white, boiled ones. And it is a spacious freezer indeed which can take a frosted, boxed and sealed cake, ready to be defrosted and served. I am inclined to freeze unfrosted cake; then thaw, and frost it just before serving. Cakes that have been frozen tend to dry out faster than those that have not.

Preparing Cakepans

Be sure to use the proper pans for the cake you are baking. Pan sizes include 8- and 9-inch round, 8-inch square, and 9- x 13-inch rectangular.

1 After you have taken the trouble to mix a perfect cake batter, it is disappointing to have a cake tear when it comes out of the pan. If you are new to cake baking, it won't hurt to take double precautions for getting the cake out whole. To do this you will need cakepan, shortening, pastry brush, flour, measuring spoons, and waxed paper (not shown).

2 Brush pan bottom and sides generously with shortening.
(Continued)

3 Using the bottom of the cakepan for a pattern, draw a line on waxed paper with tip of scissors. Then cut the circle.

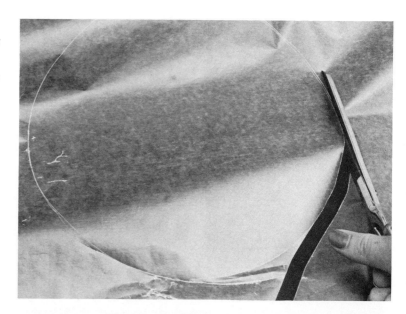

4 Fit circle into bottom of greased pan. Turn paper over so both sides are greased; press onto pan bottom.

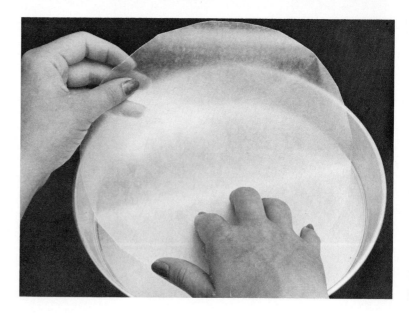

5 Toss a tablespoonful of flour into pan.

6 Shake, toss, turn, tap—whatever is necessary to coat the greased surface of pan sides and bottom with flour. Then tap pan upside down over sink to discard excess flour.

Making a Cake

COCOA LAYER CAKE

1 stick (½ cup) butter or margarine,
    softened

1 cup sugar
2 eggs, separated
1¾ cups all-purpose flour
⅓ cup cocoa

1 Combine softened butter
with sugar in large mixing
bowl.

2 Beat butter and sugar
until light and fluffy.
Underbeating will not
dissolve enough of the
sugar; overbeating will
cause butter to separate,
and make an oily,
lumpy-looking mixture.

1 teaspoon soda
   Pinch salt
1 cup buttermilk
1 teaspoon vanilla extract

---

3 Add (room temperature) egg yolks, beating until well blended.

4 Measure all dry ingredients into sifter. Sift together into a bowl or onto waxed paper.

(Continued)

5 Combine buttermilk and
vanilla, and add dry
ingredients alternately.
This means to add the milk
in 2 parts, the flour mixture
in 3 parts, beginning and
ending with flour. Beat after
each addition until mixture
looks homogeneous.

6 Wash beaters thoroughly
before beating egg whites;
if any fat is left on beaters,
whites will not reach full
volume. The standard
method for adding beaten
egg whites to any firmer
mixture, including soufflés
is to pick up a dab of
beaten white with a spatula
and add to mixture.

7 Stir the bit of white briskly into batter with rubber spatula. This loosens mixture, making it more receptive to the final, careful folding in of the remaining bulk of beaten egg whites.

8 Add remaining egg whites. Carefully, so as not to lose the air in the whites, fold into mixture with rubber spatula, bringing batter up and over, up and over, until cake batter is gently but thoroughly blended. Pour batter into 2 prepared 9-inch layer cakepans. Place on shelf in center of 375° oven, and bake about 25 minutes or until wooden pick or wire inserted into center comes out clean. When done, layers will have drawn slightly away from sides of pans. Yield: 1 (9-inch) 2-layer cake.

Making Boiled Frosting

2 cups sugar
1 cup water
2 egg whites
¼ teaspoon cream of tartar
1 teaspoon vanilla

Note: If frosting does not get firm enough, syrup is undercooked. Place it in heatproof bowl over (not in) boiling water, and beat mixture with rotary beater until it will hold peaks and be spreadable. If

1 Combine sugar with water in 1-quart saucepan. Over high heat, stir with wooden spoon until all sugar is dissolved, which should occur just as boiling point is reached. From this point, syrup is not stirred again. Have candy thermometer standing by in pan of boiling water. Cover syrup pan with lid, and boil 2 minutes to dissolve with steam any remaining sugar crystals. Insert candy thermometer, and boil to 238° (240° if it is a rainy or humid day).

2 Have egg whites ready in large bowl of mixer, with cream of tartar stirred in. As soon as syrup is cooked, gently move it to a cool burner, and let stand while you beat egg whites until they are quite foamy and start to cling to sides of bowl. The syrup has cooled for a couple of minutes by this time.

frosting sets up too soon, syrup is over-cooked. Try adding a few drops lemon juice or a teaspoon of boiling water.

3 With mixer at medium-high speed, start pouring the syrup into egg whites in a very fine stream. Continue to add syrup slowly without interruption until all is used. Do not scrape pan. Reduce speed to medium, and beat until mixture will support soft peaks when beaters are raised.

4 Beat in vanilla. When icing begins to feel dry around edges of bowl, it is ready to spread on cooled cake. Do not scrape bowl; if any sugar crystals have formed there, and you get them into the frosting on cake, entire frosting could turn sugary by chain reaction. Yield: about 2 cups.

Frosting a Layer Cake

Note: To keep frosting off the cake plate, you might like to try this: Cut a square of waxed paper into 4 triangles. Place on cake plate before adding bottom layer, so that paper will extend out and all around layer.

After frosting cake, the paper triangles may be carefully pulled out, and the little frosting disturbed by its removal can be readily touched up with a clean spatula.

1 Place first layer, top side down, on cake plate. Spread about ¼ of frosting on top.

2 Place second layer, top side down, over filling, making sure edges are straight.

3 Cover top with another ¼ of the frosting, spreading almost to edges. With spatula, pick up frosting, and, starting at bottom, bring each row of frosting up and over top edge. Continue to frost from bottom upward, until all frosting is used.

4 Finish frosting by swirling into peaks and curls. You may smooth sides, and swirl only the top.

Preparing a Jelly Roll

SPONGE CAKE

¾ cup sifted cake flour
1 teaspoon baking powder

Pinch salt
4 eggs, room temperature
¾ cup sugar
1 teaspoon vanilla extract

1 After baking Sponge Cake, remove cake like this: Sift powdered sugar generously over cake; run knife around edges, and spread a clean kitchen towel over it. Cover towel with cookie sheet, and turn the whole assembly over. Cake is now on towel. Peel off waxed paper, and trim away crisp edges with sharp knife.

2 While cake is still hot, starting with one long side, roll cake, towel and all, into a fairly tight roll. Let stand until cooled.

242

Resift cake flour with baking powder and salt. Reserve. In small bowl of mixer, beat eggs until light, using high speed. Slowly add sugar, beating until fluffy. Remove

bowl from mixer stand, and fold in sifted dry ingredients with rubber spatula. Fold in vanilla.

Prepare a jelly roll pan (9 x 13 inches, 1

3 Carefully unroll sponge cake, and spread with your choice of fillings. Strawberry cream (shown), flavored whipped cream, chocolate cream, or lemon cream are good choices.

4 Reroll cake, wrap in plastic wrap or waxed paper to hold the shape, and refrigerate until serving time.

(Continued)

inch deep) by greasing and lining with
waxed paper. Turn paper over so that both
sides are greased. Pour in batter and bake
at 400° about 13 to 15 minutes, or until it
tests done. Yield: 8 servings.

5 If desired, sift a little
powdered sugar over jelly
roll, and slice to serve. Jelly
roll usually serves 8, if cake
is baked in standard 9- x
13-inch pan.

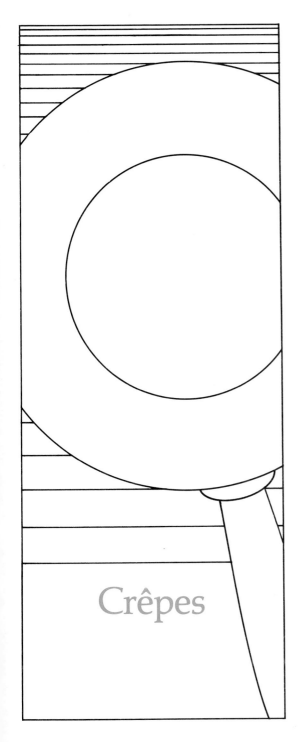

Crêpes

Once thought of as one of the international delicacies most difficult to prepare, crêpes have now become one of the most popular contributions to luncheons, dinners, and desserts. Whether prepared by the traditional, time-tested method or by using one of the new, foolproof, crêpe pans, a stack of crêpes, once prepared, can be frozen until needed; then, speedily thaw, fill, and heat for a quick company dinner with a flavor that is far from spur-of-the-moment.

Besides their ability to freeze well, crêpes offer versatility within the framework of the meal itself. For example, a basic crêpe can be filled with either a vegetable or meat mixture and thereby provide as light or as heavy a meal as you wish. Certainly a dinner composed of two or three crêpes filled with Crabmeat Filling, a leafy green salad, and a rich dessert is sure to appease the heartiest appetite.

If, on the other hand, the dinner menu has been set, choose crêpes for dessert, a cheerful change from humdrum sweets. Choices run the gamut from Vanilla Crêpes with Orange Sauce, simply stuffed and sweetly sauced, to flambéed finales such as Crêpes Suzette.

Should you prefer to entertain with a brunch or spark a Saturday breakfast for your family, crêpes again are ready to help: a meal of fresh fruit, lox or bacon, and Cheese Blintzes together with a pot of freshly brewed coffee is guaranteed to open the bleariest of early morning eyes.

Both basic and sweet crêpes are prepared in the same manner, so only a few forays into crêpe making will provide a myriad of mealtime possibilities.

Preparing Basic Crêpes

2 cups all-purpose flour
½ teaspoon salt
4 large eggs
1 cup cold milk

1 cup cold water
4 tablespoons butter, melted
 Salad oil

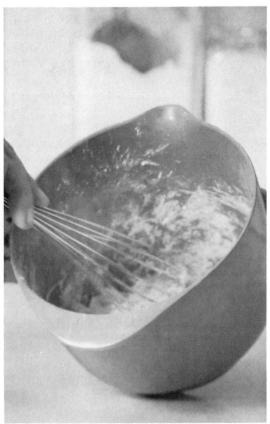

1 With a wire whisk or electric mixer, blend flour, salt, and eggs. Mixture will be stiff; blend until smooth.

2 Combine liquid ingredients except oil: add to flour mixture; blend until batter is smooth. Refrigerate for 1 to 2 hours before cooking.

246

Note: There is another, newer (and less expensive) crêpe baker on the market: a 7-inch, nonstick-coated, shallow pan. To use it, one pours batter into heated pan, then pours out excess. Using it is child's play; perfect crêpes each time. In making crêpes, if they are perfectly thin, there is no reason for turning and baking other side.

3 Brush crêpe pan with salad oil; place over medium heat. Pour in a scant ¼ cup of batter, and quickly tilt pan to cover the entire bottom thinly and evenly. Cook crêpe about 1 minute or until lightly browned.

4 Lift edge of crêpe to test for doneness. Shake crêpe free from bottom of pan. Raise pan and with a flick of the wrist, flip the crêpe, catching it neatly back in the pan. Cook about ½ minute longer. (For cheese blintzes, do not brown second side.) The "flick of the wrist" comes with practice. Feel free to turn crêpes with spatula, meanwhile, working in some practice as you find time. *(Continued)*

5 Turn crêpe out of pan. Stack between layers of waxed paper to prevent sticking; keep warm in oven. To refrigerate or freeze crêpes, stack as directed in stacks of 8 to 10; wrap in foil. Heat them in a covered dish at 300° to thaw. Yield: about 22 crêpes.

6 New and functional is this crêpe baker. If you have one, by all means use it instead of the traditional method. Heat domed crêpe pan over medium heat until water sizzles when sprinkled on surface. Pour batter into pieplate; dip pan into batter. Place pan (domed side up) over medium heat; cook crêpe about 1 minute or until browned on bottom.

Making Crêpes Suzette

Basic Crêpe batter (1 recipe)
2 tablespoons sugar
½ teaspoon vanilla or brandy extract
Orange Butter

Orange Sauce
3 tablespoons Grand Marnier or other
orange-flavored liqueur

1 Combine ingredients for Crêpe batter, and add sugar and extract. Beat until smooth. Cover, and refrigerate at least 2 hours. Cook Crêpes according to instructions given for Basic Crêpes in this chapter.

2 Prepare Orange Butter: Cream butter and sugar until light and fluffy; blend in Grand Marnier and orange rind. Yield: 2 cups.

(Continued)

Orange Butter:

¾ cup unsalted butter, softened
½ cup sugar

⅓ cup Grand Marnier or other
orange-flavored liqueur
¼ cup grated orange rind

3 Prepare Orange Sauce: Combine butter, sugar, orange rind, and orange juice in a skillet; cook over low heat about 10 minutes, stirring frequently. Add orange sections and Grand Marnier. Yield: 2¾ cups.

4 Spoon about 1 tablespoon orange butter on each crêpe, spreading evenly to outer edges. Fold crêpes in half, then into quarters.

Orange Sauce:

½ cup unsalted butter, melted
¾ cup sugar
2 tablespoons grated orange rind

⅔ cup orange juice
2 oranges, peeled and sectioned
¼ cup Grand Marnier or other
    orange-flavored liqueur

5 Spoon half of Orange Sauce into chafing dish; arrange crêpes in sauce. Spoon remaining sauce over crêpes; place over low heat until thoroughly heated. Heat Grand Marnier; ignite, and pour over crêpes.

6 Crêpes Suzette flamed at the table make a spectacular dessert. Yield: about 2 dozen to serve 6 or 8.

Recipes for
All Occasions

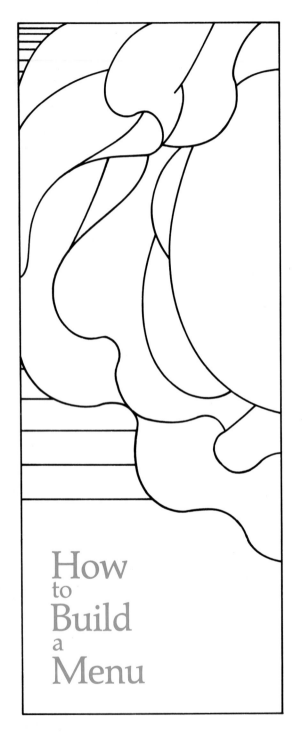

How
to
Build
a
Menu

There are some do's and some don'ts involved in the construction of a menu, and some preliminary observations may serve to loosen your thinking: It is customary to start a menu with a main dish, then plan other foods around it; but if you are planning to serve an especially elegant dessert, nothing is to prevent your working from dessert backward through the meal. The principle involved is to decide on the dish most important to you; then select other menu elements that will complement that dish. Well planned, a meal will be a composition as whole and well rounded as a painting, a sculpture, or any other work of art.

Do: Think color. Here is a reverse illustration: Envision this meal, please. Chicken and dumplings, creamed cauliflower, a salad of sliced cucumbers in sour cream, and vanilla ice cream for dessert. If there is anything nice to say about it, well, it would be invisible in a snow storm.

Do: Think flavor. Hide a few surprises in some of your dishes. Use a few drops of onion juice in a congealed fresh grapefruit salad, not enough really to taste, just enough to give it mystery. Put some chopped fresh mint in the peas; combine mashed potatoes with an equal quantity of cut-up cooked green cabbage or fresh kale greens, an idea that is old hat to the Irish who have been eating it for years and calling it colcannon. Experiment, by all means, with wine cookery.

Do: Think texture. Something crunchy, something smooth. A crisp green salad is a better complement to a main dish of creamed chipped beef on toast or turkey hash on cornbread than, say, a lettuce leaf filled with fruit swimming in mayonnaise and sour cream. If you should get trapped into a corner of this kind, use your head: remedy the impasse by freezing that soupy fruit salad, thus giving it not only a crunchy, chewy quality but also supplying an appetizing chill for the palate. Your green vegetable should not be overcooked; err on the side of crispness (and good nutrition) by using the stir-fry or steam method of cooking as often as possible. Exception: Southern cooks, go ahead and cook green beans for half a day; nothing more delicious exists.

Do: Think hot and cold. On the hottest summer day, your main dish might well be a congealed chicken salad or a bowl of greens generously overlaid with slivers of cold meat and cheeses. Nothing could be more complementary to such a meal than a pan of hot rolls fresh from the oven. Or you could serve finger sandwiches with the salad, then have a shockingly hot dessert of fresh fruit poached in port.

Do: Think of your expendable time. Attempt to build a menu in such a way that some or most of it may be made the day before. A congealed salad lends itself to early preparation, as do many desserts.

Do: Think of your expendable energy. Especially when baking, we sometimes get unnecessarily overworked. If you are going to the trouble of making yeast rolls, by all means arrange to have something from the store for dessert, such as ice cream or perhaps fruit and cheese.

However, if it is your pleasure to spend hours on a gorgeous dessert, then get your rolls from the bakery. If you enjoy baking cakes and whipping up freezers of ice cream, let those be the main part of the show, and go easy on the rest of the meal. You could serve, perhaps, hot souffléed

sandwiches (made up ready to bake the night before) and a simple green salad.

Do: Encourage your family to try new foods. Prepare dishes and combinations new to your family, especially nutritious ones.

Don't: Repeat elements in a meal. This point bears careful watching. You would not want, for example, to serve Chicken Paprika, which is made with sour cream, on the same menu with a sour cream-topped cheesecake. If your main dish is a casserole heavy on the cheese, you'd want to leave cheese out of your appetizer and dessert plans. You wouldn't want to include raw celery or mushrooms in a salad if one of your cooked dishes contains the same vegetable.

Don't: Serve bread with a meal containing such breadstuffs as dumplings, noodles, grits, rice, or barley. An exception could be made at holiday time when the "big pot goes in the little one" and you want to be most lavish.

Don't: Use vinegar in your salad dressing when you're serving wine with a meal. Use lemon juice instead. Vinegar tends almost to cauterize the palate against the delicacy of wine.

Don't: Overdo it. There was once an attitude, perhaps peculiar to the South, when the hostess or host felt affronted if guests didn't leave the table groaning and glassy-eyed from overeating. Give them a full, well-rounded meal, and let them depart in a glow of well being, not in a state of misery from ingesting too much.

Don't: Go overboard on the hors d'oeuvres. Guests may overindulge and blunt the effect of your carefully planned dinner.

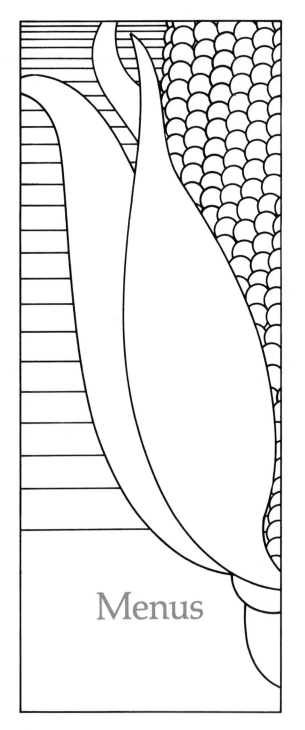

Menus

CHICKEN PAPRIKA DINNER FOR 4

Hungarian Dumplings
Chicken Paprika
Sliced Tomatoes with
Herbed Mayonnaise
Baked Summer Squash
Minted Pineapple Cup

HUNGARIAN DUMPLINGS

2½ cups all-purpose flour
  1 teaspoon salt
  1 egg
½ cup shortening, divided
  Ice water to make a soft dough
  4 quarts boiling water
  1 tablespoon salt
  Salt to taste

Stir flour and 1 teaspoon salt together in a deep bowl. Add egg and half the shortening. Working with your hands, work egg and shortening into center of flour. Gradually add enough water to make a very soft dough, too thick to pour but too soft to be rolled out as biscuits. Beat mixture with a wooden spoon until it won't cling to the sides of bowl; it will make a little snapping noise at this point.

Bring water to boil, and add the tablespoon salt. To form dumplings, drop by teaspoonfuls into boiling water, or place a third of the dough at a time on a wooden cutting board, and scrape pencil-size bits from the board into the water with a straight-bladed knife. Dumplings will rise to the top when done. To make sure, cut one open, and taste the inside. Drain; then rinse under hot tap water. Melt remaining shortening in saucepan, and stir in the dumplings. Season. Serve hot. Yield: 4 servings.

CHICKEN PAPRIKA

2 large onions, finely chopped
⅓ cup vegetable oil or
    shortening
2 tablespoons paprika
1½ teaspoons salt
¼ cup water
1 (3-pound) frying chicken,
    cut up
1 cup commercial sour cream
1 teaspoon cornstarch

Select a heavy skillet with cover. Sauté the onions in oil until they are transparent. Add paprika, salt, water, and chicken. Cover, and simmer gently until meat is very tender. Combine sour cream with cornstarch, and add to sauce, pushing chicken aside. Heat without boiling (boiling will curdle sour cream) for 5 minutes. Serve immediately on warmed platter. Yield: 4 servings.

Note: Alternate method of cooking: Assemble ingredients as above; then bake in 325° oven for 1 hour or until chicken is tender.

SLICED TOMATOES WITH HERBED MAYONNAISE

4 medium-size tomatoes
4 lettuce leaves
½ cup mayonnaise
½ teaspoon dried basil

Core, peel, and slice tomatoes from top to bottom. Place on lettuce leaf. Blend mayonnaise with basil, and spoon over tomatoes. Yield: 4 servings.

BAKED SUMMER SQUASH

4 small tender summer squash, yellow,
    zucchini, or pattypan
1 cup water
1 teaspoon salt
¼ cup firmly packed light brown
    sugar
2 tablespoons butter
1 teaspoon lemon juice

Slice squash lengthwise, and simmer in salted water, covered, until almost tender; or steam squash over boiling water, sprinkling salt over slices. Transfer drained squash to buttered 1-quart baking dish. Sprinkle with brown sugar, dot with butter, and sprinkle lemon juice over all. Bake at 350° for 20 minutes or until lightly browned. Yield: 4 servings.

MINTED PINEAPPLE CUP

1 (8-ounce) can sliced pineapple
1 cup seedless grapes
8 white cream candy mints, broken up
1 (7-ounce) bottle ginger ale, chilled

Drain, and cut pineapple into chunks. Add grapes and candy mints. Refrigerate several hours or overnight. At serving time, pour a little ginger ale over each serving. Yield: 4 servings.

SALISBURY STEAK DINNER FOR 4

Salisbury Steak
Green Salad with Thousand Island Dressing
Prospector Potatoes
Green Lima Casserole
Wine-Poached Pears

SALISBURY STEAK

1 pound ground beef
1 egg
⅓ cup half-and-half or evaporated milk
2 slices white bread, finely crumbled
1 teaspoon Worcestershire sauce
1 teaspoon prepared mustard
1 teaspoon dried parsley flakes
1 teaspoon salt
   Dash pepper
1 (4-ounce) can mushroom stems and pieces
2 teaspoons cornstarch
½ cup beef bouillon
   Chopped fresh parsley (optional)

Combine beef, egg, cream, crumbs, and seasonings. Form into 4 thick, oval patties. Sprinkle iron skillet with salt to prevent sticking, and heat to medium hot. Fry patties slowly, about 10 minutes on each side, until done and brown. Reserve on warmed platter. Mix liquid from mushrooms with the cornstarch. Pour off all fat, and place mushrooms, cornstarch mixture, and bouillon in the skillet. Cook, stirring, until sauce is transparent and slightly thickened. Pour sauce over steaks. Garnish with parsley, if desired. Yield: 4 servings.

GREEN SALAD WITH THOUSAND ISLAND DRESSING

1 small head lettuce or a combination of your favorite greens
½ cup mayonnaise
¼ cup catsup or chili sauce
   Dash lemon juice
   Dash Worcestershire Sauce
¼ cup pickle relish

Break lettuce into bite-size pieces. Combine remaining ingredients for dressing and spoon over salad greens and serve. Yield: 1 cup.

PROSPECTOR POTATOES

4 medium-size baking potatoes
   Bacon drippings
   Coarse salt to taste
   Catsup (optional)

Scrub potatoes with a brush; the skins are intended to be eaten. Cut in half lengthwise. With a sharp knife, cut down through the cut surface almost but not quite through the bottom skin, making a diamond or check pattern. With your hands, rub potatoes all over with bacon drippings. Place on cookie sheet, and sprinkle with coarse salt. Bake at 400° about 25 minutes or until potatoes are tender and brown. They are a little like French fries, so serve with catsup, if desired. Yield: 4 servings.

GREEN LIMA CASSEROLE

1 small onion, chopped
½ stick butter, divided
1 (16-ounce) can green lima beans
¼ cup tomatoes, broken up
2 slices white bread, coarsely
    crumbled

Sauté onion in half the butter until transparent. Partially drain beans, and place in 1-quart casserole. Add onion and tomatoes. Place remaining butter in skillet, and fry bread crumbs. Top casserole with crumbs,

and bake at 350° for 30 minutes. Yield: 4 servings.

WINE-POACHED PEARS

1 (16-ounce) can pear halves
½ cup liquid drained from pears
½ cup dry red wine
¼ cup sugar

Drain pears, reserving the ½ cup liquid called for in recipe, and save remainder for other uses, such as gelatin desserts. Place juice, wine, and sugar in small saucepan, and boil 5 minutes. Place pears in pint jar, and pour wine sauce over them. Cover tightly and refrigerate overnight, turning jar over occasionally to color and flavor pears uniformly. Serve pears, with their liquid, in stemmed dessert dishes. Yield: 4 servings.

BEST YET CHICKEN DINNER FOR 6

Best Yet Chicken Croquettes with Mushroom Sauce
Grapefruit Aspic
Broccoli with Lemon Butter
Self-Crusting Oatmeal Pie

BEST YET CHICKEN CROQUETTES WITH MUSHROOM SAUCE

    1 (3- to 3½-pound) frying chicken
1½ quarts water
    1 bay leaf
    1 slice lemon
    2 teaspoons salt
    2 tablespoons butter
    2 tablespoons all-purpose flour
    1 cup half-and-half
      Salt and pepper to taste
    1 cup finely chopped mushrooms
    1 (10½-ounce) can condensed cream of
        mushroom soup, divided
    2 eggs
    2 cups fine bread crumbs
      Oil for frying
      Mushroom Sauce

The day before you wish to serve the croquettes, simmer the chicken until tender in water with bay leaf, lemon, and salt. Remove meat from bones, and chop rather finely. Reserve chicken stock.

In a saucepan, melt butter, and blend in the flour. Gradually add cream, salt and pepper. Cook until thickened, stirring constantly. Add chopped chicken, mushrooms, and half the can of soup. Chill overnight in a covered container.

To finish croquettes: Beat eggs in a small bowl. Mound crumbs on waxed paper. With a knife, cut across chilled chicken mixture to divide it into 12 portions. Pick up each portion with a spoon, and shape by hand into logs about 3 inches long by 1½ inches wide. Coat with crumbs, dip into egg, then roll in crumbs again. Chill well before frying. Heat oil, enough to cover, to 375°. Fry croquettes, turning once, until nicely browned. Serve with Mushroom Sauce. Yield: 12 croquettes.

Mushroom Sauce:

    2 tablespoons butter
    1 tablespoon all-purpose flour
    1 cup reserved chicken broth
    ½ (10½-ounce) can condensed cream of
        mushroom soup

Combine butter and flour in small, heavy saucepan. Gradually add chicken broth, stirring constantly. Cook over medium heat until thickened. Add reserved ½ can soup, and stir well to blend. Yield: about 1½ cups.

GRAPEFRUIT ASPIC

    1 (3-ounce) package lemon-flavored
        gelatin
    ½ cup boiling water
    1 cup grapefruit juice
      Dash salt
    1 teaspoon sugar
    ½ teaspoon onion juice
    ½ cup slivered almonds
1½ cups fresh grapefruit sections, cut up

Dissolve gelatin in boiling water. Add grapefruit juice, salt, sugar, and onion juice. Chill until syrupy. Stir in almonds and grapefruit. Pour into eight ½-cup molds or one 4-cup mold. Yield: 8 servings.

BROCCOLI WITH LEMON BUTTER

2 (10½-ounce) packages frozen broccoli spears
½ stick butter
Grated rind and strained juice from ½ lemon
½ teaspoon sugar

Cook broccoli to crisp-tender stage according to package directions. Place drained broccoli in warmed serving bowl. In the same saucepan, melt butter, and add lemon rind, juice and sugar. Drizzle over hot broccoli. Yield: 6 servings.

SELF-CRUSTING OATMEAL PIE

3 egg whites
½ teaspoon cream of tartar
½ teaspoon cornstarch
1 teaspoon vanilla extract
1 cup sugar
6 saltine crackers, crushed
1 cup quick-cooking oats
1 cup whipping cream
1 tablespoon powdered sugar
½ teaspoon vanilla extract
1 pint fresh strawberries, sliced and sweetened

Combine egg whites with cream of tartar, cornstarch, and vanilla in large bowl of mixer, and beat until very soft peaks form. Add sugar slowly, beating constantly. With rubber spatula, fold in crackers and oatmeal. Grease a 9-inch piepan heavily and pour pie mixture into it. Bake at 375° for 25 minutes. Cool. To serve, top with whipped cream which has been flavored with powdered sugar and ½ teaspoon vanilla. Spoon crushed, sweetened berries over each serving. Yield: 6 to 8 servings.

SUMMERTIME LUNCHEON FOR 6 OR 8

Strawberry Frappé
Pumpernickel Strata with Horseradish-Ham, Crabmeat,
and Dilled Egg Fillings
Vegetable Garnishes
Demitasse Mousse

STRAWBERRY FRAPPÉ

1 (10½-ounce) package frozen
   strawberries
1 cup vodka
1½ cups finely crushed ice

Combine berries (not defrosted), vodka, and ice in electric blender. Blend until uniformly mixed, with no ice chunks showing. Serve immediately in stemmed wine or champagne glasses. Yield: 6 to 8 servings.

PUMPERNICKEL STRATA

1 round loaf pumpernickel bread
1 stick softened butter
  Horseradish-Ham Filling
  Crabmeat Filling
  Dilled Egg Filling

Horseradish-Ham Filling:

2 (4½-ounce) cans deviled ham
1 rib celery, minced
1 tablespoon horseradish
2 tablespoons mayonnaise

Combine ingredients; reserve.

Crabmeat Filling:

1 (7½-ounce) can king crabmeat
2 ounces blue cheese, crumbled
2 tablespoons butter, softened
1 green onion, chopped
1 whole pimiento, chopped

Drain, and chop crabmeat. Blend blue cheese with butter, and add to crabmeat, along with the onion and pimiento. Mix well and reserve.

Note: You may substitute a like amount of tuna or chicken for crab.

Dilled Egg Filling:

4 hard-cooked eggs
2 tablespoons mayonnaise
2 teaspoons prepared mustard
1 teaspoon dried dillweed
1 teaspoon salt
¼ teaspoon pepper

Shell and chop eggs. Blend in remaining ingredients; reserve.

To assemble sandwiches cut bread crosswise into 5 slices. Butter each slice as you build sandwich. On bottom slice, spread half the Horseradish-Ham Filling. Cover with next slice of bread, and spread with all the Crabmeat Filling. The third slice of bread goes on next; cover with all the Dilled Egg Filling. Then add the fourth slice; spread with remaining half of the Horseradish-Ham. Cover with the top slice. To serve, cut into wedges with sharp knife. Yield: 6 to 8 servings.

VEGETABLE GARNISHES FOR SANDWICH SERVINGS

Green onions
Carrot curls
Thin-sliced zucchini
Celery hearts
Olives
Pickles

DEMITASSE MOUSSE

¾ cup milk
½ teaspoon instant coffee powder
1 (6-ounce) package chocolate pieces
2 eggs
¼ cup brandy
½ cup whipping cream, whipped
1 teaspoon cocoa

Scald milk with instant coffee. Place chocolate pieces in blender jar. Add scalded milk, and blend until smooth. Without turning off motor, add eggs and brandy, and blend 2 minutes. Pour into 6 or 8 demitasse cups. Refrigerate several hours or overnight, covered with buttered waxed paper. At serving time, top with whipped cream, and sift cocoa over top for garnish. Yield: 6 to 8 servings.

Note: You may substitute rum, crème de cacao, or crème de menthe for brandy.

STANDING RIB DINNER FOR 8

Standing Rib Roast
Individual Yorkshire Puddings
Lettuce Wedges with Blue Cheese Dressing
Green Beans in Cream
Lemon Jelly Pie

STANDING RIB ROAST

1 (4- or 5-rib) roast
Salt and pepper to taste

Ask the butcher to remove the backbone (for easier carving) and tie the roast. Have him cut the backbone into several pieces to be used as a rack under the roast.

Season meat. Put reserved backbones in bottom of an open roasting pan, and place roast on top of them. Insert meat thermometer so bulb is centered in the thickest part, making sure bulb does not rest in fat or on bone. Do not add water. Do not cover. Bake at 325° to desired degree of doneness. Meat thermometer will register 140° for rare, 160° for medium, and 170° for well done.

Lacking a meat thermometer, estimate 23 to 25 minutes per pound for rare, 27 to 30 minutes for medium, and 32 to 35 minutes for well done.

For easier carving, finished roast should "rest" on a warmed platter for about 15 minutes. Since roasts continue to cook after they are taken from the oven, remove meat when thermometer registers 5° below the desired final number. Place roast on warmed platter while puddings bake. Yield: 8 servings.

INDIVIDUAL YORKSHIRE PUDDINGS

4 eggs
2¼ cups milk
½ teaspoon salt
½ cup all-purpose flour
4 tablespoons beef drippings
2 tablespoons water

Prepare batter about 15 minutes before roast is done. Beat eggs. Add milk, salt, and flour; beat well. Cover, and let stand until it is time to take the roast out of the oven. Reset oven heat to 450°, placing muffin pans in oven to preheat.

Pour pan juices into tall, narrow jar, and remove as much fat as possible with bulb baster or spoon, reserving fat. Spoon a teaspoon of drippings from roast into each hot muffin cup. Fold water into muffin batter (batter will be thin), and spoon into muffin pans filling each cup no more than halfway. Bake at 450° for 15 to 20 minutes or until well puffed and golden brown. Serve with roast. Heat remaining defatted pan juices, and serve over puddings. Yield: 12 individual puddings.

Note: Although Yorkshire pudding is traditionally served with standing rib roast, it is delicious with most other beef cuts and provides a change from potatoes or rice.

LETTUCE WEDGES WITH BLUE CHEESE DRESSING

1 large head iceberg lettuce
⅔ cup salad oil
⅓ cup wine vinegar
½ cup blue cheese, crumbled
    Salt and pepper to taste
1 small clove garlic, pressed

Wash, core, and wrap lettuce in cloth towel. Refrigerate until serving time. Combine remaining ingredients in quart jar, put on lid, and shake to blend. (You may use electric blender, if smooth dressing is desired.) Cut lettuce into 8 wedges, and top each serving with dressing. Yield: 1½ cups.

GREEN BEANS IN CREAM

2 (29-ounce) cans French-style green
    beans
1 teaspoon salt
1 cup whipping cream, warmed
½ cup salted cashews, coarsely chopped

Cook beans for 20 minutes in their own liquid with salt added. Drain. Turn into warmed serving bowl, and pour cream over them. Top with cashews. Yield: 8 servings.

Note: Whipping cream is a good dressing for any fresh, frozen, or canned vegetable when a simple dish is wanted.

LEMON JELLY PIE

2 cups sugar
2 tablespoons cornmeal
1 tablespoon all-purpose flour
    Dash salt
4 eggs
¼ cup melted butter
¼ cup milk
¼ cup lemon juice
1½ tablespoons grated rind of lemon
1 (9-inch) unbaked pie shell

Combine sugar, cornmeal, flour, and salt in mixing bowl. Turn electric mixer on medium speed. Add eggs one at a time, beating after each addition. Stir in butter, milk, juice, and rind. Pour into pie shell. Bake at 425° for 10 minutes, then reduce heat to 325°, and bake an additional 30 minutes or until filling is set. Test for doneness; shake pan gently; center should not look runny. Or insert a wooden pick in center; pick should come out clean. Yield: One (9-inch) pie.

CORNISH HEN DINNER FOR 8

Cornish Hens with Herbed Butter
Pistachio Rice
Cranberry Waldorf Mold
Skillet Zucchini
Cream Filled Nut Roll

CORNISH HENS WITH HERBED BUTTER

**8 Cornish hens (12 to 16 ounces
  each)
Salt to taste
1 lemon
1 stick (½ cup) butter, softened
1½ teaspoons thyme**

Wash and dry birds well, then rub salt inside cavities and over the outside. Cut lemon into 8 wedges, and insert one into each bird. Mix butter with thyme, and put a lump into each cavity and the remainder over the breasts of the hens. Fold wingtips underneath, and tie the legs together with string. Place in open roasting pan, and bake at 325° for 45 minutes to an hour, depending on size. They should be very tender. Baste with pan juices 2 or 3 times during cooking period. Serve with Pistachio Rice. Yield: 8 servings.

PISTACHIO RICE

**8 cups hot cooked rice
¾ cup shelled pistachio nuts
⅓ cup butter or pan drippings from
  roasted birds**

Prepare rice according to package directions. Toss with nuts and butter. Yield: 8 servings.

CRANBERRY WALDORF MOLD

**2 envelopes (2 tablespoons) unflavored
  gelatin
½ cup cold water
½ cup sugar
2¼ cups cranberry juice cocktail beverage
¼ cup lemon juice
2¼ cups chopped, unpeeled apple
¼ cup thinly sliced celery**

Sprinkle gelatin over water in saucepan. Stir over low heat until gelatin dissolves. Remove from heat, add sugar, and stir to dissolve. Add cranberry juice beverage and lemon juice. Chill until syrupy. Add apples and celery. Pour into 6-cup mold or 8 small individual molds, and refrigerate to congeal. Yield: 8 servings.

SKILLET ZUCCHINI

**About 4 small zucchini
¼ cup butter or oil
1 teaspoon salt
Dash pepper
¾ (8-ounce) can tomatoes or 1½ cups
  fresh tomatoes**

Wash, scrub with a brush, and thinly slice zucchini. Stir-fry in butter or oil for 5 minutes until lightly browned. Add salt, pepper, and tomatoes; cover. Simmer until zucchini is crisp-tender. Yield: 8 servings.

CREAM FILLED NUT ROLL

5 eggs, separated
1 cup sugar, divided
1 teaspoon vanilla
1 cup all-purpose flour
½ teaspoon baking powder
¼ teaspoon salt
1¼ cups finely grated or ground nutmeats
¼ cup powdered sugar
   Whipped-Cream Filling
   Whole nutmeats (optional)

In large electric mixer bowl, beat egg whites until soft peaks form. Slowly add half the sugar, beating until peaks are fairly firm. Without washing the beaters, beat egg yolks in smaller mixer bowl with remaining ½ cup sugar and vanilla until creamy with sugar dissolved. Sift or stir flour with baking powder and salt; then combine with nuts.

Pour half the egg-yolk mixture over egg whites and fold in. Add half the dry mixture, and fold in. Repeat with remaining egg yolk and dry mixture.

Thoroughly grease jelly roll pan (15½ x 10 inches), and line with waxed paper. Turn paper over to grease both sides. Turn cake into pan and bake at 375° for 20 minutes.

On a clean tea towel, spread the powdered sugar and turn cake out on it. Remove waxed paper, and cut away dry edges of cake. Starting with one long side, roll cake, towel and all, and cool. Gently unroll cake; remove towel, fill with Whipped Cream Filling, and reroll. Chill. To serve, slice and garnish each serving with a whole nutmeat, if desired. Yield: 8 to 10 servings.

Note: Use your favorite nuts—filberts, almonds, English or black walnuts, or pecans.

Whipped-Cream Filling:

2 cups whipping cream
1 teaspoon vanilla extract
2 tablespoons powdered sugar

Whip cream until it holds firm peaks. Fold in flavoring and sugar.

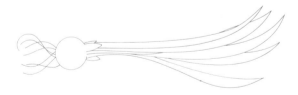

PANTRY SHELF LUNCHEON OR SUPPER FOR 4

Tuna Newburg
Asparagus Tips Vinaigrette
Crisp Oatmeal Biscuits
Dried Fruit Compote

TUNA NEWBURG

1 (10½-ounce) can condensed cream of
    celery soup
⅓ cup milk
  Dash white pepper
  Juice of ½ lemon
  Dash hot pepper sauce
1 (2-ounce) jar pimiento pieces, drained
2 hard-cooked eggs, sliced
1 (7-ounce) can water-packed white
    tuna, drained
1 (8-ounce) can whole kernel corn,
    drained
  Crisp Oatmeal Biscuits
  Hard-cooked sliced egg, black olives,
    parsley (optional)

In heavy saucepan, combine soup, milk, pepper, lemon juice, pepper sauce, pimiento, and eggs. Heat, stirring gently, until blended and hot. Add tuna, broken up, and corn. Bring to serving temperature. Serve over hot Crisp Oatmeal Biscuits. Garnish with sliced eggs, black olives, and parsley. Yield: 4 servings.

ASPARAGUS TIPS VINAIGRETTE

1 (16-ounce) can asparagus tips, drained
    and chilled
4 lettuce leaves
  Vinaigrette Dressing

Arrange cold asparagus tips in lettuce cups and spoon Vinaigrette Dressing over each serving. Yield: 4 servings.

Vinaigrette Dressing:

¾ cup salad oil
½ cup tarragon vinegar
¾ teaspoon salt
1 tablespoon minced chives
½ teaspoon dried basil
2 teaspoons capers, rinsed and chopped
1 hard cooked egg, chopped (optional)

Combine all ingredients in a pint jar, and shake until well mixed. Yield: about 1⅓ cups.

CRISP OATMEAL BISCUITS

1½ cups all-purpose flour
½ cup uncooked regular oats
1 tablespoon baking powder
1 teaspoon salt
⅓ cup margarine
⅔ cup milk

Combine dry ingredients in mixing bowl, and stir well to blend. Add margarine, and cut in with pastry blender until particles are like very coarse cornmeal. Add milk, mix, and turn out on floured dough board or canvas. Knead a few turns to smooth dough. Roll to ½-inch thickness, and cut with floured biscuit cutter. (For this purpose a doughnut cutter makes an attractive biscuit.) Transfer to lightly greased baking sheet, and bake at 450° about 10 minutes or until lightly browned. Yield: about 1 dozen biscuits, depending on size of cutter.

Note: These biscuits may be frozen after they are cut. Thaw; then bake until brown and crisp.

DRIED FRUIT COMPOTE

  1 pound mixed dried fruit
½ cup dry white wine
½ cup water
½ cup sugar
¼ lemon
  3 whole cloves

Soak fruit in mixture of wine and water for several hours or overnight. Simmer in the same liquid with sugar, lemon chunk, and cloves added just until tender, about 20 minutes. If necessary, add a little more wine during cooking so there will be enough sauce to enhance each serving. Keeps several days in refrigerator. Remove lemon before serving. Good hot or cold. Yield: 4 to 6 servings.

BLINTZ BREAKFAST OR BRUNCH FOR 4 OR 5

Hot Tomato Bouillon
Cheese Blintzes
Crisp Bacon Curls

HOT TOMATO BOUILLON

1 (10-ounce) can condensed beef
    bouillon
2 cups tomato juice
1 teaspoon Worcestershire sauce
8 paper-thin slices lemon (optional)

Combine bouillon, juice, and Worcestershire sauce in saucepan, and bring to boiling point. Serve in mugs, garnish with lemon slice on top, if desired. Yield: 4 or 5 servings.

Note: Bloody Marys may be used instead of the bouillon as a prelude to this breakfast.

CHEESE BLINTZES

4 eggs
1 cup milk
1 cup all-purpose flour
½ teaspoon salt
    Oil for making crêpes
    Cheese Filling
2 cups cherry preserves
1 cup commercial sour cream

To make crêpes combine first four ingredients in blender. Blend at high speed for a few seconds, just until mixed. Let stand in refrigerator at least 2 hours before baking to let air bubbles settle and assure smoothness in the baked crêpes.

Heat crêpe pan or six-inch iron skillet, and brush with oil. When a droplet of water sizzles when dropped in pan, it is ready for business. Add just enough batter to cover bottom of pan thinly; a ladle that holds 2 to 3 tablespoons is about right. Swirl pan so batter covers bottom evenly. Brown lightly on one side only. Stack crêpes on sheet of waxed paper, brown side up. (Crêpes may be stored in refrigerator, wrapped in plastic wrap, for a few days or, well sealed, in the freezer for a month.) To fill crêpes, place a tablespoonful of Cheese Filling on top crêpe of stack. Fold bottom third of crêpe away from you, then fold the sides over center and bring remaining side over to cover side folds. Place, fold downward, on tray lined with waxed paper. At this stage, you may hold them overnight in refrigerator, well covered, with plastic wrap.

To cook, fry in butter, lightly browning both sides. Serve with cherry preserves and sour cream. Yield: 24 six-inch crêpes.

Cheese Filling:

1 (16-ounce) package farmer cheese or
    cottage cheese, well drained
¼ cup sugar
3 tablespoons commercial sour cream
½ teaspoon ground cinnamon
½ teaspoon salt
3 egg yolks
    Dash ground nutmeg

Combine ingredients in blender jar and blend until smooth.

CRISP BACON CURLS

Bring bacon to room temperature. Pull slices apart, and drop them, in folds as they fall, into a 9- or 10-inch skillet. Make no effort to lay them straight. Turn up heat under skillet. When bacon starts to sizzle, turn heat down to medium, and start moving the bacon around with an egg turner. Do not pour off grease. Continue to stir and fry until bacon is nearly done. Turn heat very low. As slices are done, lift them out with a fork, laying them straight on absorbent paper. As you take them out, just as soon as they can be handled and before they are crisp, roll each slice around a wooden spoon handle. Transfer to warmed serving plate. With the heat very low under the skillet, the bacon stays pliable until you are ready to lift out each piece and roll it. It is essential to roll the bacon while it is still quite hot. Yield: 4 or 5 servings.

TURKEY DINNER FOR 8

Pimiento Cream Soup
Turkey Breast with Mushroom Dressing
Broccoli Soufflé
Almond Chocolate Charlotte

PIMIENTO CREAM SOUP

¼ cup butter
¼ cup all-purpose flour
2 cups milk
2 cups half-and-half
4 cups chicken stock
2 (4-ounce) cans pimiento
1 teaspoon grated onion
   Salt and pepper to taste
   Dash cayenne pepper

In a 3-quart heavy saucepan, melt butter, and blend in the flour to make a roux. Slowly add milk, stirring briskly so no lumps will form, and cook until thickened. Gradually add half-and-half and stock. Sieve pimientos or whirl in blender to puree. Add to soup along with onion, salt, pepper, and cayenne. Cook over lowest heat, not boiling, 10 minutes. Yield: 8 to 10 servings.

TURKEY BREAST WITH MUSHROOM DRESSING

1 (about 5-pound) frozen turkey breast
½ lemon
1 teaspoon rosemary, crushed
1 tablespoon salt
   Mushroom Dressing
   Gravy

Thaw turkey according to package direc-

tions. Bring it almost to room temperature; thoroughly wash and dry. Rub meat all over with cut lemon, then rub in the rosemary and salt. Place turkey in brown paper bag which is large enough to contain it and allow for a double 1-inch fold at the end. Fold over end, and secure with paper clips. Place in open shallow roasting pan. Insert meat thermometer through paper into meat. Bake in 350° oven until thermometer registers 185°. Time will vary according to size, but baking should commence 3½ to 4 hours before serving time. Yield: 8 to 10 servings.

Mushroom Dressing:

1½ pounds fresh mushrooms (about 6
      cups sliced)
1 cup commercially prepared seasoned
      stuffing mix
¾ cup half-and-half
½ cup chicken stock
3 tablespoons butter, melted
3 tablespoons dry sherry

Wash mushrooms quickly, and dry well. Slice them thin. Butter a shallow 2½-quart casserole, and add half the mushrooms. Sprinkle with half the crumbs: add remaining mushrooms, and top with remaining crumbs. Mix cream, stock, butter, and sherry, and pour over top. Cover with lid or foil, and bake at 350° for 40 minutes. Remove cover, and bake 15 minutes longer or until lightly browned. Yield: 8 servings.

Gravy:

    Pan drippings plus chicken stock to
      measure 3 cups
¼ cup cornstarch
    Salt and pepper to taste
    Few drops yellow food coloring
      (optional)

Put liquid in saucepan, reserving ½ cup. Combine the ½ cup stock with cornstarch, and add to pan. Cook, stirring, until thickened. Season and add yellow coloring. Yield: 3 cups.

BROCCOLI SOUFFLÉ

1 (10-ounce) package frozen chopped
    broccoli
1 (10½-ounce) can condensed cream of
    mushroom soup
½ cup shredded sharp cheddar cheese
¼ cup milk
¼ cup mayonnaise
3 eggs, separated
¼ cup bread crumbs
2 tablespoons melted butter or
    margarine

Cook broccoli according to package directions, but omit salt. Drain thoroughly; reserve. In top of double boiler, combine soup, cheese, milk, mayonnaise and beaten egg yolks. Cook over simmering water, stirring, for 8 to 10 minutes or until cheese is melted and mixture thickens. Cool to lukewarm, and fold in broccoli. Whip egg whites stiff, and fold in. Pour into buttered, 8-cup, straight-sided baking dish. Stir crumbs together with melted butter, and sprinkle over soufflé. Place immediately in 350° oven, and bake about 45 minutes or until set and browned. Serve immediately. Yield: 8 servings.

ALMOND CHOCOLATE CHARLOTTE

1 dozen ladyfingers, split
½ cup curaçao or orange juice
1 cup chocolate pieces
2 tablespoons (liquid) coffee
1 cup softened butter or margarine
1 cup powdered sugar
1 cup finely grated almonds
1 cup whipping cream whipped to soft
    peaks
    Shaved bitter chocolate curls
    (optional)

Select a 2-quart charlotte mold or a straight-sided pan or even a clean clay flower pot. Cut 2 strips of waxed paper or plastic wrap 2 feet long, then fold them lengthwise until they are only 2 inches wide. Lay them, crossing each other, into the mold, fitting across bottom and up to extend over the side. This is to facilitate removing the charlotte at serving time.

Working quickly, dip (do not soak) ladyfinger halves into orange liquid, and line, first, bottom of mold; then line the sides. Melt chocolate pieces with coffee, and keep warm. In electric mixer bowl, combine butter and sugar, beating until creamy. Add any orange liquid left from dipping ladyfingers, the chocolate mixture, and almonds. Fold in whipped cream. Break up remaining ladyfingers, and use them to separate layers of the charlotte mixture, making 3 or 4 layers of each. Chill all day or overnight.

To unmold, run a knife around inside edge. Invert a chilled dessert dish over top of mold, making sure the waxed paper ends are outside mold. Turn the whole assembly over, pulling on the paper, if necessary, to loosen bottom. Discard paper. Garnish with shaved chocolate, if desired. Yield: 8 servings.

PORK SHOULDER DINNER FOR 8

Pork Shoulder in Bourbon Sauce
Pure Green Salad
Creamed New Potatoes with Peas
Jelled Coffee with Pour Custard

PORK SHOULDER IN BOURBON SAUCE

  Fresh shoulder of pork (about 5
    pounds)
⅓ cup Dijon mustard
⅔ cup firmly packed light brown sugar
  3 tablespoons oil
½ cup bourbon, divided
  1 tablespoon salt
½ teaspoon pepper
¼ teaspoon each sage and marjoram
  1 tablespoon freeze-dried parsley
  1 (10-ounce) can condensed beef
    bouillon

Trim skin and excess fat from roast. Combine mustard and sugar, and rub meat all over with the mixture. Heat oil in Dutch oven, and brown meat on all sides over medium heat, taking care not to scorch, as the sugar tends to burn with too high heat. You want only to caramelize it to a nice brown color.

Pour half the bourbon over meat, and flame, using a long match and caution. When flame has died down, add salt, pepper, sage, marjoram, and parsley, turning meat to season on all sides. Add remaining bourbon and beef bouillon; cover and bake at 375° for one hour. Remove from oven; turn meat over.

Reduce heat to 325°, and return meat, covered, to oven, and bake until tender, about 2 hours. (Meat thermometer will register 170° when it is done.) Remove to warmed platter.

There should be about 1½ cups pan juices. If you have less, add water or stock to make that amount; then boil, scraping to deglaze the pan. Remove excess fat. Serve sauce in separate gravy boat. Yield: 8 servings.

Note: Leftover roast is delicious served cold with breakfast eggs.

PURE GREEN SALAD

  3 varieties of salad greens to make 2
    quarts or more
  Dressing

Select favorites from among the greens in season. Wash well, and break into bite-size pieces. Make sure the quantity is enough for the number to be served. To prepare greens in advance, shake off excess water, and wrap in a clean towel. Just before serving, toss greens with enough Dressing to coat each bit.

Dressing:

  1 teaspoon sugar
  Dash pepper
½ cup salad oil
  3 tablespoons catsup
  1 teaspoon salt
  2 teaspoons grated onion
  3 tablespoons vinegar

Combine ingredients in a pint jar, and shake well, or use electric blender to mix. Yield: about 1¼ cups dressing.

CREAMED NEW POTATOES WITH PEAS

16 or more small new potatoes
  Water
2 teaspoons salt
⅓ cup milk
1 (10½-ounce) can condensed cream of
  chicken soup
2 (16-ounce) cans tiny peas, drained

Cut a half-inch band of skin from each potato with a potato parer. Place in saucepan with just enough water to cover, and add salt. Cook until tender.

Drain potatoes, and place in warm serving bowl. In same saucepan, mix milk with soup mixture, and add peas. Slowly heat to boiling, and pour over potatoes. Yield: 8 servings.

JELLED COFFEE WITH POUR CUSTARD

2 envelopes (2 tablespoons) unflavored
  gelatin
½ cup cold water
3 cups strong, hot coffee
⅔ cup sugar
1 teaspoon vanilla extract
¼ cup coffee-flavored liqueur
¼ cup chopped walnuts (optional)
  Pour Custard

Soften gelatin in cold water. Add hot coffee, stirring to dissolve gelatin. Add sugar, vanilla, and liqueur. Chill until syrupy. Fold in walnuts, if desired. Pour into 8 individual

half-cup molds, and refrigerate to congeal. To serve, unmold each serving into a small dessert bowl. Spoon Pour Custard over each serving. Yield: 8 servings.

Note: If walnuts are not used, pour gelatin mixture into molds without chilling to syrupy consistency.

Pour Custard:

3 eggs, slightly beaten
¼ cup sugar
  Dash salt
2½ cups milk
1 teaspoon vanilla extract

Blend eggs, sugar, and salt in top of double boiler. Gradually stir in milk. In bottom of double boiler, place water at a level which will not touch pan. Bring to near-boil, not bubbling. Place custard over hot water and cook, stirring constantly, for about 20 minutes or until custard will coat a metal spoon. Cool, and stir in vanilla. Yield: 2¾ cups.

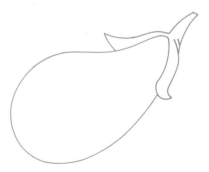

UPSIDE-DOWN TACOS BUFFET FOR 16

Upside-Down Tacos
Margaritas
Avocado Salad
Dessert

UPSIDE-DOWN TACOS

6 pounds ground beef
4 large onions, chopped
6 (15-ounce) cans chili beans
6 (10-ounce) cans enchilada hot sauce
    Salt to taste
5 heads iceberg lettuce, coarsely
    chopped
1 (8-ounce) bottle commercial Italian
    salad dressing
6 or 7 bunches green onions, chopped
10 to 12 fresh tomatoes, chopped
2 pounds shredded sharp cheddar
    cheese
3 (7-ounce) packages corn chips,
    coarsely crumbled

Select a covered roasting pan with a tight fitting cover. Place meat in roaster, and cook, stirring, over medium heat until it loses its redness. Add onions, and cook until onions become transparent. Add beans and enchilada sauce, rinsing each can with a little water, and adding the water to the pan. Bring to boil, and add salt, starting with 2 teaspoons; then taste, and add a bit more, if necessary. Cover roasting pan, and place in 225° oven. Cook at least 8 hours (overnight is better).

To assemble your Mexican buffet, place lettuce in a large salad bowl, and toss with dressing to coat each bite. Place onions, tomatoes, cheese, and corn chips in separate bowls. Guests serve themselves, starting with a plateful of lettuce, then spoonfuls of onions, tomatoes, cheese, a whopping ladle of hot chili, and a topping of corn chips. Yield: 16 servings.

Note: If possible, it is well to cook the chili a day or 2 ahead, then cool, and refrigerate. When chilled, the fat may be lifted off the top, then the chili reheated to serve.

MARGARITA

    Citrus fruit rind
    Salt
1 jigger white tequilla
½ ounce Triple Sec
1 ounce lime or lemon juice

Moisten cocktail glass rim with fruit rind; spin rim in salt. Shake ingredients with ½ cup cracked ice. Strain into glass. Drink is sipped over the salted edge. Yield: 1 serving.

AVOCADO SALAD

½ small avocado per person
    Lemon or lime juice
1 tablespoon commercial sour cream
    Wedge of lemon or lime

Cut avocados in half as close to serving time as possible. Do not peel; remove seed. Brush cut side with lemon juice. Place spoonful of sour cream in center hole and garnish with a generous wedge of lemon or lime. Eat with teaspoon, not fork. Yield: 1 serving.

DESSERT

Fill a large bowl half full with ice and cover ice with plastic wrap. Quickly unwrap 16 commercial chocolate-covered ice cream sticks, and arrange over ice. Serve immediately.

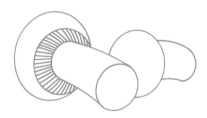

AL FRESCO LUNCHEON FOR 12

Curried Seafood Crêpes with Cheese Sauce
Green Goddess Salad
Black Walnut Carrot Cake

CURRIED SEAFOOD CREPES

1 cup cold milk
1 cup cold water
4 eggs
½ teaspoon salt
2 cups all-purpose flour
 Vegetable oil
 Curried Seafood Filling
1½ cups shredded pasteurized process
 American cheese
 Cheese Sauce

To make crêpes combine first 5 ingredients in the order given, in blender, and blend on high speed for 1 minute. Allow batter to rest in refrigerator for at least 2 hours before baking.

To cook, brush crêpe pan or 6-inch skillet with oil; heat pan so that a drop of water will sizzle when dropped into it. Add batter (about 3 tablespoons) barely to cover bottom of pan, swirling pan to cover completely. Cook until lightly brown; flip them over to cook reverse side slightly. Crêpes can be stacked on waxed paper, cooled, wrapped well, and refrigerated until ready to fill. Crêpes will keep several days in refrigerator, a month frozen.

Using about ¼ cup Filling per crêpe, fill crêpes and roll up, placing them in a buttered 3-quart rectangular glass baking dish. Cover with cheese. Bake at 350° for 45 minutes. Serve with Cheese Sauce. Yield: about 24 filled crêpes.

Curried Seafood Filling:

1 stick (½ cup) butter or margarine
1 cup chopped fresh mushrooms
1 tablespoon all-purpose flour
1 cup hot milk
1 cup diced lobster
1 cup crabmeat
1 cup diced boiled shrimp
 Curry powder to taste
 Salt and pepper to taste
1 tablespoon dry sherry

Melt butter in top of double boiler; add mushrooms. Cook stirring, five minutes over boiling water. Stir in flour, and add the milk gradually. Cook, stirring, 10 minutes. Add seafood, curry powder, salt, pepper, and sherry.

Cheese Sauce:

2 (10-ounce) cans condensed cheddar
 cheese soup
1 cup milk
 Dash curry powder

Blend ingredients and heat. Pass Sauce in gravy boat. Yield: 3⅓ cups.

GREEN GODDESS SALAD

3 small heads iceberg lettuce
 Anchovy Dressing

Wash and core lettuce. Break up into bite-size pieces, and refrigerate in plastic bag with several paper towels to absorb moisture. Toss with Dressing just before serving. Yield: 12 servings.

Anchovy Dressing:

    2 tablespoons anchovy paste
    1 cup mayonnaise
    2 tablespoons tarragon vinegar
    ¼ cup chopped chives
    ¼ cup chopped parsley
    2 green onions, chopped
    ½ teaspoon dried tarragon
    1 clove garlic

Blend anchovy paste, mayonnaise, vinegar, chives, parsley, onions, and tarragon. Cut garlic in half, and impale it on a wooden pick; place in dressing, and refrigerate. Let stand at least an hour to develop flavor. Remove garlic before serving. Yield: 2 cups.

BLACK WALNUT CARROT CAKE

1½ cups salad oil
    2 cups sugar
    4 eggs
    2 cups self-rising flour, divided
    1 teaspoon vanilla extract
    1 teaspoon ground cinnamon
    1 cup black walnuts, chopped
    4 medium-size carrots, finely grated
    Topping

Combine oil, sugar, and eggs in large bowl of mixer, and beat at medium speed for 5 minutes. Beat in 1½ cups of the flour and vanilla. Mix remaining ½ cup flour with cinnamon and nuts; add to first mixture, beating now with a wooden spoon. Blend carrots thoroughly into batter. Pour into greased 9- x 13-inch sheet cakepan, and bake at 325° for 50 to 60 minutes or until wooden pick inserted in center comes out clean. While cake is baking, prepare Topping. Pour Topping over hot cake. Yield: 12 servings.

Topping:

    1 cup sugar
    ½ cup buttermilk
    ½ teaspoon soda
    1 tablespoon white corn syrup
    1 teaspoon vanilla extract

Combine all ingredients except vanilla in saucepan; bring to a rolling boil, and boil 5 minutes. Add vanilla.

DERBY DAY BRUNCH FOR 8

Belgravia Court Appetizer
Kentucky Mint Julep
Frankfort Bibb Lettuce Salad with Celery-Seed French Dressing
Kentucky Derby Fried Country Ham with
Red-Eye Gravy or Cream Gravy
Shoepeg Pudding
Fresh-Cooked Asparagus with Unhollandaise Sauce
Fresh Strawberries with Brandy-Caramel Sauce

BELGRAVIA COURT APPETIZER

8 hard-cooked eggs, put through a ricer
2 tablespoons chopped chives
3 tablespoons minced celery
3 to 4 tablespoons mayonnaise
1 cup commercial sour cream
1 (2-ounce) jar black caviar
1 (2-ounce) jar red caviar
 Party rye bread
 Bland crackers

Mix eggs with chives and celery. Add just enough mayonnaise to moisten. Place in a shallow glass serving dish. Cover evenly with sour cream. Spoon black and red caviar over sour cream, making an attractive pattern. Serve with party rye bread or bland crackers. Yield: 8 or more servings.

KENTUCKY MINT JULEP

4 sprigs fresh mint
1 teaspoon sugar
1 teaspoon water
 Finely crushed ice
2 jiggers bourbon
 Straws

Place one sprig mint in bottom of julep cup. Add sugar and water, and stir with handle of wooden spoon until mint is well crushed and sugar completely dissolved. Add crushed ice to fill cup ¾ full. Add bourbon. Stir gently, then fill cup level with top with more crushed ice. Place in refrigerator to frost outside of cups. Place remaining mint with stems down in the ice. Insert 2 drinking straws, and trim them so that the "nose is close to the mint." Yield: 1 serving.

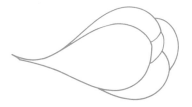

FRANKFORT BIBB LETTUCE SALAD

1 head Bibb lettuce per person
 Celery-Seed French Dressing

Cut away stalk end of lettuce and discard any withered leaves. Wash gently in cold water, and wrap loosely in a cloth towel until serving time. Serve with Celery-Seed French Dressing.

Celery-Seed French Dressing:

¼ cup sugar
¼ cup vinegar
1 teaspoon dry mustard
1 teaspoon celery seed
1 teaspoon paprika
1 teaspoon salt
1 teaspoon onion juice
1 cup salad oil, slightly warmed

Combine all ingredients, except oil, and beat until blended. (Electric blender is best.) Add warm oil very slowly, beating constantly. Refrigerate. Yield: 1½ cups.

Note: Warming the oil is the secret to this nonseparating dressing. If it should separate on long standing, shake well.

KENTUCKY DERBY FRIED COUNTRY HAM

1 center cut slice ham (¼ to ⅓ inch thick) per person
Red-Eye Gravy
Cream Gravy

Trim rind and all but ¼ inch of fat from slices. With a sharp knife, score fat at 1-inch intervals to prevent curling. Place ham in warm iron skillet or an electric fry pan set at 225°. It is all right for slices to overlap a bit, but do not stack. Just make sure the fat edges are nearest center of skillet; this assures that the fat will brown nicely without overcooking the other edge, which becomes hard with too much heat. It is better to use 2 skillets than overcrowd. Cover, and fry 15 minutes on each side, turning only once. With the electric fry pan you needn't worry. With the iron skillet, it should cook on heat so low you have to lean over it to hear it. This is as foolproof a method as you're likely to find.

Red-Eye Gravy:

2 tablespoons melted ham fat
1 cup black coffee
½ cup water

Combine ingredients in skillet, and boil for 5 minutes stirring actively to deglaze pan of all ham residue. Yield: 1½ cups.

Cream Gravy:

2 tablespoons melted ham fat
3 tablespoons all-purpose flour
1 cup water
1 cup milk

Pour off all except 2 tablespoons ham fat from the skillet in which slices have been cooked. Shake flour and water in a covered jar; pour through strainer into skillet. Add milk. Place on high heat and boil, stirring constantly for 5 minutes. Yield: 2 cups.

Note: Usually no salt is needed, but taste and make sure.

SHOEPEG PUDDING

2 eggs, separated
½ cup fine cracker crumbs
2 tablespoons melted butter or margarine
2 cups milk
½ teaspoon salt
½ teaspoon sugar
Dash pepper
1 (16-ounce) can shoepeg corn, drained

Beat egg yolks; then beat in crumbs, butter, milk, salt, sugar, pepper, and corn. Beat egg whites until stiff, and fold into first mixture. Pour into buttered 8-cup casserole, and bake at 350° about 35 minutes or until firm, puffy, and browned. Yield: 8 servings.

FRESH-COOKED ASPARAGUS

2½ to 3 pounds fresh asparagus
  1 cup boiling water
  1 teaspoon salt
  Unhollandaise Sauce

Select asparagus with tight tips and unwrinkled stem bottoms. Break off tough ends of stems at the point where they are brittle. Wash thoroughly to dislodge soil in the tips. Tie together into 8 bundles with clean string. Stand bundles upright in bottom of double boiler, add water, and cover with top part of double boiler. Cook 15 minutes or until tender. Steam will cook the tip ends. To serve, cut away string, and arrange on warmed serving bowl or platter. Sprinkle with salt. Top with Unhollandaise Sauce. Yield: 8 servings.

Unhollandaise Sauce:

  ¾ cup mayonnaise
  1 cup milk
  1 teaspoon lemon juice
  Salt and pepper to taste

In top of double boiler, combine mayonnaise and milk, and cook over simmering water for 5 minutes, stirring constantly. Season with lemon juice, salt and pepper. Yield: 1⅛ cups.

FRESH STRAWBERRIES WITH BRANDY-CARAMEL SAUCE

  2 quarts fresh strawberries
  ½ cup whole unsalted almonds

Wash, stem berries; drain well. Arrange them on a low serving dish in a mound, and sprinkle almonds over them. Refrigerate while preparing Sauce.

Sauce:

  2 cups sugar
  6 tablespoons butter
  ⅔ cup whipping cream
  ½ cup brandy

In a heavy iron skillet, place the sugar, and cook over low heat, stirring, until sugar melts (caramelizes). Add butter, and stir to melt it. Remove from heat, and stir in cream. Add brandy, and allow to cool to room temperature. Pour Sauce over berries. Yield: 8 servings.
  Note: This sauce is delicious served hot over ice cream or cake. It keeps well in refrigerator for several days.

BIRTHDAY PARTY

Coconut Cake
Fresh Lemon Ice Cream

COCONUT CAKE

2 cups sugar
1 cup commercial sour cream
3 (6-ounce) packages frozen
  coconut
1 (18½-ounce) box yellow butter cake
  mix

Thoroughly combine sugar, sour cream, and coconut. Refrigerate overnight.

Bake the 2 layers of cake according to package directions, using butter instead of margarine and milk instead of water. Cool layers on racks. When cold, split layers, making 4 thin layers. (An easy way to split cake layers evenly is to push 6 wooden picks into sides of layer just below half the height of the cake. Use a sharp, long-bladed knife or electric knife to cut just above the picks.) Place bottom layer on cake plate. With a knife, mark the filling into 4 parts, and use one fourth of the filling on each layer as you stack the cake. Store in tightly covered cake container in refrigerator for 3 days before serving. Yield: 1 (9-inch) layer cake.

Note: The cake has an attractive look with the sides not iced. If you desire, you may cover sides with swirls of commercial frozen whipped topping, thawed.

FRESH LEMON ICE CREAM

10 lemons, divided
1½ quarts milk
  1 pint whipping cream
  1 (13-ounce) can evaporated milk
3 cups sugar

Finely grate the rind of 5 lemons; reserve. Squeeze juice from all 10; then strain. Combine lemon rind and juice with remaining ingredients in a gallon-size ice-cream freezer container. Stir until sugar is completely dissolved. Chill thoroughly. Assemble freezer, packing alternate layers of coarsely crushed ice and ice-cream salt around the can. (The larger the proportion of salt to ice, the faster the ice cream will freeze; one part salt to 8 parts ice is a good combination.) Turn the handle (if manually operated) until the crank becomes very difficult to turn. Carefully remove dasher, making sure no salt falls into the ice cream. Cover open can with 2 layers of plastic wrap, and replace freezer cover. Drain water from freezer bucket, and repack with ice and salt. Cover with an old blanket, and allow to stand several hours to ripen the flavor. Yield: 1 gallon.

Note: Rind of 5 lemons yields about 2 tablespoons.

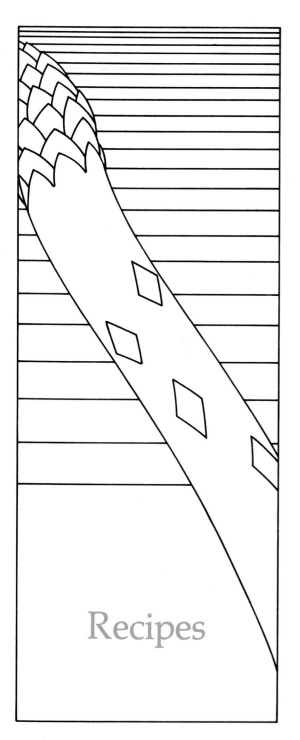

Recipes

Appetizers and Party Foods

Warning: overindulgence in "appetizers" can blunt the effect of the most meticulously prepared dinner. If you offer too many irresistibles, undereaters will fill up on them, then pick at their plates. Overeaters will wolf them down and go on to overeat at table, thus compounding their problem.

How long between arrival of guests and serving of the meal? An hour and two drinks worth? Modest appetizers are in order; perhaps fresh vegetables with a dip or simply cheese straws or wafers. More time, more drinks? Weight the appetizers with a cheese ball, guacamole with corn chips. Remember, the fat content in the appetizer has the effect of slowing the absorption of alcohol in the system.

Think of appetizers as an integral part of the meal, and do not duplicate during dinner something you have presented beforehand. For example, if you've had the vegetable-dip combination, a green salad would be repetitious.

Party foods are something else, usually standing in for a meal. Party foods can be fun and madness. Pull out all the stops. Go fancy. Go for variety. Go hot and cold. Go broke, if you're not careful.

First courses are a pleasant part of dinner, one much neglected by many hosts. Simplest of all, cups of hot soup served in the living room prepare the palate for good things to come. But a dainty first course in place on the table when the guests are seated says, "Look, I care; I bothered." And it can be a holding action while food heats or waits in the kitchen.

PARTY SEAFOOD MOLD

2 (2 tablespoons) envelopes unflavored
  gelatin
¼ cup lemon juice
¼ cup cold water
½ cup chili sauce
3 cups cooked shrimp, halved
  lengthwise
1 cup flaked crabmeat
3 hard-cooked eggs, thinly sliced
2 teaspoons salt
1 cup mayonnaise
1 teaspoon minced onion
2 cups chopped celery

Soften gelatin in mixture of lemon juice and
cold water. Stir over hot water to dissolve;
add chili sauce. Combine all remaining
ingredients in large bowl, and stir in gelatin
mixture gently but thoroughly. Pack into
a well-oiled, 2-quart, ring or fish-shaped
mold, and refrigerate overnight. To serve,
unmold on chilled platter, and garnish with
salad greens. Yield: 12 servings.

BLUE CHEESE FILLING

1 (5-ounce) jar pasteurized process blue
  cheese spread, softened
1 teaspoon Worcestershire sauce
½ cup commercial sour cream
  Cream Puffs
  Paprika (optional)
  Minced parsley (optional)

Cream blue cheese spread until smooth.
Blend in Worcestershire sauce. Fold in sour
cream; chill. Split Cream Puffs, and fill. Top
with a little of the filling or a sprinkling
of paprika or minced parsley, if desired.
Yield: 1 cup filling.

DEVILED-CHEESE FILLING

1 cup shredded pasteurized process
  American cheese
¼ teaspoon dry mustard
3 tablespoons mayonnaise
½ teaspoon Worcestershire sauce
1 teaspoon grated onion
5 to 6 drops hot pepper sauce
¼ teaspoon celery seeds
  Cream Puffs

Mix all ingredients together; split Cream
Puffs, and fill. Yield: about 1 cup filling.

SHRIMP SPREAD

2 tablespoons melted butter
1 teaspoon grated onion
2 tablespoons mayonnaise
1 teaspoon lemon juice
¼ teaspoon salt
  Dash pepper
1 (7-ounce) can shrimp, drained and
  chopped
  Cocktail Sauce

Combine melted butter with onion,
mayonnaise, lemon juice, salt, and pepper.
Fold in shrimp; chill. Serve with shredded
wheat crackers and Cocktail Sauce. Yield:
1¼ cups.

Cocktail Sauce:

¾ cup chili sauce
1 tablespoon bottled horseradish
½ teaspoon Worcestershire sauce
  Dash lemon juice

Combine ingredients, and chill before serving. Yield: about ¾ cup.

TUNA DIP

1 (1 tablespoon) envelope unflavored
    gelatin
½ cup cold water
1 (10-ounce) can condensed tomato soup
1 (8-ounce) package cream cheese,
    softened
1 cup mayonnaise
2 (7-ounce) cans white tuna fish
½ cup minced green pepper
½ cup minced celery
½ cup minced onion
½ cup sweet pickle relish

Sprinkle gelatin over cold water. In small heavy saucepan, heat soup, and stir in cut-up cheese. Stir over low heat until melted. Add gelatin, and stir until dissolved. Pour into large bowl of mixer. Add mayonnaise and beat well. Drain tuna, and place in a separate bowl, breaking it up fine. Add tuna to soup mixture, beating at low speed. Add remaining ingredients, and blend thoroughly. Refrigerate several hours or overnight before serving. Yield: about 7 cups.

PEANUT-CHEESE NIBBLES

½ cup margarine
⅓ cup shredded medium-sharp cheddar
    cheese
4 tablespoons Worcestershire sauce
2 tablespoons seasoned salt
7 slices stale bread, cubed
1 (9-ounce) jar dry roasted peanuts
5 strips bacon, fried crisp and crumbled

Melt margarine in small heavy saucepan. Add cheese, and stir to melt. Add Worcestershire and seasoned salt. Put cubed bread into roasting pan, and pour cheese mixture

over it. Stir gently to coat bread. Bake at 350° for 30 minutes, stirring occasionally. Cool. Combine with peanuts and bacon crumbles. Yield: 1 quart.

Note: You may substitute 3½ cups wheat or rice cereal that comes in little squares for the bread cubes.

ANTIPASTO PARLANTI

3 cans pitted black olives
2 jars stuffed green olives
1 jar hot pickled cauliflower
1 jar dilled green tomatoes
1 jar pepperoncini (small hot peppers)
1 large bunch fresh celery
3 red Spanish onions, sliced, separated
    into rings
2 tablespoons fennel seed
1 teaspoon oregano
4 teaspoons crushed red pepper
1½ cups salad oil or olive oil

Drain liquid from all canned and pickled products. Scrub celery ribs, and slice into 1-inch pieces. Place in large bowl or crock. A covered plastic bowl is ideal as you can shake it instead of having to stir the mixture occasionally. Add remaining ingredients, and shake or stir well. Olive oil is more authentic but rather greasy in the mixture. Refrigerate a week before using, shaking or stirring from time to time. Keeps well in refrigerator several weeks. Yield: 5 or 6 quarts.

Note: No can sizes are given here; the sizes are left to the individual taste. For instance, if you like more black than green olives, juggle things around to suit yourself.

HOT CHEESE PUFFS

1 (3-ounce) package cream cheese,
   softened
¾ teaspoon grated onion
¼ cup mayonnaise
1 tablespoon chopped chives
⅛ teaspoon cayenne pepper
2 tablespoons grated Parmesan cheese
   Bread slices, crust trimmed

Combine all ingredients except bread;
blend well. Cut each slice bread into 4
"fingers"; spread with cheese mixture. Bake
at 350° for 15 minutes. Yield: about 25
servings.

CHAFING DISH PARTY MEATBALLS

¾ cup ground beef
¼ pound ground pork
1 cup fine dry bread crumbs
1 teaspoon dried parsley flakes
1 small clove garlic
¼ cup milk
2 eggs, beaten
½ teaspoon salt
   Dash pepper
   Crimson Sauce

Combine all ingredients, working with
hands. Chill mixture to make it easier to
handle; form into about 50 to 60 balls, the
smaller the better. Place on lightly oiled
baking sheet. Bake at 400° for 15 to 20
minutes, shaking the pan once or twice
during baking. Drain on paper towels. May
be refrigerated or sealed and frozen. To
serve, put warm meatballs in chafing dish
and pour over Crimson Sauce. Ignite heat
source under chafing dish. Yield: 50 to 60
meatballs in sauce.

Crimson Sauce:

1 (16-ounce) can jellied cranberry sauce,
   cut up
1 cup chili sauce

Combine cranberry and chili sauces in
small saucepan, and stir over low heat until
cranberry sauce melts and mixture is boiling hot.

SAUERKRAUT BALLS

½ pound cooked ham
¼ pound corned beef
1 tablespoon minced onion
1 tablespoon dried parsley flakes
2 cups all-purpose flour, divided
1 cup milk
1 teaspoon prepared mustard
½ teaspoon salt
1 (16-ounce) can sauerkraut, rinsed and
   drained
2 eggs
2 tablespoons water
2 cups dry bread crumbs
   Oil for frying

Put meats through food grinder, using fine
blade. Add onion and parsley. Without
added fat, stir over medium heat until
lightly browned. Remove skillet from heat.
Thoroughly blend in 1 cup flour; slowly
stir in milk. Add mustard and salt. Return
to heat, and cook, stirring, until very thick,
5 or 6 minutes; cool. Combine with sauerkraut, and put the mixture through grinder,
using fine blade. Roll into 1-inch balls. Beat
eggs with water in small bowl. Roll balls
in remaining 1 cup flour, coat with egg, then
dredge with crumbs. Heat oil to 365°, and
fry balls until browned. Drain on absorbent
paper. Yield: about 65 balls.

BLUE CHEESE BALL

1 (4-ounce) package blue cheese,
  softened
1 (8-ounce) package cream cheese,
  softened
½ teaspoon celery salt
½ teaspoon Worcestershire sauce
1 tablespoon milk
¾ cup chopped pecans

Blend cheeses with celery salt, Worcestershire sauce, and milk. Refrigerate until firm enough to handle. Form into ball, and roll in chopped nuts. Yield: 1 (15-ounce) cheese ball.

Variation: Make up cheese mixture, and chill. Instead of rolling cheese in chopped nuts, use pecan or English walnut halves to make little party sandwiches with the cheese mixture inside.

PECAN-CHEESE WAFERS

1 pound sharp cheddar cheese, shredded
2 sticks (1 cup) butter or margarine,
  softened
3 cups all-purpose flour
1 teaspoon cayenne pepper
1 cup finely chopped pecans

Shred cheese while cold, then bring to room temperature. In large bowl of mixer, beat cheese with butter until well blended. Remove bowl from electric mixer and, with the hands, work in the flour, pepper, and nuts. Form into 4 rolls, 1 inch in diameter. Wrap separately in waxed paper, and chill at least an hour in refrigerator, preferably longer.

To bake, slice in ¼-inch thick slices, place on ungreased baking sheets, and bake at 350° for about 15 minutes. Do not brown. Yield: about 6 dozen wafers.

GARLIC-CHEESE ROLL

1 pound cheddar cheese, shredded and
  softened
1 teaspoon salt
2 (8-ounce) packages cream cheese,
  softened
⅛ teaspoon garlic powder
3 dashes hot sauce
1 tablespoon onion juice
1 tablespoon Worcestershire sauce
2 tablespoons mayonnaise
¼ teaspoon dry mustard
2 tablespoons chili powder
2 tablespoons paprika

Combine all ingredients except chili powder and paprika; blend thoroughly with an electric mixer. Shape into 1 long or 2 short rolls with a diameter about the size of a silver dollar.

Combine chili powder and paprika. Roll cheese logs back and forth in mixture until well coated; wrap in waxed paper, and refrigerate at least 24 hours. Will keep well for several weeks. Serve with crackers. Yield: 1 long or 2 short rolls.

QUICHE

½ (11-ounce) package piecrust mix
4 strips bacon
½ small onion, minced
½ cup milk
¼ cup half-and-half
2 eggs, slightly beaten
1 cup shredded Gruyère cheese
2 tablespoons grated Parmesan
¼ teaspoon salt
  Dash cayenne
  Dash ground nutmeg
1 tablespoon chopped chives
2 tablespoons chopped parsley

Make dough according to package directions; divide in half. Roll dough, and fit loosely into two 6-inch, glass pie plates (or you may use 4 foil tart pans). Trim edges; fold under and flute.

Fry bacon until crisp; drain, and set aside. Pour off all but 1 tablespoon drippings; add onion, and sauté until tender.

Heat milk and half-and-half to boiling point. Add a small amount of hot mixture to eggs, stirring until blended; then add egg mixture to remaining hot mixture. Add onion, cheese, and seasonings, blending well.

Crumble bacon into pastry shells; pour in filling. Bake at 375° about 30 minutes or until set and slightly browned. Cut into wedges, and serve immediately. Yield: 4 servings.

Note: Quiche is an excellent first course; cut into 8 servings.

A # 1 CHEESE BALL

½ pound extra sharp cheddar cheese, shredded
1 (8-ounce) package cream cheese, softened
1 medium-size onion, minced
½ green pepper, minced
1 (2-ounce) can pimientos, chopped
2 dashes thick steak sauce
½ cup finely chopped pecans

Shred cheese while cold, then allow it to come to room temperature. Beat with the cream cheese until blended. Add remaining ingredients, and mix well. Chill. When firm enough to handle, form mixture into a ball. Roll in pecans, coating it on all sides. Best made at least 24 hours ahead. Yield: 1 (1¼-pound) cheese ball.

CHEESY-BEER DIP

2 cups shredded sharp cheddar cheese, softened
1 (8-ounce) package cream cheese, softened
1 small clove garlic, crushed
⅔ cup beer
1 tablespoon poppy seeds
2 tablespoons minced dill pickle

Combine cheeses, garlic, and beer. Using an electric blender or mixer, blend until smooth and creamy. Stir in poppy seeds and minced pickle. Chill. Yield: about 2½ cups.

HOT CHEESE-BACON SQUARES

1 cup mayonnaise
2 teaspoons Worcestershire sauce
¼ teaspoon paprika
½ teaspoon instant salad blend seasoning
12 bacon slices, cooked and crumbled
2 medium-size whole green onions, chopped
1 (2½-ounce) package sliced almonds
1 (8-ounce) package sharp cheddar cheese, shredded
Bread slices

Combine mayonnaise and Worcestershire sauce, stirring until blended. Add paprika, salad blend, bacon, onion, almonds, and cheese; mix well. Thinly spread on bread and cut into squares or triangles. Bake at 400° for 10 minutes. Serve hot. Yield: about 5 dozen small squares or triangles.

ROQUEFORT-STUFFED CELERY

6 ribs celery
¼ cup crumbled Roquefort cheese
1 (3-ounce) package cream cheese, softened
Dash cayenne pepper
Paprika

Wash celery, and cut into 3-inch pieces. Combine Roquefort cheese, cream cheese, and cayenne pepper; blend well. Spread on celery and sprinkle with paprika. Yield: about 1½ dozen pieces.

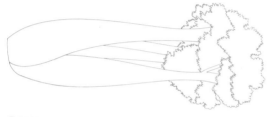

CELERY-CHEESE SWIRLS

1 bunch celery
1 (8-ounce) package cream cheese, softened
½ cup shredded pasteurized process American cheese
1 tablespoon milk
1 tablespoon finely chopped onion
1 garlic clove, minced
Salt and pepper to taste

Separate celery into stalks; trim, and wash thoroughly. Combine cream cheese and American cheese; blend until smooth. Add milk, onion, garlic, salt, and pepper; mix until well blended.

Spread cream cheese mixture on each celery stalk. Press 3 stalks together, and secure with rubber bands. Chill for 1 hour. Cut into ½- to 1-inch slices. Yield: about 3 dozen slices.

PINEAPPLE-CHEESE BALL

2 (8-ounce) packages cream cheese, softened
1 (8½-ounce) can crushed pineapple, drained
¼ cup finely chopped green pepper
2 tablespoons chopped onion
1 tablespoon seasoned salt
½ cup chopped pecans
½ cup chopped parsley

Combine cream cheese, pineapple, pepper, onion, and salt; mix well. Chill. Form mixture into a ball, and roll in mixture of pecans and parsley. Yield: about 15 servings.

PÂTÉ MOVEABLE FEAST

2 pounds bacon
3 large onions, finely chopped
6 tablespoons melted butter
4 (3-ounce) packages cream cheese, softened
1 pound Braunschweiger (liver sausage), at room temperature
2 cups port
Chopped pickles

Cook bacon in 350° oven until done. Drain on absorbent paper; crumble.

Sauté onion in butter until slightly cooked but still crunchy; add to cream cheese and Braunschweiger. Put this mixture through a food mill or blender. Add bacon and port; mix well. Pour into an oiled mold, and chill. Unmold onto platter, and garnish with pickles. Stores well in refrigerator for 1 week. Yield: 100 cocktail servings.

SAUSAGE-CRESCENT APPETIZERS

**1 (8-ounce) can refrigerated crescent
    dinner rolls
2 tablespoons prepared mustard
    (optional)
16 Vienna sausages or small cocktail
    wieners**

Separate dough into 8 triangles. If desired, spread with mustard. Cut each triangle in half, forming 16 triangles. Place a sausage on wide end of triangle. Roll up, and place on ungreased cookie sheet. Bake at 375° for 10 to 12 minutes or until golden brown. Serve hot. Yield: 16 appetizers.

CHEESE-SAUSAGE BALLS

**½ pound sharp cheddar cheese
½ pound hot pork sausage
1¾ cups commercial biscuit mix**

Melt cheese in top of double boiler over simmering water. Cool slightly. Fry sausage, breaking it up fine with a fork, until it is about half cooked. Drain well, squeezing in paper towels. Add sausage and biscuit mix to cheese, and blend. Form into 1-inch balls. Place on ungreased cookie sheet and bake at 400° for about 13 minutes until nicely browned. Yield: about 40 balls.

SAUSAGE PINWHEELS

**2 cups commercial biscuit mix
1 pound ground pork sausage
Chopped chives (optional)**

Prepare biscuit mix according to package directions for biscuit dough, using required liquid. Roll dough out on a lightly floured surface to a rectangle that measures 15 x 18 inches and about ⅛ inch thick. Dot entire surface with pieces of fresh pork sausage; sprinkle with chives. Cut dough in half crosswise and roll each half, jelly roll fashion, toward the center, making 2 rolls. Chill for easy slicing (or freeze).

Cut each roll into ½-inch slices. Arrange ½ inch apart in shallow baking pan. Bake at 450° for 15 minutes or until golden brown. Drain on absorbent paper. Serve hot. Each roll makes about 24 slices. Yield: 4 dozen.

SWEET-AND-SOUR MEATBALLS

**1 pound ground beef
½ cup uncooked regular oats
½ cup evaporated milk
1 medium-size onion, chopped
1 teaspoon pepper
¼ teaspoon salt
3 tablespoons melted shortening
⅔ cup catsup
4 teaspoons Worcestershire sauce
2 tablespoons vinegar
2 tablespoons sugar
⅓ cup water**

Combine beef, oats, milk, onion, pepper, and salt; mix well. Shape into about 30 small balls. Brown in hot shortening; drain.

Combine catsup, Worcestershire, vinegar, sugar, and water; mix well. Pour sauce over meatballs; simmer 30 minutes over low heat.

Transfer to a chafing dish set on low heat. Have toothpicks handy for serving. Yield: about 30 meatballs.

SWEET-AND-SOUR SAUSAGE BALLS

2 pounds bulk sausage
2 eggs, slightly beaten
¾ cup soft bread crumbs
   Oil for frying
1½ cups catsup
6 tablespoons firmly packed brown
   sugar
¼ cup wine vinegar
¼ cup soy sauce

Combine sausage, eggs, and bread crumbs; shape into teaspoon-size balls. Sauté in oil until brown; drain. Combine remaining ingredients; pour over sausage balls, and simmer for 30 minutes. Serve hot.

Sausage balls may be refrigerated or frozen in sauce. To serve, heat at 350° for 20 minutes. Yield: about 6 dozen.

CHICKEN LIVER PÂTÉ

1 pound chicken livers
2 sprigs fresh parsley
2 tablespoons chopped onion
¼ teaspoon thyme
½ cup melted butter
1 teaspoon salt
1 teaspoon dry mustard
   Dash pepper
3 tablespoons brandy
   Chopped parsley

Place livers, parsley, onion, and thyme in saucepan. Cover with water, and simmer 20 minutes. Drain well, and put through fine blade of food chopper. Beat butter into mixture, and add remaining ingredients. Pack firmly into an oiled 2-cup mold. Cover, and chill thoroughly. To serve, unmold, and garnish with chopped parsley. Yield: 2 cups.

SHERRIED CHOPPED LIVER

½ pound chicken livers
½ pound calf liver, sliced and skinned
3 tablespoons butter
1 small onion
2 hard-cooked eggs
   Salt and pepper to taste
2 tablespoons dry sherry
   Crackers or party rye bread

Place livers in kettle with butter, and cook over low heat until done. Put through finest blade of food grinder, along with onion and eggs. (If finer, smoother mixture is desired, put ground mixture, a little at a time, into blender, adding a little sherry to each batch to help blending.) To ground mixture, add seasonings and sherry, mixing thoroughly. Refrigerate at least 24 hours before serving. Serve with crackers or party rye bread. Yield: about 2½ cups.

SKORTHALIA

1 (16-ounce) can small whole beets,
   drained
1 (6½-ounce) can artichoke hearts,
   drained
1 (4½-ounce) can medium-size shrimp,
   drained
1 cucumber, sliced
1 (3¾-ounce) can sardines, drained
   Fried eggplant wedges
   Fried zucchini slices
   Garlic Sauce

Arrange assortment of beets, artichoke hearts, shrimp, cucumber, sardines, eggplant, and zucchini on tray. Separate hot and cold vegetables on tray with dish of Garlic Sauce to be used as a dip. Yield: 8 to 10 servings.

Garlic Sauce:

4 cloves garlic, chopped or pressed
1 teaspoon salt
1 egg
4 tablespoons white vinegar
12 slices white bread
½ cup olive oil or salad oil
    Hot water
1 potato, cooked and mashed

Combine garlic and salt, and mash to a paste with a mortar and pestle, or place in small cup, and mash to a paste with handle of wooden spoon. Scrape into mixing bowl. Beat in egg and vinegar.

Remove crusts from bread, and crumble slices into a second mixing bowl; mix with olive oil and 2 or 3 tablespoons hot water. Gradually beat bread into garlic mixture. Add additional hot water until mixture is consistency of whipped potatoes. Add mashed potato and beat until smooth. Yield: about 2 cups.

Note: 1 teaspoon garlic salt may be substituted for 4 cloves garlic and 1 teaspoon salt.

MARINATED CARROT STICKS

8 small carrots
3 tablespoons vinegar
3 tablespoons salad oil
1 small clove garlic, crushed
¾ teaspoon seasoned salt
¼ teaspoon salt
    Minced fresh parsley

Peel carrots, and cut into thin 3-inch sticks; place in a shallow dish. Combine remaining ingredients except parsley; pour over carrots, stirring gently so carrots are well coated. Cover tightly, and refrigerate 6 hours or overnight, stirring occasionally if convenient. Drain off marinade; arrange carrot sticks attractively in serving dish, and sprinkle with parsley. Yield: 6 to 8 servings.

VIENNA LIPTAUER KÄSE

1 (8-ounce) package cream cheese,
    softened
1 stick margarine, softened
¼ teaspoon paprika
¼ teaspoon caraway seeds, crushed
1 small onion, minced
6 capers, minced
1 small clove garlic, pressed

Beat cheese and margarine in small bowl of mixer at low speed. Add remaining ingredients, and blend well. Pack into 2-cup, straight-sided jar or bowl. Refrigerate, covered. Remove from refrigerator an hour before serving. Yield: about 1⅔ cups.

MINI MEATBALLS

1 pound ground pork sausage
¼ pound ground round beef
1 egg, slightly beaten
¼ cup dry bread crumbs
1 (5-ounce) can water chestnuts
1 (16-ounce) bottle barbecue sauce

Place pork sausage and ground beef in bowl; add egg and bread crumbs; mix well. Cut each water chestnut into 4 to 6 small pieces. Shape a scant tablespoon of meat around each piece. Roll in palms of hands to make balls. Place meatballs in unheated skillet; cook slowly, turning carefully until browned on all sides. Transfer meatballs to chafing dish. Add barbecue sauce, and keep warm over low flame. Serve with toothpicks. Yield: about 4 dozen.

Beverages

Coffee, tea, or milk? All of the above, please. But others, hot or cold, alcoholic and nonalcoholic, have a place in our diet and in our social life. What's a wedding reception without a stunning punch bowl, a picnic without lemonade, or a wintry afternoon of bridge without hot, spiced tea? For some, happiness is a glass of beer while watching a football game on television. A solitary cup of coffee after the children leave for school can be one of the highlights of a mother's day.

From morning OJ to preprandial cocktails or aperitifs, beverages play not only a nutritional role in our lives but also a social one. "Come for coffee" or "Drop by for a drink" are friendly rituals, part of daily living.

Facing up to the fact that instant coffee is very much with us, we will leave "how to brew a good cup of coffee" to the instruction sheet that came with your coffeemaker and touch coffee brewing with only two thoughts; keep the pot scrupulously clean, and cut down on the amount of coffee per cup called for in most instructions; otherwise, the brew is too strong for many tastes.

Tea lovers, for the most part, simply toss the tea bag into the cup and pour on boiling water. But tea is an expansive subject; there are many kinds of loose teas on the market, herbal and exotic, which are fun to experiment with. Used tea leaves, especially those with whole spices and other woody material, can cause trouble in some automatic dishwashers, tea balls are one way of coping with the problem. There are ceramic ones, if you believe metal tea balls give an off-flavor to your cup.

SANGRÍA PUNCH

2 quarts burgundy
1 cup orange juice
1 cup pineapple juice
   Juice of 1 lemon
1 cup sugar
1 lemon, thinly sliced
1 small orange halved and thinly sliced
2 quarts ginger ale, chilled

Combine wine, fruit juices, and sugar. Stir to dissolve sugar. Refrigerate until serving time. When ready to serve, pour into chilled bowl, and add sliced fruit and ginger ale. Yield: 30 (4-ounce) servings.

Note: A simple ice ring, which will not dilute the punch, may be made by mixing a 6-ounce can of frozen lemonade concentrate with water to make 1 quart. Freeze in a ring mold.

SANGRÍA SOUTHERN

1 lemon, thinly sliced
1 orange, thinly sliced
1 lime, thinly sliced
   Sugar
1 jigger Triple Sec or other orange
   liqueur
1 (4/5-quart) bottle dry red wine
½ cup club soda, chilled
   Additional lime slices

Remove seeds from sliced fruit; place slices in glass pitcher, and add 1 to 2 tablespoons sugar. Do not add too much sugar until wine has been added. Allow to stand a few minutes.

Add Triple Sec to sliced fruit; stir with wooden spoon, bruising fruit to extract juices. Add wine; more sugar may be added, if desired. Chill. Just before serving, add club soda. Serve over ice, and garnish with additional lime slices. Yield: 6 to 8 servings.

COLOR SCHEME PARTY PUNCH

    1 (3-ounce) package gelatin, any flavor
        desired
    2 cups hot water
    1½ cups sugar
    1 quart cold water
        Juice of 4 lemons, strained
    1 (46-ounce) can pineapple juice
    2 quarts ginger ale, chilled

Dissolve gelatin in hot water. Add sugar, and stir to dissolve. Add cold water and fruit juices. Chill well. Pour into punch bowl. Add ginger ale before serving. Yield: 30 servings.

Note: Part of the punch mixture may be frozen in ring mold or ice-cube trays. Used this way, ice will not weaken flavor of punch.

ROSY RUM PUNCH

    1 cup cranberry juice
    ¼ cup frozen orange juice concentrate
    2 tablespoons lemon juice
    ½ cup light rum
    1 7-ounce bottle ginger ale, chilled

Combine all ingredients, except ginger ale, and chill well. Add ginger ale just before serving. Yield: 6 servings.

HOT SPICED CRANBERRY TEA

    3 cups boiling water
    ½ cup sweetened lemon-flavored ice tea
        mix
    3 cups cranberry juice cocktail
        Lemon slices
        Whole cloves
        Cinnamon sticks

Combine water, tea mix, and cranberry juice; heat thoroughly. Serve hot in mugs or cups with a lemon slice decorated with cloves. Stir with a cinnamon stick. Yield: 6 cups.

APRICOT MILK SMOOTHEE

    1 cup milk
    ½ cup dried apricots, soaked for 30
        minutes and drained
    3 tablespoons sugar
    1 cup cracked ice

Pour milk into blender container. Add other ingredients. Cover, and blend thoroughly for 1 or 2 minutes. Yield: 2 cups.

TROPICAL COOLER

    1 (6-ounce) can frozen orange juice
        concentrate, undiluted
    1 (6-ounce) can frozen lemonade
        undiluted
    1 quart apple juice
    2 quarts ginger ale, chilled

Combine orange juice, lemonade, and apple juice; mix well. Just before serving, stir in ginger ale. Serve over crushed ice. Yield: about 3 quarts.

HOT SPICED ORANGE JUICE

 1 pint cider or apple juice
½ cup firmly packed brown sugar
½ cup sugar
 2 (2-inch) cinnamon sticks
 3 whole cloves
 1 quart orange juice
 1 cup freshly squeezed lemon juice
   Orange and lemon slices
   Cinnamon sticks

Combine first 5 ingredients; simmer for 5 minutes. Combine orange juice and lemon juice; heat to just below simmering. Add to hot cider. Serve in mugs, and garnish with orange and lemon slices on a cinnamon stick. Yield: 12 servings.

FRUIT PUNCH

 1 (46-ounce) can unsweetened pineapple
   juice, chilled
 1 (46-ounce) can red fruit juice punch,
   chilled
 1 (28-ounce) bottle ginger ale, chilled
 1 (12-ounce) can frozen orange juice
   concentrate, thawed and undiluted
   Juice of 3 lemons
¼ cup sugar

Combine all ingredients, stirring well. Serve over ice. Yield: about 3½ quarts.

HOT MULLED WINE

 1 cup sugar
 4 cups water
   Rind of 1 lemon
16 whole cloves
 1 stick cinnamon, broken up
 2 bottles (fifths or quarts) dry red wine

In large kettle, combine sugar, water, lemon rind (peel lemon with potato parer), cloves, and cinnamon. Boil mixture for 15 minutes. Reduce heat, and add wine. Heat, never boiling, to serving temperature. Serve in warm mugs or cups. Yield: about 20 servings.

BLOODY MARY

 1 jigger vodka
 2 jiggers tomato juice
⅓ jigger lemon juice
   Dash Worcestershire sauce
   Salt and pepper to taste
   Dash Tabasco sauce (optional)
   Celery sticks

Combine ingredients in shaker with ½ cup cracked ice. Shake until chilled, and strain into a 6-ounce cocktail glass. Garnish with celery sticks. Yield: 1 serving.

SPICED LEMONADE

¾ cup sugar
4¾ cups water, divided
12 whole cloves
 7 cinnamon sticks, divided
   Juice of 6 lemons
   Lemon slices

Combine sugar and ¾ cup water; boil about 5 minutes. Add cloves and 1 cinnamon stick; cook 5 minutes over medium heat. Strain into pitcher.

Add lemon juice and remaining 4 cups water. Chill. Serve over ice. Garnish each glass with a lemon slice; use remaining cinnamon sticks for stirrers. Yield: 6 servings.

TEA WALLOP

2 tablespoons black tea leaves
15 mint leaves
3 cups boiling water
5 tablespoons freshly squeezed lemon
    juice
1½ cups orange juice
1 cup grape juice
4½ cups pineapple juice
1 cup powdered sugar
    Ice

Combine tea and mint leaves, and pour boiling water over them. Let steep until water is cool; strain. Combine with fruit juices and sugar; stir until sugar is dissolved. Chill. Serve over ice. Yield: 12 servings.

SPICY ICED COFFEE

3 cups hot double-strength coffee
2 cinnamon sticks
4 whole cloves
4 whole allspice berries
    Ice
    Cream and sugar to taste

Pour coffee over cinnamon sticks, cloves, and allspice berries. Let stand for 1 hour. Strain, and pour over ice in 4 tall glasses. Add cream and sugar. Yield: 4 servings.

STRAWBERRY COOLER

1 (3-ounce) package strawberry-flavored
    gelatin
1 cup boiling water
1 cup cold water
1 cup pineapple juice
1 cup frozen lemonade (diluted
    according to directions on can)
2 cups crushed or sliced strawberries

Dissolve gelatin in boiling water. Add cold water, pineapple juice, lemonade, and strawberries. Mix well. Chill. Serve over ice in glasses. Yield: 10 servings.

Soups

Once upon a time a self-confessed gourmand was convicted of eating too richly for his station in life (he was a thatcher by trade) and condemned to choose one category of food on which he must live for the rest of his life. Quickly his mind ran down the list of things he loved, from hors d' oeuvres through desserts. In one minute flat, he cried, "Soup!" for he knew that he could have just about anything in the world he wanted to eat and call it soup.

He lived happily to a great age, and his health was superb to the end. He drank light, hot and cold soups from a cup for appetizer; fish-rich chowders, beefy stews with dumplings, chili, thick homemade bean, and chicken-vegetable soups for dinner; and he ended with one of his favorite fruit soups for dessert.

As many nourishing soups are made with cheap ingredients, he saved money, and his heirs had loads of fun on their inheritances. Granted, in those days, butchers did not charge for soup bones, and grocers gave away wilted produce, whereas nowadays those commodities command premium prices. Undoubtedly, a soup diet would cost more today. But there is no more versatility to be found under any caption than that of "Soup."

QUICK MINESTRA

3 ounces leftover cooked ham fat, diced
1 small onion, diced
1 (16-ounce) can lima beans
1 (16-ounce) can spinach or kale
   Salt and pepper to taste

In electric blender, combine ham fat and onion. Mince, but do not puree. Put mixture into heavy saucepan. Add lima beans. Run a sharp knife down through the can of spinach or kale to cut it up; add to pan. Simmer 20 to 30 minutes. Season. Yield: 4 servings.

Note: This easy, economical version of a classic Italian soup is a meal in itself, needing only cornbread and a salad of sliced green pepper, onion, and tomato with herbs and oil.

QUICK LOBSTER SOUP

3 (8-ounce) packages frozen lobster tails,
   thawed
2 hard-cooked egg yolks
1 tablespoon butter, softened
1 tablespoon all-purpose flour
   Grated rind of 1 lemon
   Dash pepper
1 quart milk
½ cup half-and-half
½ teaspoon salt
½ teaspoon cayenne pepper
1 teaspoon aromatic bitters
1 tablespoon dry sherry

Cut away underside membrane on lobster tails, and remove meat from shell. Dice lobster meat.

Mash egg yolks to a paste; blend in butter, flour, lemon rind, and pepper. Bring milk to a boil; gradually add to egg yolk mixture, blending well.

Add lobster meat to milk mixture, and simmer over low heat for 5 minutes. Add half-and-half; bring to a boil, stirring constantly. Add salt, cayenne, bitters, and sherry. Serve hot, but do not boil after adding sherry. Yield: 6 to 8 servings.

FROSTY SEABREEZE SOUP FOR TWO

1 (10¾-ounce) can condensed tomato
    soup
1 soup can water
½ cup diced cooked shrimp or flaked
    cooked crab
2 tablespoons dry vermouth
1 tablespoon chopped parsley
4 drops hot sauce

Blend soup and water; add remaining ingredients. Place in refrigerator for at least 4 hours; serve in chilled bowls. Yield: 2 to 3 servings.

DAUGHDRILL'S SEAFOOD DELUXE

¼ cup salad oil
¼ cup all-purpose flour
2 large onions, chopped
2 cloves garlic, minced
1 green pepper, chopped
4 stalks celery, chopped
    Fish Stock (Court Bouillon)
2 (16-ounce) cans tomatoes
4- to 6-pound firm redfish, grouper,
    snapper, or catfish, fileted and
    cubed
    Salt to taste
2 bay leaves
1 to 2 teaspoons seafood seasoning
2 hard-cooked eggs, sliced
1 lemon, sliced
    Cooked rice

Heat oil in a heavy saucepan or Dutch oven over medium heat; add flour very slowly, stirring constantly with a wooden spoon until roux is very brown.

Add onions, garlic, green pepper, and celery to the roux; cook until vegetables are limp. Add Fish Stock and tomatoes; simmer 30 minutes. Add fish, salt, bay leaves, and seafood seasoning; simmer 20 minutes.

Just before serving, stir in egg and lemon slices; remove bay leaves. Spoon over rice in soup bowls. Yield: 8 to 10 servings.

QUICK CRAB GUMBO

1 (7-ounce) can crabmeat
1 (16-ounce) can stewed tomatoes
1 (16-ounce) can okra
7 or 8 dashes hot pepper sauce
    Freshly ground pepper to taste
1 teaspoon salt
¼ teaspoon dried thyme
2 cups cooked rice
    Paprika (optional)

Combine ingredients, except rice, in saucepan, and cook until boiling. Serve in soup bowls, and place a large mound of cooked rice in center of each serving. If desired, sprinkle rice mounds with paprika. Yield: 2 to 3 servings.

FISH STOCK (COURT BOUILLON)

6 cups water
    Backbone and head from 4- to
        6-pound fish
2 bay leaves
1½ teaspoons salt
½ teaspoon pepper
2 to 3 teaspoons seafood seasoning

Combine all ingredients in a large saucepan or Dutch oven; simmer 1 hour. Strain stock. Yield: about 5 cups.

ICED AVOCADO SOUP

1 large avocado, peeled and coarsely
    chopped
1 (10¾-ounce) can condensed chicken
    broth
1 soup can water
1 cup half-and-half
    Salt and pepper to taste
    Dash hot sauce
6 thin lemon slices (optional)

Combine avocado, chicken broth, and water
in container of electric blender. Cover, and
blend 15 seconds or until smooth. Pour into
a saucepan, and stir in half-and-half. Season with salt, pepper and hot sauce. Heat
well, but do not boil. Chill thoroughly
before serving. Garnish with thin lemon
slices. Yield: 6 servings.

ALMOND CREAM SOUP

2 cups blanched almonds, ground
1 stick butter or margarine
1 quart milk, divided
1 quart Chicken Stock
2 tablespoons cornstarch
    Pinch sugar
    Salt to taste
2 tablespoons toasted slivered almonds
    (optional)

Sauté ground almonds in butter until just
browned. Stir in all but ¼ cup of milk; add
Chicken Stock. Dissolve cornstarch in
reserved milk, and stir into soup. Cook over
low heat, stirring frequently, until slightly
thickened. Season with sugar and salt. To
serve, ladle into warmed soup plates or
bowls, and garnish with almonds. Yield: 8
to 10 servings.

CHEESE-ASPARAGUS SOUP

1 tablespoon butter
1 tablespoon all-purpose flour
2 cups milk
1 cup cut cooked asparagus
1 teaspoon salt
    Dash white pepper
¾ cup shredded cheddar cheese

Melt butter; blend in flour, and cook until
bubbly. Gradually add milk, stirring until
well blended. Cook over low heat, stirring
constantly, until smooth and thickened.

Add asparagus and seasonings. Mix well.
Add cheese; stir until cheese is melted.
Yield: 4 servings.

ITALIAN SPLIT PEA SOUP

1 (16-ounce) package dried split peas
5 quarts water
    Salt to taste
1 (16-ounce) can peas, undrained
1 head cauliflower, separated into
    flowerets
1 small head cabbage, cut into 1-inch
    cubes
¾ cup olive oil
2 small cloves garlic, crushed
½ teaspoon cayenne

Wash dried peas; cook in boiling salted
water until soft.

Mash a small amount of cooked peas into
a fine paste to thicken cooking liquid; add
to remaining cooked peas along with
canned peas, cauliflower, cabbage, olive oil,
garlic, and cayenne. Simmer over low heat
1½ to 2 hours or until vegetables are tender.
Yield: about 12 servings.

CREAMY CUCUMBER SOUP

1 cup chopped onion
1 tablespoon melted butter or margarine
1 cucumber, peeled
3 cups chicken stock
½ to 1 cup commercial sour cream
   Salt to taste
¼ cup finely chopped green onion

Sauté onion in butter until tender. Remove seeds from cucumber, and coarsely chop; add to onion. Cook about 3 minutes, stirring constantly. Add chicken stock, and simmer about 15 minutes. Puree cucumber mixture; chill.

Stir in sour cream and salt just before serving. Pour into chilled cups; garnish with green onion. Yield: 6 servings.

SLAVIC CABBAGE SOUP

2 pounds beef bones
1 medium-size onion, coarsely cut
3 carrots, scrubbed and sliced
2 cloves garlic, minced
2 small bay leaves
2½ to 3 pounds beef chuck, fat trimmed
1 teaspoon thyme
1 teaspoon paprika
2 quarts water
2 quarts (1 large head) shredded cabbage
2 (16-ounce) cans tomatoes
2½ teaspoons salt
½ teaspoon cayenne pepper
¼ cup chopped fresh parsley
   Juice of 1 lemon
3 tablespoons sugar
1 (16-ounce) can sauerkraut

Place beef bones, onion, carrots, garlic, and bay leaves in open roasting pan. Add chuck, thyme, and paprika. Bake at 450°, uncovered, for 20 minutes or until meat is brown. Transfer meat and vegetables to a large soup kettle. Add water, cabbage, tomatoes, salt, and cayenne. Bring to a boil. Simmer, covered, 1½ hours. Skim off fat. (If possible, cool, and refrigerate overnight at this point. Fat can then be lifted off entirely.) Add parsley, lemon juice, sugar, and sauerkraut. Simmer, uncovered, 1½ hours. Remove meat and bones from kettle. Remove meat from bones, shred, and put meat back into soup. Remove bay leaves before serving. Yield: 12 servings.

CREAM OF CELERY SOUP

2 cups chopped celery
1 large onion, chopped
½ bay leaf
1 clove garlic, minced
2 cups water
2 tablespoons margarine
¼ cup all-purpose flour
1 cup instant nonfat dry milk solids
½ teaspoon salt
   Dash pepper
½ teaspoon Worcestershire sauce

Combine celery, onion, bay leaf, garlic, and water; cook about 15 minutes or until celery is tender. Remove bay leaf; drain, reserving liquid. Set vegetables aside. Add enough water to reserve liquid to make 2 cups.

Melt margarine in a heavy saucepan; stir in flour and dry milk. Slowly add reserved liquid to flour mixture, stirring constantly, until smooth and thickened. Add salt, pepper, and Worcestershire sauce, stirring well.

Combine vegetables and cream sauce; process in blender until smooth. Remove from blender; heat to serving temperature. Yield: 4 servings.

CHICKEN STOCK

4 pounds chicken pieces
1 onion, quartered
2 stalks celery
½ teaspoon dried parsley
1 bay leaf
¼ teaspoon thyme
⅛ teaspoon marjoram
2 quarts water
Salt and pepper to taste

Combine chicken and remaining ingredients in a large kettle. Cover and bring to a boil; reduce heat and simmer 3 hours or until meat falls from bones. Strain broth; reserve chicken and vegetables for other uses. Cool and skim off fat. Cover and refrigerate until ready to use. Yield: about 1½ quarts.

Note: Canned chicken broth, chicken broth made with bouillon cubes, or chicken concentrate may be substituted for freshly made chicken broth. Also, turkey pieces may be substituted for chicken in the above recipe to make turkey broth.

ONION SOUP WITH PUFFY CHEESE CROUTONS

4 cups thinly sliced onion
¼ cup melted butter
2 tablespoons all-purpose flour
2 (10½-ounce) cans condensed beef broth
1 (10¾-ounce) can condensed chicken broth
1 soup can water
Puffy Cheese Croutons

Sauté onion in butter until limp but not brown; blend in flour. Add broths and water; stir until smooth. Simmer about 30 minutes. Serve soup with Puffy Cheese Croutons. Yield: 6 to 8 servings.

Puffy Cheese Croutons:

¼ cup butter
1 tablespoon milk
1 cup (¼ pound) shredded cheddar cheese
2 egg whites
French bread

Melt butter in top of double boiler over hot, but not boiling, water or in a saucepan over very low heat. Add milk and cheese, stirring constantly until cheese is melted. Remove from heat.

Beat egg whites until stiff but not dry; gently fold into cheese mixture. Cut 30 bite-size cubes of French bread; dip into egg-cheese mixture. Bake on ungreased cookie sheets at 400° for 10 to 15 minutes or until lightly browned. Remove immediately. Yield: 30 croutons.

CREAM OF CORN SOUP FOR TWO

2 teaspoons butter
2 teaspoons all-purpose flour
1½ teaspoons instant minced onion
¼ teaspoon salt
Dash pepper
¼ teaspoon ground nutmeg
1 cup evaporated milk or half-and-half
1 (8½-ounce) can whole kernel corn, undrained

Melt butter in saucepan over low heat; remove from heat. Blend in flour; add onion and seasonings. Gradually stir in milk. Cook, stirring constantly, until mixture thickens. Add corn. Heat to serving temperature. Yield: 2 servings.

BLOODY MARY SOUP

4 to 5 ripe tomatoes
2 cloves garlic
1 medium-size onion, sliced
1 small green pepper, cut into small
    pieces
2 cups tomato juice
   Salt and pepper to taste
½ cup vodka, chilled
4 celery sticks (optional)

Peel and seed tomatoes; place in blender container with garlic, onion, and green pepper. Blend to a smooth paste; gradually blend in tomato juice. Season. Chill thoroughly.

Just before serving, stir in vodka. Serve over ice in large goblets; use celery sticks for stirrers. Yield: 4 servings.

POTATO-FRANKS SOUP FOR TWO

1 medium-size onion, finely chopped
1 small carrot, chopped
1 rib celery, chopped
3 tablespoons melted butter or
    margarine
1½ cups diced potato
3 cups water
1 teaspoon salt
   Dash pepper
4 cooked frankfurters, sliced
   Chopped parsley

Sauté onion, carrot, and celery in butter about 10 minutes. Add potato, water, salt, and pepper; bring to a boil. Cover, and simmer 45 minutes. Add frankfurters; heat thoroughly. Sprinkle with parsley before serving. Yield: 2 to 3 servings.

Salads

We might put the vitamin manufacturers out of business if we added more salads to our diets. But, while Americans are much more given to salad eating than most other countries, there are enough of us who neglect fresh raw fruits and vegetables to keep vitamin companies comfortably in the black.

Salad greens should be utterly fresh, which goes (or should go) without saying. They can be washed ahead of time and stored in a clean towel or (large quantities) in a large plastic bag, with paper towels mixed in to absorb moisture. Or you can spend some money for a centrifugal-action basket to whirl the water out. When washed greens are properly dried, dressing will adhere, and there will be no dilution.

The care and feeding of wooden salad bowls is the subject of a hardy perennial debate.

Washing: pro and con. I'm pro; many are the beautiful salad bowls I've sniffed that reeked so of stale garlic and rancid oil that I dreaded eating the contents. Those against washing the prized bowl claim water will not only warp it but also remove the oil with which many of them are finished. My compromise is to wash the inside after each use; essentials are cool water, a drop of detergent, and lightning speed. Follow with a quick, cool rinse and thorough drying.

When the bowl feels dry to the touch, rub in a little salad oil; then scrub it down with a towel; don't do it after each use, or you could bring on that rancid build-up.

Some molded fruit salads can double as desserts. Indeed they should, especially the overly sweet ones laden with whipped cream and (heaven forbid) those little marshmallows.

CHICKEN SALAD WITH GRAPES

    4 cups chopped, cooked chicken
    1 cup chopped celery
    ⅓ cup sweet pickle relish
    2 cups seedless white grapes, halved
    1 cup chopped pecans
    1 cup commercial sour cream
    1 cup mayonnaise
    6 hard-cooked eggs, thinly sliced
    2 teaspoons salt
      Pepper to taste
      Salad greens

Place first 8 ingredients in large mixing bowl in the order listed. Sprinkle with salt and pepper. Toss lightly (clean hands are the gentlest mixer) to blend. Chill several hours. Serve on salad greens. Yield: 12 servings.

CRANBERRY NUT MOLD

    1 (6-ounce) package cherry-flavored
       gelatin
    1 pint boiling water
    2 cups raw cranberries, ground
    1 cup sugar
    1 cup chopped English walnuts
    1 tablespoon grated orange rind
      Salad greens

Dissolve gelatin in boiling water. Chill until syrupy. Meanwhile, combine cranberries with sugar, and stir to dissolve all sugar. When gelatin reaches the consistency of unbeaten egg white, fold in all remaining ingredients except salad greens, and spoon into 12 individual molds or one 6-cup mold. To serve, unmold, and garnish with salad greens. Yield: 12 servings.

TOMATO ASPIC HÉLÈNE

1 envelope (1 tablespoon) unflavored
gelatin
¼ cup water
¼ teaspoon grated onion
1 (12-ounce) can mixed vegetable juice
½ teaspoon salt
Dash red pepper
½ teaspoon celery salt
1 tablespoon lemon juice
Salad greens
Half-and-half Dressing

Sprinkle gelatin over water in small bowl, and let stand 5 minutes. Combine onion, vegetable juice, salt, pepper, celery salt, and lemon juice in small saucepan. Bring to boiling point. Pour over softened gelatin, and stir until gelatin is dissolved. Pour into 4 or 5 individual molds. Chill to set. Unmold on salad greens; garnish with Half-and-half Dressing. Yield: 4 or 5 servings.

SPICED ORANGE MOLD

1 (11-ounce) can mandarin oranges
¼ cup sugar
½ cup water
1 stick cinnamon
6 whole cloves
1 (3-ounce) package lemon-flavored
gelatin
½ cup orange juice
Juice of 1 lemon, strained
Salad greens
Half-and-half Dressing

Drain liquid from oranges into small saucepan; add sugar, water, and spices. Bring to a boil, and simmer 5 minutes. Place gelatin in bowl, and pour hot liquid through a strainer into gelatin; discard spices. Stir until gelatin is completely dissolved. Add fruit, orange juice, and lemon juice. Spoon into 6 individual molds. Chill until set. Unmold, and serve on salad greens. Garnish with Half-and-half Dressing. Yield: 6 servings.

Half-and-half Dressing:

½ cup mayonnaise
½ cup commercial sour cream

Combine ingredients. Yield: 1 cup.
Note: Make any quantity you wish, using half mayonnaise, half sour cream.

BLUEBERRY SALAD

1 (8¼-ounce) can crushed pineapple
2 (3-ounce) packages
blackberry-flavored or black
raspberry-flavored gelatin
3 cups boiling water
1 (15-ounce) can blueberries, drained
1 (8-ounce) carton commercial sour
cream
1 (8-ounce) package cream cheese,
softened
½ cup sugar
Chopped pecans

Drain pineapple, reserving juice. Dissolve gelatin in boiling water; stir in pineapple juice. Chill until consistency of unbeaten egg white. Stir in pineapple and blueberries. Pour into a 10- x 6- x 1¾-inch pan. Chill until firm.

Combine sour cream, cream cheese, and sugar; mix until smooth and well blended. Spread over salad, and top with pecans. Yield: 8 servings.

STRAWBERRY-BANANA SALAD

3 (3-ounce) packages
    strawberry-flavored gelatin
1 cup boiling water
1 (10-ounce) package frozen
    strawberries, thawed and undrained
1 (15¼-ounce) can crushed pineapple,
    undrained
3 bananas, sliced
2 cups commercial sour cream, divided
½ cup chopped pecans or walnuts

Dissolve gelatin in boiling water; stir in fruit. Pour half of gelatin mixture into an 8-inch pan, and refrigerate until firm; store remaining gelatin mixture at room temperature.

Spread congealed gelatin with 1 cup sour cream. Spoon remaining gelatin over sour cream, and refrigerate until firm. Top with remaining sour cream, spreading evenly; sprinkle with pecans. Yield: 8 to 10 servings.

LETTUCE CUP SALAD

4 hard-cooked eggs
2 tablespoons mayonnaise
1 (2¼-ounce) can deviled ham
2 cups chopped cabbage
½ cup grated carrots
½ cup mayonnaise
4 lettuce cups
¼ cup chopped chives

Split hard-cooked eggs; remove yolks, and blend with 2 tablespoons mayonnaise and deviled ham. Stuff egg halves with mixture.

Mix cabbage, carrots, and mayonnaise; place in lettuce cups. Top each with 2 ham-stuffed egg halves, and garnish with chives. Yield: 4 servings.

CARIBBEAN FRUIT SALAD

¼ large fresh pineapple, cut into chunks
1 small ripe avocado, sliced
1 small sweet onion, sliced
¼ cup mayonnaise
4 lettuce cups or 1 head Bibb lettuce

Combine pineapple, avocado, and onion that has been separated into rings. Add mayonnaise, and toss very gently. Serve in lettuce cups or on Bibb lettuce leaves. Yield: 4 servings.

FROZEN FRUIT SALAD

2 envelopes (2 tablespoons) unflavored
    gelatin
½ cup cold water
¾ cup orange juice
¾ cup pineapple juice
⅓ cup whipping cream, whipped
3 tablespoons mayonnaise
¾ cup drained pineapple chunks
½ cup halved orange sections
½ cup drained sliced peaches
2 bananas, sliced
¼ cup maraschino cherries
½ cup chopped pecans
    Lettuce

Soak gelatin in cold water. Combine fruit juices; bring to a boil. Add gelatin, stirring until dissolved; chill until consistency of unbeaten egg white.

Combine whipped cream and mayonnaise; fold into gelatin mixture along with fruit and pecans. Spoon into a 4-cup mold; freeze. Unmold on lettuce, and garnish as desired. Yield: 6 servings.

RED APPLE SALAD

1½ cups sugar
¼ teaspoon salt
½ cup red cinnamon candies
3 cups water
4 firm tart apples, peeled and cored
1 (3-ounce) package cream cheese,
    softened, or ½ cup cottage cheese
¼ cup chopped green pepper or celery
    Lettuce

Combine sugar, salt, candies, and water; heat until candies are dissolved. Add apples; cover and cook slowly 15 to 20 minutes or until tender, turning occasionally to color evenly. Drain, and chill.

Combine cream cheese and pepper; spoon into apples. Serve on lettuce. Yield: 4 servings.

TABOOLEY SALAD

3 cups cold water
½ cup cracked wheat
4 cups coarsely chopped parsley
12 green onions, including tops chopped
½ cup chopped fresh mint
5 large ripe tomatoes, peeled, cubed
    small, and drained
½ cup lemon juice
½ cup olive oil
    Salt and pepper to taste

Place cold water in bowl, and add cracked wheat. Soak several hours or overnight before putting salad together. Drain well, squeezing out all possible water. Wash parsley thoroughly, and discard most of the stems before chopping it. In salad bowl, combine all ingredients, including salt and pepper. This is excellent with lamb. Yield: 10 to 12 servings.

FROZEN SPRING SALAD

1 envelope unflavored gelatin
1 cup cold water
⅓ cup sugar
½ teaspoon dry mustard
2 tablespoons freshly squeezed lemon
    juice
1 (8-ounce) carton commercial yogurt
2 (3-ounce) packages cream cheese,
    softened
1 (11-ounce) can mandarin oranges,
    drained
1 (16-ounce) can sliced peaches, drained
1 (17-ounce) can pitted dark sweet
    cherries, drained
½ pint whipping cream, whipped
    Lettuce

Soften gelatin in cold water; place over hot water to dissolve gelatin. Combine gelatin, sugar, mustard, lemon juice, yogurt, and cream cheese; beat until well blended. Chill until mixture thickens and begins to set. Beat until smooth. Fold in fruits and whipped cream. Pour into two 1-quart refrigerator trays or a 2-quart mold. Freeze. Unmold, and serve on lettuce. Yield: 6 to 8 servings.

GOLDEN SALAD

1 cup seedless raisins
¼ cup sherry
1 (20-ounce) can pineapple chunks,
    drained
2 cups shredded carrots
⅓ cup yogurt
    Lettuce or watercress

Soak raisins in sherry for 1 to 2 hours; drain. Combine pineapple, carrots, and raisins; add yogurt, and toss well. Chill, and serve on lettuce. Yield: 8 servings.

PASTA SALAD

 5 ounces vermicelli
 5 hard-cooked eggs, chopped
1½ cups finely chopped celery
 1 cup finely chopped sweet pickle
 2 to 2½ teaspoons onion salt
 1 cup mayonnaise
   Lettuce leaves
 1 (7½-ounce) can crabmeat, drained and
   flaked
   Paprika

Break vermicelli into pieces, and cook according to package directions. Drain, and rinse; let cool. Add eggs, celery, pickle, onion salt, and mayonnaise to vermicelli. Mix lightly, and chill. To serve, mound vermicelli mixture on bed of lettuce leaves. Top with crabmeat, and sprinkle with paprika. Yield: 6 to 8 servings.

HONEYDEW MELON BOATS

 ¾ cup seedless green grapes
 1 cup strawberry halves
 1 cup fresh orange sections
 1 honeydew melon, cut into quarters

Arrange fruit in melon quarters. Chill until ready to serve. Yield: 4 servings.

TEXAS COLESLAW

 1 cup sugar
 1 large cabbage, shredded
 1 large onion, thinly sliced
⅔ cup salad oil
 1 cup wine vinegar
 1 tablespoon celery seed
 1 tablespoon dry mustard

Sprinkle sugar over shredded cabbage and sliced onion; mix well. Combine oil, vinegar, celery seed, and dry mustard in saucepan; bring to a boil, stirring constantly. Pour hot sauce over cabbage-onion mixture, and toss well. Cover; refrigerate at least 8 hours. Yield: 8 servings.

PINEAPPLE-MINT SALAD

 1 (3-ounce) package lime-flavored
   gelatin
 1 cup boiling water
 1 cup pineapple juice
 2 drops of oil of peppermint
 1 cup crushed pineapple
 1 cup finely shredded white cabbage
   Dash salt
   Shredded lettuce

Dissolve gelatin in boiling water. Let cool; then add pineapple juice and oil of peppermint. Congeal until almost firm, and add crushed pineapple, cabbage, and salt. Turn into a wet 5-cup ring mold, and chill until firm. Unmold, and garnish with shredded lettuce. Yield: 6 servings.

YOGURT

 1 quart milk at room temperature
 1 teaspoon yogurt culture
   or 3 to 4 tablespoons commercial
   yogurt

Any kind of milk may be used except raw milk. If you have only raw milk, boil it 10 to 15 minutes before making yogurt. The caloric content will depend on the milk; skim milk will be lowest; half-and-half will make a very rich yogurt; evaporated milk, diluted, works, as does dry skim milk, reconstituted.

Stir culture (available at health food store) or yogurt into milk, and pour into glass or glazed ceramic containers. Do not fill to top. Place jars in pan of warm water (110°), and set pan in a place to maintain an even temperature of 100° to 110°, such as an unlit gas oven with a pilot light or a glass-doored electric oven with a light in it; in the latter case, just turn on the light, not the oven. Allow to stand without being jarred or disturbed for 4 hours. Examine it and if the yogurt has not yet reached the characteristic custardlike consistency, allow 2 to 3 more hours, checking each hour. If it stands in the heat too long, it becomes more acid in flavor. Yield: 1 quart.

Note: Yogurt sweetened with fruit makes an excellent low-calorie dessert. If fruit-flavored yogurt is desired, place crushed fruit in bottom of containers before adding yogurt. Do not stir. Five partially filled 1-cup containers will hold a quart of yogurt.

BUTTERMILK DRESSING FOR GREEN SALADS

1 small clove garlic, pressed for juice
½ green pepper, finely chopped
2 radishes, finely chopped
2 hard-cooked egg yolks, sieved
½ cup buttermilk
¼ teaspoon paprika
½ cup small-curd cottage cheese
1 teaspoon salt
  Juice of 1 lemon

Combine all ingredients in bowl, and mix well. If a very smooth dressing is desired, puree mixture in blender. Good on any green salad or on lettuce wedges. Yield: about 1⅔ cups.

BUTTERMILK SALAD DRESSING

1 tablespoon cornstarch
1 tablespoon dry mustard
  Dash paprika
¼ teaspoon onion salt
  Salt and white pepper to taste
1 cup buttermilk
2 eggs, beaten
½ cup vinegar
¼ cup lemon juice
  Sugar to taste

Combine cornstarch, dry mustard, paprika, onion salt, salt, and pepper in top of double boiler. Gradually stir in buttermilk and eggs. Cook, stirring constantly, over hot, not boiling, water until mixture begins to thicken. Remove from heat.

In a separate bowl, combine vinegar, lemon juice, and sugar. Gradually add to hot buttermilk mixture, beating well after each addition. Chill before serving. Good on fruit salads. Yield: 2 cups.

CLASSIC SALAD DRESSING

⅔ cup salad oil
¼ cup cider vinegar
2 tablespoons water
1 teaspoon salt
1 teaspoon sugar
¼ teaspoon pepper
2 cloves garlic, mashed
1 teaspoon prepared mustard
1 teaspoon creamy horseradish

Combine all ingredients in a jar, and shake well. Refrigerate at least 24 hours before using. Yield: about 1¼ cups.

GARLIC FRENCH DRESSING

⅓ cup vinegar
⅓ cup catsup
⅓ cup sugar
 1 small clove garlic, peeled and
    quartered
    About 1 teaspoon chopped onion
½ teaspoon salt
 1 cup salad oil, room temperature

Combine vinegar, catsup, sugar, garlic, onion, and salt in jar of electric blender. Blend until garlic and onion have disappeared. Without turning off motor, slowly add oil in a small but steady stream. Store in refrigerator. Shake before each use. Yield: 2 cups.

CREAMY FRENCH DRESSING

 1 teaspoon salt
½ teaspoon dry mustard
 3 to 4 tablespoons sugar
 3 tablespoons catsup
¼ cup undiluted evaporated milk
½ cup corn oil
 3 tablespoons vinegar

Combine all ingredients except vinegar in mixing bowl. Beat with rotary beater until smooth and well blended. Add vinegar all at once, beating until thoroughly mixed. Dressing will be creamy thick. Yield: about 1¼ cups.

AVOCADO SALAD DRESSING

 1 cup whipping cream, whipped
½ cup powdered sugar
⅛ teaspoon salt
¾ cup sieved, ripe avocado
 3 drops green food coloring

Whip cream, and add sugar; mix well. Add salt and avocado, and mix well. Stir in food coloring. Serve over fruit salads. Yield: 1¼ cups.

POPPY-SEED DRESSING FOR FRUIT

1¼ cups sugar
1½ teaspoons salt
 ½ cup wine vinegar
1½ teaspoons dry mustard
 2 tablespoons onion juice
 2 tablespoons poppy seeds
1½ cups salad oil, slightly warmed

Place all ingredients, except poppy seeds and oil, in electric blender jar, and blend for a few seconds. Without stopping motor, add poppy seeds and (very slowly) the oil. Keeps well in refrigerator and may be beaten again if it separates. Good with all fruit salads. Yield: about 3 cups.

LEMON-POPPY-SEED DRESSING

 2 tablespoons poppy seeds
¼ cup honey
½ cup salad oil
½ teaspoon ground cinnamon
¼ teaspoon ground coriander
¾ teaspoon salt
⅓ cup lemon juice

Put poppy seeds into blender; blend on high speed for 1 minute or until seeds are crushed. Add honey, salad oil, cinnamon, coriander, and salt. Blend until well mixed. Add lemon juice, and blend until creamy. Store in a tightly covered jar in refrigerator until ready to use. Yield: 1 cup.

HONEY FRUIT SALAD DRESSING

½ cup honey
¼ cup hot water
¼ cup lemon juice
¼ cup salad oil
¼ teaspoon salt
¼ teaspoon ground ginger

Combine all ingredients in small mixer bowl; beat until well blended. Store in a covered jar in refrigerator. Shake well before using. Yield: 1¼ cups.

HORSERADISH-CREAM SALAD DRESSING

½ cup whipping cream, whipped
¼ cup bottled horseradish, drained
¾ teaspoon salt
2 teaspoons sugar
  Dash cayenne pepper
4 drops hot pepper sauce
3 drops Worcestershire sauce
1 cup mayonnaise

Fold first 7 ingredients into the mayonnaise. Chill before serving. Use on fruit or vegetable salads. Yield: 2 cups.

PEANUT BUTTER-FRUIT DRESSING

½ cup orange juice
½ cup pineapple juice
¼ cup lemon juice
½ cup smooth or crunchy peanut butter
½ teaspoon salt
2 tablespoons honey or sugar

Combine fruit juices; gradually add to peanut butter, blending well. Stir in salt and honey. Store in covered container in refrigerator. Serve on fruit salads. Yield: 1½ cups.

EMERALD DRESSING

1 cup salad oil
⅓ cup vinegar
¼ cup chopped onion
¼ cup minced parsley
2 tablespoons finely chopped green
  pepper
2 tablespoons powdered sugar
1½ teaspoons salt
2 teaspoons dry mustard
½ teaspoon red pepper

Combine all ingredients in a jar; shake until well blended. Refrigerate at least an hour. Shake well before using. Serve with seafood, cottage cheese, or tossed green salad. Yield: about 1½ cups.

CREAM SALAD DRESSING

½ teaspoon salt
4 tablespoons sugar
1 teaspoon dry mustard
1 teaspoon all-purpose flour
1 egg, beaten
1 cup commercial sour cream
⅓ cup wine vinegar

Combine all ingredients except vinegar in top of double boiler; place over boiling water. Add vinegar slowly, stirring constantly as mixture cooks. Cook until mixture coats a spoon and is slightly thickened. Yield: about 1½ cups.

Seafood

Remember Botticelli's glorious painting of Venus standing demurely in the scallop shell? Not being an erudite student of art, I sometimes enjoy that painting by imagining a voluptuous scallop lolling in the shell.

People accustomed to the coastal regions, who take for granted the wealth of good seafood there, would have only to live inland for a month to know the depressing difference. Some landlocked cities are blessed with good markets that have fish flown in daily from the coasts. But many of us have to rely on the dubious largesse of the frozen food bins at the supermarket, or cans of what I think of as Neptune's leftovers. Many's the time I've dined on creamed tuna on oatmeal biscuits and dreamt of eating fresh crabmeat cocktail along Fisherman's Wharf in San Francisco.

Seafood in almost any form is high in protein and low in fat. Some forms of seafood are higher in fat than others, however. A few of the fattier ones (15 or more percent fat), in case you need to avoid them, are mackerel, pompano, salmon, sardines, and trout. Eel, running to 25 or 30 percent fat, you will just have to give up entirely.

SCALLOPED OYSTERS

2 cups cracker crumbs
⅛ teaspoon pepper
½ cup melted butter
1 pint standard-size oysters, drained
¼ teaspoon Worcestershire sauce
1 cup milk

Combine cracker crumbs, pepper, and butter; sprinkle one-third of mixture in a but-

tered 2-quart casserole, and cover with a layer of oysters. Repeat layers.

Add Worcestershire sauce to milk; pour over oysters. Sprinkle remaining crumbs over top. Bake at 350° for 30 minutes or until crumbs are brown. Yield: 6 to 8 servings.

CLAM PIE

2 (7-ounce) cans minced clams
1 cup chopped onion
¼ cup melted butter or margarine
¼ cup all-purpose flour
    Dash pepper
½ cup diced cooked carrots
½ cup chopped cooked celery
3 hard-cooked eggs, chopped
1½ cups seasoned mashed potatoes

Drain clams and reserve liquid. Add water to clam liquid to make 2 cups. Cook onion in butter until tender. Blend in flour and pepper; add clam liquid, and cook until thickened, stirring constantly. Add carrots, celery, eggs, and clams. Place in a well-greased 1½-quart casserole. Cover with mashed potatoes, and bake at 425° for 20 to 25 minutes or until brown. Yield: 6 servings.

LEMON-GARLIC BROILED SHRIMP

2 pounds unpeeled raw shrimp, fresh or frozen
2 cloves garlic, finely chopped
½ cup melted butter or margarine
3 tablespoons lemon juice
½ teaspoon salt
    Dash freshly ground pepper
    Chopped parsley

Thaw frozen shrimp. Peel shrimp; make a shallow cut lengthwise down the back of each and remove sand veins. Rinse shrimp with cold water; drain thoroughly.

Cook garlic in butter until tender. Remove from heat. Add lemon juice, salt, and pepper.

Arrange shrimp in a single layer in a 15- x 10- x 1-inch baking pan. Pour sauce over shrimp. Broil about 4 inches from heat for 8 to 10 minutes or until shrimp are tender. Baste once during broiling with sauce in pan. Sprinkle with parsley. Yield: 3 to 4 servings.

Note: If raw, shelled, deveined shrimp are used, use 1½ pounds.

CURRIED SHRIMP AND RICE CASSEROLE

Water
1 tablespoon salt
1 thick slice unpeeled lemon
1 bay leaf
4 pounds large raw shrimp
5 cups water
1 tablespoon salt
1½ cups regular white long grain rice
  Sauce
  Paprika

Bring a large pot of water to a boil; add salt, lemon slice, and bay leaf. Add shrimp to rapidly boiling water and, after water returns to a boil, cook shrimp for 10 minutes; drain, shell, and devein. Refrigerate until needed.

To cook rice, bring water to a boil in a large saucepan which has a tight-fitting lid; add 1 tablespoon salt; stir in the rice and boil rapidly, uncovered, for 18 to 20 minutes. Start tasting at 18 minutes; rice may be done at that point—it must not be mushy. Drain rice; return to the hot saucepan; cover with several paper towels; then place the lid on tightly, and return to the still warm eye on the stove, but with the heat turned off. Allow to stand until ready to use. (The paper towels will absorb all the moisture, and rice will be dry.)

Butter a large casserole. Starting with rice, arrange rice and shrimp in layers, pouring some of the Sauce over each layer, ending with rice. Sprinkle with paprika; cover, and bake at 350° for 30 to 40 minutes. Yield: 12 to 15 servings.

Note: For added glamor, reserve about 8 shrimp; place over top of casserole, and drizzle melted butter over them before baking the casserole.

Sauce:

6 tablespoons butter or margarine
3 tablespoons grated onion
5 tablespoons all-purpose flour
1 teaspoon curry powder
3 cups warm milk or half-and-half
1 teaspoon salt
  Dash white pepper
  Generous dash ground nutmeg
¼ cup dry sherry
1 tablespoon minced parsley

Heat butter in a large saucepan, and sauté onion until golden. Blend in flour and curry powder; cook for a few minutes, stirring constantly. Very slowly add warm milk, stirring constantly until thickened. Remove from heat; stir in salt, pepper, nutmeg, sherry, and parsley. Taste; add more seasonings, if mixture is too bland.

SHRIMP MEUNIERE

1½ pounds unpeeled raw shrimp, fresh or
frozen
¼ cup melted butter or margarine
1 tablespoon lemon juice
¼ teaspoon salt
Dash pepper

Thaw frozen shrimp. Peel shrimp, and remove sand veins. Wash thoroughly, and drain on absorbent paper. Sauté shrimp in butter, turning frequently, about 10 minutes or until lightly browned. Remove shrimp to platter.

Add lemon juice and seasonings to browned butter; pour over shrimp. Yield: 3 to 4 servings.

Note: You can use 1 pound uncooked shrimp already shelled and deveined.

SHERRIED SEAFOOD

2 cups oysters
5 tablespoons melted margarine, divided
1 cup sliced mushrooms
4 cups cooked, peeled, and deveined
shrimp
1 cup cooked, chopped chicken
2 (10¾-ounce) cans condensed cream of
mushroom soup
1 tablespoon grated onion
½ teaspoon pepper
1 teaspoon salt
1 tablespoon finely chopped parsley
2 tablespoons sherry
¼ teaspoon cayenne pepper
Hot cooked rice

Sauté oysters in 3 tablespoons margarine until edges curl; drain and set aside. Sauté mushrooms in remaining 2 tablespoons margarine; drain.

Combine all ingredients except rice; simmer over low heat 5 minutes, stirring occasionally. Transfer to a chafing dish set on low heat. Serve over rice. Yield: 10 to 12 servings.

HOT SEAFOOD SALAD

2 tablespoons butter or oil, divided
1 cup chopped celery
½ cup chopped onion
1 cup sliced fresh mushrooms
1 cup shrimp, cooked, canned or frozen,
cut up
1 cup crabmeat, cooked, canned or
frozen
1 cup mayonnaise
Salt and pepper to taste
½ teaspoon Worcestershire sauce
½ cup crushed saltines

Heat 1 tablespoon butter in skillet, and stir-fry the vegetables only until thoroughly heated. Remove from heat and add shrimp, crabmeat, mayonnaise, and seasonings. Spoon into 6 buttered individual shells or buttered 1½ quart casserole. Heat remaining butter, and combine with crumbs. Top seafood with buttered crumbs. Bake at 350° for 20 minutes or until thoroughly hot and lightly browned. Yield: 6 servings.

LOBSTER WAFFLES

½ pound cooked lobster meat
3 cups waffle mix
Cheese Sauce

Chop lobster meat. Prepare waffle mix as directed on package. Add lobster meat. Bake in hot waffle iron until brown. Serve with Cheese Sauce. Yield: 6 (7-inch) waffles.

Cheese Sauce:

1 (11-ounce) can condensed cheddar
    cheese soup
⅓ cup milk

Combine cheese soup and milk. Heat.
Yield: about 1¾ cups.

JELLIED ROCK LOBSTER MEDALLIONS

4 (8-ounce) packages frozen rock lobster
    tails
½ cup milk
½ envelope (1½ teaspoons) unflavored
    gelatin
½ cup mayonnaise
1 teaspoon lemon juice
1 cucumber, thinly sliced
1 (4-ounce) can broiled mushroom slices
    Shredded lettuce
    Creamy Wine Sauce

Drop frozen lobster tails into boiling salted
water. When water reboils, cook lobster 2
to 3 minutes. Drain immediately, and
drench with cold water.

Cut away underside membrane. Remove
meat from shells in one piece; reserve any
leftover bits of lobster to use in Creamy
Wine Sauce; chill. Retain shells for later
use.

Put milk in top of double boiler; sprinkle
gelatin over milk, and let stand a few minutes until softened. Gradually heat milk,
stirring constantly, until almost at the boiling point. Do not boil. Add mayonnaise and
lemon juice; mix thoroughly until smooth
and creamy. Cool.

Cut lobster meat crosswise into 1-inch
thick slices. Dip each slice into gelatin mixture, coating thoroughly on all sides. Place
a thin slice of cucumber and a slice of
mushroom on top of each slice. Chill.

To serve, arrange lobster shells on platters. Place a layer of shredded lettuce in
shells and top with jellied lobster slices.
Serve with Creamy Wine Sauce. Yield: 8
to 10 servings.

Creamy Wine Sauce:

    Leftover pieces of lobster meat
½ cup mayonnaise
½ cup commercial sour cream
    Few drops onion juice
    Salt and pepper to taste
¼ cup white wine

Grind leftover pieces of lobster meat; add
remaining ingredients, and blend well.
Yield: about 1¼ cups.

CREAMED LOBSTER ON TOAST

2 cups cooked lobster meat
4 tablespoons butter or margarine
2 tablespoons all-purpose flour
1 cup milk or half-and-half
2 tablespoons finely minced onion
½ teaspoon salt
¼ teaspoon white pepper
    Toast

Cut lobster meat into bite-size pieces; set
aside. Melt butter in skillet; stir in flour.
Add milk gradually; cook, stirring constantly, until smooth and thickened. Add
onion, salt, pepper, and lobster. Heat
thoroughly. Serve over toast. Yield: 6 servings.

CHICKEN AND LOBSTER MADEIRA

¼ cup butter
¼ cup minced onion
¼ cup all-purpose flour
1¼ cups milk
½ cup half-and-half
2 chicken bouillon cubes, crumbled
¾ cup fresh cooked or canned lobster, cubed
1½ cups cubed cooked chicken
1 (4-ounce) can mushrooms, drained
½ cup Madeira
Salt and pepper to taste
1 egg yolk, beaten
Cooked rice
Almonds (optional)

Melt butter in heavy 3-quart saucepan; add onion, and cook until transparent. Blend in flour, and add milk gradually, stirring. Add half-and-half and bouillon cubes. Cook, stirring constantly, until thickened and smooth. Add lobster, chicken, and mushrooms. Stir in wine, salt and pepper. Spoon out some of the hot liquid, and beat with the egg yolk; then stir back into pan. Cook over low heat, stirring gently, until sauce is thickened and serving temperature is reached. Serve over hot, cooked rice. Garnish, if desired, with almonds. Yield: 6 servings.

CRAB À LA DEWEY

4 scallions, chopped
2 tablespoons melted margarine
1 pound cooked crabmeat
1 cup dry white wine
1 (4-ounce) can mushrooms
½ cup mayonnaise
2 tablespoons all-purpose flour
¼ cup milk
4 baked tart shells

Sauté scallions in margarine about 5 minutes, stirring frequently. Add crabmeat and wine; cook 5 minutes and set aside. Drain mushrooms and reserve liquid.

Combine mayonnaise and flour in saucepan; add mushroom liquid and milk, stirring constantly, until mixture thickens; add mushrooms. Pour over crabmeat mixture; mix gently. Heat for 5 minutes. Serve in tart shells. Yield: 4 servings.

CREAMED CRABMEAT

4 tablespoons butter or margarine
4 tablespoons all-purpose flour
1 (13¾-ounce) can condensed chicken consommé
¼ cup sauterne
4 eggs, well beaten
4 tablespoons freshly squeezed lemon juice
1 cup crabmeat
Patty shells or toast points

Melt butter in blazer pan of chafing dish over direct heat. Stir in flour, and keep stirring until smooth. Gradually add chicken consommé and wine, stirring constantly until sauce is thickened and smooth. Remove from direct heat and place over hot, but not boiling, water.

Beat eggs in small bowl. Add lemon juice gradually, beating constantly. Gradually beat in about a cup of the warm sauce. Slowly stir this mixture into the rest of the sauce in chafing dish; mix well. Add crabmeat, and heat. Serve in patty shells. Yield: 4 servings.

CRAB STEW

1 dozen blue crabs, boiled
½ cup finely chopped celery
1 tablespoon finely chopped onion or
    chives
3 tablespoons butter
1 (10¾-ounce) can condensed cream of
    mushroom soup
1 cup milk
  Salt and pepper to taste
1 to 2 teaspoons dry sherry
  Lemon slices

Remove meat from bodies and claws of crabs. Sauté celery and onion in butter; add crabmeat, mushroom soup, and milk. Cook over low heat for 15 to 20 minutes, stirring frequently. Season to taste with salt and pepper.

Before serving, add sherry. Garnish with lemon slices. Yield: 4 servings.

CRABMEAT ROYALE

1 pound crabmeat
1 (4-ounce) can mushrooms, drained
¼ cup butter or margarine
1 tablespoon chopped onion
1 teaspoon Worcestershire sauce
¼ cup dry sherry (optional)
3 tablespoons all-purpose flour
1 cup milk
  Salt and pepper to taste
  Shredded cheese for topping

Remove all cartilage from crabmeat. Sauté drained mushrooms in butter for about 5 minutes. Add onion, and cook until onion is tender. Add crabmeat, Worcestershire sauce, and sherry, if desired.

Make a paste of flour and milk; add to crabmeat mixture, and cook until sauce thickens. Add salt and pepper. Spoon mix-ture into a 1-quart baking dish or individual shells or ramekins. Sprinkle shredded cheese over the top.

Bake at 350° for 5 minutes or until cheese melts, and mixture is bubbly. Yield: 6 serv-ings.

CRABMEAT FILLING FOR CRÊPES

½ cup chopped green pepper
2 tablespoons butter
4 tablespoons all-purpose flour
1 cup half-and-half
1 egg yolk, beaten
1 pound crabmeat
1 cup commercial sour cream
2 tablespoons grated Romano cheese
  Salt and pepper to taste
  Hollandaise sauce (optional)

Sauté green pepper in butter. Add flour and half-and-half, stirring constantly, cooking until thickened. Add a little of the hot mix-ture to the egg yolk; then stir back into the mixture in the saucepan. When quite thick, add crabmeat, sour cream, and cheese. Sea-son to taste, and heat to serving tempera-ture. Spoon over crêpes, and roll up. Top rolled crêpes with hollandaise sauce, if desired. Yield: 3½ cups.

BROILED BLUFFTON FLOUNDER

¼ cup dry white wine
2 pounds boned and fileted flounder
  Salt
  Lemon pepper

Pour wine into a greased, shallow baking dish. Place filets, skin side down, in dish; sprinkle with salt and lemon pepper. Broil 5 minutes or until fish flakes easily when tested with a fork. Yield: 4 servings.

TANGY BAKED SNAPPER

6 tablespoons tomato sauce
1 tablespoon lemon juice
2 tablespoons melted margarine
　Dash herb seasoned salt
2 (1½- to 2-pound) dressed red snappers
　Parsley
　Lemon slices

Combine tomato sauce, lemon juice, margarine, and salt. Wash, and dry fish; place in a lightly greased baking pan. Brush fish with sauce, inside and out.

　Bake at 350° for 1 hour or until fish flakes easily when tested with a fork. Garnish with parsley and lemon slices. Yield: 4 servings.

DILLY TROUT

2 pounds pan-dressed trout, fresh or
　frozen
1½ teaspoons salt
¼ teaspoon pepper
½ cup butter or margarine
2 teaspoons dillweed
3 tablespoons freshly squeezed lemon
　juice

Thaw frozen fish. Wash, and dry fish. Cut fish almost through lengthwise, and spread open. Sprinkle with salt and pepper. Melt butter in a 10-inch frying pan. Add dillweed. Place fish in a single layer, flesh side down, in the hot dill butter. Fry over moderate heat for 2 to 3 minutes. Turn carefully. Fry 2 to 3 minutes longer or until fish flakes easily when tested with a fork. Place fish on a warm serving platter. Keep warm. When all the fish have been fried, turn heat very low, and stir in lemon juice. Pour sauce over fish. Yield: 6 servings.

SALMON ROLL

1 (9¼-ounce) package piecrust sticks
1 (1-pound) can salmon, drained and
　flaked
1 small onion, chopped
1 medium-size green pepper,
　chopped
　Salt and pepper to taste
¼ cup milk

Prepare piecrust sticks according to directions on package, and roll out to ¼-inch thickness.

　Combine salmon, onion, green pepper, salt, pepper, and milk in a large bowl. Mix well, and spread to edges of dough. Roll carefully, jelly roll fashion, and cut into ¾-inch slices. Place on greased baking sheets. Bake at 400° for 30 minutes or until lightly browned. Yield: about 2 dozen.

SOUTHERN FAVORITE FISH

2 pounds flounder or other fish filets
1 teaspoon salt
　Dash pepper
1 cup all-purpose flour
½ cup melted butter or margarine
½ cup blanched slivered almonds
2 tablespoons chopped parsley

Cut filets into serving-size portions; sprinkle with salt and pepper, and dredge in flour. Sauté in melted butter. When fish is brown on one side, turn carefully, and brown other side. Total cooking time should be 7 to 10 minutes, depending on thickness of fish. Remove fish from pan, and place on a hot platter. Sauté almonds until lightly browned; add parsley, and serve over fish. Yield: 6 servings.

Game

A few years ago, when I ran a menu featuring quail, I was taken to task by one of my state's most ardent and effective conservationists. There followed a few exchanges of letters, during the course of which we became friends, agreeing that hunting seasons are stringently enforced, and the game and fish restocked on schedule by the state's fish and game conservation department. Now I count that gentleman among the most discerning critics, in the best sense of the word, of my work.

Not all of us are fortunate enough to number hunters among our friends and relations. But what joy it is to be a guest at a quail dinner or a feast of roast venison. The gift of wild duck or goose, complete with feathers and entrails, can seem a mixed blessing to the novice. Several years ago, a friend slowed down on his way home from a hunting trip and pitched a pair of wild ducks on my porch. An unforgettable experience was dressing them, with my brother telling me blow by blow, feather by feather, how to do it, by long distance telephone.

Game of any sort is a rare treat, worth any amount of trouble it takes to get it ready for cooking. Thrice happy is the recipient of freshly dressed, ready to cook, wild meat.

DOVE PILAU

12 doves
½ pound lean salt pork
4 medium-size onions, diced
4 cups uncooked regular rice
Salt and pepper

Cook doves in boiling water until meat comes off bones easily; drain, reserving stock. Dice meat, and set aside.

Fry salt pork until crisp; remove from skillet, and set aside. Add onion to drippings in skillet, and sauté until brown; add dove and salt pork.

Add enough water to reserved stock to make 8 cups liquid; bring to a boil. Add rice, and cook until tender. Season to taste with salt and pepper; stir in dove mixture. Yield: 6 to 8 servings.

Note: Quail, grouse, or chicken can be substituted for dove.

DOVE BREASTS STROGANOFF

12 to 18 dove breasts
1 medium-size onion, chopped
2 tablespoons melted butter or
    margarine
1 (10¾-ounce) can condensed cream of
    celery soup
1 (4-ounce) can mushrooms
½ cup sauterne
½ teaspoon oregano
½ teaspoon rosemary
    Salt and pepper to taste
1 teaspoon bottled brown bouquet sauce
1 cup commercial sour cream
    Cooked wild rice

Arrange meat in a large baking dish; do not crowd.

Sauté onion in butter. Add remaining ingredients, except sour cream and rice. Pour mixture over meat. Cover dish lightly with foil. Bake at 325° for 1 hour, turning occasionally.

Add sour cream; stir into sauce. Bake, uncovered, an additional 20 minutes. To serve, spoon over wild rice. Yield: 6 to 9 servings.

DOVES TEXAS STYLE

6 doves
⅔ cup minced onion
2 cloves garlic, minced
½ bay leaf
1 teaspoon peppercorns
½ cup melted margarine
1 cup white wine
1 cup water
2 cups whipping cream
½ teaspoon salt
⅛ teaspoon pepper
1 teaspoon chives

Clean doves, and set aside. Cook onion, garlic, bay leaf, and peppercorns in margarine until onion is tender. Add doves, and sauté until browned. Add wine and water, and simmer for 30 minutes. Remove doves; strain sauce into a 2-quart casserole, and gradually add cream to sauce. Stir remaining seasonings into sauce; add doves. Cover, and heat just to boiling. Serve hot. Yield: 6 servings.

RANCH-STYLE CREAMED QUAIL

Salt and pepper
12 quail, cleaned and dressed
1 pound butter or margarine
4 cups half-and-half
1 to 1½ cups toasted bread crumbs

Salt and pepper quail; simmer slowly in butter until tender. Add cream and continue simmering about 30 minutes until done. Remove quail to hot platter, and sprinkle with bread crumbs. Pour cream gravy over all. Yield: 12 servings.

QUAIL WITH WILD RICE

10 quail
1¼ cups melted butter or margarine, divided
1½ pounds chicken livers
2 large onions, chopped
1 green pepper, chopped
2 cloves garlic, minced
2½ cups cooked wild rice
2 cups chicken broth
1½ cups port

Truss body cavity of quail using wooden picks instead of nails. Sauté in ½ cup butter until quail are browned. Place in baking dish. Cover, and bake at 350° about 30 minutes.

While quail are baking, sauté livers, onion, pepper, and garlic in ¾ cup butter. Do not let vegetables brown, but cook until transparent. Stir in rice, chicken broth, and wine.

Spoon rice mixture into a 3-quart baking dish; cover, and bake at 325° about 20 minutes or until liquid is absorbed. Serve quail over rice. Yield: 8 to 10 servings.

SMOTHERED WILD DUCK

1 duck
1 teaspoon salt
¼ teaspoon pepper
½ cup all-purpose flour
½ cup salad oil
1 cup milk

Cut duck into 6 or 7 pieces. Season, and dredge in flour. Sauté duck slowly in hot oil about 30 minutes or until brown on both sides, turning only once.

Add milk; cover, and simmer slowly 1 hour, or bake at 325° for 1 hour. Yield: 3 to 4 servings.

DUCK WITH WILD RICE STUFFING

  1 (4-pound) duck
1½ cups uncooked wild rice
  ⅓ cup butter
  ½ cup chopped celery
  3 small onions, chopped
  2 teaspoons curry powder
  2 teaspoons salt
    Pepper to taste
    Orange Gravy
    Grapes
    Commercial cranberry sauce

Roast duck at 450° for 20 minutes. Pour off drippings, and reserve for Orange Gravy. Set duck aside. Cook wild rice according to directions.

Melt butter; add celery, onion, curry powder, salt, and pepper. Cook until celery and onion are wilted. Pour over wild rice, and mix well.

Stuff duck loosely with wild rice mixture (remainder of stuffing may be baked in a separate pan). Truss duck, and return to oven. Roast at 375° for 1½ hours. Serve with Orange Gravy. Garnish with grapes and slices of cranberry sauce. Yield: 4 to 6 servings.

Orange Gravy:

  3 tablespoons thin strips orange peel
  1 cup orange juice
  1 cup reserved pan drippings
  ½ teaspoon dry mustard
    Salt to taste
    Dash cayenne
  ⅓ cup red wine
  2 tablespoons currant jelly
  ¾ cup orange sections

Cover orange peel with orange juice, and simmer 20 minutes. Add drippings, sea-sonings, wine, and jelly; cook, stirring constantly, until jelly melts. Add orange sections just before serving.

ROAST WILD DUCK WITH CHESTNUT DRESSING

  8 chestnuts, cooked and mashed
  ¼ cup melted butter
  ½ cup bread crumbs
  ½ cup milk
  ¼ cup diced celery
  1 or 2 shallots
    Pinch sage
    Pinch rosemary
  ¼ cup white seedless raisins
    Salt and pepper to taste
  1 (2- to 3-pound) mallard
    Clove garlic
    Ground ginger
  3 slices bacon

Cut an X into the bottom of each chestnut with a sharp knife. To cook, either simmer for 20 minutes or bake for 20 minutes at 325°; then shell and mash.

To make dressing, combine chestnuts, butter, bread crumbs, milk, celery, shallots, sage, rosemary, raisins, salt and pepper; mix well.

Season cavity of duck with salt and pepper; rub outside with garlic, and sprinkle with ginger. Stuff cavity with dressing mixture; place bacon over breast.

Preheat oven to 450°, place duck in oven, and reduce oven temperature to 350°. Roast for 30 minutes, basting frequently. Remove bacon. Roast duck 30 minutes longer, basting frequently.

Remove dressing from cavity before serving. Serve dressing separately. Yield: 4 servings.

ROASTED WILD TURKEY

  1 (8- to 10-pound) turkey
    Salt and pepper
  8 cups dry bread cubes
  ¾ cup finely chopped celery
  ½ cup chopped walnuts
  2 to 3 teaspoons sage
  1 teaspoon salt
  ¼ teaspoon pepper
1½ cups chopped onion
  ¼ cup melted butter or margarine
  ¼ cup water
  4 slices bacon
    Bacon drippings

Rub turkey inside and out with salt and pepper.

Combine bread cubes, celery, walnuts, and seasonings. Sauté onion in butter until tender but not brown; pour over bread mixture. Add water, and toss lightly.

Lightly stuff turkey with dressing. (Put remaining dressing in a greased casserole. Cover, and bake in oven with turkey during last 30 minutes of roasting time.)

Truss bird. Cover breast with bacon slices and cheesecloth soaked in bacon drippings. Place turkey, breast up, on rack in roasting pan. Roast at 325° for 20 to 25 minutes per pound or until tender, basting frequently with bacon drippings in pan. Remove dressing from turkey. Yield: 8 to 10 servings.

VENISON ROAST

  4- to 5-pound venison roast
  ½ cup red wine
  1 bay leaf
  1 small onion (left whole)
  1 stalk celery (left whole)
  2 or 3 whole cloves or dash of ground
    cinnamon
    Juice of 1 lemon
  ¼ pound beef suet
    Pepper to taste
    Beef stock, defatted
    All-purpose flour

Put roast into a deep pan or Dutch oven; add wine and enough water to cover. Add remaining ingredients except beef stock and flour; cover, and simmer until roast is tender.

Remove roast to serving platter. Strain, and measure cooking liquid. Combine cooking liquid and an equal amount of beef stock; thicken with a small amount of flour to make a gravy. (For a medium-thick gravy, use 1½ tablespoons flour per cup measured liquid. Blend flour with cold water to make thin paste, and pour through strainer into pan liquid.) Serve with roast. Yield: 8 servings.

Note: Before slicing roast, you can cover it with bacon strips and place under broiler until bacon is crisp.

Beef and Veal

Red meat is apparently the American staff of life. Have you ever stood in line at the supermarket and heard a woman say, "My husband must have his steak, no matter what it costs"? Beef is delicious, and we love it. But in the light of the world food picture, would it not make sense for us to use more fish and poultry, more grain-legume combinations as an occasional substitute for a beef meal? Consider the ground beef with soy protein added; it is cheaper, and tastes as good as pure beef when used in combination dishes such as chili and meat loaf.

Veal, a staple in Switzerland, where it is difficult to winter-over cattle, is very scarce in this country. If you have a craving for Veal Scallopini, you may have to put your order in with the butcher days ahead of time. When circumstances conspire to get it on the table, there is no loftier morsel than veal. Treat it with respect in preparation; don't overseason and wreck the delicacy of flavor.

MEAT-LOAF MIDGETS

½ pound ground beef
½ cup soft bread crumbs
¼ cup chopped walnuts
2 tablespoons chili sauce
1 teaspoon seasoned salt
¼ cup milk

Mix all ingredients just until blended. Shape into 2 loaves. Bake at 350° for 35 minutes or until a rich brown. Yield: 2 servings.

MARINATED FLANK STEAK

1 cup soy sauce
½ cup water
1 tablespoon Worcestershire sauce
1 teaspoon sugar
1 teaspoon salt
1 clove garlic, crushed
1 jigger whiskey
⅛ teaspoon pepper
1 (1¼-pound) flank steak

Combine first 8 ingredients, mixing well; pour over steak. Cover, and marinate in refrigerator overnight, turning once.

Drain meat; broil to desired doneness. Slice across grain in thin slices. Yield: 4 to 6 servings.

Note: Leftover marinade may be stored in refrigerator and used again. This is also a good marinade for chuck roast.

UPSIDE-DOWN MEAT LOAF

½ cup sliced cooked carrots, diagonally cut
2 eggs
½ cup water
1 (1⅜-ounce) envelope dry onion soup mix
⅔ cup fine dry bread crumbs
⅓ cup snipped parsley
2 pounds ground lean beef

Arrange carrot slices in bottom of buttered 9- x 5- x 3-inch loaf pan. Beat eggs; mix in water, onion soup mix, bread crumbs, and parsley. Mix in ground beef. Pack meat mixture into loaf pan. Bake at 375° for 45 minutes.

Remove from oven, and let stand 15 minutes. Invert on serving dish. Yield: about 8 servings.

BURGER BAKE

1 pound ground beef
½ cup finely chopped green pepper
½ cup finely chopped onion
½ cup mayonnaise
1 teaspoon salt
1 egg, beaten
1 tablespoon water
¾ cup instant potato flakes
¼ cup salad oil
3 slices sharp pasteurized process
    American cheese
1 (10¾-ounce) can condensed cream of
    celery soup
⅓ cup milk
3 large English muffins, sliced and
    toasted

Combine beef, green pepper, onion, mayonnaise, and salt. Shape into 6 large patties. Combine egg and water. Dip patties into egg mixture; then coat with potato flakes. Brown lightly in hot oil.

Arrange patties in a shallow baking dish. Cut cheese into 6 triangles; place a triangle on each patty.

Combine soup and milk; heat and pour around patties. Bake at 350° for 12 to 15 minutes or until thoroughly heated. Serve on English muffin halves. Yield: 6 servings.

MEAT-FILLED GERMAN PANCAKES

6 eggs
1 cup all-purpose flour
½ cup milk
    Meat Filling
    Topping

To make pancakes, beat eggs, and add flour and milk alternately, beating to keep mixture smooth. Heat, and grease an 8-inch skillet. Pour in just enough batter (¼ to ⅓ cup) to cover bottom thinly. Rotate skillet to cover uniformly. When pancake is lightly browned, turn carefully, and brown other side very lightly. Stack pancakes on a warm plate as they are cooked. Spread one portion of Filling on each pancake, roll up, and place in oiled, 3-quart, rectangular casserole. Add Topping. Bake at 350° for 25 minutes or until piping hot and bubbly. Yield: 10 servings.

Meat Filling:

2 pounds ground chuck or
    round
2 eggs
1 tablespoon salt
½ teaspoon pepper
2 teaspoons ground nutmeg
¼ cup fine dry bread or cracker
    crumbs
¼ cup finely chopped onion
¼ cup finely chopped parsley
½ cup milk

Blend all ingredients, using hands. Mixture should resemble meat loaf, but be thinner so it will spread. Shape into a flat cake on waxed paper, and mark into 10 equal portions with a knife.

Topping:

1 pound Swiss cheese, shredded
2 cups commercial sour cream
¾ cup milk

Sprinkle cheese uniformly over stuffed pancakes. Mix sour cream with milk and pour over top.

CHUCK ROAST STEAK

1 (5-pound) chuck roast
½ cup salad oil
½ cup wine vinegar
½ cup catsup
1 teaspoon salt
1 teaspoon pepper
1 clove garlic, minced

Punch holes in roast with ice pick or sharp fork; place in a glass dish or enamel pan.

Make a marinade by combining remaining ingredients: pour over roast. Cover, and place in refrigerator for at least 12 hours. Cook on grill for 30 minutes on each side, basting with marinade. Reduce cooking time if well-done meat is not desired. Yield: 8 to 10 servings.

BEEF POT ROAST

½ teaspoon marjoram
2 bay leaves, crushed
1 clove garlic, crushed
1 small green pepper, minced
1 small onion, minced
¼ cup olive oil
1 (3- to 4-pound) chuck roast
1 (1-pound) can tomatoes
¼ teaspoon ground cinnamon
⅛ teaspoon ground cloves
2 cups red wine
2 teaspoons salt

Combine herbs, green pepper, onion, and olive oil; mash to a paste, and rub into roast. Let stand 1 hour. Brown roast in a heavy saucepan; add remaining ingredients. Cover, and simmer gently 3 to 4 hours or until very tender. Yield: 6 servings.

CUBE STEAKS WITH WINE SAUCE

2 (½-pound) cube steaks
Salt and pepper to taste
¼ teaspoon salad oil
1½ tablespoons melted butter or margarine
2 carrots, cut into strips
2 small onions, halved or quartered
1 teaspoon chopped parsley
¼ cup dry rosé
¼ cup evaporated milk
¼ teaspoon instant beef bouillon

Season steaks with salt and pepper; brown in oil and butter. Remove from skillet, and set aside.

Add carrots, onions, and parsley to skillet; sauté 5 minutes, stirring frequently. Add wine and steaks; cover, and cook over low heat until steaks are tender. Remove with slotted spoon, reserving cooking liquid.

Add evaporated milk and beef bouillon to cooking liquid; cook, stirring constantly, until smooth. Return steaks and vegetables to skillet; heat thoroughly. Yield: 2 servings.

BEEF TERIYAKI

¼ cup commercial Italian dressing
¼ cup soy sauce
2 tablespoons sugar
½ teaspoon ground ginger
2 pounds round steak, cut into ½-inch strips

Combine all ingredients except steak in a glass bowl; add steak, and toss well. Marinate about 30 minutes in refrigerator. Thread steak on skewers. Grill quickly, turning once and basting with remaining marinade. Yield: 6 servings.

COLONIAL POT ROAST

1 (3- to 4-pound) beef blade pot roast
¼ cup all-purpose flour
1½ teaspoons salt
⅛ teaspoon pepper
3 tablespoons salad oil
¼ cup water
1 medium-size onion, cut into quarters
1 beef bouillon cube
⅓ cup hot water
1 butternut squash, pared and sliced
2 medium-size tart apples, quartered
and cored

Dry meat with paper towel. Combine flour, salt, and pepper. Dredge meat in seasoned flour, reserving leftover flour. Brown meat in oil. Pour off drippings; add ¼ cup water and onion. Cover tightly; cook slowly for 2½ hours.

Dissolve bouillon cube in ⅓ cup hot water. Add bouillon, squash, and apples to meat. Cover tightly; cook for 30 to 35 minutes or until meat and vegetables are tender. Remove meat and vegetables to heated platter.

Thicken cooking liquid with reserved flour dissolved in a small amount of water. Serve with roast. Yield: 6 to 8 servings.

BRISKET IN BEER

1 (12-ounce) can beer
1 bay leaf
2 cloves garlic
½ teaspoon sage
¼ teaspoon ground cumin
2 teaspoons salt
1 small pod red pepper
1 (4-pound) piece fresh brisket of beef
2 tablespoons butter
2 tablespoons all-purpose flour

Make a marinade of beer, bay leaf, garlic (split and impaled on wooden picks), sage, cumin, salt, and pepper. Pour over beef, and refrigerate overnight. Next day, remove meat from marinade, and dry thoroughly. Remove garlic from marinade.

Heat butter in Dutch oven (or other heavy pot with cover), and brown the brisket on all sides. Pour marinade over meat, cover, and simmer 2½ hours or more, until quite tender. Remove meat to cutting board. Strain pan liquid into glass jar or measuring pitcher. Remove as much fat as possible from top. Return liquid to pan, reserving ¼ cup to combine with flour for thickening gravy. Make a smooth paste of the flour and liquid, and stir into pan juices. Cook and stir until thickened.

Slice meat very thin, diagonally across the grain; return to gravy and reheat. Yield: 8 to 10 servings.

Note: Easy way to marinate meat: Use a heavy nonleaking plastic bag; set in a bowl. Add meat and marinade; then close the plastic down, forcing out air. Fasten. Keep meat covered with liquid.

CORN BEEF HASH RING

2 (16-ounce) cans corn beef hash
2 tablespoons Worcestershire sauce
1 teaspoon dry mustard
2 (3½-ounce) cans French fried onions

Combine hash with seasonings; mix well. Pack into a well-greased ring mold. Bake at 375° about 50 minutes. Loosen ring carefully around edges, and invert on serving platter. Fill center with warmed, canned, French fried onion. Yield: 6 to 8 servings.

VEAL SCALLOPINI

⅓ cup all-purpose flour
1 teaspoon salt
⅛ teaspoon pepper
1½ pounds veal round steak
¼ cup shortening
½ cup water or chicken stock
1 clove garlic, crushed
1 teaspoon freshly squeezed lemon juice
1 medium-size onion, sliced
1 (4-ounce) can sliced mushrooms
8 medium-size stuffed olives, sliced
2 tablespoons grated Parmesan cheese

Combine flour, salt, and pepper. Pound seasoned flour into steak, and cut into serving-size pieces. Brown meat in shortening; remove from skillet, and put in casserole. Add water, garlic, and lemon juice to meat. Arrange onion, mushrooms, and olives over meat; sprinkle cheese on top. Cover tightly, and bake at 300° for 45 minutes to 1 hour or until meat is tender. Yield: 6 servings.

VEAL RUMP ROAST

3- to 4-pound veal rump roast
Salt
Pepper
4 to 6 slices bacon

Season roast with salt and pepper.

Place on rack in open roasting pan. Insert a meat thermometer so the tip reaches the center of the roast, but be sure that the tip does not rest in fat or on bone. Place bacon slices on roast. Do not add water. Do not cover. Roast at 300° for about 2 hours or until the meat thermometer registers 170°. Allow about 40 minutes per pound for roasting. Yield: 6 to 8 servings.

ROLLED VEAL SHOULDER-APRICOT GLAZE

3- to 4-pound rolled veal shoulder roast
1 (12-ounce) can apricot nectar
2 tablespoons frozen concentrated
    grapefruit juice, undiluted
½ cup firmly packed brown sugar

Place roast on rack in open roasting pan. Insert a meat thermometer so that the tip reaches the center of the roast. Do not add water or cover. Roast at 300° for 1½ hours.

While veal is cooking, prepare apricot glaze by combining remaining ingredients; simmer about 10 minutes. Cool. Remove veal from oven after cooking 1½ hours. Spoon about one-third of the glaze over roast. Continue cooking 20 minutes. Spoon another third of glaze over roast. Allow to cook another 20 minutes. Spoon remaining glaze over roast, and continue cooking until meat thermometer registers 170°. Allow about 40 minutes per pound total cooking time. Serve drippings as sauce with roast, if desired. Yield: 6 to 8 servings.

BREADED VEAL CHOPS

1 egg
2 tablespoons milk
6 veal rib chops, cut ½ inch thick
1 cup fine bread crumbs
¼ cup shortening
1 teaspoon salt
⅛ teaspoon pepper

Beat eggs slightly, and add milk. Dip chops in crumbs, then in egg mixture, and then in crumbs again. Brown in hot shortening, and season. Cook at moderate temperature until done, turning occasionally. Yield: 6 servings.

VEAL STEW

**2 pounds boneless veal shoulder, cut
    into 1½-inch cubes**
3 tablespoons shortening
1½ teaspoons salt
⅛ teaspoon pepper
½ teaspoon paprika
2½ cups water or chicken stock, divided
**4 medium-size carrots, cut into 1-inch
    pieces**
1 (4-ounce) can mushrooms
1 (10-ounce) package frozen peas
3 tablespoons all-purpose flour

Brown meat in shortening. Add seasonings
and 2 cups water. Cover, and simmer for
1½ hours. Add carrots and mushrooms,
and cook 15 minutes. Add peas, and cook
15 minutes longer. Combine flour and ½
cup water; add to stew, and cook over
medium heat until thickened. Yield: 6 to
8 servings.

STUFFED VEAL BIRDS IN SOUR
CREAM GRAVY

½ cup diced celery
¼ cup chopped onion
½ cup butter, divided
2 cups soft bread cubes
¾ teaspoon salt, divided
⅛ teaspoon sage
    Dash pepper
1 tablespoon chopped parsley
¼ cup milk
**8 (4- to 5-ounce) boneless veal cutlets,
    flattened**
⅓ cup all-purpose flour
¼ cup water
¼ cup white wine
1 cup commercial sour cream
1 (4-ounce) can mushrooms, drained

Sauté celery and onion in ¼ cup butter
until onion is tender. Combine with bread
cubes, ¼ teaspoon salt, sage, pepper, parsley, and milk; toss lightly.

Divide dressing evenly among cutlets,
placing dressing in center of each. Roll meat
around dressing, and fasten with wooden
picks or skewers. Roll meat in flour, saving
leftover flour. Brown meat in remaining ¼
cup butter, turning as necessary to brown
on all sides. Add water and wine; cover
tightly, and cook slowly until meat is
tender, about 45 minutes. Remove meat to
serving platter, and keep warm.

Blend together leftover flour and sour
cream. Stir into drippings; add mushrooms
and remaining ½ teaspoon salt. Cook, stirring constantly, until gravy is heated and
thickened. Serve with veal birds. Yield: 8
servings.

Note: Place each cutlet between sheets of
waxed paper. Flatten with mallet or foil-
wrapped brick.

BLANQUETTE OF VEAL

2½ pounds veal, cut into 1-inch cubes
    Salt and pepper
    All-purpose flour
**6 tablespoons melted butter or
    margarine**
3½ tablespoons all-purpose flour
5 cups chicken broth
2 tablespoons dried parsley flakes
¼ cup wine vinegar
1 teaspoon salt
¼ teaspoon pepper
¼ teaspoon thyme
¼ teaspoon rosemary
⅛ teaspoon ground cloves
**2 (16-ounce) cans small white onions,
    drained**

Sprinkle veal with salt and pepper; coat lightly with flour. Brown meat in butter in a heavy skillet; using a slotted spoon, transfer to a Dutch oven.

Blend 3½ tablespoons flour into butter remaining in skillet; stir constantly over low heat until smooth. Gradually add broth; cook, stirring constantly, until smooth.

Pour broth mixture over veal; add remaining ingredients except onions. Cover, and simmer 2 hours. Add onions just before serving; heat thoroughly. Yield: 6 servings.

Note: If a thicker gravy is desired, make a paste of 2 to 3 tablespoons additional flour and a small amount of cooking liquid. Gradually stir into veal; cook over low heat, stirring constantly, until smooth and thickened.

SESAME VEAL CHOPS

1 egg, beaten
2 tablespoons milk
¼ cup all-purpose flour
1 teaspoon salt
⅛ teaspoon pepper
1 teaspoon paprika
2 tablespoons sesame seeds, toasted if desired
6 rib veal chops, cut ½ to ¾ inch thick
⅓ cup shortening
2 (10-ounce) packages frozen or 2 (6-ounce) cans, drained, green beans, cooked
2 tablespoons finely chopped onion
1 (10½-ounce) can condensed celery soup
¼ cup milk
1 teaspoon salt

Combine egg and milk. Mix together flour, salt, pepper, paprika, and sesame seeds. Dip chops in egg mixture, then in flour mixture. Brown chops in shortening; pour off drippings. Combine green beans, onion, celery soup, milk, and salt; pour mixture into a 12- x 8-inch baking dish. Place veal chops on top. Cover, and bake at 300° for 45 minutes. Uncover, and continue baking 15 minutes. Yield: 6 servings.

SAVORY VEAL CHOPS WITH LIMAS

¼ cup all-purpose flour
1 teaspoon salt
⅛ teaspoon pepper
¼ teaspoon ground nutmeg
⅛ teaspoon savory
6 veal chops, cut ½ inch thick
¼ cup shortening
1 (10½-ounce) package frozen baby lima beans
1 cup tomato juice
1 bouillon cube

Combine flour, salt, pepper, nutmeg, and savory. Dredge chops in seasoned flour. Sprinkle any remaining seasoned flour over chops; brown in hot shortening. Remove chops from skillet, and pour off drippings. Place lima beans in skillet; add tomato juice and bouillon cube and place chops on top. Cover tightly and simmer 45 minutes to 1 hour or until chops and limas are tender. Yield: 6 servings.

Lamb

To me, one of life's mysteries is that Kentucky spring lamb, so coveted in Chicago, New York, and other cities, is almost without honor in its native state. Kentuckians will rave about their cured hams, but seldom mention that exquisite lamb they produce. Or someone will say, "I love lamb chops, but they're so expensive."

There is more to lamb than lamb chops. There are shanks; ask your butcher to collect them for you ahead of time. There are lamb fries, a delicacy so many overlook, and ground lamb patties, all of which come under the heading of less expensive ways to consume lamb. Leg of lamb, simply rubbed with salt and pepper, and seasoned with slivers of garlic inserted into slits in the meat has only to be roasted to be incredibly delicious.

Always a mainstay in the Middle East, lamb is used there in some ways unknown in this country. A vegetable such as green beans may be seasoned with lamb and a pinch of nutmeg. If you've never used your outdoor grill for a leg of lamb, boned and butterflied (opened up flat), marinated in a blend of oil, lemon juice, mint, salt, and garlic, you have a delicious treat in store. Serve it with a parsley based Tabooley salad. It is a feast you can envision being served by a wealthy desert sheik, with a luxurious tent and squealing camels in the background.

WALNUT GLAZED LAMB CHOPS

 4 loin lamb chops (1 inch thick)
   Salt to taste
 ¼ cup honey
 ¼ cup ground walnuts

Place chops on broiling rack 3 to 4 inches from source of heat; broil 5 to 7 minutes. Season with salt; turn and broil 5 to 7 minutes longer or to desired doneness. Season with salt.

Combine honey and walnuts; spread on chops. Broil 2 to 3 minutes longer. Yield: 2 to 4 servings.

LAMB CHOPS WITH ONIONS

 8 shoulder or loin lamb chops
   Salt and pepper to taste
 2 tablespoons melted margarine
 1 (16-ounce) can small white onions, drained
 1 (6-ounce) can frozen orange juice concentrate, thawed and undiluted

Season lamb chops; place chops in skillet, and brown lightly on both sides in margarine. Place chops and onions in a shallow roasting pan. Deglaze skillet with orange juice. Boil, stir, and pour over chops. Cover, and bake at 350° for 30 minutes. Uncover, and bake an additional 15 minutes or until tender, basting often. Yield: 8 servings.

GRILLED SIRLOIN LAMB CHOPS

 1 (1-inch thick) sirloin lamb chops
 ¼ cup salad oil
 3 tablespoons lemon juice
 ⅓ cup chopped stuffed olives
 1 clove garlic, crushed
 ½ teaspoon salt
 ¼ teaspoon oregano
 ¼ teaspoon basil
 ⅛ teaspoon pepper

Put lamb chops in a shallow dish. Combine oil, lemon juice, olives, and seasonings; pour over lamb chops. Marinate in refrigerator 2 or 3 hours, turning chops once.

Grill chops 3 to 4 inches from source of heat 8 minutes on each side or until desired degree of doneness. Heat marinade in a small saucepan, and pour over chops before serving. Yield: 4 servings.

MARINATED ROAST LEG OF LAMB

 5 cups red wine
½ cup gin
¼ cup olive oil
 2 teaspoons dried thyme
 3 whole cloves
 2 to 3 small cloves garlic, crushed
10 peppercorns, crushed
 1 (5-pound) leg of lamb

To make marinade, combine first 7 ingredients in a saucepan. Bring to a boil; lower temperature, and simmer 5 minutes. Cool.

Put leg of lamb in double bag (use either heavy plastic bags or large oven bags). Pour marinade over lamb and seal bag tightly. Place in refrigerator to marinate for 5 days. Turn several times each day.

Remove lamb from marinade, and place on rack in a shallow roasting pan. Do not cover. Insert meat thermometer into thickest part of leg, being sure bulb does not rest in fat or on bone.

Roast at 325° to desired degree of doneness. Meat thermometer will register 165°–170° for medium rare, 175° for medium and 180° for well done. Allow 30 to 35 minutes per pound for roasting; total roasting time should be 2½ to 3 hours. Yield: 6 to 8 servings.

Note: Lamb is at its best when served medium-rare, slightly pink at center.

CURRIED LAMB STEW

 2 pounds lamb shank, neck, or shoulder
 3 tablespoons all-purpose flour
 2 tablespoons chopped onion
 2 tablespoons salad oil
1½ cups boiling water
 1 (8-ounce) can tomato sauce
1½ cups 1-inch celery strips
 1 to 1½ teaspoons curry powder
 1 teaspoon salt
 1 green pepper, cut into strips
 3 cups cooked rice

Cut meat into 1-inch cubes; trim off excess fat. Dredge meat in flour, and cook very slowly with onion in salad oil until meat is brown on all sides. Add water slowly. Add tomato sauce, celery, curry, and salt; cover, and simmer for 1½ hours. Add green pepper; cover, and continue cooking until vegetables and meat are tender. Serve over hot cooked rice. Yield: 6 servings.

ARNI PSITO

 1 (5- to 7-pound) leg spring lamb
 3 cloves garlic, thinly sliced
 1 tablespoon oregano
   Salt and pepper
¼ cup melted butter
   Juice of 3 lemons

Remove all fell (tissue-like covering) from lamb. Insert garlic in slits made with a sharp knife at 2- or 3-inch intervals on lamb. Combine oregano, salt, pepper, butter, and lemon juice; brush lamb with this mixture. Bake at 350° for 30 to 35 minutes per pound or until thermometer registers 165°-170° for medium rare, or 175° for medium well done. Yield: 6 to 8 servings.

KRAUT-BARBECUED LAMB

1 cup sauerkraut juice
1 medium-size onion, sliced
2 cloves garlic, cut into halves
¼ teaspoon celery seeds
¼ teaspoon pepper
1 (5- to 6-pound) leg of lamb
⅓ cup honey
1 teaspoon lemon juice

Prepare marinade by combining kraut juice, onion, garlic, celery seeds, and pepper. Put lamb in a shallow glass dish, and pour marinade over meat; cover, and chill 1 day. Turn lamb occasionally.

Skewer lamb on rotisserie spit. Place spit about 8 inches above heat, and cook 30 minutes per pound for medium. Blend honey and lemon juice; heat, and brush on lamb during last 30 minutes of cooking time. Yield: 8 servings.

GRILLED BUTTERFLIED LEG OF LAMB

Leg of lamb, 6 to 7 pounds
2 cloves garlic, minced
2 teaspoons salt
¾ teaspoon dried mint, or fresh mint to
      make ½ teaspoon juice when put
      through garlic press
½ teaspoon coarsely ground black pepper
2 tablespoons onion, finely minced
⅔ cup olive oil
⅔ cup lemon juice

Have the butcher bone and "butterfly" the lamb. He will make a few cuts and spread the meat so that the thickness is fairly uniform and the meat shaped somewhat like a butterfly. Combine all remaining ingredients to make marinade. Place a strong plastic bag in a bowl, add the meat, and pour in the marinade. Shape, squeeze, and pull bag tightly around the meat so all is covered by marinade. Tie top. Marinate at least 2 hours at room temperature or overnight in refrigerator.

At cooking time, drain off marinade, saving some for basting meat as it cooks.

Grill over medium-hot coals 1½ to 2 hours, turning and basting every 15 minutes; meat should be slightly pink, not too well done. To carve, remove skewers, and slice thinly, diagonally. Yield: 10 to 12 servings.

KABOBS OF LAMB

6 tablespoons lemon juice
¼ cup salad oil
2 tablespoons grated onion
½ teaspoon cayenne
1 teaspoon ginger
1 clove garlic, crushed
2 teaspoons curry powder
1 tablespoon salt
4 pounds lamb, cut into 1-inch cubes
20 fresh mushroom caps
2 green peppers, cut into 1-inch squares
2 tablespoons melted butter
20 cherry tomatoes
4 onions, quartered
1½ cups pineapple chunks
      Cooked brown rice

Combine lemon juice, salad oil, grated onion, cayenne, ginger, garlic, curry powder, and salt; add lamb cubes, and marinate 24 hours.

Sauté mushrooms and green peppers in butter. Alternate meat, vegetables, and pineapple on skewers; brush with marinade. Grill 10 to 15 minutes over medium heat, basting with marinade and turning occasionally. Serve over brown rice. Yield: 8 servings.

ROCKY MOUNTAIN LAMB RIBLETS

1 (12-ounce) bottle hot catsup
½ cup orange juice
¼ cup chopped parsley
¼ teaspoon celery seeds
¼ teaspoon crushed rosemary leaves
3 pounds lamb riblets

Combine catsup, orange juice, parsley, celery seeds, and rosemary. Put riblets in a glass dish; add sauce and marinate overnight.

Remove lamb to a large skillet; reserve marinade. Brown riblets thoroughly. Arrange riblets in a 2-quart flat baking dish; add marinade. Cover; bake at 375° for 35 to 40 minutes or until tender. Yield: 4 to 6 servings.

JIFFY LAMB DINNER

6 slices bacon
6 lamb patties
  Salt and pepper
6 canned pineapple slices
6 large tomatoes
1 cup whole kernel corn
6 potatoes, peeled and boiled
2 tablespoons shredded cheddar cheese

Wrap bacon around lamb patties, securing with toothpicks. Season patties with salt and pepper, and place on broiling rack with pineapple slices. Broil until patties are browned. Turn patties, placing them browned side down on pineapple slices.

Core tomatoes, and fill with corn; place on broiling rack along with potatoes. Sprinkle potatoes with cheese. Broil until patties are done and tomatoes and potatoes are thoroughly heated and slightly brown. Yield: 6 servings.

LAMB KABOBS

1 (3- to 4-pound) loin of lamb
1 cup red wine
¼ cup olive oil
3 cloves garlic, crushed
  Salt and pepper to taste
  Dash oregano

Cut lamb into 2-inch squares. Combine remaining ingredients in a glass dish or enamel pan. Place lamb in marinade. Cover and keep in refrigerator for 2 or 3 days.

Remove meat from marinade, and thread on skewers. Reserve marinade. Cook over low heat about 25 to 30 minutes for well-done lamb. Brush often with marinade while meat is cooking. Yield: 6 to 8 servings.

SHERRIED LAMB IN PATTY SHELLS

¼ cup sliced scallions
¼ pound mushrooms, sliced
¼ cup melted butter or margarine
¼ cup all-purpose flour
1½ teaspoons salt
¼ teaspoon rosemary
⅛ teaspoon pepper
1 cup half-and-half
¾ cup milk
2 cups diced cooked lamb
2 tablespoons chopped pimiento
2 tablespoons dry sherry
1 (10-ounce) package frozen patty shells

Sauté scallions and mushrooms in butter until tender; stir in flour and seasonings. Gradually add half-and-half and milk; cook, stirring constantly, until sauce thickens and boils. Stir in lamb, pimiento, and sherry; heat thoroughly.

Bake patty shells according to package directions; fill with hot sherried lamb. Yield: 6 servings.

Pork

Everyone has his favorite foods; one of mine is country ham. To my mind, southern cured ham is reason enough for pork's existence. But there are others; possibly I'm partisan because of my rural southern Kentucky upbringing during the Depression. Everyone who could raised his own pork, and our homemade sausage, sugar-cured hams, bacon, and canned pork tenderloin stand out in my mind as luxuries in the midst of deprivation. Beef was almost unknown to our table; it took a visitor of unbounded importance to bring about the purchase of beef, as we did not raise our own.

Unfortunately, pork has a reputation for containing an overabundance of fat. The fact is that nutritious pork, trimmed of all visible fat, is as lean as beef (leaner than prime, well-marbled steak), because pork is not marbled with fat as is beef. A fresh or "green" roast of ham or shoulder is food for the angels, and I've always looked forward to breakfast the day after the roast is served, for cold roast of pork is unparalleled as an accompaniment for breakfast eggs.

THREE-IN-ONE HAM

Purchase shank half of smoked ham. Have butcher cut ¾- to 1-inch slice from large end and a generous piece of shank for use in soup recipe to follow. Have him weigh the large center piece to be used as a roast.

Ham and Potatoes in Cream Sauce:

> 1 (¾- to 1-inch thick) slice ham
> 1 (16-ounce) can white potatoes, drained
> 1 (10¾-ounce) can condensed cream of mushroom soup
> 1 soup can milk

Place ham slice in shallow baking dish. Arrange potatoes around it. Combine soup with milk, and pour over ham and potatoes. Bake at 350° for about 1¼ hours or until ham is very tender. Yield: 4 servings.

Roast Ham:

> Large center cut of ham, weighed
> Orange juice
> Whole cloves

Refer to pork roasting chart to find roasting time for the size of the meat. Roast uncovered. When done, brush with orange juice, and stud with cloves. Return to oven 15 minutes to glaze. Yield: Depends on size. Estimate ¼ to ⅓ pound per person.

Ham Shank Soup:

> Ham shank from Roast Ham recipe
> 1 cup split peas or lentils
> 1 medium-size onion, chopped
> 1 medium-size carrot, chopped
> 1 tablespoon dried parsley
> 1 teaspoon celery salt
> Dash pepper
> Cold water to cover
> Salt to taste

Place ham shank in large kettle with remaining ingredients. Bring to boil, reduce heat, and simmer for 2 hours. Lift out ham shank and, when cool enough to handle, pick lean meat from bone, and return to soup. Discard bone and fat. Add salt, if necessary: some ham cures are saltier than others. Yield: 4 to 6 servings.

Note: This soup freezes well.

SPICED COTTAGE HAM

1 (2-pound) boneless shoulder butt ham
1 tablespoon pickling spice
2 or 3 additional whole cloves
  Cold water to cover

Remove wrapping from ham; place in a pan with a well-fitting lid. Place pickling spice in palm of the hand, and rub over the ham. Add cloves. Cover with cold water, put on lid, and simmer gently 2 hours or until very tender. Serve hot or cold. Yield: 6 servings.

HAM WITH RED WINE AND GRAPES

2 tablespoons butter or margarine
2 tablespoons sugar
¼ teaspoon ground cloves
1 (1½-inch thick) center slice (about 2½ pounds) smoked ham
¾ cup dry red wine
1 tablespoon cornstarch
¼ cup cold water
1 cup seedless green grapes

Melt butter in large skillet; add sugar and cloves. Quickly brown ham on both sides in the skillet mixture. Remove ham. Pour wine into skillet and cook, stirring, until it boils. Combine cornstarch with water, and stir into wine; then cook until thickened, stirring constantly. Return ham to skillet, and heat gently 15 minutes. Add grapes, and cook 2 minutes, just until grapes are hot. Transfer ham to warm platter, and spoon grapes and wine sauce over meat. Yield: 6 servings.

MISSISSIPPI STUFFED HAM AND DRESSING

Bake ham half-done. Skin; remove all but ¼ inch fat. Turn over, and insert boning knife at the hock and split, following the bone carefully. Cut bone out of the meat, leaving as little meat on it as possible. When bone is removed, fill cavity with Dressing, pressing it well into all cut places. Pour in a little melted butter. Sew up the ham with a cord. Make enough Dressing to cover entire ham (½-inch thick). Moisten with juice of ham, and wrap in cheesecloth. Bake at 275°. Leave cheesecloth on until ham is cold. Yield: Depends on size. Estimate ¼ to ⅓ pound per person.

Dressing:

1 pound bread crumbs
3 cups crumbled corn bread
1 teaspoon ground cloves
1 teaspoon ground allspice
1 teaspoon ground ginger
1 teaspoon ground mace
1 teaspoon onion salt
1 teaspoon garlic salt
1 teaspoon pepper
½ cup molasses
2 tablespoons mustard
3 eggs, well beaten

Mix the crumbs, corn bread, and all spices well. Add molasses, mustard, and eggs. Moisten with juice of ham, and fill cavity.

HAM LOAF MARY ANN

2 pounds smoked ham
2 pounds fresh pork shoulder
2 cups graham cracker crumbs
2 eggs, beaten
1½ cups milk
1 cup canned condensed tomato soup
½ cup vinegar
1 cup firmly packed brown sugar
1 tablespoon dry mustard

Grind the meats once separately, then grind them together, using fine blade. Mix ground meats with crumbs, eggs, and milk. Form mixture into 2 oval loaves, and place in open roasting pan. Mix soup, vinegar, brown sugar, and mustard; pour over loaves. Bake at 300° for 2 hours. Yield: 8 to 10 servings.

BARBECUED HAM MONIQUE

1 (8- to 10- pound) picnic ham (smoked shoulder)
2 tablespoons whole cloves
1 (1⅛-ounce) can red pepper*
1 cup vinegar
1 cup firmly packed brown sugar
1 (4-ounce) bottle liquid smoke
1 (14- to 16-ounce) bottle commercial barbecue sauce

Put ham into a large pot with enough water to almost cover it. Add cloves, pepper, vinegar, and sugar. Bring to boil; then reduce heat to medium, and cook about 2½ hours or until tender.

Drain water from ham. Skin ham and score it in a pattern of squares or diamonds. Pour the liquid smoke and barbecue sauce over it and bake at 200°, uncovered, with meat thermometer inserted so tip touches

neither bone nor fat. Thermometer will register 160° when ham is done. Yield: about 20 servings.

*You *do* use the entire can.

HERBED ROAST OF PORK

1 tablespoon all-purpose flour
1 (4-pound) center-cut pork loin roast
¼ teaspoon marjoram
¼ teaspoon thyme
¼ teaspoon rosemary
    Dash pepper
1½ teaspoons salt
1 or 2 medium-size onions, sliced
½ cup cider, apple juice, or dry white wine
    Oven Sauerkraut

Put flour into small (10- x 16-inch) oven bag; shake to coat evenly. Place bag in a 2-inch deep roasting pan.

Trim excess fat from roast. Sprinkle roast with herbs, pepper, and salt; pat in firmly, and set aside.

Place onion slices in bag. Slide in roast; add cider. Close bag with twist tie, and puncture six ½-inch slits in top. Insert meat thermometer through bag into thickest part of roast; do not let thermometer touch bone. Cook at 325° for 2 to 2½ hours or until thermometer registers 170°. Serve with Oven Sauerkraut. Yield: 6 to 8 servings.

Oven Sauerkraut:

1 tablespoon all-purpose flour
2 pounds sauerkraut, drained
1 tart apple, sliced
1 onion, sliced
1 bay leaf
1 teaspoon caraway seeds
1½ cups cider or apple juice

Put flour into small (10- x 16-inch) oven bag; shake to coat evenly. Place bag in 2-inch deep pan. Place all ingredients in bag. Close bag with twist tie and puncture six ½-inch slits in top. Cook at 325° for 1 hour. Yield: 6 to 8 servings.

PORK AND SAUERKRAUT

1 (16-ounce) can sauerkraut, drained
1 (3½- to 4-pound) pork loin roast
2 medium-size onions, sliced
  Salt and pepper to taste

Put half of sauerkraut into Dutch oven, and place roast on kraut; cover with onion and remaining sauerkraut. Season with salt and pepper.

Cover, and place in 375° oven. Bake for 2 to 2½ hours or until meat is very tender. If sauerkraut becomes dry while cooking, add a small amount of hot water. Yield: 6 to 8 servings.

PORK ROAST PLATTER

1 pork loin roast (4 to 5 pounds)
2 cloves garlic, cut into slivers
  Salt and pepper
1 (23-ounce) can sweet potatoes packed in syrup
6 canned pineapple slices
6 canned crabapples

Make small slashes in roast, and stuff each with slivers of garlic. Sprinkle roast with salt and pepper. Place, fat side up, on rack in shallow open pan. Insert meat thermometer in center of roast (do not let thermometer touch bone). Roast at 325° for 2½ to

3 hours or until thermometer reaches 170°. Remove from oven, and let stand 20 minutes for easier slicing; remove garlic slivers.

Heat sweet potatoes in mixture of their syrup and juice drained from pineapple slices. Arrange roast on a heated serving platter; surround it with sweet potatoes, pineapple rings, and crabapples. Glaze sweet potatoes and fruit with hot syrup. Yield: 6 servings.

PORK RIBS WITH ONION SAUCE

4 pounds pork ribs or pork tips, cut into serving-size pieces
2 cups sliced onion
2 cloves garlic, minced
1 tablespoon salad oil
¼ cup vinegar
¼ cup chili sauce
3 tablespoons firmly packed brown sugar
2 tablespoons lemon juice
2 tablespoons Worcestershire sauce
1 teaspoon dry mustard
½ cup water
1½ teaspoons salt

Place ribs, meaty side down, in a shallow roasting pan. Roast at 450° for 30 minutes. Drain off excess fat. Turn ribs meaty side up.

Sauté onion and garlic in hot oil until tender; add remaining ingredients. Simmer 10 minutes. Pour sauce over ribs.

Reduce oven temperature to 350°; bake ribs about 1½ hours or until tender, basting occasionally with sauce. If sauce gets too thick, add more water. Yield: 6 servings.

OVEN-BARBECUED SPARERIBS

4 pounds spareribs
1 large onion, sliced
1 lemon, sliced
1 cup catsup
⅓ cup Worcestershire sauce
1 teaspoon bottled commercial chili
  sauce
1 teaspoon salt
2 dashes hot pepper sauce
2 cups cold water
2 small garlic cloves, minced
1 tablespoon olive oil
1 teaspoon vinegar
½ teaspoon dry mustard

Cut ribs into serving-size pieces, and place in shallow baking pan, meaty side up. On each piece place a thin slice of onion and of lemon. Roast in 450° oven, uncovered, for 30 minutes. Drain off all fat.

Combine remaining ingredients in saucepan, and bring to rolling boil. Pour over ribs, and bake, uncovered, at 350° for 45 minutes or until tender. Baste with pan juices every 15 minutes, adding a little water, if necessary. Yield: 4 servings.

GLAZED PORK KABOBS

½ cup apricot preserves
½ cup tomato sauce
¼ cup firmly packed brown sugar
¼ cup dry red wine
3 tablespoons lemon juice
2 tablespoons salad oil
1 teaspoon onion juice
4 large carrots, cut into 1-inch slices
1½ pounds lean boneless pork, cut into
    1-inch cubes
  Fresh pineapple chunks
  Salt and pepper

Combine apricot preserves, tomato sauce, brown sugar, wine, lemon juice, salad oil, and onion juice; boil, uncovered, 10 to 15 minutes.

Parboil carrots about 5 minutes. Alternate pork, pineapple, and carrots on skewers; season. Grill 10 minutes over medium heat, turning occasionally. Baste with apricot sauce, and grill 5 additional minutes.

PORK CHOPS WITH APPLE-ONION SAUCE

4 center-cut pork chops, cut ¾ inch thick
  Salad oil
¼ cup water
  Salt and pepper to taste
2 cups diced apple
½ cup chopped onion
2 tablespoons melted butter or
    margarine
½ cup commercial sour cream
1 teaspoon lemon juice
½ teaspoon onion salt
  Paprika
  Chopped parsley

Brown chops on both sides in a small amount of salad oil. Pour off drippings, and add water, salt, and pepper. Cover and cook over low heat for 45 minutes. Put chops on platter and keep warm.

Sauté apple and onion in butter over low heat for 5 minutes. Add sour cream, lemon juice, and onion salt; cook about 5 minutes. Spoon over chops, and garnish with paprika and parlsey. Yield: 4 servings.

HERB-FLAVORED PORK CHOPS

8 (1-inch thick) loin pork chops
3 cups tomato juice
1 teaspoon salt
½ teaspoon pepper
1 to 2 tablespoons basil

Put pork chops into flat container. Combine remaining ingredients, and pour over chops. Marinate in refrigerator for several hours.

Remove chops carefully from marinade so that basil clings to chops. Cook over low heat on grill until meat is done, basting with marinade as meat cooks. Turn chops often. Yield: 8 servings.

SWEET AND PUNGENT PORK

2 tablespoons salad oil
1 teaspoon salt
1 clove garlic, minced
1 pound lean pork, cut in ½-inch cubes
1 cup chicken consommé, divided
1 (8½-ounce) can pineapple tidbits, drained
1 green pepper, cut into strips
2 cups sliced celery
2 tablespoons cornstarch
2 teaspoons soy sauce
⅓ cup vinegar
¼ cup sugar
Hot cooked rice

Heat salad oil, salt, and garlic in skillet; add pork cubes and sauté until brown. Add ⅓ cup consommé, pineapple, green pepper, and celery. Cover; and simmer 15 minutes. Blend together remaining ingredients except rice with ⅔ cup consommé; add to pork mixture, stirring until thickened. Serve with rice. Yield: 4 servings.

HAWAIIAN BAKED PORK

2 cups crushed pineapple
3 medium-size sweet potatoes
2 tablespoons firmly packed brown sugar
4 pork shoulder steaks
Salt and pepper
4 strips bacon

Place pineapple in 1 large baking dish or 4 individual ones. Pare and slice sweet potatoes; place over pineapple, and sprinkle with brown sugar.

Season pork steaks with salt and pepper, and place on top of sweet potatoes. Arrange bacon strips on top.

Cover, and bake at 350° until sweet potatoes and chops are tender (about 1 hour). To brown steaks and bacon, remove cover, and increase temperature to 450° during the last 10 minutes of cooking. Yield: 4 servings.

COUNTRY SKILLET

1 pound bulk sausage
½ cup thinly sliced onion
2 (14¾-ounce) cans macaroni and cheese
1 cup cooked cut green beans
¼ teaspoon caraway seeds

Shape sausage into 4 patties; brown in skillet. Add onion. Cover; cook over low heat for 20 minutes or until sausage is done. Remove sausage; pour off drippings. Stir remaining ingredients into skillet. Top with sausage. Cover; heat, stirring occasionally. Yield: 4 servings.

Poultry

Where would we be without chicken? You could buy a truckload of the critters, and cook each one in a tantalizingly different way. Prices fluctuate, but chicken and turkey generally are among the best meat buys in the market, year in and year out.

High in protein and low in fat (take off the skin before broiling or baking if you have a low-fat diet to contend with), poultry can be as simple or as dressy as the occasion demands. The penny-wise cook will bake poultry with bread dressing in it or under it, or she may simmer it with plenty of flavorful additives, take off the meat for casseroles and salads, and save the broth to use instead of water to augment flavor in soup and vegetable cookery.

Cornish game hens are a good buy per serving if you purchase the 20-ounce frozen birds and have the butcher saw them into halves. The halves, baked on a savory rice mixture, make an excellent dinner for most select company. In menu planning, remember that poultry is especially complemented by fruit accompaniments, such as baked curried fruit or congealed salad. And if the recipe you are using for your bird is a bland one, that is a signal to serve with it one of the stronger-flavored vegetables, such as Brussels sprouts or broccoli.

BAKED MUSTARD CHICKEN

1 teaspoon salt
1 broiler-fryer chicken, quartered
¼ cup prepared mustard
1 tablespoon vinegar
1 tablespoon water
1 tablespoon salad oil
½ teaspoon dried leaf thyme

Sprinkle salt on both sides of chicken. Place, skin side up, in foil-lined shallow baking pan. Combine other ingredients, and spoon over chicken. Bake, uncovered, at 375° for 50 to 60 minutes, basting occasionally. Yield: 4 servings.

CHICKEN AND RICE MEXICALI

2 tablespoons all-purpose flour
1 teaspoon garlic salt
1 teaspoon paprika
8 large pieces frying chicken
  Salad oil
1 cup finely chopped onion
1 clove garlic, minced
½ cup finely chopped green pepper
1 teaspoon chili powder
2 cups regular rice
1 (30-ounce) can tomatoes
1 (4-ounce) can green chiles, chopped
1 (10-ounce) package frozen whole kernel corn
3½ cups chicken broth
1 teaspoon salt
½ teaspoon pepper

Combine flour, garlic salt, and paprika; dredge chicken in flour mixture and brown slowly in hot salad oil. Remove chicken. Measure oil left in pan, and return ¼ cup to pan. Add onion, garlic, green pepper, and chili powder. Cook until vegetables are soft.

Add rice to vegetables; cook a few minutes until heated, stirring occasionally. Stir in all remaining ingredients except chicken. Spoon into shallow casserole.

Tuck chicken pieces into rice mixture. Cover. Bake at 375° about 50 to 60 minutes until rice is tender and liquid is absorbed. Yield: 8 servings.

COUNTRY CAPTAIN

3½ to 4 pounds chicken thighs, legs, and
    boned breasts
  All-purpose flour
  Salt and pepper to taste
1 cup shortening
2 onions, finely chopped
2 green peppers, chopped
1 small clove garlic, minced
1½ teaspoons salt
½ teaspoon white pepper
3 teaspoons curry powder
2 (16-ounce) cans tomato wedges,
    undrained
½ teaspoon chopped parsley
½ teaspoon ground thyme
¼ cup currants
  Hot cooked rice
¼ pound slivered almonds, toasted
  Parsley for garnish

Remove skin from chicken. Combine flour,
salt and pepper. Dredge chicken in flour
mixture, and brown in hot shortening.
Remove chicken from skillet, but keep it
hot (this step is important for the success
of the dish).

Pour off all but ¼ cup drippings from
skillet. Add onion, green pepper, and garlic;
cook very slowly, stirring constantly, until
vegetables are tender. Season with 1½ teaspoons salt, ½ teaspoon white pepper, and
curry powder (amount of curry powder may
be varied according to taste). Add tomatoes,
½ teaspoon parsley, thyme, and currants;
stir gently to mix.

Put chicken in a roaster or large casserole;
add sauce. If sauce does not cover chicken,
add water. Cover tightly and bake at 350°
about 45 minutes or until the chicken is
tender.

Place chicken in center of a large platter,
and pile rice around it. Spoon sauce over
rice; sprinkle almonds on top. Garnish with
parsley. Yield: 8 to 10 servings.

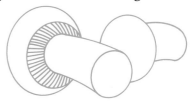

OLD-STYLE CHICKEN TETRAZZINI

1 (4-pound) chicken, cut up
1 medium-size onion
1 teaspoon peppercorns
  Salt
1 teaspoon sugar
1 bay leaf
1 stalk celery with tops
5 quarts water
1 (16-ounce) package spaghetti
2 cups sliced mushrooms
1 large onion, chopped
1 green pepper, chopped
1 (2-ounce) jar pimiento, chopped
2 tablespoons melted margarine
  Velouté Sauce
  Grated Parmesan cheese

Combine chicken, whole onion, peppercorns, 1 tablespoon salt, sugar, bay leaf,
celery, and water; simmer about 3 hours
or until chicken is tender. Remove chicken
from bones, and cut into small pieces; set
aside.

Strain broth, reserving 2 cups for Velouté
Sauce; bring remaining broth to a boil, and
add salt to taste. Cook spaghetti in boiling
broth until tender.

Sauté mushrooms and chopped vegetables in margarine; set aside. Combine
chicken, spaghetti, vegetables, and Velouté
Sauce. Spoon mixture into a 3-quart casserole; top with Parmesan cheese. Bake at
400° for 20 minutes. Yield: 10 to 12 servings.

CUBAN CHICKEN WITH RICE

1 large frying chicken, cut up
3 tablespoons shortening
1 medium-size onion, chopped
2 cloves garlic, minced or pressed
1 small green pepper, finely
    chopped
1½ tablespoons olive oil
1 (8-ounce) can tomato sauce
1 small bay leaf
¼ teaspoon oregano
    Pinch cumin
    Dash pepper
    Dash saffron
2 cups water
½ cup beer
1 cup uncooked long grain regular
    rice
½ (8½-ounce) can green peas
1 (2-ounce) jar pimiento pieces
1 (16-ounce) can asparagus spears

Soak cut-up chicken in enough salted water to cover overnight. Dry well, and brown, a few pieces at a time, in hot shortening. Transfer to small roaster or Dutch oven. Combine onion, garlic and green pepper with olive oil in small skillet, and sauté until onion is transparent. Add, along with tomato sauce, to chicken.

Add bay leaf, oregano, cumin, pepper, and saffron. Add water, and cook over medium heat 15 minutes. Add beer and rice. Bring to boiling; then reduce heat to low. Stir mixture once at this point; do not stir again. Cook, covered, until rice is done (about 45 minutes). Remove from heat, add peas, and replace lid. Let stand 15 minutes.

To garnish and serve, arrange chicken and rice on warm platter, and top with drained pimiento pieces. Drain asparagus spears, and arrange, tips toward center, like spokes in a wheel. Yield: 4 servings.

CHICKEN FILLING FOR CRÊPES

3 tablespoons chopped onion
6 tablespoons butter
½ cup all-purpose flour
2 cups milk or 1 cup milk and 1 cup
    chicken stock
    Salt to taste
    Dash pepper
    Dash paprika
3 tablespoons chopped chives (optional)
6 tablespoons sherry
1 (4-ounce) can sliced mushrooms,
    drained
1 cup shredded Swiss cheese
3 cups diced, cooked chicken
    Sauce

Sauté onion in butter. Blend in flour. Add milk; cook, and stir until mixture boils thoroughly. Add salt, pepper, paprika, chives, sherry, mushrooms, and cheese. Lightly mix with chicken. Chill for easier handling. This mixture should be very thick. Spoon filling on crêpes, and roll up. Place rolled crêpes in buttered dish. Cover with Sauce. Yield: filling for 14 crêpes.

Sauce:

3 tablespoons chopped onion
6 tablespoons butter
½ cup all-purpose flour
2⅔ cups milk or 1⅓ cups milk and 1⅓ cups
    chicken stock
    Salt to taste
    Dash pepper
    Dash paprika
3 tablespoons chopped chives (optional)
6 tablespoons sherry
1 (4-ounce) can sliced mushrooms,
    drained
1 cup shredded Swiss cheese
    Grated Parmesan cheese

Combine all ingredients as directed. Pour thin sauce over crêpes, and bake at 375° for 15 to 20 minutes. Sprinkle with grated Parmesan cheese. Serve immediately. Yield: sauce for 14 crêpes.

CHICKEN BREASTS SUPREME FOR TWO

  2 chicken breasts
  ½ (10¾-ounce) can condensed cream of
      mushroom soup
  3 tablespoons dry onion soup mix

Place each chicken breast on a square of heavy-duty aluminum foil. Combine soup and soup mix; spread half on each chicken breast. Wrap foil securely. Bake at 350° for 1 hour. Yield: 2 servings.

CHICKEN BREASTS WELLINGTON

  6 whole chicken breasts, boned and split
    Seasoned salt
    Seasoned pepper
  1 (6-ounce) package long grain and wild
      rice
  ¼ cup grated orange peel
  2 eggs, separated
  3 (8-ounce) cans refrigerated crescent
      dinner rolls
  1 tablespoon water
  2 (10-ounce) jars red currant jelly
  1 tablespoon prepared mustard
  3 tablespoons port
  ¼ cup lemon juice

Flatten chicken breasts with foil wrapped brick or meat mallet; sprinkle each with seasoned salt and pepper.

Cook rice according to package directions; add orange peel. Cool. Beat egg whites until soft peaks form; fold into rice mixture.

On floured surface, roll 2 triangular pieces of dinner roll dough into a circle. Repeat with remaining rolls until you have 12 circles. Place a chicken breast in center of each circle. Spoon about ¼ cup rice mixture over chicken; roll chicken jelly roll fashion. Bring dough up over stuffed breast. Moisten edges of dough with water and press together to seal. Place, seam side down, on large baking sheet. Slightly beat egg yolks with water; brush over dough. Bake, uncovered, at 375° for 45 to 50 minutes or until breasts are tender. If dough browns too quickly, cover loosely with foil.

Heat currant jelly in saucepan; gradually stir in mustard, wine, and lemon juice. Serve warm with chicken. Yield: 12 servings.

CHICKEN IN WINE

  4 whole chicken breasts, split
  ¼ cup soy sauce
  ¾ cup red wine
  ¼ teaspoon ground oregano
  1 clove garlic, minced
  ¼ cup salad oil
  4 tablespoons water
  1 teaspoon ground ginger
  1 tablespoon firmly packed brown sugar
    Parsley flakes

Place chicken breasts, flat side down, in a shallow casserole dish. Combine remaining ingredients; pour over chicken. Bake, covered, at 350° for 1 hour. Yield: 4 servings.

BAKED CHICKEN AND RICE FOR TWO

2 chicken breasts
  Melted butter or margarine
½ cup uncooked regular rice
1 (10¾-ounce) can condensed chicken
  broth
⅛ teaspoon celery seeds
⅛ teaspoon celery salt
½ teaspoon parsley flakes
½ teaspoon green pepper flakes
1 (6-ounce) can water chestnuts, sliced
  Salt and pepper to taste

Brush chicken with butter; place in a flat casserole, and bake at 350° about 20 minutes. Add remaining ingredients; cover, and bake at 350° about 40 minutes or until chicken is tender and rice is done. Yield: 2 servings.

STUFFED CHICKEN BREASTS SAVANNAH

4 whole chicken breasts, skinned,
  boned, and halved
4 thin slices boiled ham, cut in half
4 thin slices Swiss cheese, cut in half
½ cup all-purpose flour, divided
1 egg, slightly beaten
⅔ cup fine dry bread crumbs
½ cup plus 2 tablespoons melted butter
  or margarine, divided
1 cup dry white wine
¼ cup finely chopped onion
½ teaspoon salt
  Pepper to taste
1 cup milk
1 cup half-and-half
  Chopped fresh parsley
  Hot cooked rice or noodles

Place chicken breasts between sheets of waxed paper and flatten with meat mallet or foil wrapped brick. Place a slice of ham and cheese on each chicken breast; roll up, and secure with toothpicks. Dredge rolls in ¼ cup flour, and dip in egg; coat well with bread crumbs.

Lightly brown on all sides in ¼ cup butter. Add wine; simmer, covered, 20 minutes. Place rolls in a shallow baking dish, reserving drippings.

Sauté onion in 6 tablespoons butter until tender, stirring occasionally; blend in ¼ cup flour, salt, and pepper. Gradually add milk and half-and-half, stirring constantly, until smooth. Add reserved drippings; simmer, stirring constantly, until smooth and thickened.

Pour sauce over rolls; bake, uncovered, at 325° for 20 minutes. Garnish with parsley. Serve over rice. Yield: 8 servings.

CHICKEN ORIENTAL

1 (4-ounce) package blanched slivered
  almonds
3 tablespoons peanut or salad oil
½ cup chopped onion
4 chicken breasts, boned and thinly
  sliced
1 (6- to 8-ounce) can bamboo shoots,
  drained
1 (6-ounce) can water chestnuts, drained
  and sliced
1 cucumber, unpeeled and thinly sliced
½ cup chicken stock or broth
2 teaspoons sherry or dry white wine
¼ teaspoon ground ginger
1 teaspoon soy sauce
½ teaspoon cornstarch
1 tablespoon cold water
  Dash salt
  Dash pepper
  Cooked rice or noodles

Place almonds in shallow pan, and brown in oven at 400° for 8 to 12 minutes. Pour oil into wok or skillet; heat at 375° for 3 minutes. Add onion, and stir-fry for 1 minute; push onion up sides of wok. Add one-fourth of chicken, and stir-fry for 1 minute; push up sides of wok. Repeat with remaining chicken. Add bamboo shoots and water chestnuts; stir-fry for 1 minute, and push up sides of wok. Add cucumber, and stir-fry for 1 minute.

Combine chicken stock, sherry, ginger, and soy sauce; add to wok and cook for 1 minute, uncovered. Combine cornstarch and water in small bowl; slowly stir into hot liquid in wok. Add salt and pepper. Stir, and heat about 2 minutes until liquid thickens. Reduce heat to warm for serving, and gently stir all foods together with sauce. Serve over cooked rice or noodles; sprinkle with the toasted almonds. Yield: 4 to 6 servings.

TART 'N' TANGY CHICKEN

  2 whole chicken breasts, split
    Salt and pepper to taste
½ cup melted butter or margarine
    Juice of 2 lemons
  1 tablespoon prepared mustard
  1 teaspoon seasoned salt
⅓ cup ground pepperoni, salami, or
    pastrami

Sprinkle chicken breasts with salt and pepper; place, meaty side down, in a shallow baking pan.

Combine butter, lemon juice, mustard, and seasoned salt; pour over chicken. Sprinkle with ground meat. Cover pan with heavy-duty aluminum foil, and bake at 400° for 45 minutes.

Remove foil; turn chicken over. Broil for a few minutes to brown. Drippings may be served over green vegetables. Yield: 4 servings.

20-MINUTE TURKEY À LA KING

1½ cups cooked turkey (or chicken), cut
    into bite-size pieces
  1 (10½-ounce) can condensed cream of
    mushroom soup
½ teaspoon dried green onion
¼ teaspoon paprika
⅛ teaspoon freshly ground white pepper
  1 tablespoon dried or frozen chopped
    parsley
  1 (2-ounce) jar pimiento, drained and
    finely chopped
  1 (4-ounce) can button or sliced
    mushrooms (optional)
  2 tablespoons sherry
    Paprika
    Parsley

Place all ingredients except the sherry in the top of a double boiler over rapidly boiling water. Cook for 10 to 12 minutes. Taste to see if salt is needed. Add sherry, and remove from heat. Serve over melba toast, corn bread squares, or toasted English muffins. Sprinkle a little paprika over each serving, and add a sprig of fresh parsley, if available. Yield: 6 to 8 servings.

Note: Keep a supply of frozen cooked turkey on hand, and unexpected company will never catch you unaware. You can buy a turkey when it is cheap, cook it, cut into bite-size pieces, and freeze in packages of 1½ to 2 cups each. Dump the frozen meat directly into the double boiler and this adds only 10 minutes more to the preparation of 20-Minute Turkey à la King.

TURKEY ENCORE

2 cups diced cooked turkey
½ cup boiled chopped chestnuts
½ cup cranberry sauce
1 teaspoon paprika
½ teaspoon tarragon
½ teaspoon thyme
½ teaspoon marjoram
6 tablespoons mayonnaise
1 tablespoon Worcestershire sauce
½ teaspoon hot sauce
4 chicken bouillon cubes
1 cup boiling water
3 envelopes (3 tablespoons) unflavored
    gelatin
3 tablespoons cold water
Sliced stuffed olives

Combine first 10 ingredients in a large mixing bowl.

Dissolve bouillon cubes in boiling water. Sprinkle gelatin into cold water; add to boiling bouillon mixture, and cook until gelatin has dissolved. Cool.

Add gelatin mixture to turkey mixture; mix well, and spoon into a 9- x 5-inch loaf pan. Chill until firm. Unmold, and garnish with olives. Yield: 8 servings.

TURKEY SPANISH RICE

2 slices bacon
1 medium-size onion, chopped
½ green pepper, chopped
½ cup uncooked regular rice
1 (16-ounce) can tomatoes
1½ cups tomato juice
½ teaspoon paprika
1 teaspoon salt
¼ teaspoon pepper
2 cups cubed cooked turkey

Fry bacon until crisp; drain, and crumble, reserving drippings. Sauté onion and pepper in bacon drippings until tender. Add bacon and remaining ingredients; bring to a boil. Pour into a greased 2-quart casserole. Cover, and bake at 350° about 1 hour or until rice is tender. Garnish as desired. Yield: 6 to 8 servings.

Eggs

Often the novice cook who is willing to attempt almost anything else pauses with apprehension at the prospect of preparing an omelet or other egg dish. And, true, a tough, dry omelet or a plate of rubbery scrambled eggs can be most unappetizing. But a well-prepared egg dish has many pluses: such dishes can have great eye appeal; they are quickly and easily made for a last minute meal for the family or drop-in guests; and egg main dishes provide the protein which each of us needs in a form that is lighter and cheaper and a change of pace from our standard protein source, meat. In addition, eggs work well in a humble meal and just as well in an elaborate menu—from the lowly fried egg to the picnic-time deviled egg to the elegance of Eggs Benedict, whose preparation is illustrated in Part II.

Banish your hesitation; the main trick in preparing egg dishes is the timing: the eggs, whether poached, fried, scrambled, coddled, or whatever, should cook slowly long enough to "set" but not long enough to dry out and harden. That is, the finished product should be firm enough to hold its outside shape, yet moist inside. Pay careful attention to timing as you practice and you will soon find yourself adept at producing perfect eggs and omelets.

CAVIAR OMELET

3 eggs
3 tablespoons water
⅜ teaspoon salt
⅛ teaspoon pepper
1 tablespoon butter, margarine, or oil
2 tablespoons red caviar
Commercial sour cream

Mix eggs, water, salt, and pepper with a whisk or fork until yolks and whites are blended.

Heat butter in a 7- or 8-inch omelet pan or heavy skillet until it is just hot enough to sizzle a drop of water. Pour in egg mixture all at once.

With a fork, lift cooked portions at the edges so uncooked portions flow underneath. Slide pan rapidly back and forth over heat to keep mixture in motion and sliding freely to avoid sticking.

When the mixture is set properly, it no longer flows freely and is moist and creamy on top. Spread caviar over surface. Cook omelet about 1 more minute to brown bottom slightly. Fold or roll, and top with sour cream. Serve immediately. Yield: 1 to 2 servings.

SALMON EGG FOO YUNG

6 eggs
½ cup finely chopped onion
¼ cup milk
1 teaspoon salt
Dash pepper
1 (8-ounce) can salmon, drained and flaked
1 (16-ounce) can bean sprouts, drained
Butter or margarine
Soy sauce (optional)

Combine eggs, onion, milk, salt, and pepper; beat until well blended but not foamy. Add salmon and bean sprouts.

Melt butter on griddle over medium heat. Pour salmon mixture onto hot griddle, allowing ¼ cup per patty. Cook until browned on bottom; turn and brown other side. Serve with soy sauce, if desired. Yield: about 14 patties.

CHINESE OMELET

1 (16-ounce) can Chinese vegetables
1 (4-ounce) can sliced mushrooms,
    drained
½ cup finely chopped green onion
2 teaspoons chopped parsley
1 cup chopped cooked shrimp
6 tablespoons butter or margarine,
    divided
2 teaspoons soy sauce
1 teaspoon salt
1 teaspoon pepper
8 eggs, divided
4 tablespoons milk, divided
    Salt and pepper to taste

Combine vegetables, parsley, shrimp, 2 tablespoons butter, soy sauce, 1 teaspoon salt, and 1 teaspoon pepper; cook until liquid is absorbed.

For each omelet, combine 2 eggs, 1 tablespoon milk, and salt and pepper to taste; beat well.

Melt 1 tablespoon margarine in a 9-inch skillet; pour in eggs, and cook until set. Spread one-fourth of vegetable mixture over half of omelet; fold over, and cook about 3 minutes. Serve immediately, or keep hot until time to serve. Repeat until all omelets are cooked. Yield: 4 servings.

COOL WEATHER OMELET

6 eggs, separated
⅓ cup milk
2 teaspoons dried chopped chives
    Dash pepper
3 tablespoons butter or
    margarine
½ cup shredded Swiss cheese
    Sauce

Beat egg whites until stiffened. Beat egg yolks until thickened and lemon colored; beat in milk, chives, and pepper; fold into whites.

Melt butter in an ovenproof skillet; pour in eggs. Cook over low heat about 5 minutes or until lightly browned on bottom. Then bake in 350° oven for 10 minutes or until top springs back when pressed with fingers.

Transfer omelet to platter. Make a shallow cut down center; sprinkle with cheese, and pour on part of sauce. Fold omelet in half; pour more sauce over top. Serve extra sauce in a sauceboat. Yield: 4 servings.

Sauce:

1 (4-ounce) can sliced mushrooms,
    drained
1 tablespoon melted butter or margarine
1 (10½-ounce) can chicken giblet gravy
½ cup thin strips cooked ham

Sauté mushrooms in butter in a saucepan. Add gravy and ham. Heat, stirring occasionally. Yield: about 2 cups.

CUBAN EGGS

8 hard-cooked eggs
½ teaspoon salt
    Dash pepper
1 teaspoon dry mustard
1 tablespoon half-and-half
1 cup shredded sharp cheddar cheese,
    divided
1 small onion, minced
½ medium-size green pepper, minced
2 tablespoons melted butter or
    margarine
2 (8-ounce) cans tomato sauce
    Hot cooked rice

Cut eggs in half lengthwise, and remove yolks. Mash yolks; add seasonings, half-and-half, and half the cheese. Mix well, and stuff whites. Place stuffed eggs in shallow baking dish.

Sauté onion and green pepper in butter for 5 minutes. Add tomato sauce; heat. Pour over eggs. Sprinkle with remaining cheese. Bake at 400° about 15 minutes. Serve over rice. Yield: 4 servings.

A LITTLE EGG FOO YUNG FOR TWO

3 eggs
½ (16-ounce) can Chinese vegetables, well drained
¼ cup finely chopped cooked meat or shrimp
2 teaspoons soy sauce, divided
2 teaspoons sherry, divided
3 tablespoons oil
1 chicken bouillon cube
¾ cup hot water
1 teaspoon cornstarch
1 (8-ounce) can tiny peas
Salt and pepper to taste
2 teaspoons butter

Beat eggs with fork. Blend in Chinese vegetables (freeze the other half can of vegetables for next time), meat, 1 teaspoon soy sauce, and 1 teaspoon sherry.

Heat oil in heavy 9- or 10-inch skillet. Ladle egg mixture to form patties in the hot oil; mixture should make about 8 patties. Do not crowd. Fry only until lightly browned on both sides. Remove to 2 warmed plates. Keep warm while sauce is made.

In small saucepan, crush bouillon cube, and add hot water. Combine cornstarch with 1 teaspoon soy sauce and 1 teaspoon sherry. Add to bouillon and cook, stirring, until transparent and slightly thickened. Pour over egg patties. Garnish plates with peas which have been seasoned with salt and pepper and butter. Yield: 2 servings.

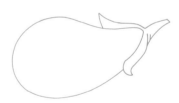

Casseroles

Think of the following recipe as a formula for building a casserole. Even the novice cook can create a masterpiece using her imagination to combine ingredients accordingly.

Casseroles are among the most economical dishes you can prepare and are a great way to use leftovers. Be it a main dish or accompanying one, the casserole is fun to prepare and even more fun to eat.

YOUR SIGNATURE CASSEROLE FOR 4

1 cup (or more) cooked meat, cut up
1 cup satellite ingredient
1½ cups (approximately) bready or starchy ingredient
1½ cups binder
¼ cup surprise ingredient
½ cup crumb topping
1 tablespoon butter

The *meat* ingredient may be any leftover pork, beef, seafood, poultry, or perhaps a can of tuna.

The *satellite* or *secondary ingredient* can be sliced celery, peas, mushrooms, or any compatible vegetable. A leftover vegetable is also good to use. If a raw vegetable is used, cook it before adding.

A *bready* or *starchy ingredient* is needed to give substance to the mixture and to stretch the meat. One cup cooked rice, macaroni, or noodles will do. But if you are using crushed corn chips, potato chips, or Chinese noodles, use 2 cups. Seasoned stuffing mix is especially good in a poultry casserole.

The *binder*, which holds everything together in a savory way, can be a well-seasoned medium white sauce, leftover gravy, or a can of cream soup extended with milk to total 1½ cups.

The *surprise ingredient* can be sliced water chestnuts, almonds, sliced stuffed olives, black olives, or pimiento. Use your imagination.

Crumb topping can be bread crumbs made in the blender, or perhaps crushed cereal, corn chips, potato chips, or Chinese noodles. Stir them in a skillet with butter.

Mix up everything but the topping, pitch it into a buttered 1½ quart casserole, top with crumbs, and bake at 350° about 25 minutes or until thoroughly hot and bubbly. Yield: 4 servings.

SWISS-SAUSAGE CASSEROLE

6 slices bread
2 pounds mild bulk sausage
1 teaspoon prepared mustard
½ pound Swiss cheese, shredded
3 eggs
1¼ cups milk
¾ cup half-and-half
¼ teaspoon salt
Dash pepper
Dash ground nutmeg
2 teaspoons Worcestershire sauce

Arrange bread in a lightly greased 13- x 9-inch pan. Sauté sausage; drain thoroughly. Combine sausage and mustard; sprinkle over bread. Place cheese over sausage.

Combine remaining ingredients; beat well. Pour mixture over sausage; refrigerate overnight.

Allow to come to room temperature, and bake at 350° for 30 to 40 minutes. Yield: 8 servings.

EGGPLANT CASSEROLE

1 medium-size eggplant, peeled and
    cubed
2 medium-size onions, finely chopped
2 stalks celery, finely chopped
¼ cup finely chopped green pepper
1 cup tomato sauce or tomato soup
2 cups shredded cheddar cheese
¾ cup corn chips

Combine eggplant, onions, celery, and
green pepper. Cook in a small amount of
boiling salted water until tender; drain. Add
tomato sauce, stirring well.

Combine cheese and corn chips, tossing
well.

Spoon eggplant mixture into a lightly
greased 1½-quart casserole. Stir in half of
cheese mixture; top with remaining cheese
mixture. Bake at 350° for 20 to 30 minutes
or until cheese is melted. Yield: 8 servings.

CHICKEN ALMOND BAKE

1 (10-ounce) can condensed cream of
    celery soup
½ cup milk
1 cup diced cooked chicken
½ cup minced celery
1 small onion, minced
½ cup slivered almonds
¼ teaspoon Worcestershire sauce
1 (3-ounce) can (2 cups) Chinese
    noodles, divided

Blend celery soup with milk. Add chicken,
celery, onion, almonds and Worcestershire
sauce. Cover bottom of 1-quart baking dish
with half the noodles. Pour in chicken mixture, and top with remaining noodles. Bake
at 350° for 30 minutes. Yield: 4 servings.

PANTRY-SHELF CHICKEN CASSEROLE

1 (10½-ounce) can chicken à la king
1 (15¼-ounce) can macaroni and cheese
1 (4-ounce) can mushrooms, drained
1 tablespoon grated onion
¼ cup sliced stuffed olives
¼ cup slivered almonds
1 cup grated sharp cheddar cheese

Combine first 5 ingredients in buttered
1½-quart casserole. Top with almonds and
cheese. Bake at 450° about 15 minutes or
until bubbling hot. Yield: 6 servings.

Note: May be made the day before,
refrigerated, then reheated. It also freezes
well.

DERBY EGG CASSEROLE

2 tablespoons butter or margarine
1 medium-size onion, chopped
2 tablespoons all-purpose flour
1¼ cups milk
1 cup shredded sharp cheddar cheese
8 hard-cooked eggs, sliced and divided
1½ cups coarsely crushed potato chips,
    divided
8 slices crisp fried bacon, crumbled and
    divided

Melt butter, and sauté onion until it is
transparent. Stir in flour, and stir to blend.
Gradually stir in milk, and cook over
medium heat, stirring constantly, until
thickened. Add cheese, and stir to dissolve.
Butter a 2-quart casserole. Add half the
sliced eggs, cover with half the cheese
sauce, half the potato chips, and half the
bacon. Repeat layers. Bake at 350° for 30
minutes. Yield: 6 to 8 servings.

EGG AND NOODLE CASSEROLE

1 (8-ounce) package egg noodles
8 hard-cooked eggs, sliced
2 cups sliced mushrooms
1 (10¾-ounce) can condensed cream of
    mushroom soup
1 cup commercial yogurt
½ cup milk
¼ cup chopped parsley
1 teaspoon salt
    Paprika

Cook noodles according to package directions; drain. Pour noodles into a greased shallow 2-quart casserole. Top with eggs and mushrooms. Combine mushroom soup, yogurt, milk, parsley, and salt; mix well. Pour over eggs and mushrooms. Sprinkle with paprika. Bake at 350° for 30 minutes. Yield: 6 servings.

SCALLOPED EGGS AND HAM

3 tablespoons butter or margarine
2 tablespoons minced onion
4 tablespoons all-purpose flour
1 teaspoon salt
1 teaspoon dry mustard
⅛ teaspoon pepper
3 teaspoons Worcestershire sauce
2 cups milk
1 cup cheese cracker crumbs, divided
6 hard-cooked eggs, sliced
2 cups cubed cooked country ham

Melt butter in a saucepan; add onion, and cook until softened. Blend in flour, salt, mustard, pepper, and Worcestershire sauce. Add milk slowly; cook, stirring constantly, until thickened.

Sprinkle half the cracker crumbs in a buttered 1½-quart casserole. Alternate layers of sliced eggs, ham, and sauce, ending with eggs. Sprinkle with remaining crumbs. Bake at 350° for 30 minutes or until sauce bubbles and crumbs are browned. Yield: 6 servings.

EGG-TUNA AMANDINE

4 tablespoons melted butter or
    margarine
¼ cup all-purpose flour
½ teaspoon salt
⅛ teaspoon pepper
2 cups milk
1 tablespoon freshly squeezed lemon
    juice
1 (7-ounce) can tuna fish, drained and
    flaked
¼ cup chopped almonds
1 pimiento, chopped
4 hard-cooked eggs, diced
½ cup buttered bread crumbs

Combine butter and flour in saucepan over medium heat; cook, stirring constantly, until bubbly. Add seasonings and milk; cook until smooth and thickened, stirring constantly. Add lemon juice, tuna, almonds, pimiento, and eggs.

Spoon into a greased casserole; top with buttered bread crumbs. Bake at 375° for 30 minutes. Yield: 4 servings.

BAKED BEAN CASSEROLE

1 (16-ounce) can red kidney beans
1 (16-ounce) can lima beans
1 (16-ounce) can pork and beans
1 cup firmly packed brown sugar
¾ cup catsup
½ teaspoon dry mustard
1 tablespoon lemon juice
1 medium-size onion, thinly sliced

Drain kidney and lima beans. Combine all ingredients except onion in greased 2-quart casserole. Separate onion slices into rings, and scatter over top of casserole. Bake, uncovered, at 350° for 30 minutes. Yield: 6 servings.

BROCCOLI SURPRISE

¾ cup uncooked macaroni
1 (10-ounce) package frozen broccoli
1 (12-ounce) can luncheon meat or leftover cooked ham cut into bite-size pieces
¼ cup margarine, melted
1 cup shredded cheddar cheese
1 cup milk
2 heaping tablespoons commercial sour cream

Cook and drain macaroni. Cook broccoli according to package directions, and drain. Brown luncheon meat in melted margarine. Combine macaroni, broccoli, luncheon meat, and cheese in casserole; pour in milk. Gently stir in sour cream. Bake at 350° until bubbly, about 20 minutes. Serve at once. Yield: 6 servings.

MASHED SOUR CREAM BEETS

12 fresh beets
½ teaspoon salt
½ medium-size green pepper, minced
1 tablespoon lemon juice
½ cup commercial sour cream
1 small clove garlic
2 slices fresh bread, coarsely crumbled
¼ cup butter, melted

Cut all but an inch of leaves away from beets, and leave roots on. Cook in boiling water until quite tender. When cool enough to handle, peel and mash or put through a ricer. Add salt, green pepper, lemon juice, and sour cream. Cut the garlic clove in half, and rub it over the inside of a 2-quart baking dish. Stir crumbs with melted butter. Pour beet mixture into prepared casserole, and top with buttered crumbs. Bake at 350° for 20 minutes. Yield: 8 servings.

SPINACH CASSEROLE

1 pound fresh spinach
2 tablespoons minced onion
3 tablespoons melted butter
3 tablespoons all-purpose flour
2 cups milk
¼ teaspoon ground nutmeg
3 hard-cooked eggs, sliced
  Salt and pepper to taste
½ cup shredded pasteurized process American cheese
½ cup buttered bread crumbs
  Paprika

Wash spinach thoroughly. Cover, and cook slowly until tender in only the water clinging to it from final rinse; drain, and chop.

Cook onion in butter until transparent. Add flour and blend well; add milk, and cook and stir until smooth and thickened. Fold in spinach, nutmeg, and eggs; season with salt and pepper.

Spoon into a buttered shallow baking dish; top with mixture of cheese and bread crumbs, and sprinkle with paprika. Bake at 375° for 20 minutes or until lightly browned. Yield: 6 servings.

SPINACH BAKE

1 (10-ounce) package frozen chopped
    spinach
1 cup commercial sour cream
1 (1⅓-ounce) envelope dry onion soup
    mix
6 water chestnuts, thinly sliced
1 (4-ounce) can mushroom pieces,
    drained

Cook spinach as directed on package; drain well. Combine sour cream, soup mix, water chestnuts, and mushrooms in mixing bowl. Stir in spinach. Pour into buttered 1-quart casserole; cover, and bake for 1 hour at 350°. Yield: 4 servings.

CHINESE CASSEROLE

1 (10¾-ounce) can condensed cream of
    mushroom soup
2 tablespoons soy sauce
½ cup milk
1 pound ground beef
1 (2½-ounce) can mushroom pieces,
    drained
½ cup slivered almonds
1 teaspoon seasoned salt
1 cup crushed potato chips
1 (16-ounce) can Chinese vegetables,
    drained
1 (5-ounce) can Chinese noodles

Combine soup, soy sauce, and milk; set aside.

Brown meat; drain. Stir in mushrooms, almonds, and salt.

Layer all ingredients in a lightly greased 2½-quart casserole in this order: potato chips, soup mixture, meat mixture, and Chinese vegetables. Top with Chinese noodles. Bake at 350° for 45 minutes. Yield: 8 to 10 servings.

BEEF 'N' VEGETABLE CASSEROLE

1 pound ground beef
3 tablespoons melted shortening
¼ teaspoon salt
1 (16-ounce) can mixed vegetables,
    drained
2½ cups cooked, drained tomato wedges
2 cups seasoned mashed potatoes
½ cup shredded cheddar cheese

Sauté ground beef in shortening until brown; drain. Add salt, mixed vegetables, and tomatoes; cook 10 minutes. Spoon into a shallow casserole.

Drop mashed potatoes by spoonfuls around edge of casserole; sprinkle with cheese. Bake at 400° until cheese melts.

Yield: 4 to 6 servings.

HIGH PROTEIN
COTTAGE CHEESE CASSEROLE

1 cup cream-style cottage cheese
1 (8-ounce) package medium-width
    noodles, cooked
1 cup commercial yogurt
1 (12-ounce) package cheddar cheese,
    shredded
½ teaspoon salt
1 teaspoon pepper
⅓ cup snipped chives
1 tablespoon margarine

Combine all ingredients except margarine. Spoon into a buttered 1½-quart casserole; dot with margarine. Cover, and bake at 350° for 30 minutes. Yield: 6 servings.

CARIBBEAN CASSEROLE

4 slices canned pineapple, divided
2 (16-ounce) cans pork and beans
1 tablespoon prepared mustard
6 frankfurters
8 whole cloves
¼ cup pineapple syrup, drained from
   canned pineapple

Cut 2 pineapple slices into small wedges; combine with beans and mustard in a 1½-quart casserole. Arrange frankfurters on top. Cut remaining pineapple slices in half; place on franks. Insert 2 cloves in each pineapple half. Pour syrup over all. Bake at 375° for 45 minutes or until bubbly. Yield: 5 to 6 servings.

LIVER CASSEROLE

2 tablespoons all-purpose flour
½ teaspoon salt
¼ teaspoon pepper
1 pound liver, skinned and cut into
   2-inch pieces
2 tablespoons melted shortening
1 medium-size onion, chopped
½ cup coarsely chopped celery
1 cup coarsely chopped carrots
½ cup coarsely chopped green
   pepper
2 cups tomato juice

Combine flour, salt, and pepper; rub into liver. Brown liver on both sides in hot melted shortening. Arrange liver in greased 2-quart casserole dish. Brown onion, celery, carrots, and green pepper in remaining shortening. Spoon vegetables over liver and pour tomato juice over mixture. Cover; bake at 350° for 1½ hours. Yield: 6 servings.

POTATO-TUNA BAKE

1 (10¾-ounce) can condensed cream of
   celery soup
⅓ cup milk
¼ cup mayonnaise
2 tablespoons chopped parsley
1 teaspoon lemon juice
⅛ teaspoon dry mustard
4 cups cubed cooked potatoes
2 (7-ounce) cans tuna fish, drained and
   flaked
½ cup shredded pasteurized process
   American cheese

Combine soup, milk, mayonnaise, parsley, lemon juice, and mustard in a 1½-quart casserole. Stir in potatoes and tuna. Bake at 400° for 30 minutes or until hot; stir.

Top with cheese. Bake 5 additional minutes or until cheese melts. Yield: 6 servings.

SCALLOPED CABBAGE

1 small head cabbage, coarsely shredded
2 teaspoons salt, divided
¼ teaspoon pepper, divided
2 teaspoons sugar, divided
2 tablespoons all-purpose flour, divided
½ cup shredded mild cheddar cheese,
   divided
2 tablespoons butter or margarine,
   divided
½ cup bread crumbs
1¼ cups hot milk

Boil cabbage for 15 minutes; drain. Put half the cabbage into buttered 1½-quart casserole. Sprinkle with half the salt, pepper, sugar, and flour; then add half the cheese and butter. Repeat layers. Top with bread crumbs and pour milk over all. Bake at 400° for 20 minutes or until crumbs are well browned. Yield: 6 servings.

Vegetables

There must be literally thousands of us who wouldn't know the difference between a truly fresh vegetable and a helping of restaurant succotash dipped from a #10 can. Quick-food chains line our streets and pick our pockets for burgers and fries. Where have the fresh vegetables and fruits gone? They are still around, if we take the trouble to look.

Realistically, however, ours is a fast-moving society. Canned or frozen produce is as close as some of us can get to freshness, because we work outside the home. And there is no knocking those products. Yet we owe it to ourselves occasionally to buy some fresh spinach, or broccoli, or Brussels sprouts just to keep alive the memory of true freshness. The Chinese are the best teachers of vegetable cookery; they steam or stir-fry them or combine the two methods so that fewer nutrients are discarded than in our usual superfluous cooking water.

CURRIED VEGETABLES WITH FRIED RICE

  2 pounds assorted vegetables, sliced
  ¼ cup safflower or peanut oil
  1 clove garlic, minced
  1 slice fresh gingerroot, minced
  1 tablespoon curry powder
     Brown Rice
  2 eggs
  2 tablespoons tamari sauce or soy sauce

The more varieties of vegetables you use, the more interesting the dish. Choose among these: carrots (parboiled 5 minutes), celery, Chinese cabbage, asparagus, mushrooms, green onions, green pepper, zucchini.

Heat oil in wok (use a heavy skillet if wok is not available), and stir-fry garlic, ginger, and curry powder for about a minute. Add vegetables in order of decreasing hardness, carrots and celery first, etc. Stir-fry until crisp-tender. Stir in cooked Brown Rice. Beat eggs with sauce, and stir into mixture. Stir-fry just to incorporate eggs. Serve hot. Yield: 4 to 6 servings.

Brown Rice:

  1 cup brown rice, washed
  2½ cups water
  1 teaspoon salt

Allow 1 hour for cooking. Combine ingredients in heavy 2-quart saucepan; cover. Boil hard 5 minutes, lower heat, and simmer 45 minutes. Let stand off heat, covered, 10 minutes.

YUGOSLAVIAN SKILLET GARDEN

  3 tablespoons olive oil
  2 medium-size onions, chopped
  2 green peppers, diced
  1 medium-size eggplant, peeled and
     cubed
  2 medium-size zucchini, sliced
  1 (10-ounce) package frozen artichoke
     hearts or 1 (16-ounce) can artichoke
     hearts
  2 tablespoons salt
  1 cup uncooked rice
  1 (29-ounce) can tomatoes, broken up
  3 cups water

Heat oil in Dutch oven or electric skillet. Sauté onions until transparent; add green peppers and eggplant. (You may need to add more oil at this point.) Cook, stirring, until well heated. Add zucchini and artichokes. Sprinkle salt and rice over mixture. Add tomatoes and water. Cover; bring to boil. Reduce heat, and cook slowly until rice is tender, 35 to 45 minutes. Yield: 12 servings.

Note: Especially good with pork or chicken. No other vegetable need be served with the meal. Freezes well.

ASPARAGUS WITH NEW POTATOES

    6 to 8 new potatoes
1½ pounds fresh asparagus
    4 tablespoons butter or margarine,
        divided
    2 tablespoons all-purpose flour
    ¼ teaspoon salt
        Dash white pepper
    ⅛ teaspoon ground nutmeg
1½ cups milk
    ½ cup shredded Gruyère or Swiss cheese

Scrub potatoes; peel a small band around the center of each. Cook in boiling water about 20 minutes or until tender. Drain and set aside.

Wash asparagus thoroughly; snap off tough end. Cut stalks in long diagonal slices, but leave the tips whole. Stir-fry asparagus in 2 tablespoons butter about 5 minutes or until crisp-tender.

Melt remaining 2 tablespoons butter over low heat, and stir in flour, salt, pepper, and nutmeg; add milk. Cook, stirring constantly, until sauce thickens. Add cheese, and stir until melted. Combine potatoes and asparagus in a serving bowl, and pour sauce over all. Yield: 5 to 6 servings.

ASPARAGUS SANDWICH PUFFS

    6 slices bread, toasted
    ¼ cup softened butter
    1 (16-ounce) can stewed tomatoes,
        drained
    6 slices pasteurized process pimiento
        cheese
    1 (16-ounce) can asparagus spears,
        drained
    3 eggs, separated
    ¼ teaspoon salt
        Dash pepper
    1 tablespoon bottled commercial French
        dressing

Spread toast with butter, and place slices close together on baking pan. Spoon tomatoes over toast, and top each with a cheese slice. Distribute asparagus spears over each sandwich. Beat egg yolks with salt, pepper, and dressing. Beat egg whites until stiff; fold together with yolk mixture and use to top sandwiches, covering them evenly. Bake for 15 minutes at 350° or until puffed and golden. Yield: 6 sandwiches.

RUSSIAN BEETS

    2 (16-ounce) cans cubed beets
    1 teaspoon salt
    1 cup yogurt
    6 or 8 green onions

Heat and drain beets; place in warmed serving bowl. Sprinkle with salt. Warm yogurt by stirring in top of double boiler over simmering water. Spoon over beets. Chop onions, green tips included, and sprinkle over yogurt. Yield: 6 to 8 servings.

Note: To use fresh beets, cut off leaves, leaving an inch of leaves and the roots. Simmer until tender. Peel and cube.

OVEN BEETS

2 (16-ounce) cans sliced beets
2 tablespoons sugar
1 tablespoon cornstarch
¼ teaspoon salt
⅓ cup vinegar
¼ cup melted butter or margarine
Onion slices

Drain beets, and reserve liquid; add water to beet liquid to make 1 cup.

Combine sugar, cornstarch, salt, and vinegar; stir until blended. Combine butter, beet liquid, and vinegar mixture. Place beets in a 2-quart casserole; pour in liquid mixture. Cover, and bake at 350° for 1 hour. Garnish with onion slices. Yield: 6 servings.

BEETS IN ORANGE SAUCE

2 cups sliced, cooked beets
2 tablespoons butter or margarine
1 tablespoon sugar
1 tablespoon cornstarch
½ teaspoon salt
⅛ teaspoon paprika
½ cup reserved beet juice
½ cup orange juice
1 teaspoon grated lemon rind

Drain beets, reserving ½ cup juice. Place beets in a 1-quart casserole, and set aside.

Melt butter in saucepan. Remove from heat, and stir in sugar, cornstarch, salt, and paprika. Cook over low heat until mixture bubbles. Remove from heat, and gradually stir in beet juice. Cook rapidly, stirring constantly, until mixture thickens. Blend in orange juice and lemon rind. Pour over beets. Bake at 350° for 15 to 20 minutes. Yield: 4 to 6 servings.

BRUSSELS SPROUTS IN CHEESE SAUCE

1 (10-ounce) package frozen Brussels sprouts
2 eggs, lightly beaten
1½ cups soft bread crumbs, divided
1 (10½-ounce) can condensed cream of mushroom soup
1 cup shredded sharp cheddar cheese
2 tablespoons minced onion
Dash cayenne pepper
2 tablespoons melted butter or margarine

Cook sprouts crisp-tender according to package directions. Drain; cool. Cut each sprout in half. In a mixing bowl, combine eggs, half the crumbs, soup, cheese, onion, and cayenne. Turn into a 1½-quart baking dish. Pour butter over remaining bread crumbs; toss together, and use to top casserole. Bake at 350° for 50 minutes. Yield: 6 servings.

CREAMED BROCCOLI BAKE

2 (10½-ounce) packages frozen, chopped broccoli
1 (8-ounce) package cream cheese, softened
1 stick butter or margarine, melted, divided
1 cup commercial or homemade croutons

Cook broccoli according to package directions. Drain. Combine cheese with half the butter. Stir into hot broccoli. Pour into 1½-quart casserole. Pour remaining butter over top, and scatter croutons over all. Bake at 350° about 20 minutes or just until piping hot. Yield: 6 to 8 servings.

MARINATED ARTICHOKE HEARTS

½ cup vinegar
½ cup salad oil
1 small clove garlic, crushed
1 teaspoon seasoned salt
¼ teaspoon salt
1 (16-ounce) can artichoke hearts,
    drained
  Minced fresh parsley
1 (2-ounce) jar pimiento, drained

Combine all ingredients except artichokes, parsley, and pimiento in saucepan; bring to boil. Split artichokes, and add to mixture. Bring mixture to boil; cover and simmer for 10 minutes. Add parsley and pimiento.

Refrigerate artichokes in marinade overnight in a covered dish or jar. Drain well before serving. Yield: 6 servings.

CAULIFLOWER WITH PIMIENTO SAUCE

1 large cauliflower
2 tablespoons melted butter or
    margarine
2 tablespoons all-purpose flour
1 cup milk
½ teaspoon salt
1 teaspoon minced onion
¼ cup mashed pimiento
¼ cup shredded cheddar cheese

Wash cauliflower, and remove large outer leaves, leaving tender green ones. Cook, covered, in a small amount of boiling salted water until just tender (about 20 minutes), or steam over boiling water.

Combine butter and flour in saucepan, stirring until smooth. Slowly add milk, stirring constantly over low heat until slightly thick. Add salt, onion, pimiento, and cheese.

Drain cauliflower; place in a warm serving dish. Pour warm sauce over cauliflower. Yield: 6 to 8 servings.

CRUSTY TOPPED CAULIFLOWER

1 large head cauliflower
½ cup mayonnaise
2 teaspoons Dijon mustard
½ to ¾ cup shredded cheddar cheese

Cook cauliflower whole in a small amount of boiling salted water about 20 minutes; drain carefully. Put cauliflower in flat pan.

Combine mayonnaise and mustard; spread over the cooked cauliflower. Sprinkle with cheese and bake at 350° about 10 minutes or until cheese melts. Yield: 6 servings.

BRAISED CELERY WITH CHIVE-BUTTER SAUCE

10 stalks celery
  Chicken Stock
¾ teaspoon salt, divided
¼ cup butter or margarine
2 tablespoons chopped fresh chives
  Dash of freshly ground black pepper

Cut celery into pieces 4 inches long. Place in a saucepan with ½ inch boiling chicken stock and ½ teaspoon salt. Cover, and cook only until crisp-tender, about 15 minutes. Drain, if necessary. Melt butter; add chives, pepper, and ¼ teaspoon salt. Pour over celery. Serve hot. Yield: 6 servings.

CELERY AMANDINE

½ cup butter, divided
4 cups diced celery
  Salt and pepper to taste
2 tablespoons finely chopped fresh
  chives
1 cup blanched chopped almonds
1 small clove garlic, minced
2 tablespoons dry white wine

Melt ¼ cup butter in a saucepan; add celery, salt, and pepper. Cover, and cook over low heat until celery is tender. Stir frequently while cooking to prevent scorching; add chives.

  Melt remaining butter in a heavy pan; add almonds, and cook over medium heat until brown. Add garlic and wine; cook 1 minute. Pour over celery, and serve immediately. Yield: 6 servings.

SAUCY BAKED BEANS

6 slices bacon, cut into 1-inch pieces
3 (16-ounce) cans pork and beans or
  baked beans
1 (8-ounce) can seasoned tomato sauce
1 cup chopped onion
½ cup catsup
¼ cup firmly packed dark brown sugar
2 tablespoons prepared mustard
1 teaspoon salt
4 drops hot sauce

Cook bacon until almost crisp; remove from pan. Combine bacon and beans. Add remaining ingredients; mix well. Spoon mixture into a greased 2-quart casserole or beanpot; bake, uncovered, at 300° for 3 to 5 hours. Yield: 6 servings.

BUCKAROO BEANS

1 pound dried red beans or pinto beans
½ pound smoked salt pork, cut into small
  cubes
1 clove garlic, minced
1 large onion, coarsely chopped
1 small bay leaf
½ cup chopped green pepper
2 teaspoons chili powder
2 tablespoons firmly packed brown
  sugar
½ teaspoon dry mustard
½ teaspoon crushed oregano leaves
2 cups canned tomatoes
  Salt to taste

Wash beans thoroughly in several changes of water. Put beans in a 3-quart Dutch oven, and cover with water. Let soak overnight.

  The next day, add salt pork, garlic, onion, and bay leaf; bring to boiling point. Reduce heat; cover, and simmer for 1 to 1½ hours or until beans are almost tender. Add remaining ingredients except salt. Allow to simmer, covered, for 2 hours; stir once or twice. Add salt, if needed. Remove bay leaf. Yield: 8 to 10 servings.

SAVORY GREEN BEANS

3 tablespoons melted butter or
  margarine
3 tablespoons all-purpose flour
2 cups milk
  Salt and pepper to taste
½ pound cheddar cheese, shredded and
  divided
3 cups cooked, seasoned, drained green
  beans
3 hard-cooked eggs, coarsely chopped
⅓ cup chopped onion

Combine butter and flour, blending until smooth; cook over low heat until bubbly. Gradually add milk; cook, stirring constantly, until smooth and thickened. Season with salt and pepper.

Set ½ cup cheese side, and stir remaining cheese into sauce.

Place beans in a shallow 2-quart casserole; cover with sauce. Stir in egg and onion; sprinkle with ½ cup cheese. Bake at 350° for 15 minutes or until bubbly. Yield: 6 to 8 servings.

ARMENIAN GREEN BEANS WITH MEAT

1 teaspoon salt
1 pound ground beef
1 medium-size onion, chopped
1 (16-ounce) can tomatoes
1 (29-ounce) can green beans
1 cup water
½ teaspoon salt
  Dash pepper
  Baked potatoes (optional)

Sprinkle 1 teaspoon salt in iron skillet, add beef and onion, and cook, stirring, until meat loses its color. Add remaining ingredients. Cover, and simmer for 1 hour. This dish is still good reheated the second or third day after preparation. Serve with baked potatoes, if desired. Yield: 4 servings.

LIMA BEANS IN TOMATO SAUCE

2 cups dried lima beans
2 quarts water
½ pound sliced bacon
1 large onion, chopped
2 tablespoons all-purpose flour
2 cups canned tomatoes
  Salt and pepper to taste

Wash beans, and put into a large saucepan. Cover with water, and let soak overnight. Pour off this water, and cover beans with 2 quarts fresh water. Bring to a boil quickly; lower temperature, and simmer about 2 hours or until beans are very tender. Remove from heat; drain.

Cook bacon until crisp; remove from skillet, and keep warm. Brown onion in bacon drippings; add flour, and stir until mixture is smooth. Add tomatoes and drained beans; cook until mixture thickens. Season to taste with salt and pepper. Serve hot with bacon strips on top. Yield: 6 to 8 servings.

DEVILED GREEN BEANS

1 to 1½ pounds green beans, cut into
    1-inch pieces
3 tablespoons butter or
    margarine
1 medium-size onion, finely
    chopped
1 clove garlic, minced
½ green pepper, chopped
1 (4-ounce) jar chopped pimiento
2 teaspoons prepared mustard
1 (8-ounce) can tomato sauce
1 cup shredded pasteurized process
    American cheese

Wash beans thoroughly. Cook in a small amount of boiling salted water until tender. Drain, and set aside.

Melt butter in a heavy skillet. Add onion, garlic, green pepper, and pimiento; cook until tender. Remove from heat and stir in mustard, tomato sauce, and cheese.

Combine beans and tomato sauce mixture; place in a greased 1-quart casserole, and bake at 350° for 25 minutes. Yield: 4 servings.

CABBAGE PLUS

½ cup butter or margarine
1 medium-size head cabbage, chopped
1 green pepper, cut into strips
2 stalks celery, chopped
2 carrots, thinly sliced
1 large onion, sliced
1 (6-ounce) can evaporated milk
  Salt and pepper to taste

Melt butter in a large skillet, and add vegetables; cover, and cook over medium heat for 10 minutes. Stir in milk; heat thoroughly. Season. Yield: 6 to 8 servings.

POLISH-STYLE STUFFED CABBAGE LEAVES

1 large head cabbage
  Water
1 tablespoon salt
2 pounds ground beef
1 medium-size onion, chopped
1 cup cooked regular rice
½ teaspoon salt
  Dash pepper
2 eggs
½ cup saltine cracker crumbs
1 (16-ounce) can sauerkraut, rinsed and
    drained
1 (16-ounce) can tomatoes, broken up
2 (8-ounce) cans tomato sauce
2 (10½-ounce) cans condensed tomato
    soup
½ cup water
  Mashed potatoes or buttered noodles

Wash and core cabbage. Bring water to boil in large kettle; add salt and cabbage. Simmer 25 minutes. Drain cabbage, and separate leaves. (It helps to run cold water into the hole left by the core's removal, possibly enlarging the hole.) Drain leaves. Combine beef, onion, rice, salt, pepper, eggs, and crumbs. Form meat mixture into 24 balls.

Starting with the largest cabbage leaves, wrap meat balls in cabbage, folding leaves to enclose filling. Fasten each with wooden pick. Arrange in rows in large baking pan or a 10- x 16- x 2½-inch casserole. Arrange remaining cabbage leaves over rolls, and distribute sauerkraut over top. Pour on tomatoes, tomato sauce, and soup. Add water. Bake at 350° at least 1½ to 2 hours, basting occasionally. Serve with mashed potatoes or buttered noodles. Yield: 12 servings.

OLD-WORLD CABBAGE CAKE WITH EGG SAUCE

1 small head cabbage
  Water
2 teaspoons salt
1 pound ground pork
1 cup fine bread crumbs
1 egg
1 teaspoon salt
  Dash pepper
¼ cup milk
6 to 8 slices bacon
  Egg Sauce

Wash and core cabbage; drop into boiling salted water to cover. Simmer 10 minutes. Drain, cool, and separate leaves. Blend pork with crumbs, egg, salt, pepper, and milk. Line, and cover the bottom of a heavy, 6-inch deep saucepan with bacon; allow bacon to extend up the sides as far as it will.

Place ⅓ of the cabbage leaves in bacon-lined pot, cover with half the pork mixture, then ⅓ of the cabbage, remaining pork, and top with remaining cabbage. Place pan on medium heat, and let bacon sizzle 2 minutes. Press cabbage down using plate. Then add boiling water to cover cabbage; cover, reduce heat to low, and cook 1¼ hours. Drain, reserving liquid. Place cabbage cake on warmed serving plate while Egg Sauce is made. Yield: 6 servings.

Egg Sauce:

  2 tablespoons butter
1½ tablespoons all-purpose flour
  2 cups reserved cooking liquid
  1 egg
  1 tablespoon cold water
    Salt and pepper to taste

Melt butter in small heavy saucepan. Stir in flour. Slowly add reserved liquid, and cook, stirring, until thickened. In small bowl, beat egg with water. Slowly stir half the hot mixture into egg, then return all to saucepan and cook, not boiling, for 2 or 3 minutes. Season. Serve in sauce boat. Yield: 6 servings.

CABBAGE QUICKIE

  2 cups milk, divided
  6 cups shredded cabbage
1½ tablespoons all-purpose flour
1½ tablespoons butter or
      margarine
1¼ teaspoons salt
  ¼ teaspoon white pepper

Heat 1½ cups milk; stir in cabbage. Cover and cook 3 minutes. Make a paste of flour and ½ cup cold milk; strain into cabbage, and add other ingredients. Cover, and cook an additional 6 minutes. Yield: 8 to 10 servings.

MINT-COOL CARROTS

 12 large carrots
  2 teaspoons chicken broth
  1 teaspoon crushed mint flakes
1½ teaspoons minced onion
  ¼ teaspoon pepper
  1 teaspoon seasoned salt
  2 teaspoons sugar
  ½ cup water
  4 tablespoons margarine

Scrape carrots, and slice diagonally about 1 inch thick. Combine carrots and all ingredients, except margarine, in a skillet. Bring to a boil, cover tightly, and simmer 12 minutes. Drain; add margarine, and mix well. Yield: 10 to 12 servings.

HONEY-GLAZED CARROTS

  4 cups sliced carrots
  1 cup boiling water
  ¼ teaspoon salt
  2 teaspoons cornstarch
  ½ cup orange juice
  2 tablespoons butter
  2 tablespoons honey
  1 teaspoon grated orange rind

Put carrots, water, and salt in medium-size saucepan. Cook rapidly, covered, just until tender, 8 to 10 minutes; keep hot.

  Combine cornstarch and orange juice in a small saucepan; blend until smooth. Add butter and honey. Stir constantly over medium heat until thickened and clear. Add orange rind.

  Drain hot carrots; add honey glaze, and mix well. Yield: 4 to 6 servings.

363

BAKED CARROTS WITH APPLES

8 medium-size carrots, pared and cut
    into 1-inch pieces
1 (20-ounce) can pie-sliced apples,
    drained
½ cup sugar
2 tablespoons butter or margarine
    Paprika

Cook carrots in a little salted water until tender, about 12 to 15 minutes, with lid on pan. Drain, and combine with apples. Turn into 9-inch pie plate; sprinkle with sugar, dot with butter, and top with several dashes paprika. Bake at 375° for 30 to 40 minutes or until tender and syrupy. Yield: 6 to 8 servings.

CREAMY WHOLE KERNEL CORN

1 (3-ounce) package cream cheese,
    softened
¼ cup milk
1 tablespoon butter or margarine
½ teaspoon onion salt
    Dash white pepper
1 (16-ounce) can shoepeg or whole
    kernel corn
    Chopped parsley or paprika
    (optional)

Combine cheese, milk, butter, and seasoning in small heavy saucepan. Stir over low heat until cheese melts. Drain corn, reserving liquid. Add corn to cheese mixture; then add as much of the corn liquid as desired. Heat thoroughly. To serve, top with parsley or paprika, if desired. Yield: 4 servings.

BAKED CORN AND TOMATOES

2 cups freshly grated corn
2 cups chopped tomatoes
2 teaspoons sugar
1 teaspoon salt
¼ teaspoon pepper
3 tablespoons melted butter or
    margarine
1 cup dry bread crumbs

Combine corn and tomatoes; add sugar, salt, pepper, and melted butter. Spoon into a greased 1-quart baking dish. Cover with bread crumbs and bake at 350° for 30 to 40 minutes or until corn is done. Yield: 4 or 5 servings.

CORN FRITTERS

1 (8-ounce) can whole kernel corn,
    drained
½ teaspoon salt
    Dash pepper
¼ cup all-purpose flour
1 egg, separated
    Salad oil

Combine corn, salt, pepper, flour, and egg yolk. Beat egg white until stiff; fold into corn mixture. Drop mixture by tablespoonfuls into hot oil; cook until lightly browned, turning once. Yield: 4 servings.

GRILLED EGGPLANT

½ cup olive or salad oil
3 cloves garlic, crushed
1 large eggplant
    Salt and pepper to taste

Combine oil and garlic, and let stand for an hour before using. Slice eggplant into thick slices, and brush generously with oil mixture. Put slices in a hinged broiler, and grill slowly over hot coals. Brush with the garlic-oil mixture occasionally. Sprinkle with salt and pepper to taste. Yield: 4 to 6 servings.

SCALLOPED EGGPLANT

1 green pepper
1 small onion, chopped
2 tablespoons melted margarine
1 large eggplant, peeled and cubed
4 cups chopped fresh or canned
    tomatoes
2 teaspoons salt
   Pepper to taste
1 cup buttered bread crumbs

Sauté green pepper and onion in margarine until tender. Add eggplant, tomatoes, salt and pepper; simmer 10 minutes. Place mixture in a greased shallow casserole; sprinkle with bread crumbs. Bake at 350° for 15 minutes or until eggplant is tender and crumbs are brown. Yield: 6 to 8 servings.

STUFFED EGGPLANT

1 large eggplant
1 small onion, finely chopped
4 tablespoons butter or margarine,
    divided
3 tablespoons chopped fresh parsley
1 (10½-ounce) can condensed cream of
    mushroom soup
   Dash Worcestershire sauce
1 teaspoon salt
   Pepper to taste
1 cup coarsely crushed butter crackers
    (not saltines)

Allow whole eggplant to balance itself; then slice off the top third. Carefully spoon out meat from bottom, leaving ¼-inch thick bowl of shell to be filled for baking. Scoop meat from top third but do not save top skin.

Place eggplant pieces in saucepan with enough boiling salted water to half cover. Put on lid, and simmer until tender. Drain thoroughly, and chop. Sauté onion in half the butter until transparent; add chopped parsley. Mix with eggplant, soup, seasonings, and enough cracker crumbs to make a consistency similar to turkey stuffing. Pile into reserved eggplant shell. Dot with remaining butter, and bake at 375° for 35 minutes. Yield: 4 servings.

TOMATOES VINAIGRETTE

2 medium-size tomatoes, sliced
1 medium-size cucumber, thinly
    sliced
¼ cup chopped green onion
½ cup salad oil
¼ cup wine vinegar
¼ teaspoon ground savory
¼ teaspoon ground tarragon
¼ teaspoon crumbled bay leaf
⅛ teaspoon pepper
¼ teaspoon celery salt
½ teaspoon salt
   Shredded lettuce
2 tablespoons chopped parsley

Alternate layers of tomato and cucumber slices and onion in a shallow glass dish. Combine salad oil, vinegar, and seasonings; beat well. Pour over vegetables. Cover and chill several hours. Drain and serve on shredded lettuce. Sprinkle with chopped parsley. Remove bay leaf. Yield: 6 servings.

TOMATO-RICE PARMESAN

1 large onion, chopped
1 clove garlic, minced
2 tablespoons melted butter or
    margarine
1 cup uncooked regular rice
1 (10¾-ounce) can condensed cream of
    tomato soup
1½ cups water
½ teaspoon salt
⅛ teaspoon pepper
¼ cup grated Parmesan cheese

Sauté onion and garlic in butter until onion is tender but not brown. Add rice, and cook until golden, stirring constantly. Add soup, water, salt, and pepper. Heat to boiling; stir. Reduce heat; cover, and simmer over low heat 20 to 25 minutes or until rice is tender and liquid is absorbed. Remove from heat; stir in Parmesan cheese. Serve hot. Yield: 4 servings.

JAMBALAYA-STYLE STUFFED PEPPERS

6 large green peppers
1½ cups boiling water, divided
1¼ teaspoons salt, divided
1¼ cups diced cooked ham
1 (4½-ounce) can diced shrimp
½ cup finely chopped celery
1 tablespoon finely chopped onion
1½ cups soft bread crumbs, divided
1 cup diced tomato
1 teaspoon dry mustard
⅛ teaspoon pepper
1 tablespoon melted butter or margarine
6 cooked shrimp

Cut tops from green peppers and scoop out seeds, leaving shells intact. Combine 1 cup

boiling water and ½ teaspoon salt in saucepan; add peppers. Cover, and parboil about 5 minutes. Drain peppers, and place in a 9-inch square baking dish; set aside.

Combine ham, diced shrimp, celery, onion, 1 cup bread crumbs, tomato, mustard, ¾ teaspoon salt, and pepper. Spoon mixture into peppers.

Combine butter and remaining ½ cup bread crumbs; sprinkle over peppers. Pour remaining ½ cup boiling water in baking dish. Bake at 350° for 40 to 50 minutes or until done. Garnish with shrimp. Serve hot. Yield: 6 servings.

SAUTÉED GREEN PEPPERS

12 medium-size green peppers
2 medium-size onions, sliced
1 cup sliced celery
½ cup chopped parsley
3 tablespoons melted butter or
    margarine
¼ cup beef broth
1¼ teaspoons salt
¼ teaspoon pepper

Remove seeds from green peppers, and cut peppers into rings ¼ inch thick. Sauté green pepper, onion, celery, and parsley in butter; cover, and cook about 5 minutes. Add remaining ingredients; cover, and simmer about 20 to 25 minutes or until tender. Yield: 6 servings.

MARINATED MUSHROOMS

1 pound small fresh mushrooms
½ teaspoon salt
¼ teaspoon freshly ground black pepper
1 teaspoon oregano
⅓ cup wine vinegar
⅔ cup olive oil or salad oil

Wipe mushrooms with a damp cloth; or wash quickly under running water; dry with towel; trim stem end of mushrooms. Mix remaining ingredients; add to mushrooms, and toss until mushrooms are well coated with the marinade. Let stand at room temperature for at least 4 hours. Yield: about 4 cups.

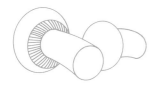

BAKED STUFFED MUSHROOMS

24 medium-size mushrooms
1 tablespoon lemon juice
1 teaspoon instant minced onion
1 teaspoon water
2 tablespoons melted butter or
  margarine
½ cup dry bread crumbs
¼ cup sliced Brazil nuts
2 slices bacon, fried and crumbled
1 teaspoon poultry seasoning
¼ teaspoon salt
½ cup Chicken Stock or water, divided

Clean mushrooms with a damp cloth; remove stems, and reserve, leaving caps intact. Brush caps with lemon juice; set aside. Combine onion and water; let stand 5 minutes.

Chop mushroom stems; add onions, and sauté in melted butter about 3 to 4 minutes. Combine sautéed mushroom and onion with bread crumbs, nuts, bacon, poultry seasoning, and salt; mix well. Add 6 tablespoons chicken stock to moisten. Stuff mixture into mushroom caps. Place in buttered baking dish; add 2 tablespoons stock. Bake at 350° for 8 to 10 minutes. Serve hot. Yield: 6 to 8 servings.

SAUTÉED MUSHROOMS

4 tablespoons melted butter or
  margarine
2 teaspoons freshly squeezed lemon
  juice
1 pound fresh mushrooms, cleaned and
  sliced, or 2 (6- to 8-ounce) cans
  sliced mushrooms, drained
½ teaspoon salt
½ teaspoon oregano
⅛ teaspoon pepper

Combine melted butter and lemon juice; add mushrooms, and sauté over medium heat 3 to 5 minutes or until tender. Add salt, oregano, and pepper. Serve hot. Yield: 4 to 6 servings.

PEAS AND ONION BAKE

2 tablespoons all-purpose flour
½ teaspoon salt
⅛ teaspoon pepper
2 tablespoons melted butter or
  margarine
1½ cups milk
2 teaspoons Worcestershire sauce
2 (16-ounce) cans green peas,
  drained
1 (3½-ounce) can French fried
  onions
Paprika

Stir flour, salt, and pepper into butter. Gradually add milk and Worcestershire sauce. Bring to a boil, stirring constantly; cook until smooth and thickened. Place peas in a shallow 2-quart casserole; add sauce. Bake, uncovered, at 350° for 20 minutes. Top with onions, and sprinkle with paprika; bake an additional 5 minutes. Yield: 8 servings.

DEVILED PEAS

1 cup finely chopped celery
1 green pepper, finely chopped
1 (10¾-ounce) can condensed tomato
   soup
1 (17-ounce) can English peas
1 (4-ounce) can sliced mushrooms,
   drained
1 (2-ounce) jar chopped pimiento
½ cup chili sauce
1 teaspoon Worcestershire sauce
   Sauce
1 cup shredded mild cheddar cheese
6 hard-cooked eggs, sliced
   Buttered bread crumbs

Combine celery, pepper, and soup; simmer until vegetables are tender. Add peas, mushrooms, pimiento, chili sauce, and Worcestershire sauce. Set aside.

Combine White Sauce and cheese in saucepan; cook and stir over medium heat until cheese melts.

Alternate layers of peas mixture, eggs, and White Sauce in a 3-quart casserole. Sprinkle with bread crumbs, and bake at 350° for 40 minutes. Yield: 8 to 10 servings.

Sauce:

5 tablespoons butter or
   margarine
4 tablespoons all-purpose
   flour
¼ teaspoon salt
½ teaspoon pepper
1½ cups milk

Melt butter in a small saucepan; stir in flour, salt, and pepper. Remove from heat, and slowly stir in milk. Return to heat, and cook, stirring constantly, until mixture is smooth and thick. Yield: 1½ cups.

SOUTHERN BROWNED OKRA

½ cup chopped onion
1 tablespoon bacon drippings
2 cups sliced okra
3 tomatoes, peeled and sliced
1 (3-ounce) can sliced mushrooms,
   undrained
½ cup water
   Salt and pepper to taste

Sauté onion in bacon drippings. Add remaining ingredients. Cover, and simmer about 1 hour. Yield: 4 servings.

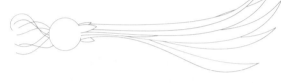

GOLDEN NUGGET CREAMED ONIONS

1 orange, peeled
1 (16-ounce) can small whole onions,
   undrained
2 tablespoons butter or margarine
2 tablespoons all-purpose flour
1 teaspoon salt
1¼ cups milk
2 teaspoons finely grated orange peel
1 teaspoon Worcestershire sauce
¼ teaspoon dry mustard
   Paprika

Cut orange into segments, and drain thoroughly. Simmer onions until heated; drain.

Melt butter in a small saucepan, and stir in flour to form a smooth paste; add salt. Gradually add milk, stirring until mixture is smooth. Bring to a boil over medium heat; boil for 3 minutes, stirring constantly.

Stir in grated orange peel, Worcestershire sauce, and mustard.

Pour hot sauce over drained onions; gently stir in orange pieces. Sprinkle with paprika. Serve at once. Yield: 6 servings.

BARBECUED ONIONS

6 large yellow onions, peeled
¼ cup bottled commercial French
   dressing
1 teaspoon Worcestershire sauce
1 (8-ounce) can tomato sauce
¼ teaspoon chili powder
   Dash cayenne pepper
   Chopped fresh parsley for garnish

Cook onions in salted water to cover until almost tender. Drain, and place in buttered baking dish. Mix remaining ingredients except parsley, and pour over onions. Bake at 400° for about 45 minutes, basting several times. Test with sharp fork and, if necessary, bake longer until onions are tender. Serve sprinkled with fresh parsley. Yield: 6 servings.

FRENCH FRIED ONIONS

4 large white onions
1 cup milk
2 eggs, beaten
2 cups self-rising flour
   Salad oil
   Salt

Cut onions into ¼-inch slices, and separate into rings. Combine milk and eggs; soak onion rings in milk-egg mixture for 2 hours. Drain. Dredge onion rings in flour, and dip again in milk-egg mixture. Dredge in flour again, and deep fry in oil heated to 365°. Drain on absorbent paper. Salt, and serve immediately. Yield: 6 servings.

HOT POTATO SALAD

6 medium-size potatoes
2 cups shredded cheddar cheese
6 tablespoons margarine,
   divided
1½ cups commercial sour cream
3 green onions, chopped
1 teaspoon salt
¼ teaspoon pepper

Cook potatoes in skins; cool. Peel, and shred on a coarse grater.

Combine cheese and 4 tablespoons margarine in saucepan; heat and stir until cheese is almost melted. Remove from heat; blend in sour cream, onions, salt, and pepper. Fold in potatoes, and spoon into a greased 2-quart casserole. Dot with 2 tablespoons margarine. Cover, and bake at 300° about 25 minutes. Yield: 6 servings.

POTATOES ON THE HALF-HOUR

6 medium-size potatoes, pared and
   cubed
   Salt to taste
   Water
¼ cup butter or margarine
   Dash pepper
½ pound sharp cheddar cheese,
   cubed
1 cup commercial sour cream
   Paprika

Cook potatoes in salted water until tender. Drain. Add butter, pepper, and cheese cubes, and shake pan over low heat until cheese has melted. Remove from heat, pour sour cream over; cover, and let stand until cream is hot. Sprinkle with paprika, and serve immediately. Yield: 6 servings.

POTATO-RUTABAGA FLUFF

4 large potatoes, peeled and cubed
1 large rutabaga, peeled and cubed
7 tablespoons butter or margarine,
    divided
1 teaspoon freshly ground black pepper
3 tablespoons melted butter or
    margarine

Boil potatoes and rutabaga separately in salted water until tender; drain. Combine potatoes, 3 tablespoons butter, and pepper; mash. Mash rutabaga with 4 tablespoons butter.

Combine potatoes and rutabaga; spoon into a 3-quart casserole dish. Pour 3 table- spoons melted butter over mixture; bake at 350° about 10 to 15 minutes. Yield: 6 to 8 servings.

PARSLIED POTATOES

1½ pounds small potatoes, peeled
¼ cup melted butter or margarine
4 tablespoons chopped parsley

Cook potatoes in boiling salted water about 15 minutes or until tender. Drain; add melted butter combined with parsley. Serve hot. Yield: 6 to 8 servings.

HOLIDAY YAMS

1 cup firmly packed light brown sugar
¼ cup melted butter or margarine
⅓ cup water
2 cups fresh cranberries
¾ teaspoon salt
6 medium-size yams, cooked, peeled,
    and quartered or 3 (16-ounce) cans
    yams, drained

Combine all ingredients, except yams, in a 2-quart shallow baking dish. Bake at 350° about 5 minutes. Remove from oven, and add yams; stir gently to mix well. Return to oven; bake 25 minutes or until mixture bubbles at edges. Yield: 6 servings.

SWEET POTATO PUDDING

2 pounds sweet potatoes, cooked and
    peeled
¼ cup melted butter or margarine
    Honey
¼ cup firmly packed brown sugar
3 tablespoons dark rum
½ teaspoon salt
    Chopped pecans

Combine potatoes, butter, honey, sugar, rum, and salt; beat until smooth. Spoon into a lightly greased 2-quart casserole; sprinkle with pecans. Bake at 350° for 30 minutes. Yield: 6 servings.

SWEET POTATOES IN APPLESAUCE

1 (16-ounce) can sweet potatoes, well
    drained
¼ teaspoon salt
1 (8-ounce) jar applesauce
¼ cup firmly packed brown sugar
2 tablespoons butter or margarine
¼ teaspoon ground cinnamon

Place sweet potatoes in a 1-quart casserole. Sprinkle with salt. Spoon applesauce over potatoes. Sprinkle with brown sugar; dot with butter. Sprinkle with cinnamon. Bake at 375° for 30 to 35 minutes. Yield: 4 serv- ings.

CANDIED SWEET POTATOES

6 medium-size sweet potatoes
6 tablespoons butter or margarine
  Salt to taste
½ teaspoon vanilla extract
1 cup dark corn syrup

Cook potatoes in the skin until tender; peel. Cut potatoes into halves and place in a shallow baking dish. Dot with butter, and add salt. Add vanilla to corn syrup and pour over potatoes. Bake at 350° for 15 to 20 minutes, basting frequently with syrup. Yield: 6 servings.

PEANUT-SWEET POTATO BALLS

2 cups cooked or canned, mashed sweet
    potatoes
½ cup crunchy-style peanut butter
3 tablespoons firmly packed brown
    sugar
1 egg, beaten
2 tablespoons molasses
  About ½ cup cornflake crumbs

Combine all ingredients except cornflake crumbs; blend well. Shape into 12 balls; roll each in cornflake crumbs.
  Place on a greased baking sheet; bake at 375° for 15 to 20 minutes. Yield: 6 servings.

SPINACH-STUFFED ONIONS

4 medium-size red onions
1 pound fresh spinach, stems removed
2 tablespoons melted butter
¼ cup half-and-half
  Salt and white pepper to taste
  Grated Parmesan or Gruyère cheese

Peel onions and cut in half horizontally; steam about 12 minutes or until tender but not soft and mushy. Cool; remove center of onions, and dice. Leave shells intact.
  Wash spinach and cook 1 minute, using only the water that clings to leaves; drain, and chop.
  Sauté spinach and diced onion in butter and half-and-half until fairly dry; season with salt and pepper. Fill onion shells with spinach mixture; sprinkle with cheese. Bake in a greased shallow pan at 350° until onions are thoroughly heated. Yield: 8 servings.

SPINACH MADELEINE

2 (10-ounce) packages frozen chopped
    spinach
2 tablespoons chopped onion
4 tablespoons melted butter
2 tablespoons all-purpose flour
½ cup evaporated milk
½ teaspoon pepper
¾ teaspoon garlic salt
¾ teaspoon salt
1 teaspoon Worcestershire sauce
1 (6-ounce) roll of jalapeño cheese, cut
    into small pieces
  Buttered bread crumbs

Cook spinach according to package directions; drain, and reserve ½ cup liquid.
  Sauté onion in butter until tender. Add flour, stirring until blended and smooth. Slowly add reserved spinach liquid and milk, stirring constantly; cook until smooth and thickened. Add pepper, garlic salt, salt, Worcestershire sauce, and cheese; stir until cheese is melted.
  Combine sauce and spinach. Pour into a 2-quart casserole; top with buttered bread crumbs. Bake at 350° about 30 minutes or until bubbly. Yield: 8 servings.

SPINACH SUPREME

  2 pounds fresh spinach
  4 tablespoons butter, divided
  1 teaspoon lime juice
  1 teaspoon Worcestershire sauce
  ½ cup commercial sour cream
  ¼ pound fresh mushrooms, washed and
    sliced
  3 or 4 tablespoons Madeira
    Salt and pepper to taste

Wash spinach in tepid water. Lifting spinach out of water each time, change water, and give it several washings in cold water. Lift out of final rinse, and place in saucepan with only the water clinging to the leaves. Cover, and cook on low heat about 10 minutes, until barely tender. Drain, and finely chop with French knife (or put through coarse blade of grinder).

   Combine spinach with 2 tablespoons butter, lime juice, Worcestershire sauce, and sour cream. Stir thoroughly, and keep warm; do not boil or sour cream will become thin and curdle.

   Sauté mushrooms in remaining butter. Add to spinach along with wine and seasonings. Mix, and simmer 2 or 3 minutes. Serve at once. Yield: 6 to 8 servings.

SWISS PIE FLORENTINE

  1 cup shredded sharp cheddar cheese
  ¾ cup all-purpose flour
  ½ teaspoon salt
  ¼ teaspoon dry mustard
  ¼ cup melted butter or margarine
    Filling

Combine cheese with flour and seasonings. Add melted butter. Pour into 9- or 10-inch piepan, and spread with the fingers to form piecrust. Pour Filling into unbaked crust. Bake 15 minutes at 400°; then reduce heat to 325°, and bake 20 to 25 minutes longer or until silver knife inserted in center comes out clean. Yield: 4 main-dish servings.

   Note: Makes an excellent first course for 8 to 10.

Filling:

  1 (10-ounce) package chopped frozen
    spinach
  ½ cup milk
  ½ cup half-and-half
  ½ cup finely chopped onion
  1 (4-ounce) can mushroom pieces,
    drained
  1 teaspoon salt
  ¼ teaspoon nutmeg
    Dash pepper
  3 eggs, slightly beaten

Cook spinach according to package directions; drain. Combine milk, half-and-half, onion, mushrooms, salt, nutmeg, and pepper in saucepan, and simmer 1 minute. Stir half the hot mixture, a spoonful at a time, into the eggs. Pour back into pan, and blend in the spinach.

ORANGE SQUASH

  2 cups cooked squash (yellow or
    zucchini)
  ½ teaspoon salt
  2 tablespoons melted butter or
    margarine
  2 tablespoons sugar
  ⅓ to ½ cup orange juice
  ½ cup finely chopped pecans

Mash squash or put through a food mill or blender. Add salt, butter, sugar, and orange juice. Add more orange juice, if mixture is too dry. Spoon into a buttered 1-quart casserole, and top with chopped pecans. Bake at 350° for 20 minutes. Yield: 4 servings.

BEER BATTER SQUASH

¾ cup beer
1 to 1½ cups all-purpose flour
1 tablespoon grated Parmesan cheese
½ to 1 teaspoon salt
  Dash of garlic powder
1½ teaspoons olive oil
1 egg, separated
  Salad oil
2 medium-size zucchini, sliced
1 pattypan squash, sliced

Let beer stand at room temperature 45 minutes. Combine flour, Parmesan cheese, salt, and garlic powder. Stir in olive oil, beaten egg yolk, and beer; beat until smooth. Fold in stiffly beaten egg white.

Heat salad oil to 400°. Dip vegetables in batter; fry 2 to 5 minutes or until golden brown, turning once. Yield: 8 servings.

ZUCCHINI WITH CHEESE

3 medium-size zucchini, cut into thick
  slices
¼ cup all-purpose flour
  Salt and pepper
4 tablespoons salad oil, divided
3 tablespoons pickle relish
4 tablespoons grated Parmesan cheese,
  divided
½ cup commercial sour cream
2 firm tomatoes, sliced

Dredge zucchini slices in flour seasoned with salt and pepper. Sauté in 3 tablespoons salad oil about 4 minutes, stirring carefully.

Use remaining oil to grease a shallow baking pan. Cover bottom of pan with half of squash; top with pickle relish and half of grated cheese. Add remaining squash; spread with sour cream. Top with tomato slices, and sprinkle with remaining cheese.

Bake at 350° about 20 minutes; then brown under broiler. Yield: 4 servings.

PARTY SQUASH

4 zucchini
1 cup water
  Salt and pepper to taste
2 tablespoons melted butter
½ cup chopped celery
½ cup chopped onion
¼ green pepper, minced
6 slices bacon, crisply fried and
  crumbled
2 tablespoons chopped pimiento
¾ cup shredded cheddar cheese
½ cup buttered bread crumbs

Trim ends from zucchini; cut in half lengthwise. Simmer zucchini in water 20 minutes or until tender; drain. Scoop out pulp, leaving shells intact (discard 2 half shells). Drain pulp thoroughly, and season with salt and pepper; chop.

Brush shells with butter, and season with salt and pepper. Sauté celery, onion, and green pepper in remaining butter until tender; add salt and pepper to taste.

Combine pulp and sautéed vegetables; stuff squash shells with pulp mixture. Sprinkle each with bacon, pimiento, and cheese. Top with bread crumbs.

Place under broiler until crumbs brown. Bake at 250° for about 10 minutes or until thoroughly heated. Yield: 8 servings.

SQUASH WITH WALNUTS

¾ pound zucchini
¾ pound yellow squash
½ cup diced onion
½ cup salad oil
¼ cup dry white wine
**2 tablespoons freshly squeezed lemon
   juice**
½ teaspoon salt
½ cup water
½ cup coarsely chopped walnuts

Wash squash, and cut crosswise into ½-inch slices. Sauté squash and onion in hot salad oil for 5 minutes. Add wine, lemon juice, salt, and water; simmer, covered, for 5 minutes. Add walnuts. Serve hot. Yield: 6 servings.

BAKED ACORN SQUASH WITH APPLES

**2 small acorn squash
   Water**
3 cups peeled grated apple
½ teaspoon salt
**¼ cup firmly packed brown sugar
   Ground nutmeg**
2 tablespoons butter or margarine

Cut squash in half; scoop out seeds. Place, cut sides down, in a baking dish containing ¼ inch water. Cover, and bake at 350° for 30 minutes or until partially done.

Remove from oven, fill with apples, and sprinkle with salt, sugar, and nutmeg; dot with butter. Bake, uncovered, 45 minutes longer or until squash and apples are tender. Yield: 4 servings.

STUFFED ZUCCHINI

6 small zucchini
½ pound ground chuck
½ cup chopped onion
1 clove garlic, minced
½ cup minced green pepper
2 teaspoons oregano
2 tablespoons olive oil
**1 (10¾-ounce) can condensed tomato
   soup, divided**
¾ cup grated Parmesan, divided
**½ cup crushed commercial herb stuffing
   mix**

Cut squash in half lengthwise; scoop out seeds and pulp, leaving a ½-inch shell. Chop seeds and pulp and set aside.

Sauté meat, onion, garlic, pepper, and oregano in oil until onion is tender. Add chopped pulp and seeds, ¼ cup soup, ½ cup cheese, and stuffing mix, blend well. Spoon mixture into zucchini shells.

Arrange stuffed zucchini in a 13- x 9- x 2-inch baking dish. Pour remaining soup over and around zucchini; sprinkle with remaining cheese. Cover, and bake at 375° about 45 minutes or until zucchini is tender. Uncover, and bake 5 minutes longer. Yield: 6 servings.

Soufflés

The mystique surrounding the baked soufflé (as opposed to the fail-safe, gelatin-based refrigerated soufflé) is almost as difficult to dispel as the supposed mystery of pastry making. A soufflé, in the first place, is composed of the most ordinary ingredients. The base is invariably a very thick white sauce or a variation thereof; then there is flavor and bulk, most often in the form of cheese, although sometimes a combination of cheese and meat or vegetables is used; egg yolks are added for richness, and stiffly beaten egg whites, to hold it up, light and airy. Do not be intimidated.

Sometimes a cook can be put off by the prospect of making a "collar" that goes around the top of the dish to support the part of the soufflé that rises above the dish in baking. A baked soufflé doesn't even need that collar, although the gelatin dessert kind does look much more stately from having been jelled with the collar on.

Make the classic "top-hat" effect by the simple act of running a wooden spoon handle into the top 1 inch deep and 1 inch in from the sides of the dish. This not only makes it look pretty, it makes for more even rising and gives added height to the center eliminating the need for the "collar."

Almost nobody has a graduated set of soufflé dishes in order to whip out a 5-cup or 6-cup dish at will. However, any straight-sided glass or ceramic casserole will do, if it is of the right capacity.

Remember: Prepare the soufflé dish, and preheat the oven in advance of starting the recipe. Have eggs at room temperature. And do not use an aluminum saucepan; it will discolor pale mixtures. Have the consumers nearby; the soufflé must go from oven to table posthaste.

BASIC CHEESE SOUFFLÉ FOR 4

¼ cup butter
¼ cup all-purpose flour
1⅓ cups milk, warmed
½ teaspoon salt
½ teaspoon prepared mustard
2 cups shredded cheddar (or combination of favorite cheeses)
4 eggs, separated
1 or 2 additional egg whites

Set oven to 375°. This temperature results in a fairly moist soufflé. For a drier one, set temperature at 325°. Prepare 6-cup soufflé dish by buttering it well and dusting it with Parmesan cheese or fine cracker crumbs.

Melt butter in heavy, nonaluminum saucepan. Stir in flour. Remove pan from heat, and gradually beat in the milk with wire whisk or wooden spoon. Return to heat and cook, stirring constantly, until white sauce is very thick. Beat in salt and mustard. Stir in cheese until it melts. Let stand, covered, until it comes to room temperature. Beat in egg yolks thoroughly, one at a time. Beat egg whites until quite stiff but not dry. Stir a spoonful or the whites into the heavy sauce mixture; then pour sauce over the whites, folding gently with a rubber spatula until whites have been incorporated.

Pour mixture into prepared baking dish. Make an inch deep groove in soufflé, 1 inch in from sides of dish. Place on shelf in center of oven, and bake at 375° for about 30 minutes or at 325° about 50 minutes. In either case, when done, the top will be golden brown, and a skewer inserted in center will come out clean. Serve immediately. Yield: 4 servings.

YOUR SIGNATURE CHEESE SOUFFLÉ FOR 4

After one or two basic cheese soufflés, you will see the principles clearly. Then you can make any sort of soufflé that strikes your fancy. You will find it an excellent way to wrap leftover vegetables or meat in a cloak of glamour. You will need:

1¼ to 1⅓ cups heavy white sauce
½ teaspoon salt
½ teaspoon seasoning
1 cup grated or shredded cheese of your choice
4 eggs, separated
1 cup signature ingredient
1 or 2 additional egg whites

Make the heavy white sauce (béchamel) with milk as in Basic Cheese Soufflé for 4; (use stock instead of milk for velouté sauce). Or perhaps you will think of using a can of condensed cream soup, undiluted. If you decide on the soup, heat it gently to boiling, as though you had just made it; add salt and seasoning, such as mustard, Worcestershire sauce, thick steak sauce, or a dash of cayenne. Stir in cheese until it melts; and cool to room temperature. Beat in egg yolks thoroughly.

Add signature ingredient using your imagination. Just remember to chop it fine, so it won't sink in the light mixture. Choose from among cooked broccoli, spinach, carrots, onion; or from leftover meats, seafood, or poultry, so long as they are also finely chopped. Try to fit the cheese to the signature ingredient, as in Swiss cheese/minced ham. Try cream of chicken or mushroom soup with poultry or fish. Another tasty combination is condensed cream of asparagus soup and chopped cooked asparagus. Fold in stiffly beaten egg whites.

Bake as directed in Basic Cheese Soufflé for 4. Any of these is a delicious luncheon or supper with salad and French bread. Yield: 4 servings.

CHEESE AND RICE SOUFFLÉ

2 tablespoons butter or margarine
3 tablespoons all-purpose flour
¾ cup milk
½ pound sharp cheddar cheese, shredded
4 eggs, separated
½ teaspoon salt
Dash cayenne
1 cup cooked rice

Wrap greased aluminum foil collar around top of lightly greased 1½-quart soufflé dish.

Melt butter over low heat; stir in flour until smooth. Slowly stir in milk; cook, stirring constantly, until thickened. Add cheese and cook, stirring constantly, just until cheese melts. Beat egg yolks slightly; add salt and cayenne. Add a small amount of the hot cheese sauce to egg yolks, and slowly pour egg mixture back into the sauce, stirring rapidly to prevent lumping. Remove from heat and stir in rice.

Beat egg whites just until stiff peaks form; gently fold egg whites into cheese mixture. Pour into soufflé dish. Using a spoon, make a 1-inch deep indentation around cheese mixture, 1 inch from side of dish. (Center part of soufflé will form a "hat.") Bake at 325° for 40 minutes or until puffy and golden brown. Remove collar, and serve immediately. Yield: 5 servings.

BROCCOLI-CHEESE SOUFFLÉ

¼ cup quick-cooking tapioca
1 teaspoon salt
1⅓ cups milk
1 cup shredded cheddar cheese
4 eggs, separated
½ teaspoon marjoram
1 cup chopped cooked broccoli

Wrap a greased aluminum foil collar around top of a lightly greased 1½-quart soufflé dish.

Combine tapioca, salt, and milk in a 1-quart saucepan. Stir over medium heat until mixture comes to a boil. Remove from heat; add cheese and stir until melted.

Beat egg yolks in a large mixing bowl until thickened and lemon colored. Add tapioca mixture and marjoram; blend well. Add broccoli.

Beat egg whites until stiff but not dry; fold in cheese mixture. Pour into soufflé dish; set in a pan of hot water. Bake at 325° for 1 hour. Remove collar and serve at once. Yield: 6 servings.

FOUR-EGG CHEESE SOUFFLÉ

3 tablespoons margarine
3 tablespoons all-purpose flour
Dash salt
Dash cayenne
¾ cup milk
½ pound pasteurized process American cheese, shredded
4 eggs, separated

Wrap a greased aluminum foil collar around top of a lightly greased 1½-quart soufflé dish.

Melt margarine in saucepan; stir in flour and seasonings until smooth. Slowly stir in milk; simmer, stirring constantly, until thickened. Add cheese; stir until melted.

Remove from heat, and gradually add slightly beaten egg yolks; cool. Fold in stiffly beaten egg whites, and pour mixture into soufflé dish. Bake at 300° for 1 hour. Remove collar, and serve immediately. Yield: 4 to 6 servings.

EGG SOUFFLÉ

3 tablespoons butter or margarine
3 tablespoons flour
⅛ teaspoon pepper
1 cup milk
4 eggs, separated
¾ teaspoon salt

Preheat oven to 325°. Set a 1½-quart casserole in a shallow baking pan; place in oven. Pour boiling water around casserole to a depth of at least 1 inch; let casserole heat while soufflé is prepared.

Melt butter in a saucepan; blend in flour and pepper, and cook until bubbly. Add milk all at once; cook, stirring constantly, until smooth and thickened.

Beat egg yolks until thick and lemon colored; add a small amount of hot sauce, blending well. Stir egg yolk mixture into remaining hot sauce. Add salt to egg whites; beat until stiff but not dry; fold in yolk mixture. Pour into heated casserole.

For an attractive appearance, cut into soufflé mixture with a spoon about 1 inch from side of casserole and about 1 inch deep, completely circling the mixture. Bake at 325° for 55 to 60 minutes or until a knife inserted in center comes out clean and soufflé is delicately browned. Serve immediately. Yield: 3 to 4 servings.

CRABMEAT SOUFFLÉ

8 slices bread, divided
2 cups fresh, frozen, or canned crabmeat
½ cup mayonnaise
1 small onion, finely chopped
1 teaspoon salt
1 cup finely chopped celery
3 cups milk
4 eggs, beaten
1 (10-ounce) can condensed cream of
   mushroom soup
1 cup shredded mild cheddar cheese
   Paprika

Cube 4 slices of the bread and spread in 9- x 13-inch casserole. Mix crab, mayonnaise, onion, salt, and celery, and spread over diced bread. Trim crusts from remaining bread, and arrange over crab mixture. Combine milk and eggs; pour over bread layer. Refrigerate overnight.

Two hours before serving time, remove casserole from refrigerator, and allow to stand at room temperature 45 minutes. Bake 15 minutes at 325°. Remove from oven, and spoon undiluted soup over top, sprinkle cheese over it, and dust with paprika. Return to oven, and bake, uncovered, 1 hour. Yield: 8 servings.

JIFFY TUNA SOUFFLÉ

1 (10¾-ounce) can cream of celery soup
1 cup shredded sharp natural cheddar
   cheese
1½ cups cooked rice
1 (7-ounce) can tuna fish, drained and
   flaked
2 tablespoons chopped pimiento
¼ teaspoon pepper
3 eggs, separated

Wrap a greased aluminum foil collar around top of a lightly greased 1½-quart soufflé dish.

Heat soup in saucepan. Add cheese; stir until melted. Remove from heat and add rice, tuna, pimiento, and pepper. Gradually add slightly beaten egg yolks; cool. Fold stiffy beaten egg whites into tuna mixture; pour into soufflé dish. Bake at 350° for 50 minutes. Remove collar, and serve immediately. Yield: 6 servings.

CHOCOLATE SOUFFLÉ

2 tablespoons margarine
2 tablespoons all-purpose flour
½ teaspoon salt
1 cup milk
1 (8-ounce) package cream cheese,
   cubed
2 (1-ounce) squares unsweetened
   chocolate, melted
1½ teaspoons vanilla extract
4 eggs, separated
⅔ cup sugar

Wrap a collar of greased aluminum foil around top of a lightly greased 1½-quart soufflé dish.

Melt margarine in saucepan; stir in flour and salt until smooth. Slowly stir in milk; simmer, stirring constantly, until thickened. Add cream cheese, chocolate, and vanilla; stir until cream cheese is melted. Remove from heat.

Beat egg yolks until thickened and lemon colored; gradually add sugar. Stir into chocolate mixture; cool slightly. Fold into stiffly beaten egg whites; pour into soufflé dish. Bake at 325° for 1 hour. Remove collar, and serve immediately. Yield: 6 to 8 servings.

Grits, Rice, and Pasta

What is the second thing you plan, after the entrée, in a menu? If not a potato dish, you will probably want a hearty, filling accompaniment such as buttered grits, a rice casserole, or a macaroni-cheese combination. True, they are high in calories and in carbohydrates, but these foods carry plus values too: they are especially rich in potassium and phosphorus.

Used correctly, none of the above should throw anybody's diet out of kilter. Grain products such as these not only add bulk to the diet, but they also serve to fill the hungry economically, and have the added talent of making a small amount of meat seem like more than it is. That, of course, is good news for the food budget. Remember, too, that any of these foods stand in for bread on any menu on which they are used.

BOILED GRITS DELUXE

Follow instructions on the box to make amount desired. But instead of using plain water, use chicken broth. This is especially delicious when served with fried chicken.

FRIED GRITS

    1 cup grits, cooked by package
        directions
    Flour for dredging
    Bacon drippings for frying

Pour cooked grits into greased 9- x 15-inch loaf pan. Refrigerate until cold and firm. Slice into ½-inch slices. Dredge with flour.

Heat about ¼-inch bacon drippings in iron skillet, and fry slices over medium heat, turning once, until brown on both sides. Serve hot. Yield: about 8 servings.

GARLIC GRITS CASSEROLE

    1 (6-ounce) roll garlic cheese, cut up
    1 stick margarine, divided
    1 cup quick-cooking grits, prepared by
        package directions
      Milk to make 1 cup when added to egg
    1 egg, beaten
    1 cup coarse, fresh bread crumbs or
        crumbled butter crackers

Stir cheese and about ⅔ of the margarine into the hot, cooked grits. Add milk mixed with egg. Pour into buttered casserole. Melt remaining margarine in small skillet, and sauté crumbs briefly. Top grits with crumbs. Bake at 350° about 30 minutes, or until mixture is quite hot and crumbs browned. Yield: 6 servings.

Variation: Cheddar Cheese Grits—follow Garlic Grits recipe, substituting 6 ounces sharp cheddar cheese, shredded, for garlic cheese.

HERBED RICE

    ¼ cup butter or margarine
    1 cup uncooked regular rice
    2 cups chicken broth
    3 tablespoons instant minced onion
    1 teaspoon salt
    ½ teaspoon rosemary
    ½ teaspoon marjoram
    ½ teaspoon thyme

Combine all ingredients in saucepan. Heat to boiling; stir once. Cover; simmer for 20 minutes or until tender. Yield: 6 servings.

CHEESE-RICE CAKES

1 cup cottage cheese, sieved
1 egg, slightly beaten
½ cup milk
1 cup cooked regular rice
1 tablespoon prepared mustard
½ cup all-purpose flour
½ teaspoon baking powder
¼ teaspoon salt
½ cup drained whole kernel corn
  Mint jelly

Combine cottage cheese and egg; stir in milk, rice, and mustard. Combine flour, baking powder, and salt. Add to cottage cheese mixture; stir until smooth. Stir in corn.

Drop by heaping tablespoonfuls onto a hot, greased griddle; cook until brown on both sides. Serve with mint jelly. Yield: 2 dozen.

FRIED RICE

3½ cups cooked regular rice, chilled
1 cup diced cooked pork, ham, chicken, or beef
¼ cup diced green onion
1 (8-ounce) can water chestnuts, drained and sliced
1 (9-ounce) can sliced mushrooms, drained
3 tablespoons melted margarine
2 eggs, slightly beaten
2 tablespoons soy sauce
½ teaspoon sugar

Stir-fry rice, meat, onion, water chestnuts, and mushrooms in margarine. Add eggs and stir constantly as mixture heats. Stir in soy sauce and sugar. Serve hot. Yield: 4 to 6 servings.

SIMPLY GOOD RICE

1 stick butter or margarine
1 medium-size onion, finely chopped
1 cup plus 2 tablespoons uncooked regular rice
1 cup chicken broth
1 (10-ounce) can condensed beef bouillon
1 tablespoon Worcestershire sauce
½ teaspoon pepper
½ teaspoon salt

Melt butter in skillet. Add onion and rice. Sauté, stirring, for 5 minutes. Add remaining ingredients, and bring to boil. Place in greased 1-quart casserole (or use skillet if it has a close-fitting lid), cover, and bake at 350° for 1 hour. Yield: 5 to 6 servings.

CALVES LIVER PILAF

4 bacon slices
1 medium-size onion, thinly sliced
4 stalks celery, diced
1½ pounds calves liver, thinly sliced
1 (16-ounce) can tomatoes
1 cup water
1 cup uncooked regular rice
1 teaspoon salt
1 bay leaf
  Pinch thyme
1 tablespoon vinegar
1 teaspoon Worcestershire sauce

Cook bacon until done but not crisp; drain. Sauté onion and celery in bacon drippings until wilted; drain.

Lightly brown liver in bacon drippings; stir in all ingredients. Cook 30 minutes over low heat. Discard bay leaf. Yield: about 6 servings.

GREEN RICE

1 cup chopped onion
1 cup finely chopped celery
6 tablespoons melted margarine
1 (10-ounce) package frozen chopped
   broccoli, thawed
1 (8-ounce) package pasteurized
   processed American cheese, cubed
1 (10¾-ounce) can condensed cream of
   mushroom soup
⅔ cup water
2 cups uncooked regular rice
   Dash garlic powder
1 teaspoon parsley flakes
   Salt and pepper to taste

Sauté onion and celery in melted margarine until clear. Add broccoli and cheese; heat until cheese melts. Add remaining ingredients, and blend well. Spoon into a 2-quart casserole; cover, and bake at 350° for 45 minutes. Uncover; reduce heat to 300°, and bake an additional 10 minutes. Yield: 8 to 10 servings.

HUNGARIAN RICE

4 cups chopped cabbage
   Salt and pepper
1 cup uncooked regular rice
1½ cups chicken bouillon
1 tablespoon sugar
6 tablespoons melted butter or
   margarine
2 eggs, beaten
¾ cup half-and-half
1 teaspoon paprika

Sprinkle cabbage with salt and pepper, and let stand about 20 minutes; drain.

Combine rice and bouillon; cover and cook slowly over low heat until liquid is absorbed.

Combine sugar and cabbage; sauté in melted butter until tender, stirring occasionally. Combine cabbage, rice, eggs, half-and-half, paprika, salt, and pepper. Pour mixture into a 2-quart casserole. Cover; bake at 300° for 35 minutes. Yield: 5 to 6 servings.

PASTA CON HAM AND SPINACH

1 tablespoon salt
1 tablespoon olive oil
12 ounces thin spaghetti or fettucini
1 stick butter, divided
1 pound fresh spinach
½ pound fresh mushrooms, washed,
   dried, and sliced
½ cup cooked ham, shredded
¼ cup grated Romano or Parmesan
   cheese

Half fill a large kettle with hot water, and add a tablespoon each, salt and oil; bring to rapid boil. Add spaghetti, and cook al dente. Pour into colander. Into empty kettle, place half the butter, and stir in hot, drained pasta. Reserve.

Wash spinach through several rinses. Lift into heavy saucepan, and cover. Add no water. Cook over low heat just until limp; do not overcook. Drain, and reserve.

Sauté mushrooms in remaining butter, along with the ham. Again, cook lightly so mushrooms retain their character. Lightly press spinach to extract excess water, then toss spinach with mushrooms and ham. Add mixture to pasta, tossing to distribute ingredients. Sprinkle cheese over top, and serve hot. Yield: 4 servings.

Note: An excellent dinner if you add French bread, white wine, and a salad.

SPANISH NOODLES

2 slices bacon, diced
½ pound ground beef
1 medium-sized onion, chopped
1 green pepper, diced
4 ounces wide noodles, uncooked
1 (29-ounce) can tomatoes, broken up
½ cup commercial chili sauce
1 teaspoon dried parsley flakes
1 teaspoon salt
Dash pepper

In Dutch oven or other skillet with a tight cover, fry bacon until crisp. Add meat, and cook until it loses its color, stirring to break it up. Scatter onion and green pepper on top, and cover with noodles. Do not stir; meat and vegetables form a "cushion" under noodles to prevent their sticking. Add remaining ingredients, cover, and bring to a boil. Reduce heat, and simmer 30 to 40 minutes. Do not remove cover for 30 minutes. If not done, replace cover and continue to cook until noodles are tender. Yield: 4 servings.

Note: The dish may also be prepared by assembling as above, then baking it in covered casserole at 350° for 1 hour.

SPAGHETTI WITH SHORT-CUT CLAM SAUCE

1 (16-ounce) package spaghetti
1 (10-ounce) can Manhattan-style clam chowder
2 (7½-ounce) cans minced clams
3 tablespoons olive oil
2 tablespoons chopped fresh parsley
1 large clove garlic, minced
¼ cup dry white wine

Cook spaghetti according to package directions. At the same time, combine remaining ingredients in another saucepan, and simmer while spaghetti cooks. Drain spaghetti; serve on warm plates topped with clam sauce. Yield: 4 servings.

SAVORY DOUBLE-CHEESE MACARONI

1 (8-ounce) package rigatoni or other macaroni
4 tablespoons butter or margarine, divided
Freshly ground pepper to taste
⅓ cup pitted black olives, whole or sliced
1 (4-ounce) jar pimiento, chopped
½ cup chopped parsley, divided
1 (16-ounce) carton creamed cottage cheese
1 (8-ounce) carton commercial sour cream or yogurt
½ cup milk
⅓ cup commercial chili sauce
1 teaspoon salt
¾ cup soft bread crumbs
¼ cup chopped walnuts
½ cup shredded Gouda cheese

Cook rigatoni according to package directions; drain. Melt 2 tablespoons butter in large saucepan. Add pepper, olives, pimiento, rigatoni, and ¼ cup parsley. Toss lightly, and pour into a shallow 2-quart baking dish.

Combine cottage cheese, sour cream, milk, chili sauce, and salt; mix well. Pour over rigatoni mixture. Sauté crumbs and walnuts in remaining butter until lightly browned. Sprinkle crumbs, nuts, remaining parsley, and cheese over rigatoni. Bake at 375° about 30 minutes. Yield: 8 servings.

Breads

Was Heidi's grandmother wrong, coveting white bread, when all the time she probably owed her longevity to the strong peasant bread of her rural Alpine homeland? Maybe. Led by the enthusiasm of our own youth, we are seeing a full circle closing with the popularity of baking whole grain bread like that of Heidi's grandmother and our own grandparents.

Quick breads are a joy, as anyone who has ever buttered a feather light biscuit will attest. But a cook about to try yeast baking for the first time is on the brink of an exciting and sensuous experience. Yeast is alive! It fights back when you knead it; what better way to work out aggression and be creative at the same time? Many a proud baker nowadays, both male and female, will boast of not buying commercial bread at all, for the nutritive value inherent in whole grains is so superior. Toast a slice of that homemade whole-wheat loaf in the morning, and join the "In" group.

Many an inexperienced baker, anxious to go the whole route with whole grains, has baked a leaden loaf because of lack of understanding of the *gluten factor*. Gluten is a high-protein and starch-free product of hard wheat. Rye and other heavy non-wheat flours (or cracked wheat, which isn't ground but chopped) must have gluten added, either in the form of plain (preferably unbleached) flour or gluten flour (available at health food stores) to make the dough elastic. Gluten must have moisture and agitation (kneading) to develop it. The elastic quality we feel when we knead a yeast dough into fighting is the gluten making it come alive in our hands. As a rule of thumb, use at least 1 part wheat flour to two parts rye or cracked wheat. And

branch out; experiment. Juggle recipes; find your own unique combinations, and enjoy, enjoy.

QUICK STICKY BUNS

1 (10-ounce) can refrigerated biscuits
½ cup firmly packed light brown sugar
1 teaspoon ground cinnamon
⅓ cup chopped nuts
2 tablespoons butter, melted and cooled slightly
2 tablespoons honey, warmed

Cut each biscuit in half, and form each piece into a ball. Combine sugar, cinnamon, and nuts in small bowl. Dip each biscuit half into butter, then into sugar mixture. Place in greased 8-inch cakepan. Sugar mixture and unused butter should be mixed and spooned over the biscuit balls. Drizzle warm honey over all. Bake at 450° 10 to 12 minutes. Turn out on warm serving plate. Yield: 20 small buns.

SOUR CREAM BISCUITS

2 cups self-rising flour
1 cup commercial sour cream
1 teaspoon water or milk (optional)

Put flour in a large bowl. Add sour cream; stir to make a soft dough. Add water, if necessary. Turn out on a lightly floured surface; knead about 30 seconds. Roll to ½ inch thick, and cut with floured biscuit cutter. Bake on ungreased baking sheets at 450° for 10 to 15 minutes or until lightly browned. Yield: 12 biscuits.

SWEET POTATO BISCUITS

1 cup all-purpose flour
3 teaspoons baking powder
½ teaspoon salt
⅓ cup margarine
1 cup mashed, cooked sweet potatoes
About 3 tablespoons milk

Combine dry ingredients. Cut in margarine with 2 knives or a pastry blender. Add sweet potatoes and enough milk to make a soft dough. Knead lightly, if desired.

Roll dough to ½-inch thickness; cut in rounds, and place on a lightly greased baking sheet. Bake at 425° for 15 to 20 minutes. Yield: 12 medium-size or 15 small biscuits.

HOT YEAST ROLLS

1 cake yeast
½ cup lukewarm water
1 cup mashed potatoes
⅔ cup shortening
½ cup sugar
1 teaspoon salt
2 eggs, beaten
1 cup warm milk
5 to 6 cups all-purpose flour

Crumble yeast into warm water, and stir well. In large mixing bowl, combine mashed potatoes, shortening, sugar, and salt. Beat on medium speed of electric mixer until well blended. Beat in eggs. Add dissolved yeast and milk. Stir in flour enough to make a soft workable dough. Form dough into ball; place in greased bowl, and turn dough over to grease both sides. Cover with damp towel, and let rise in warm place until doubled in bulk. Punch dough down, and turn out on floured surface. Knead until smooth

and satiny. Return dough to greased bowl, and let rise again until doubled in bulk. Refrigerate until 1½ hours before using. (This gives you ½ hour to shape them and 1 hour for rolls to rise before baking.)

Working with half the dough at a time, roll out, and shape. (See *Shaping Dinner Rolls* for directions.) Let rise in warm place until doubled. Bake at 400° 12 to 15 minutes or until brown. Yield: about 4 dozen rolls.

REFRIGERATOR ROLLS

¾ cup hot water
½ cup sugar
1 tablespoon salt
3 tablespoons margarine
2 packages dry yeast
1 cup very warm water
1 egg, beaten
About 5¼ cups all-purpose flour
Melted butter

Combine hot water, sugar, salt, and margarine; cool to lukewarm.

Soften yeast in very warm water. Add sugar mixture, egg, and half of flour; beat until smooth. Add enough remaining flour to make a soft dough.

Turn dough out on a lightly floured board; knead about 10 minutes or until smooth and elastic. Place in a greased bowl, turning to grease top. Cover tightly with waxed paper or aluminum foil. Store in refrigerator until doubled in bulk or until needed. (Dough may be kept 4 to 5 days.)

To use, punch dough down, and turn out on a lightly floured board, and shape.

Cover; let rise until doubled in bulk. Brush with melted butter. Bake at 400° about 10 to 15 minutes. Yield: 2½ to 4 dozen rolls, depending on shape.

LIGHT AND TENDER ROLLS

1½ cups scalded milk
2 tablespoons sugar
1½ teaspoons salt
⅓ cup shortening
2 packages dry yeast
⅓ cup very warm water
1 egg, well beaten
4½ to 5 cups all-purpose flour
    Melted margarine

Combine milk, sugar, salt, and shortening; let stand until lukewarm.

Dissolve yeast in very warm water; add to milk mixture. Stir in egg. Gradually add enough flour to make a soft dough that leaves sides of bowl.

Cover with a towel, and let rise in a warm place until doubled in bulk.

Punch dough down, and turn out on a lightly floured board or pastry cloth; knead lightly, and shape. Brush with melted margarine. Let rise until doubled in bulk (about 45 minutes). Bake at 425° for 10 to 15 minutes. Yield: about 3 dozen rolls, depending on shape.

DRESSING FOR TURKEY

4 cups bread crumbs (half corn bread
    and half biscuit and light bread)
2 cups diced celery
1 cup chopped onion
2 tablespoons freshly squeezed lemon
    juice
1 teaspoon salt
¼ teaspoon red pepper
½ teaspoon Worcestershire sauce
½ teaspoon steak sauce
1 to 1½ cups butter
1 cup hot water or stock

Combine bread crumbs, celery, onion, lemon juice, salt, and pepper. Blend Worcestershire sauce and steak sauce with butter, and add to mixture. Stuff turkey, and place in roaster with 1 cup hot water. Cover, and bake at 325° for 30 minutes to the pound. When turkey is almost tender, remove cover, and brown. Make gravy from drippings when bird is done. Yield: 6 to 8 servings.

Note: Do not stuff until ready to bake; then be to sure separate leftover poultry and dressing. Or bake dressing in separate greased casserole.

FAVORITE BREAD DRESSING

1½ cups minced onion
3 cups diced celery
1 cup shortening
1 tablespoon salt
½ teaspoon pepper
2 teaspoons poultry seasoning
4 quarts bread crumbs
1½ to 2 cups broth or water

Cook onion and celery in shortening over low heat until onion is soft but not browned, stirring occasionally. Meanwhile, blend seasonings with bread, which has been crumbled. Add the onion, celery, and shortening and blend. Pour the broth gradually over surface, stirring lightly. Add more seasoning as desired. Bake, uncovered, in a 13- x 9- x 2-inch pan at 325° about 45 minutes. Yield: dressing for a 14- to 18-pound turkey.

CHOCOLATE WAFFLES

3 eggs
1½ cups buttermilk
1 teaspoon soda
1½ cups all-purpose flour
¼ cup cocoa
2 teaspoons baking powder
½ teaspoon salt
1 stick softened butter or margarine,
    melted and cooled
Powdered sugar
Cocoa

Preheat waffle iron. Beat eggs until light; then beat in the buttermilk. Sift dry ingredients together, and beat into the liquid mixture. Add melted butter, beating until smooth. The batter is fairly thin. Bake in hot waffle iron. To serve, pass softened butter and a bowl of powdered sugar that has been sifted with cocoa (use about a cup of sugar to a tablespoon cocoa). Yield: 8 waffles.

STRAWBERRY PANCAKES

2 eggs
½ cup flour
½ teaspoon salt
½ teaspoon baking powder
2 tablespoons melted butter or oil
½ cup milk
2 tablespoons oil
½ cup powdered sugar, divided
¼ teaspoon cinnamon
1 quart fresh strawberries, sliced
1 cup whipping cream, whipped
½ teaspoon vanilla extract
2 teaspoons sugar

Beat eggs just until blended. Stir flour, salt, baking powder together; beat into eggs. Add butter and milk, and beat until smooth. Let stand while oven heats to 450° with a 10-inch iron skillet inside. Put the 2 tablespoons oil in hot skillet, and immediately pour in batter. Bake at 450° for 15 minutes, using bottom shelf of oven. Pull skillet out, and prick the large bubbles with a sharp fork. Replace pancake in oven on top shelf for another 4 or 5 minutes.

Sift powdered sugar with cinnamon. Sprinkle half the mixture over hot pancake. Add other half to the strawberries. Pour strawberries over hot pancake. Top with cream which has been flavored with vanilla and sugar. Slice, and serve immediately. Yield: 4 large breakfast servings or 8 dessert servings.

GOOD MORNING COFFEE CAKE

½ cup butter or margarine
1 cup sugar
2 eggs
1 teaspoon vanilla extract
2 cups all-purpose flour
1 teaspoon soda
1 teaspoon baking powder
½ teaspoon salt
1 cup commercial sour cream
    Filling-Topping Mixture

In large bowl of mixer, combine butter and sugar, beating until light and fluffy. Beat in eggs, and add vanilla. Sift or stir dry ingredients together and add, alternately with sour cream, to original mixture, beating only until smooth. Pour half the batter into greased 9- x 13-inch baking pan. Sprinkle with half the Filling-Topping Mixture. Drop remaining batter over the dry layer, and spread carefully. Top with remaining half the Filling-Topping Mixture. Bake at 325° for 40 to 45 minutes. Yield: 10 or 12 servings.

Filling-Topping Mixture:

⅓ cup firmly packed light brown sugar
½ cup sugar
1 teaspoon cinnamon
1 cup finely chopped pecans

Mix ingredients, and set aside.

ORANGE FRENCH TOAST

1 long loaf French bread
2 cups milk
4 eggs
¼ cup orange marmalade
1 stick butter
Orange Syrup

Slice bread into pieces ¾ to 1 inch thick. Place close together in a large baking pan with 1-inch sides. In jar of electric blender, place milk, eggs, and marmalade, and blend until marmalade has almost disappeared. Pour evenly over bread slices. Cover with plastic wrap and refrigerate overnight. Turn bread once. Heat butter in large iron skillet, and fry toast over medium heat until nicely browned on both sides. Serve with Orange Syrup. Yield: 6 to 8 servings.

Orange Syrup:

1 (6-ounce) can frozen orange juice
   concentrate
1 (6-ounce) can water
¾ cup light corn syrup

Combine ingredients in saucepan, and simmer 10 minutes. Serve, hot, over Orange French Toast. Yield: about 2 cups.

CRISPY CORNMEAL CRACKERS

1½ cups all-purpose flour
½ cup cornmeal
1½ teaspoons salt
1½ teaspoons dry mustard
½ cup shortening
1 tablespoon prepared horseradish
2 tablespoons cold water
½ cup buttermilk

Combine flour, cornmeal, salt, and mustard. Cut in shortening and horseradish until mixture resembles coarse crumbs. Blend water and buttermilk; add to dry ingredients, stirring lightly until just dampened (dough will be sticky).

Turn out on lightly floured surface. Knead gently a few times. Divide dough in half. Roll each half of dough paper thin; cut with floured, 2-inch, round cookie cutter. Place on ungreased cookie sheets; prick with fork. Bake at 375° for 10 to 12 minutes or until lightly browned. Yield: 8½ dozen crackers.

GEORGIA HUSH PUPPIES

2 cups self-rising cornmeal
½ cup finely chopped onion
1½ to 2 cups boiling water
1 egg, beaten
Oil

Combine cornmeal and onion. Stir in 1½ cups boiling water, mixing until well blended. Stir in egg. Add more water, if necessary, to make a thick batter.

Drop by rounded tablespoonfuls into oil for frying and fry until golden brown (about 3 to 4 minutes), turning once. Drain on absorbent paper. Serve hot. Yield: 2 dozen hush puppies.

CRACKLING CORN BREAD

1 cup cracklings, finely chopped
1½ cups water (or enough to cover
cracklings)
2 cups commercial corn bread mix
½ cup buttermilk
1 tablespoon fat or bacon drippings

Place 9- or 10-inch skillet in oven, and preheat oven to 450°.

In heavy saucepan, place cracklings, and cover with water. Bring to boil. Remove from heat and add corn bread mix, beating it in well. Add buttermilk, and beat well again. Take skillet from oven, and grease it with fat; rotate skillet to coat bottom. Pour in batter, and bake 25 to 30 minutes until golden brown. Yield: 8 servings.

SPOONBREAD

3 cups milk
1½ teaspoons salt
2 tablespoons butter or margarine
1 cup white cornmeal
3 eggs

Warm milk in heavy saucepan. Add salt and butter. Gradually stir in cornmeal. Increase heat, and cook, stirring, until well thickened, about 10 minutes. Beat eggs in large bowl of electric mixer. Slowly pour or spoon hot mixture into eggs, beating constantly. Pour batter into buttered 1½-quart baking dish. Bake 35 to 40 minutes at 400°. Bread is done when center doesn't look soft when dish is shaken. Yield: 6 servings.

PUMPKIN MUFFINS

¾ cup firmly packed light brown sugar
¼ cup molasses
½ cup butter or margarine, softened
1 egg
1 cup canned or cooked, mashed
pumpkin
1 teaspoon soda
½ teaspoon salt
1¾ cups unbleached flour
½ cup chopped nuts

In large bowl of mixer, combine sugar, molasses, and butter. Beat until creamy. Add egg and pumpkin, and beat well. Stir soda and salt into flour, and beat into pumpkin mixture. Fold in nuts. Spoon into well-greased muffin tins, and bake at 375° for approximately 20 minutes. Yield: 1½ to 2 dozen muffins.

BRAN MUFFINS BY THE GALLON

1½ cups sugar
1 cup butter or margarine, softened
4 eggs, beaten
1 teaspoon salt
1 quart buttermilk
5 teaspoons soda
2 cups boiling water
4 cups bran flakes
2 cups 100% bran cereal
5 cups unbleached flour

In a very large bowl, beat sugar and butter together; blend in eggs and salt. Mix buttermilk, soda, and water; add to butter mixture. Add flakes, cereal, and flour. Stir until thoroughly blended. To bake, grease muffin cups, and fill them ⅔ full with batter. Bake at 400° for 15 to 20 minutes, depending on size of muffin tins. Remainder of batter will keep up to a month refrigerated, to be used as needed. Yield: 1 gallon batter.

FRESH ORANGE MUFFINS

 2 tablespoons butter or margarine,
   softened
¼ cup firmly packed brown sugar
 1 egg
 2 tablespoons grated orange rind
¼ cup orange juice
¼ cup milk
 1 cup unbleached flour
1½ teaspoons baking powder
¼ teaspoon salt

Cream butter and sugar until light and fluffy. Add egg; beat well. Stir in orange rind, orange juice, and milk. Combine flour, baking powder, and salt; add to creamed mixture, stirring just enough to moisten dry ingredients.

Fill greased muffin pans two-thirds full, and bake at 400° for 20 minutes or until lightly browned. Yield: 6 muffins.

COTTAGE CHEESE DILL BREAD

 1 package dry yeast
¼ cup warm water
 1 cup small curd cottage cheese
 1 tablespoon butter or margarine
 1 tablespoon sugar
 1 tablespoon dehydrated onion
 1 teaspoon dillweed (or seed)
 1 teaspoon salt
¼ teaspoon baking soda
 1 egg, beaten
   About 2½ cups all-purpose flour

Dissolve yeast in warm water. Heat cottage cheese to lukewarm, and stir in butter.

Remove from heat. In large bowl of mixer, combine cottage cheese mixture, sugar, onion, dill, salt, soda, and egg. Beat well. Add dissolved yeast, continuing to beat. Gradually beat in flour, enough to make a soft dough. Form into ball, and place in greased bowl. Oil top of dough, and cover with damp cloth. Allow to rise in warm place until doubled in bulk. Punch down.

Turn out on floured surface, and work dough just enough to form it into a loaf; for a round loaf, use a well-greased, 1½-quart casserole. For regular loaf, use a greased 9- x 5-inch loaf pan. (This is a rather soft dough; no kneading required except to form the loaf.) Oil top of loaf. Allow to rise again until doubled. Bake at 350° for 35 to 40 minutes or until it tests done. Yield: 1 loaf.

NO-YEAST CHEESE BREAD

 2 cups unbleached flour
½ teaspoon soda
¾ teaspoon salt
 2 teaspoons baking powder
1½ cups finely shredded sharp cheddar
   cheese
 2 teaspoons caraway seeds
 1 cup evaporated milk
 1 tablespoon vinegar
 1 egg, slightly beaten
 1 tablespoon vegetable oil

Into large bowl, sift or stir flour with soda, salt, and baking powder. Blend in cheese and caraway. Combine milk, vinegar, egg, and oil. Add to flour mixture, and stir just until moistened throughout. Pour into greased 9- x 5-inch loaf pan, and bake at 350° for 50 minutes or until it tests done. Yield: 1 loaf.

GLAZED LEMON NUT BREAD

½ cup butter or margarine
¾ cup sugar
2 eggs
2 teaspoons grated lemon rind
2 cups all-purpose flour
2½ teaspoons baking powder
1 teaspoon salt
¾ cup milk
½ cup chopped walnuts
2 teaspoons lemon juice
2 tablespoons powdered sugar

Combine butter and sugar in large bowl of mixer and beat until creamy. Beat in eggs and lemon rind. Sift, or stir the flour with baking powder and salt. Add, alternately with milk, to original mixture. Fold in nuts. Pour batter into well-greased, 8½- x 4½- x 2½-inch loaf pan. Bake at 350° for 50 to 55 minutes or until wooden pick inserted in center comes out clean. Remove from pan; turn right side up on rack. To glaze, combine lemon juice with powdered sugar. Spoon over hot bread. Glaze will harden. Yield: 1 loaf.

LEMON BREAD

1⅔ cups all-purpose flour
1 teaspoon soda
½ teaspoon salt
½ cup shortening
1 cup sugar
2 eggs, slightly beaten
½ cup milk
½ cup chopped nuts
1 tablespoon grated lemon rind
1 tablespoon freshly squeezed lemon juice
¼ cup sugar

Combine flour, soda, and salt. Cream together shortening and sugar; add eggs, and mix well. Add dry ingredients to creamed mixture alternately with milk. Stir in nuts and lemon rind. Spoon mixture into a greased 9- x 5- x 3-inch loaf pan. Bake at 350° for 1 hour.

Combine lemon juice and sugar; heat until sugar is dissolved. Remove bread from oven, and let cool for 5 minutes before removing from pan. Remove from pan, and pour lemon-sugar mixture over warm loaf. Finish cooling on cake rack. Yield: 1 loaf.

CRUSTY OAT BREAD

2 cakes or 2 packages dry yeast
½ cup warm water
2 cups boiling water
3 tablespoons sugar
1 tablespoon salt
3 tablespoons softened shortening
5½ to 6½ cups unbleached flour, divided
1½ cups plus 2 tablespoons regular oats, uncooked
2 tablespoons milk

Soften yeast in warm water. (Dry yeast takes warmer water than yeast cakes.) Pour boiling water over sugar, salt, and shortening in large mixing bowl. Stir to melt shortening. Cool to lukewarm. Beat in 1 cup flour. Add yeast and 1½ cups oats. Gradually add flour. Unless you have a dough hook on your mixer, you will have to work in the remainder of the flour by hand or with a wooden spoon. Add enough flour to make a soft but workable dough. Turn out on floured surface, and knead until smooth, about 10 minutes. Round dough into ball, place in large greased bowl, and turn dough over to grease all sides. Cover with damp towel, and set to rise in warm place until doubled in bulk, an hour or more. Punch down, cover, and let rest 10 minutes.

Divide dough in half; form into loaves. Place, smooth sides up, in two greased 8½- x 4½- x 2½-inch loaf pans. Brush with milk, and sprinkle 2 tablespoons dry oats over tops. Let rise about 45 minutes until dough fills pans. Bake at 375° about 50 minutes or until bread is brown and tests done. Yield: 2 loaves.

YOUR SIGNATURE BREAD LOAF

    1 envelope dry yeast
1¼ cups warm water
    1 tablespoon honey, brown sugar, or
        molasses
    1 egg
    2 tablespoons safflower oil or melted
        butter
    1 teaspoon salt
    ½ cup dry milk solids
2½ cups grains
    2 cups (approximately) unbleached flour

In large bowl of mixer, stir yeast with water that is warmer than lukewarm. When dissolved, beat in honey, egg, oil, salt, and dry milk solids.

Here's where you make the recipe your own. Make up a total of 2½ cups, choosing and combining regular uncooked oats, wheat germ, whole wheat flour, cornmeal, bran, and soya grits. About a cup of the mix should be whole wheat. Beat the mixture into original wet mix. When the electric mixer begins to overload (unless you have a dough hook on it), remove bowl, and stir

in remaining unbleached flour by hand or wooden spoon, adding enough to make a good workable dough. Turn out on floured surface; knead 10 minutes or until smooth and elastic. Form into ball, place in greased bowl, and turn to grease all sides. Cover with damp towel, and let rise in warm place until doubled in bulk. Punch down, let rest 15 minutes; then form into loaf. Place in large greased 9½- x 5½-inch loaf pan, oil top, and cover with damp towel. Let rise again until dough reaches top of pan. Bake at 350° about an hour (340° if using oven-proof glass pan) or until it tests done. Cool on rack. Yield: 1 loaf.

APRICOT-NUT BREAD

    ½ cup dried apricots
    2 cups all-purpose flour
    2 teaspoons baking powder
    1 teaspoon soda
    1 cup sugar
    ¼ teaspoon salt
        Boiling water
        Juice and grated rind of 1 large orange
    1 egg, beaten
    2 tablespoons melted margarine
    1 teaspoon vanilla extract
    ½ cup chopped dates
    ½ cup chopped nuts

Cover apricots with cold water; let stand 30 minutes. Drain and chop; set aside.

Combine dry ingredients. Add enough boiling water to orange juice to make 1 cup liquid; add to dry ingredients, and mix well. Combine egg, margarine, and vanilla; add to batter, mixing well. Stir in dates, nuts, orange rind, and apricots. Pour into a well-greased and floured 9- x 5- x 3-inch loaf pan. Bake at 350° for 50 minutes. Yield: 1 loaf.

BANANA BREAD

1 stick butter or margarine, softened
2 cups sugar
2 eggs
2 cups all-purpose flour
1 teaspoon soda
3 bananas, well mashed

Place softened butter in large bowl of electric mixer; add sugar. Beat until creamy. Add eggs, and beat 1 minute. Sift, or stir flour and soda together. Beat flour mixture alternately with bananas into egg mixture; beat 1 minute. Grease a 9- x 5- x 3-inch loaf pan, and pour batter into it. Bake at 350° for 30 minutes or until a wooden pick inserted in center comes out clean. Cool before cutting. Yield: 1 loaf.

Note: This is a good recipe for those who must control their salt intake as there is no salt in the recipe.

HIGH PROTEIN BREAD

1 cup 2% milk, scalded
2 tablespoons honey
3 tablespoons solid shortening
1 tablespoon salt
1 cup cold water
½ cup soy granules
1 cup whole wheat flour
4 cups unbleached flour
2 packages dry yeast
  Melted butter or oil

In large bowl of mixer, combine milk, honey, shortening, and salt. Stir to dissolve shortening. Add water. Combine in another bowl the soy granules, whole wheat, unbleached flour, and dry yeast.

Gradually beat dry mixture into milk mixture until mixer begins to sound "labored." If you have a dough hook, you may add all flour by machine. If not, take bowl from mixer and add remaining flour mixture with wooden spoon or by hand. Do not use quite all the flour, if it makes mixture too dry. Mix well. Form into ball, place in greased bowl, turn ball over to grease both sides. Cover with damp towel in warm place, and set to rise until doubled in bulk which will take about an hour at 80-85°.

Punch down dough; knead on floured surface about 10 minutes or until dough feels smooth and elastic. Divide dough, and form into 2 loaves. Place in greased 9- x 5-inch loaf pans. Brush tops with melted butter. Set in warm place to rise until dough fills pans, about 45 minutes at 80-85°.

Bake at 375° for about 45 to 50 minutes or until well-browned loaves sound hollow when thumped with finger. Turn out of pans. If soft crust is desired, cool loaves in paper bag. If not, cool on racks. Yield: 2 loaves.

WHOLE-WHEAT HONEY BREAD

3¾ cups whole wheat flour
2½ cups unbleached flour
  2 packages dry yeast or 2 cakes yeast
  ½ cup warm water
1¾ cups lukewarm milk
  ½ cup honey
  1 tablespoon salt
  ¼ cup softened shortening

Combine flours. Soften yeast in warm water.

In large bowl of mixer, combine milk, honey, and salt, stirring to dissolve. Beat in shortening, yeast mixture, and 1 cup of the flour. Beat until smooth. Gradually add remaining flour, beating with electric mixer as long as possible; then finish blending by hand. It may take a little more or less than the given measurement of the flour. What is wanted is a soft but workable dough. Turn dough out on floured surface, and knead until smooth and elastic, about 10 minutes. Place in greased bowl, and turn dough to grease top. Cover with damp towel, and let rise in warm place until doubled in bulk, 1 to 1½ hours. Punch down, and let rise again for about an hour.

Punch down dough, and divide into 2 equal portions. With rolling pin, roll each half into a rectangle about 8 x 15 inches. Roll up tightly, starting at narrow end. Place, seam side down, in two 9- x 5- x 3-inch greased loaf pans. Brush with melted butter. Cover with waxed paper, and let rise in warm place until dough fills pan, 1 to 1½ hours. Bake at 375° for 45 to 50 minutes or until it tests done. Remove loaves to rack to cool. Yield: 2 loaves.

NOVA SCOTIA OAT CAKES

3 cups unbleached flour
3 cups regular oats, uncooked
1 cup butter, softened
1 cup shortening, softened
½ cup sugar
½ teaspoon salt
¼ cup water

Mix by hand all ingredients in the order stated. Working with half the dough at a time, form into flat rectangle, and place between two sheets of waxed paper. Roll out to a thickness of about ½ inch. Cut into squares or diamonds. Bake on ungreased cookie sheets in 375° oven for 15 to 20 minutes or until lightly browned. Yield: 3 to 4 dozen oat cakes.

BOSTON BROWN BREAD

¾ cup raisins
Boiling water
1½ cups chopped English walnuts
¼ cup all-purpose flour
½ cup firmly packed light brown sugar
3 tablespoons shortening
½ cup molasses
1 egg
1 teaspoon soda
2½ cups buttermilk
1 teaspoon salt
4 cups graham flour

Cover raisins with boiling water, and let stand to plump for 10 minutes. Drain on paper towels. Combine with nuts, and dredge with ¼ cup flour.

In large bowl of mixer, cream the sugar and shortening. Beat in molasses and egg. Dissolve soda in buttermilk and add, along with the salt, to batter. Blend in graham flour thoroughly. Fold into the raisin-nut mixture. Divide batter among 5 well-greased 1-pound cans. Stand cans in pan containing 1 inch water, and bake at 350° for 1 hour or until wire inserted in center comes out clean. Cut around bottom of can, and use the loosened covering to push bread up and out. Yield: 5 loaves.

Desserts

Time was, dessert, pastries, and cakes were the hallmark of a fine cook. Now, thanks to America's national disease, obesity, a host or hostess is likely to feel ill at ease in offering a high-calorie dessert. Still there are people and occasions to demand them, so you'll find plenty of mouth-watering pies and cakes in this section. You will also find a number of non-pastries, such as fruit concoctions flavored with a little wine. In some of the latter, where sugar is not a factor in the bulk or thickening of a dish, you could substitute your favorite artificial sweetener.

The fledgling cake or pie baker will find help in the *Art of Preparation* section of the book. Cast out fear, and bake away. Remember this: much of cooking is rescue work. I once served a lemon meringue pie, whose filling didn't thicken, by spooning it into parfait glasses. The family thought it divine, that stately swirl of flaky pastry, lemon "sauce," and pale brown meringue. If you can't use it, laughing, pitch it out.

Guidance is something you can scrape off a page with your eyes; experience is not. Make a dish again if you are not successful the first time. You'll quickly come to realize that recipes are an inexact ruler. Flour for bread, for example, cannot be stated exactly because of such factors as the dryness of flour or the size of eggs. Baking time can throw you off; your oven thermostat may need adjusting or you may be using a deeper or shallower pan than the one called for. Experience will nurture your common sense until you'll know by "feel" when there is enough water in the piecrust and enough flour in the bread. Soon you'll be swashbuckling with the best of them.

COFFEE-CHARLOTTE SQUARES

2 tablespoons instant coffee
1 cup hot water
½ pound (about 32) marshmallows, cut up
1 cup whipping cream, whipped
18 ladyfingers, split

In saucepan, dissolve coffee in water. Add cut marshmallows. Place over low heat and stir until marshmallows dissolve. Chill until slightly thickened. Fold in whipped cream. Grease and line bottom of a shallow rectangular dish or 6-cup mold with ladyfingers. Cover with layers of coffee mixture and ladyfingers, ending with the coffee mixture on top. Cover with greased waxed paper, and refrigerate 8 hours or overnight. Cut into squares. Yield: 8 to 10 servings.

PEPPERMINT BAVARIAN

1½ envelopes (1½ tablespoons) unflavored gelatin
⅓ cup cold water
6 egg yolks
¾ cup sugar
    Pinch salt
1½ cups milk
1¼ cups finely crushed peppermint sticks, divided*
2 drops oil of peppermint (optional)
1½ cups whipping cream

Sprinkle gelatin over water to soften. In top of double boiler, beat egg yolks until light and lemon colored. Slowly beat in sugar and salt. In another saucepan, heat milk with 1 cup of the candy, and stir over low heat to dissolve. Stir hot mixture slowly into egg yolks. Cook stirring, over hot (not boiling) water, until it will coat a metal spoon.

Stir in softened gelatin. Set aside to cool. Add flavoring, if desired. Whip cream until stiff. Fold cooled custard into whipped cream. Pour into a 6-cup mold, and refrigerate overnight or all day. To serve, unmold on chilled serving plate and garnish with remaining ¼ cup crushed peppermint candy. Yield: 8 or more servings.

*Electric blender makes short work of crushing candy.

Note: For an added grace note, drizzle a little chocolate syrup over each serving.

BOURBON MOUSSE

2 envelopes (2 tablespoons) unflavored gelatin
1 cup cold water
8 eggs, separated (room temperature)
¾ cup bourbon
2 tablespoons vanilla extract
1 cup sugar
1 cup whipping cream, whipped to Chantilly stage, flavored
Nutmeg

Sprinkle gelatin over cold water. When softened, place over hot water, and stir to dissolve completely. Using smaller bowl of mixer beat egg yolks until light and fluffy. Beating at slow speed, add bourbon, vanilla, and dissolved gelatin.

In large bowl of mixer, beat egg whites until they hold very soft peaks. Gradually add sugar, beating until mixture is quite stiff. Stir a spoonful of whites into yolk mixture. Pour yolk mixture over whites, and fold together gently but thoroughly. (Sometimes it helps keep an egg white-gelatin mixture from separating while it

jells if you refrigerate for a few minutes at this point, then fold again before pouring into mold; however, don't let it jell completely in the bowl.)

Pour into 7- or 8-cup mold, and refrigerate several hours or overnight to jell firmly. To serve, dip mold quickly up to rim in hot water, and place chilled, wet dessert plate over it. Turn over the whole assembly; give it a quick shake to deposit dessert on plate. (The point of wetting a dish to receive gelatin is that if the gelatin happens to land off-center, it can be moved by sliding it with your hands. It will not slide on a dry plate.) Cut, and serve on chilled dessert dishes. Garnish each serving with Chantilly cream and a dash of nutmeg. Yield: 8 servings.

CHOCOLATE ANGEL FANCY

1 (12-ounce) package semisweet chocolate pieces
2 tablespoons water
3 eggs, separated
1 teaspoon vanilla
½ teaspoon salt
1 tablespoon sugar
1 cup whipping cream, whipped
1 (8-inch) angel food cake

In top of double boiler, melt chocolate with water. Beat egg yolks, and blend into chocolate. Cook and stir a few seconds. Add vanilla and salt; cool. Blend sugar into whipped cream, and fold into chocolate. Whip egg whites until stiff, and fold into chocolate mixture. Slice cake thinly, and place in bottom of a 13- x 9- x 2-inch baking dish, overlapping as necessary. Pour chocolate mixture over cake. Refrigerate several hours or overnight. Cut into squares to serve. Yield: 10 to 12 servings.

CREAM SQUARES

⅓ cup sugar
⅓ cup cornstarch
  Pinch salt
2 cups milk
½ cinnamon stick, halved
1 egg
1 tablespoon water
1 cup fine bread crumbs
¼ cup butter or margarine
1 tablespoon sugar
½ teaspoon cinnamon

In a heavy saucepan, combine sugar, cornstarch, and salt. Add milk gradually, stirring. Add cinnamon stick, and cook over medium heat, stirring constantly, until quite thick and smooth. Remove cinnamon. Pour into buttered 8-inch square pan, and smooth top. Cover with plastic wrap, and refrigerate several hours or overnight. Turn out on waxed paper, and cut into 16 squares. Beat egg with water. Dip cream squares into egg, then into crumbs. Heat butter in heavy skillet, and fry breaded cream squares until lightly brown on both sides. Place on 4 individual dessert plates and sprinkle with sugar mixed with cinnamon. Serve hot. Yield: 4 servings.

VANILLA CRÊPES WITH ORANGE SAUCE

1 cup milk
2 tablespoons vanilla extract
½ cup sugar
3 tablespoons all-purpose flour
3 eggs, separated
16 crêpes
2 tablespoons melted butter
  Orange Sauce

Scald milk and vanilla. Set aside. Combine sugar, flour, and egg yolks. Stir in milk mixture. Cook over medium heat, stirring constantly, until mixture comes to a boil. Cook a few seconds; remove from heat. Beat egg whites until stiffened; fold gently into egg yolk mixture. Place about 3 tablespoons batter on each crêpe; roll crêpes loosely over batter. Place on cookie sheet; brush crêpes with melted butter. Bake at 350° for 20 to 25 minutes. Arrange crêpes on platter; serve immediately with Orange Sauce. Yield: 8 servings.

Orange Sauce:

⅔ cup sugar
3 egg yolks
1 cup scalded milk
2 tablespoons orange extract

Combine sugar and egg yolks in saucepan. Stir in scalded milk and orange extract. Cook over medium heat, stirring constantly, until sauce thickens and coats the spoon. Do not let it boil. Remove from heat. Serve hot or cold. Yield: 2 cups.

RHUBARB CRUNCH

1 cup all-purpose flour
¾ cup regular oats, uncooked
1 cup firmly packed light brown
  sugar
½ cup melted butter or
  margarine
4 cups sliced rhubarb
1 cup water
1 cup sugar
2 tablespoons cornstarch
1 teaspoon vanilla extract

Stir together the flour, oats, and brown sugar. Add butter. Mix well, and press half the mixture into 9-inch square pan. Distribute rhubarb over crumb mixture. Combine water, sugar, and cornstarch in small saucepan and cook, stirring, until thickened, about 5 minutes. Add vanilla, and pour over rhubarb. Top evenly with remaining crumb mixture. Bake 1 hour at 350°. Best served warm. Yield: 9 servings.

Note: Almost any fruit juice may be substituted for water. If it is syrup drained from canned fruit, reduce sugar to ¾ cup.

BASIC PASTRY CREAM

⅓ cup sugar
¼ cup cornstarch
   Pinch salt
2 cups milk, warmed
3 egg yolks
1 teaspoon vanilla extract

Combine sugar, cornstarch, and salt in top pan of double boiler over boiling water, or use a heavy saucepan. Add a little milk, and mix until smooth. Add remaining milk, stirring constantly, to keep the mixture smooth. Stir and cook over medium heat until quite thick. Beat egg yolks, and slowly pour about half the hot mixture into them. Add back to pan, stirring rapidly; reduce heat, and cook until thick as mayonnaise. Remove from heat, and add vanilla. Yield: about 2 cups. (Filling for 8 tarts or 8 large cream puffs.)

Variations: Coffee pastry cream: Add 2 teaspoons instant coffee to original dry mixture; then proceed with recipe.

Chocolate pastry cream: Add 2 squares semisweet chocolate, grated, after combining egg yolks with cornstarch mixture.

Coconut pastry cream: Add ½ cup flaked coconut after cooking, along with vanilla.

Almond pastry cream: Add ½ teaspoon almond extract instead of vanilla, and stir in ¼ cup finely chopped almonds.

OATMEAL CARMELITAS

32 light-colored caramel
   candies
5 tablespoons evaporated milk or
   half-and-half
1 cup all-purpose flour
1 cup quick-cooking rolled
   oats
¾ cup firmly packed light brown
   sugar
½ teaspoon soda
¼ teaspoon salt
¾ cup butter or margarine,
   melted
1 (6-ounce) package chocolate
   pieces
½ cup chopped nuts

In top of double boiler, combine caramels with milk, and melt over simmering water. Cool slightly, but keep mixture pourable. In a large bowl, combine flour, oats, sugar, soda, salt, and butter. Stir well to blend. Press half the crumb mixture into bottom of a 9-inch square pan. Bake 10 minutes at 350°. Take from oven and sprinkle chocolate pieces and nuts over baked layer. Carefully pour the caramel over all; then add remaining crumb mixture evenly over the top. Bake 15 to 20 minutes at 350°. Chill 1 to 2 hours. Cut into bars or squares. Yield: 1 (9-inch) square cake.

BANANA SPLIT CAKE

1 cup margarine, divided
1½ cups vanilla wafer crumbs
2 cups powdered sugar
2 eggs
1 teaspoon vanilla extract
3 or 4 bananas, sliced
1 (20-ounce) can crushed pineapple,
    drained
1 (9-ounce) carton frozen whipped
    topping, thawed
½ cup chopped pecans or walnuts

Melt ½ cup margarine, and add to crumbs. Mix well, and pat into a 13- x 9- x 2-inch pan.

Combine sugar, eggs, ½ cup softened margarine and vanilla; beat until smooth and creamy. Spread over crust. Add a layer of banana slices and pineapple; spread whipped topping evenly over fruit. Sprinkle with nuts. Refrigerate until set. Yield: 12 to 15 servings.

CHERRY PINK CAKE

2¼ cups sifted cake flour
3 teaspoons baking powder
½ teaspoon salt
1⅓ cups sugar
½ cup butter or margarine, softened
16 maraschino cherries, chopped
¼ cup juice from cherries
½ cup milk
4 egg whites, unbeaten
½ cup chopped walnuts

Combine cake flour, baking powder, salt, and sugar; sift together into a large bowl. Add butter, cherries, cherry juice, and milk; blend well at medium speed of electric mixer or mix by hand. Add egg whites; beat 2 minutes at medium speed of electric mixer or 300 strokes by hand. Fold in nuts.

Spoon batter into 2 well-greased and floured 8-inch cakepans. Bake at 350° for 30 minutes. Cool, and frost with your favorite white frosting. Yield: 2 (8-inch) layers.

APPLE-NUT CAKE

1¼ cups salad oil
2 eggs
2 cups sugar
3 cups all-purpose flour
1 teaspoon salt
1 teaspoon soda
3 cups diced apples, peeled
1 cup chopped nuts
1 teaspoon vanilla extract
    Topping

Combine salad oil, eggs, and sugar; mix well. Combine flour, salt, and soda; dredge apples and nuts with 1 cup of flour mixture. Add remaining flour to sugar mixture, and blend well; add apples, nuts, and vanilla. Batter will be thick.

Spoon batter into a greased and floured 10-inch tube pan. Bake at 350° for 1¼ hours. Cool for 30 minutes; remove from pan. Spread Topping over warm cake. Yield: 1 (10-inch) cake.

Topping:

½ cup firmly packed light brown sugar
2 tablespoons milk

Combine all ingredients; boil 2 to 3 minutes over medium heat. Spread over warm cake. Yield: about ¾ cup.

PINEAPPLE-FILLED JAM CAKE

1 cup shortening
2 cups sugar
3 eggs
3 cups all-purpose flour
½ teaspoon salt
1 teaspoon soda
1 teaspoon ground cinnamon
½ teaspoon ground allspice
½ teaspoon ground nutmeg
1 cup buttermilk
1 cup blackberry, boysenberry, or
    strawberry jam
1 teaspoon vanilla extract
1 cup raisins
1 cup chopped pecans
    Pineapple Filling
    White Frosting

Cream shortening and sugar until light and fluffy. Add eggs, one at a time, beating well after each addition. Combine dry ingredients; add to creamed mixture alternately with buttermilk, beating well after each addition. Add jam, vanilla, raisins, and pecans; stir to mix.

Spoon batter into 3 greased and floured 9-inch cakepans. Bake at 350° for 30 minutes or until done. Cool on cake racks. Put layers together with Pineapple Filling; frost with White Frosting. Yield: 1 (9-inch) layer cake.

Pineapple Filling:

1 cup sugar
3 tablespoons all-purpose flour
1 (8¼-ounce) can crushed pineapple,
    undrained
2 tablespoons butter or margarine

Combine all ingredients, and cook over low heat, stirring constantly, until thickened (about 5 to 6 minutes). Cool slightly. Spread between layers of cake.

White Frosting:

¾ cup sugar
⅓ cup light corn syrup
2 tablespoons cold water
½ teaspoon salt
2 egg whites
1 teaspoon vanilla extract

Combine all ingredients, except vanilla, in top of double boiler. Place over boiling water. Beat at high speed of electric mixer for 6 minutes or until frosting is fluffy and holds its shape. Remove from heat, and add vanilla.

CHERRY UPSIDE-DOWN CAKE

3 tablespoons butter
½ cup sugar
¼ teaspoon salt
½ teaspoon ground cinnamon
2 cups canned sour red cherries, drained
1 (18-ounce) package yellow or white
    cake mix
    Whipped cream (optional)

Melt butter in a 2-quart casserole. Add sugar, salt, and cinnamon; mix well. Spread evenly in bottom of casserole. Arrange canned cherries over sugar mixture. Prepare cake mix according to package directions, and pour over the cherries. Bake at 350° for 1 hour or until cake tests done. Allow to cool a few minutes in dish; then invert on serving dish, and allow to stand 5 minutes. Garnish with whipped cream, if desired. Yield: 10 to 12 servings.

OLD-FASHIONED GINGERBREAD

½ cup shortening
½ cup sugar
1 cup molasses
2 eggs
2½ cups all-purpose flour
1 teaspoon salt
2 teaspoons baking powder
½ teaspoon soda
1 teaspoon ground ginger
2 teaspoons ground cinnamon
½ teaspoon ground cloves
1 cup hot water

Cream shortening and sugar; blend in molasses. Add eggs, one at a time, beating well after each addition.

Combine flour, salt, baking powder, soda, and spices. Add to creamed mixture alternately with hot water.

Spoon batter into a greased 9- x 9- x 2-inch baking pan. Bake at 350° for 40 minutes or until gingerbread tests done. Cool. Yield: 9 to 12 servings.

Note: Substitute 1 cup buttermilk for 1 cup hot water, if desired. Omit baking powder, and increase soda to 1½ teaspoons.

TROPICAL FRUIT LAYER CAKE

½ cup butter or margarine
1½ cups sugar
1 tablespoon lemon juice
¾ teaspoon salt
2 cups cake flour
2 teaspoons baking powder
¾ cup milk
4 egg whites
Tropical Filling
Apricot Icing

In large bowl of mixer, combine butter, sugar, lemon juice, and salt. Beat until light and fluffy. Sift flour and baking powder together. Add, alternately with milk, to first mixture, beating constantly. (Begin and end with the liquid when adding wet and dry ingredients.) Beat egg whites until stiff but not dry, and fold into batter, first stirring in a spoonful of the egg white to loosen batter before folding in the rest. Pour into 2 well-greased and floured 8-inch layer cakepans. Bake on middle shelf of 350° oven for 25 to 30 minutes. When done, layers will shrink slightly from sides of pan, and a wooden pick inserted in center will come out clean. Turn out and cool, right side up, on wire racks. Fill and top with Tropical Filling, and cover with Apricot Icing. Yield: 1 (8-inch) layer cake.

Tropical Filling:

1½ cups mashed, cooked apricots
½ cup sugar
½ cup drained, crushed pineapple
1 (3½-ounce) can flake coconut, divided

Combine apricots, sugar, and pineapple in small saucepan. Cook, stirring, until thickened. Add ¼ cup coconut; cool.

Apricot Icing:

1½ cups sugar
2 egg whites, unbeaten
⅓ cup strained apricot pulp
Coconut

Place ingredients in top of double boiler, and place over gently simmering water. Cook, beating constantly with rotary beater or electric hand-held beater, until mixture will hold peaks when beater is raised. Cooking will take 7 to 10 minutes. Spread either all over cake beginning always with sides, or on sides only to allow contrast between top and sides. Sprinkle with remainder of can of coconut.

STRAWBERRY SHORTCAKE WITH CARAMEL SAUCE

2¼ cups commercial biscuit mix
  2 tablespoons sugar
  2 tablespoons melted butter
  1 egg
    Milk
  2 tablespoons softened butter
  3 cups strawberries, divided
  ½ cup sugar
  1 cup whipping cream or 2 cups
    commercial whipped topping
  1 tablespoon powdered sugar
  ½ teaspoon vanilla extract
    Caramel Sauce

Combine biscuit mix, sugar, and butter in a bowl. Break egg into measuring cup, beat, and add milk to total ½ cup liquid. Add to first mixture, and stir with a fork until a soft dough forms. Press dough into lightly greased 9-inch round layer cakepan. Bake at 425° about 15 minutes or until done and lightly browned. Turn out of pan and split crosswise while warm. Spread each half with a tablespoon of softened butter.

Reserve 8 fresh whole berries for garnish; slice the rest thin, and combine with sugar. Let stand until juice forms. Whip cream until soft peaks form; add powdered sugar and vanilla. Beat until flavors blend.

To assemble, place bottom shortcake layer on serving plate, and spoon half the berries on it. Spread with half the whipped cream. Repeat layers. To serve, cut into 8 wedges and top each serving with Caramel Sauce. Yield: 8 servings.

Caramel Sauce:

1½ cups firmly packed light brown sugar
1½ teaspoons cornstarch
    Pinch salt
 ¾ cup water

Combine ingredients in the order given in a small saucepan. Cook, stirring, over medium heat, until thickened, which takes about 10 minutes. Cool.

BROWN SUGAR CAKE

  2 cups sifted cake flour
  1 teaspoon baking powder
  1 teaspoon salt
  ¼ teaspoon soda
  ½ cup butter or margarine, softened
1¼ cups firmly packed brown sugar
  ¾ cup milk
  2 eggs
1½ teaspoons vanilla extract

Sift flour with baking powder, salt, and soda; add to butter along with brown sugar and milk. Mix until all flour is moistened; then beat 2 minutes at medium speed of electric mixer or 300 vigorous strokes by hand, scraping bowl occasionally. Add eggs and vanilla. Beat 1 minute longer with electric mixer or 150 vigorous strokes by hand.

Spoon batter into two 9-inch paperlined cakepans. Bake at 375° for 20 to 25 minutes or until cake tester inserted in center comes out clean. Cool cake in pans 10 minutes. Remove from pans, and finish cooling on racks. Frost as desired. Yield: 2 (9-inch) layers.

WHITE CAKE WITH BURNT SUGAR FROSTING

¾ cup solid shortening
2 cups sugar
3 cups cake all-purpose flour
¾ teaspoon salt
1 tablespoon baking powder
½ cup milk
½ cup water
½ teaspoon vanilla extract
½ teaspoon lemon extract
6 egg whites
   Burnt Sugar Frosting

Cream shortening and sugar together thoroughly. Sift dry ingredients together, and add alternately with combined milk and water to sugar mixture. Beat in flavorings. Fold in egg whites that have been stiffly beaten. Pour batter equally into 2 prepared 9-inch layer pans. Bake at 350° for 35 minutes or until they test done. Cool in pans 5 minutes, turn out, and cool right side up. Frost with Burnt Sugar Frosting. Yield: 2 (9-inch) layers.

Burnt Sugar Frosting:

2½ cups sugar, divided
1¼ cups sweetened condensed milk
   2 tablespoons margarine
   1 teaspoon vanilla extract

Place ½ cup sugar in heavy skillet. Over medium heat, and using a wooden spoon, stir the sugar until it melts. Add condensed milk; mixture will be lumpy. Cook, and stir over high heat until smooth, add remaining sugar, and cook until a soft ball is formed when tested in cold water. A candy thermometer will read 238° when syrup is ready. Remove from heat, add margarine, and vanilla. Cool 10 minutes, then beat until thick and creamy. Spread between layers, on top and sides of cake. Yield: icing for 2-layer cake.

SUGAR BUSH WALNUT CAKE

7 eggs, separated
2¼ cups all-purpose flour
1½ cups sugar
1 tablespoon baking powder
1 teaspoon salt
½ cup vegetable oil
¾ cup cold water
1 teaspoon vanilla extract
1 teaspoon maple extract
⅔ cup finely chopped English walnuts
1 teaspoon cream of tartar
   Autumn Mist Topping
12 English walnut halves

In large bowl of mixer, beat egg yolks until light and lemon colored. Sift or stir together flour, sugar, baking powder, and salt. Beat oil into egg yolks; then add dry mixture alternately with water, beating constantly. Beat in flavorings. Fold in walnuts.

Beat egg whites with cream of tartar in a large bowl until stiff. Stir a large spoonful of whites into batter; then pour batter over whites, and fold together lightly but thoroughly. Pour batter into ungreased 10-inch tubepan. Bake at 325° for 55 minutes; increase heat to 350° and bake 20 minutes longer. Test for doneness by inserting wooden pick in center of cake; it should come out clean. Hang pan upside down until cool. (If pan has no "legs," place hole over neck of a heavy bottle.) Run sharp knife around sides and tube of pan. Turn cake out on serving plate. Fifteen minutes before serving, frost with Autumn Mist Topping, and garnish with walnut halves. Yield: 1 (10-inch) cake.

Autumn Mist Topping:

1 cup whipping cream
1 tablespoon dry instant coffee
1 tablespoon sugar

Whip cream until soft peaks form. Sprinkle coffee and sugar gradually over cream, beating constantly until quite stiff.

PINEAPPLE UPSIDE-DOWN CAKE

⅓ cup butter
½ cup firmly packed brown sugar
1 (20-ounce) can sliced pineapple, drained
  Maraschino cherries
  Pecan halves
1⅓ cups sifted all-purpose flour
1 cup sugar
2 teaspoons baking powder
½ teaspoon salt
⅓ cup shortening
⅔ cup milk
1 teaspoon vanilla extract
½ teaspoon lemon extract
1 egg

Melt butter in a heavy 10-inch skillet. Spread brown sugar evenly over butter. Arrange pineapple slices in attractive pattern on sugar. Put cherries in center of slices, and fill in spaces with pecan halves.

Combine flour, sugar, baking powder, and salt in mixing bowl. Add shortening, milk, and flavorings. Beat 2 mixtures at medium speed of electric mixer or 300 vigorous strokes by hand. Add egg. Beat 2 more minutes, scraping bowl frequently.

Pour batter over fruit. Bake at 350° for 40 to 50 minutes or until cake tests done. Turn upside down on cake plate. Yield: 1 (10-inch) layer.

Note: In a hurry? A 9-ounce (1-layer size) box yellow cake mix may be substituted for the cake part of this recipe. Just mix according to package directions, and pour over fruit. Bake as directed above.

DEVIL'S FOOD CAKE

1 cup margarine, softened
1½ cups sugar
2 eggs
3 squares unsweetened chocolate, melted
2 cups all-purpose flour
1 teaspoon soda
1 cup milk
  Chocolate-Coffee Frosting

Cream margarine and sugar until light and fluffy. Add eggs, and beat well. Add chocolate, mixing until blended.

Combine flour and soda; add to creamed mixture alternately with milk. Pour into 2 greased and floured 9-inch cakepans. Bake at 350° for 30 minutes or until cake tests done. Cool, and frost with Chocolate-Coffee Frosting. Yield: 1 (9-inch) layer cake.

Chocolate-Coffee Frosting:

1 (16-ounce) package powdered sugar
2 tablespoons cocoa
2 tablespoons melted margarine
5 tablespoons cold strong coffee
1 teaspoon vanilla extract
1 tablespoon milk (optional)

Sift powdered sugar and cocoa together. Add margarine, coffee, and vanilla; blend until smooth and creamy. If too thick to spread, add 1 tablespoon milk. Fill and frost cooled cake. Yield: frosting for 1 (9-inch) layer cake.

BLACK RUSSIAN CAKE

1 (18½-ounce) package dark chocolate
    cake mix
½ cup salad oil
1 (4½-ounce) package instant chocolate
    pudding and pie filling
4 eggs, at room temperature
¾ cup strong coffee
¾ cup combined Kahlua and crème de
    cacao
    Topping

Combine cake mix, salad oil, pudding, eggs, coffee, and Kahlua-crème de cacao mixture in a large mixing bowl. Beat about 4 minutes at medium speed of electric mixer or until smooth.

Spoon into a well-greased Bundt pan, and bake at 350° for 45 to 50 minutes. Remove cake from pan when cool. Punch holes in cake with cake tester or meat fork; spoon topping over cake. Yield: 1 (10-inch) cake.

Topping:

1 cup sifted powdered sugar
2 tablespoons strong coffee
2 tablespoons Kahlua
2 tablespoons crème de cacao

Combine all ingredients, mixing well, and spoon over cake. Yield: about 1½ cups.

OLD-FANGLED BREAD PUDDING

1½ cups firmly packed light brown sugar
    Softened butter or margarine
6 slices white bread
½ cup raisins
4 eggs
1 teaspoon vanilla extract
    Dash salt
3 cups milk

Put sugar into top of double boiler. Butter bread, stack, and cut into cubes. Place on top of sugar. Sprinkle raisins over bread. Slightly beat eggs. Add vanilla, salt, and milk. Pour over bread cubes; do not stir. Cover, and place over simmering water. Cook 1¼ hours. To serve, run knife around edges; invert serving dish (with 1-inch sides) over pudding. Quickly invert. Cool slightly; sugar forms caramel sauce over pudding. Yield: 8 servings.

COFFEE-BREAD PUDDING

1 cup strong coffee
1 cup half-and-half
2 cups milk
6 thin slices raisin bread
    Soft butter or margarine
2 eggs
½ cup sugar
½ teaspoon salt
1 teaspoon vanilla extract
¼ teaspoon ground nutmeg
    Plain or whipped cream

Combine coffee, cream, and milk. Bring to scalding boil. Spread bread slices lightly with butter or margarine. Do not trim off crusts. Cut into ½-inch cubes, and add to coffee mixture. Beat eggs slightly. Add sugar and salt. Mix well. Add bread mixture and vanilla extract. Pour into a 1½-quart casserole. Sprinkle with nutmeg. Set casserole in pan of warm water. Bake at 325° for 1 hour and 15 minutes or until knife inserted near rim of casserole comes out clean. Chill. Serve with plain or whipped cream. Yield: 8 servings.

ICED RASPBERRY PUDDING

1 (10-ounce) package frozen raspberries
⅓ cup currant jelly
1½ cups plus 1 tablespoon water
3 tablespoons quick-cooking tapioca
  Whipped cream

Combine all ingredients except whipped cream in a heavy saucepan; bring to a rolling boil over medium heat, stirring constantly. Remove from heat, and cool at room temperature, stirring occasionally. Refrigerate for several hours before serving. Garnish with whipped cream.

Note: Pudding may be served as a sauce over ice cream.

CHRISTMAS PLUM PUDDING

1 cup all-purpose flour
1 teaspoon soda
1 teaspoon salt
1 teaspoon ground cinnamon
½ teaspoon ground nutmeg
½ teaspoon ground allspice
1½ cups chopped raisins
1½ cups currants
1 cup diced dates
¾ cup diced candied orange peel
½ cup chopped almonds
1½ cups soft bread crumbs
1 cup firmly packed brown sugar
3 eggs, beaten
⅓ cup blackberry jelly
¼ cup sherry or brandy
2 cups ground suet
  Hard Sauce

Combine flour, soda, salt, and spices. Add fruit, almonds, and bread crumbs; mix well.

Combine brown sugar, eggs, jelly, and sherry; add to fruit mixture along with suet, mixing well. Pack mixture into a well-buttered and sugared 1½-quart mold; cover tightly.

Place mold on shallow rack in a large, deep kettle with enough boiling water to come halfway up the mold. cover kettle; steam pudding about 5½ hours in continuously boiling water (replace water as needed). Unmold, and serve with Hard Sauce. Yield: 12 servings.

Hard Sauce:

½ cup butter or margarine, softened
1 cup powdered sugar
¼ cup brandy

Combine butter and powdered sugar; beat until smooth. Add brandy, and beat until fluffy. Chill. Yield: ¾ cup.

BLUEBERRY PUDDING

½ cup butter or margarine
1 cup all-purpose flour
1 cup sugar
⅛ teaspoon salt
2 teaspoons baking powder
1 cup milk
1 pint fresh blueberries, washed and
  drained
2 tablespoons lemon juice

Melt butter in an 8-inch square pan; set aside. Combine flour, 1 cup sugar, salt, and baking powder; stir in milk, blueberries, and lemon juice. Pour batter over melted butter. Bake at 350° about 45 to 50 minutes. Yield: 6 to 8 servings.

Note: Two cups of fresh peaches, blackberries or other canned fruit, drained, may be used.

PINEAPPLE PUDDING

1½ cups sugar
¼ cup cornstarch
1½ cups milk
3 egg yolks, slightly beaten
1 (20-ounce) can crushed pineapple,
    drained
Vanilla wafers
Meringue

Combine sugar and cornstarch. Gradually add milk and egg yolks; cook over medium heat, stirring constantly, until thickened. Add pineapple, and blend well.

Line a 2-quart casserole with vanilla wafers; cover with half of pudding. Repeat layers; cover with Meringue. Bake at 400° for 8 to 10 minutes or until golden brown. Yield: 6 servings.

Meringue:

3 egg whites
¼ teaspoon cream of tartar
6 tablespoons sugar
¼ teaspoon vanilla extract

Beat egg whites and cream of tartar until frothy. Gradually add sugar, and continue beating until stiff and glossy. Beat in vanilla.

LEMON CHIFFON PUDDING

3 tablespoons butter or margarine,
    softened
3 egg yolks
5 tablespoons sifted all-purpose flour
¼ teaspoon salt
⅔ cup sugar
¼ cup lemon juice
1 cup milk
3 egg whites, stiffly beaten

Combine butter and egg yolks; beat with electric mixer until well blended. Add remaining ingredients except egg whites; beat until smooth. Fold in egg whites.

Pour mixture into a 1-quart casserole. Place casserole in a pan of warm water, and bake at 375° for 45 minutes or until firm. Serve warm or cold. Yield: 4 servings.

WOODFORD PUDDING WITH BUTTERSCOTCH SAUCE

½ cup softened butter
1 cup sugar
3 eggs
1 teaspoon soda
½ cup buttermilk
1 cup all-purpose flour
1 teaspoon cinnamon
1 cup blackberry jam
Butterscotch Sauce

In large bowl of mixer, beat butter with sugar until fluffy. Add eggs, one at a time, beating well after each addition. Stir soda into buttermilk; stir flour and cinnamon together. Add milk and flour alternately to egg mixture. Blend in jam. Pour into greased 8- x 12-inch baking dish. Bake at 325° for 45 minutes. Cut into 8 squares and top each serving with Butterscotch Sauce. Best served warm. Yield: 8 servings.

Butterscotch Sauce:

1½ cups firmly packed light brown sugar
4 tablespoons all-purpose flour
Pinch salt
1 cup boiling water
¼ cup butter
2 tablespoons half-and-half or
    evaporated milk

Combine sugar, flour, and salt in small saucepan. Add water gradually, stirring constantly. Cook, stirring, about 8 to 10 minutes or until thickened. Remove from heat, and stir in butter and cream.

LIME PUDDING

1 cup sugar
3 tablespoons all-purpose flour
3 tablespoons butter, softened
2 eggs, separated
3 tablespoons lime juice
1 teaspoon grated lime rind
1 cup milk
Whipped cream (optional)

Combine sugar, flour, and butter in a mixing bowl. Add unbeaten egg yolks, lime juice, lime rind, and milk; blend well. Beat egg whites until stiff; fold into yolk mixture. Pour into a greased 1-quart mold or 6 custard cups. Place in pan of hot water, and bake at 325° for 1 hour (35 minutes for custard cups).

This pudding has a cakelike top with a smooth, delicious lime sauce beneath. Serve warm or cold with whipped cream, if desired. Yield: 6 servings.

OLD-FASHIONED BLACKBERRY PUDDING

2 cups sugar, divided
⅓ cup butter, softened
2 cups all-purpose flour
2 teaspoons baking powder
1 teaspoon salt
1 cup milk
2 cups blackberries
2 cups boiling water
Ice cream

Cream 1 cup sugar and butter until light and fluffy. Add flour, baking powder, salt, and milk; mix well, and spoon batter into a greased 3-quart casserole.

Sprinkle blackberries and 1 cup sugar over batter. Add water. Bake at 350° about 1 hour or until done. Serve warm; top with ice cream. Yield: 6 servings.

SAUCY RHUBARB PUDDING

1 (8-ounce) can crushed pineapple, drained
4 cups rhubarb, cubed
3 drops mint flavoring
1 egg, beaten
1½ cups sugar, divided
2 tablespoons all-purpose flour
1 tablespoon lemon juice
1 cup all-purpose flour
¼ teaspoon salt
⅓ cup softened butter or margarine

Combine pineapple, rhubarb, and mint flavoring; mix well. Spoon into a lightly greased 8-inch square pan.

Combine egg, 1 cup sugar, 2 tablespoons flour, and lemon juice; beat until smooth. Pour over fruit.

Combine 1 cup flour, ½ cup sugar, and salt; cut in butter with pastry blender or 2 knives until coarse crumbs form. Sprinkle over batter; press down gently with back of spoon.

Bake at 350° for 50 to 55 minutes or until lightly browned. Yield: 8 servings.

NO-FAIL PIE CRUST

4 cups all-purpose flour
2 teaspoons salt
1½ cups solid shortening
1 egg
6 tablespoons cold
    water

Sift or stir flour and salt together in large mixing bowl. Add shortening and, with pastry blender, cut into flour until mixture resembles very coarse meal. Beat the egg with water in a cup until thoroughly mixed. Add, a splash at a time, tossing with a fork, until mixture will hold together in a loose ball. The emphasis here is that the liquid measure is variable: the flour may take all of it or not quite all. It may even need another spoonful or so of water to make it right for rolling. You want no dry flour on the bottom of the bowl. When it is right, you can pick up a handful, squeeze it, and it will stay in a lump.

Divide pastry into quarters. Roll out one piece at a time on floured surface. Place loosely in pie pans, leaving ½ inch over-hanging edge, and cutting away excess with scissors. Save all the scraps in a stack; do not wad them up. Your 5th pie crust is made of those trimmings, or you can use the scraps, rolled out, and make enough strips of them to top 2 pies. Strips may be stacked, wrapped, and refrigerated or frozen. Turn the overhang underneath, and flatten on rim. Crimp with fork, if you wish to stack them to refrigerate or freeze. Or make standing fluted edge. Yield: 5 (8- or 9-inch) pie shells.

Note: This is a fine recipe for beginners because it can be overhandled and still remain tender. You may want to buy reus-able aluminum pie tins, and keep a stack in freezer.

APPLE PIE WITH NUT TOPPING

3 cups chopped cooking apples
1 (9-inch) unbaked pie shell
¾ cup sugar
1 teaspoon aromatic bitters
½ cup firmly packed brown sugar
½ cup chopped nuts
¾ cup all-purpose flour
¼ cup melted margarine

Put apples into pie shell; sprinkle with ¾ cup sugar and bitters. Mix brown sugar, nuts, flour, and melted margarine; spread over apples. Bake at 350° about 45 minutes or until apples are tender. Yield: 1 (9-inch) pie.

APPLE-COCONUT PIE

Cream Cheese Pastry
3½ cups thinly sliced tart apples
¾ cup sugar
2 tablespoons all-purpose flour
½ teaspoon salt
1 (3½-ounce) can flaked coconut
1 teaspoon vanilla extract
2 tablespoons margarine

Line a 10-inch piepan with half the pastry rolled ⅛ inch thick.

Arrange apples in unbaked pie shell. Combine sugar, flour, and salt; sprinkle over apples, mixing well. Cover with coconut, sprinkle vanilla over top, and dot with margarine.

Roll out remaining pastry, and place over filling; seal, and flute edges. Cut slits in top to allow steam to escape. Bake at 400° for 10 minutes; reduce heat to 300°, and bake an additional 35 to 40 minutes. Yield: 1 (10-inch) pie.

Cream Cheese Pastry:

1 cup margarine, softened
2 (3-ounce) packages cream cheese,
    softened
2 cups all-purpose flour
    Dash salt

Combine margarine and cream cheese; mix well. Cut in flour and salt with pastry blender. Shape dough into a ball; chill. Yield: pastry for double crust 10-inch pie.

APPLE PIE WITH STREUSEL TOPPING

½ cup sugar
    Dash salt
½ teaspoon ground cinnamon
6 cups sliced, pared apples
1 unbaked 9-inch pie shell
¾ cup firmly packed brown sugar
½ cup all-purpose flour
6 tablespoons butter or margarine,
    softened

Combine ½ cup sugar, salt, and cinnamon; mix with apples. Spoon into pie shell.

Combine brown sugar and flour; cut in butter. Sprinkle over apples. Bake at 425° for 30 minutes or until apples are tender and topping is browned. Yield: 1 (9-inch) pie.

VINEGAR PIE

1 stick margarine, melted and cooled
1½ cups sugar
2 tablespoons all-purpose flour
1 tablespoon vanilla extract
2 tablespoons vinegar
3 eggs
1 (9-inch) unbaked pie shell

Combine first 6 ingredients, blending well; pour into pie shell. Bake at 400° for 10 minutes. Reduce heat to 300°, and bake 30 minutes or until set. Yield: 1 (9-inch) pie.

CHOCOLATE FUDGE PIE

1 cup sugar
¼ cup cocoa
3 tablespoons all-purpose flour
3 egg yolks, beaten
1 cup milk
3 tablespoons butter or margarine
1 teaspoon vanilla extract
½ cup chopped pecans (optional)
1 (9-inch) baked pie shell
    Chocolate Meringue

Combine sugar, cocoa, and flour in a saucepan. Combine egg yolks and milk, blending well; add to dry ingredients. Cook slowly over low heat, stirring constantly, until very thick. Add butter, vanilla, and nuts; blend well.

Pour into pie shell; top with Meringue. Bake at 325° for 20 to 30 minutes until meringue is slightly browned. Chill 6 hours before serving. Yield: 1 (9-inch) pie.

Chocolate Meringue:

3 egg whites
¼ teaspoon cream of tartar
6 tablespoons powdered sugar
2 teaspoons cocoa
½ teaspoon vanilla extract

Combine egg whites and cream of tartar; beat until frothy. Add sugar sifted with cocoa, a small amount at a time, and continue beating until mixture is thickened and glossy. Fold in vanilla. Yield: meringue for 1 (9-inch) pie.

RUN-FOR-THE-ROSES PIE

4 eggs
1 cup sugar
¼ cup melted butter
2 tablespoons bourbon
1 cup white corn syrup
½ cup chocolate pieces
¾ cup chopped pecans or English
     walnuts
1 (9-inch) pie shell, unbaked
     Whipped cream (optional)

Beat eggs and sugar together only until well blended. Add butter, bourbon and syrup. Beat only to blend. Stir in chocolate pieces and pecans. Pour into unbaked pie shell, and bake at 425° for 10 minutes; reduce heat to 350°, and continue baking about 30 minutes or until set in the middle. Serve at room temperature or when slightly warmed, with whipped cream, if desired. Yield: 1 (9-inch) pie.

RHUBARB MERINGUE PIE

2 cups sugar
4 tablespoons all-purpose flour
¼ teaspoon salt
3 eggs, separated
4 cups rhubarb, thinly sliced
1 unbaked 9-inch pie shell
2 tablespoons butter
     Meringue

Mix sugar, flour, and salt. Beat egg yolks, and add, along with the rhubarb, to the dry mixture. Pour into pie shell, and dot with butter. Bake 10 minutes at 400°; reduce heat to 350°, and bake for 40 minutes longer. Remove from oven, and let stand while Meringue is prepared. Spread Meringue over warm rhubarb pie, sealing it well to edges of crust. Swirl Meringue slightly higher in center than on sides. Return to 350° oven, and bake 8 to 10 minutes to brown lightly. Yield: 1 (9-inch) pie.

Meringue:

3 egg whites
     Pinch cream of tartar
¼ teaspoon cornstarch
¼ cup sugar

Beat egg whites with cream of tartar and cornstarch until they hold soft peaks. Add sugar slowly, beating constantly with mixer at slow speed. When mixture holds fairly firm peaks, Meringue is ready.

EASY LEMON PIE

1 (3¼-ounce) package regular lemon
     pudding mix (not instant)
6 tablespoons sugar
3 egg yolks, beaten
1½ cups water
2 tablespoons butter
1 (9-inch) baked shell
4 egg whites
8 tablespoons sugar

Put pudding mix and sugar in top of a double boiler; stir in egg yolks. Put pan over simmering water and gradually stir in water. Cook slowly, stirring constantly, until mixture thickens. Add butter, and spoon mixture into baked pie shell.

Beat egg whites, adding sugar gradually. Spread meringue on top of pie, checking to see that meringue completely covers pie to edge of pie shell. Bake at 350° about 15 minutes or until browned. Yield: 1 (9-inch) pie.

KEY WEST LIME PIE

1 envelope (1 tablespoon) unflavored
    gelatin
¼ cup cold water
4 eggs, separated
1 cup sugar, divided
⅓ cup lime juice
½ teaspoon salt
2 teaspoons grated lime rind
    Green food coloring
1 (9-inch baked pie shell
    Halved white grapes (optional)
    Mint sprigs (optional)

Soften gelatin in cold water. Beat egg yolks; add ½ cup sugar, lime juice, and salt. Cook egg mixture over hot water, stirring constantly until thickened. Add grated rind and gelatin; stir until gelatin is dissolved. Tint pale green with food coloring. Cool.

Beat egg whites until stiff but not dry; add remaining sugar slowly, beating after each addition; fold into lime mixture. Pour into baked 9-inch pie shell; chill until firm. If desired, garnish the top with halved white grapes and mint sprigs to resemble grape clusters. Yield: 1 (9-inch) pie.

FRESH BLUEBERRY PIE

5 cups fresh blueberries, washed and
    well drained, divided
¾ cup sugar
¾ cup water
1 teaspoon grated lemon rind
¼ cup water
¼ cup sugar
3 tablespoons cornstarch
1 (9-inch) baked pie shell

In saucepan, combine 1 cup blueberries, ¾ cup sugar, ¾ cup water, and 1 teaspoon lemon rind. Bring mixture to a boil.

Mix ¼ cup water, ¼ cup sugar, and cornstarch, and add to hot mixture. Cook until clear and thickened. Cool. Pour thickened mixture over 4 cups blueberries in baked pie shell. Chill until ready to serve. Yield: 1 (9-inch) pie.

DUTCH PEACH PIE

10 to 12 ripe peaches
1 (9-inch) unbaked pie shell
1 egg
1 cup commercial sour cream
¼ teaspoon salt
¾ cup sugar
2 tablespoons all-purpose flour
½ teaspoon ground cinnamon
½ teaspoon ground nutmeg
    Peach Pie Topping

Peel peaches, slice, and arrange in pie shell. Beat egg slightly; mix with sour cream, salt, sugar, flour, cinnamon, and nutmeg. Pour over peaches. Bake at 350° for 20 minutes. Then sprinkle with Peach Pie Topping, and bake 15 to 20 minutes longer. Yield: 1 (9-inch) pie.

Peach Pie Topping:

¼ cup firmly packed brown sugar
3 tablespoons all-purpose flour
2 tablespoons butter
½ cup chopped pecans

During the first 20 minutes while pie is baking, mix topping ingredients together. Yield: topping for 9-inch pie.

HEAVENLY PIE

**1 (8-ounce) package cream cheese,
    softened
1 (14-ounce) can sweetened condensed
    milk
⅓ cup lemon juice
1 (9-ounce) carton frozen whipped
    topping, thawed
½ cup chopped pecans
1 cup drained fruit (pineapple, peaches,
    or fruit cocktail)
2 (9-inch) Graham Cracker Pie Shells**

Combine cream cheese, condensed milk, and lemon juice; beat until smooth. Fold in whipped topping. Stir in pecans and fruit; pour into pie shells, and refrigerate for several hours. Yield: 2 (9-inch) pies.

Graham Cracker Pie Shell:

**18 single graham crackers, crushed
¼ cup melted butter
2 tablespoons sugar**

Combine all ingredients. Press into 9-inch shell. Yield 1 (9-inch) pie shell.

BOSTON CREAM PIE

**1 (9-ounce) box yellow cake mix
1 tablespoon all-purpose flour
1 tablespoon sugar
½ cup hot milk
2 tablespoons butter
1 egg
½ teaspoon vanilla extract
    Shiny Chocolate Frosting**

Bake 1 (9-inch) layer cake according to package directions; cool and split crosswise.

In top pan of double boiler, combine flour and sugar. Add hot milk gradually, stirring until smooth. Add egg, and beat well. Add vanilla. Place pan over boiling water and cook, stirring, until mixture is very thick. Add butter, and cool somewhat before spreading on bottom half of cake layer. Cover with top layer. Frost with Shiny Chocolate Frosting. Yield: 1 (9-inch) layer cake.

Shiny Chocolate Frosting:

**3 tablespoons hot milk
3 tablespoons butter
½ teaspoon vanilla extract
2 to 2½ cups sifted powdered sugar
2 ounces unsweetened chocolate, melted**

Combine ingredients in the order given. Adjust amount of sugar, using the cups first, then more if mixture is too thin. Let stand 15 minutes before spreading on cake. Pour and spread over top, letting it drizzle down sides. If frosting dulls before spreading, a few drops of hot water will bring back the gloss. Yield: frosting for one cake layer.

SOUTHERN SWEET POTATO-FIG PIE

**1 (9-inch) pie shell
1 (24-ounce) can sweet potatoes (or
    yams)
3 eggs
1 cup milk
⅓ cup firmly packed light brown sugar
½ cup drained, chopped fig preserves
1 teaspoon lemon juice
    Gingered Whipped Cream**

Bake pie shell 10 minutes at 425°. (This is called "blind baked" and is done to set the crust without browning so filling will not soak in.)

While crust bakes, drain and mash sweet potatoes; you should have about 1½ cups. Beat in eggs, milk, sugar, fig preserves and lemon juice. Pour into pie shell, and bake 10 minutes at 425°. Reduce heat to 350°, and bake 45 minutes longer or until center is set. Cool. Just before serving, top with Ginger Whipped Cream. Yield: 1 (9-inch) pie.

Note: If fresh yams are used, increase sugar to ½ cup.

Gingered Whipped Cream:

    1 cup whipping cream
  ¼ teaspoon vanilla extract
    1 tablespoon sugar
    1 tablespoon candied ginger, chopped

Whip cream until soft peaks form, add vanilla, and gradually add sugar, beating until sugar is dissolved and cream holds shape. Swirl on cooled pie. Sprinkle with ginger.

PRUNE-COTTAGE CHEESE PIE

    1 cup chopped pitted prunes
  ¼ cup firmly packed light brown sugar
  ½ teaspoon ground cinnamon
  ¼ teaspoon ground nutmeg
    Juice of 1 lemon, divided
    1 (10-inch) unbaked pie shell
    1 (12-ounce) carton cottage cheese
  ½ cup sugar, divided
    2 tablespoons all-purpose flour
  ½ teaspoon salt
    3 eggs, separated
  ½ cup whipping cream
    Grated rind of 1 lemon

Combine prunes, brown sugar, cinnamon, nutmeg, and half the lemon juice; mix well, and spread over bottom of pie shell.

Put cottage cheese through a sieve, or process in electric blender; add ¼ cup sugar, flour, and salt, mixing well. Beat in egg yolks, whipping cream, remaining lemon juice, and lemon rind. Beat egg whites until soft peaks form. Gradually add ¼ cup sugar, beating until stiff; fold into cottage cheese mixture. Carefully spoon over prunes; bake at 300° for 1 hour. Increase temperature to 350°, and bake 20 to 30 minutes longer or until lightly browned. Yield: 1 (10-inch) pie.

GOLD-FILLED JELLY BARS

    1 cup all-purpose flour
    6 tablespoons powdered sugar, divided
  ½ cup butter or margarine
    2 tablespoons sugar
    2 eggs, lightly beaten
    2 tablespoons frozen concentrated
      orange juice
    2 tablespoons all-purpose flour
  ½ teaspoon baking powder

Combine flour, 4 tablespoons powdered sugar, and butter. With pastry blender, chop together until texture resembles coarse meal. Press into 9-inch square pan. Bake 15 minutes at 350°.

Beat together 2 tablespoons sugar, eggs, juice, flour, and baking powder, and pour over baked crust. Bake 25 minutes at 350°. Cool, sift remaining 2 tablespoons powdered sugar over top, and cut into squares or bars. Yield: about 16 bars.

APPLE-COOKIE SQUARES

½ cup shortening
1 cup sugar
2 eggs
1 teaspoon vanilla extract
½ cup chopped nuts
1 tart apple, coarsely chopped
2 cups all-purpose flour
2 teaspoons baking powder
½ teaspoon salt
1 teaspoon ground cinnamon
   Whipped cream (optional)

Cream shortening and sugar. Add eggs, one at a time, beating well after each addition. Add vanilla, nuts, and apple; mix well. Combine dry ingredients, and add to creamed mixture; mix well.

Bake in a greased and floured 13- x 9- x 2-inch pan at 350° about 30 minutes. Cool, and cut into squares. Serve with whipped cream, if desired. Yield: 30 squares.

BUTTER-NUT BALLS

1 cup butter, softened
2 cups all-purpose flour
¼ cup sugar
½ teaspoon salt
2 teaspoons vanilla extract
1½ cups finely chopped pecans, walnuts,
    filberts or almonds
   Granulated sugar

Beat butter until almost liquified. Sift together flour, sugar, and salt. Beat gradually into the butter. Add vanilla and nuts, mixing well. Dough will be crumbly. Shape into ¾-inch balls. Place on greased cookie sheets, and bake 30 minutes at 350°. Roll in granulated sugar while warm. Yield: about 5 dozen balls.

SNOWFLAKES

1 cup all-purpose flour
1 teaspoon baking powder
¼ teaspoon salt
2 ounces unsweetened chocolate, melted
¼ cup butter
1 cup sugar
2 eggs, well beaten
½ teaspoon almond extract
3 tablespoons bourbon
1 cup nuts, finely chopped
   Powdered sugar

Sift or stir together flour, baking powder, and salt. In small saucepan, melt chocolate and butter together. Add sugar, stirring to dissolve; pour into large bowl of mixer, and set aside to cool. When cool, beat in the eggs, flavoring, and bourbon. Quickly stir in dry ingredients and chopped nuts. Chill dough at least 4 hours. Form dough into balls about ¾ to 1 inch in diameter. Dredge in powdered sugar. Place on greased cookie sheet, and bake 15 to 20 minutes, depending on size, in 350° oven. Dredge warm cookies again in powdered sugar. Yield: 3 to 4 dozen cookies.

CHOCOLATE NUT-FILLED COOKIES

⅔ cup shortening
⅔ cup sugar
2 eggs
2 cups all-purpose flour
1½ teaspoons baking powder
½ teaspoon salt
   Chocolate-Nut Filling

Cream shortening and sugar until light and fluffy; add eggs, and beat well. Add flour, baking powder, and salt; mix well. Chill dough 2 to 4 hours.

Roll out dough to ⅛-inch thickness on a lightly floured board. Cut half of dough into 36 circles with a 2-inch cookie cutter. Using a 2-inch doughnut cutter, cut remaining dough into 36 circles.

Place solid circles on lightly greased cookie sheet. In center of each circle, place a teaspoon of Chocolate-Nut Filling; spread almost to the edges. Top with a circle cut with doughnut cutter; seal edges with fork tines. Bake at 350° for 10 to 12 minutes. (Cookies may be filled with jam.) Yield: 3 dozen cookies.

Chocolate-Nut Filling:

¼ cup sugar
1 tablespoon cornstarch
½ cup chocolate syrup
¼ cup chopped pecans

Combine all ingredients; cook over low heat until thickened and smooth. Cool. Yield: about 1 cup.

PEANUT BUTTER COOKIE CHIPS

1 cup chunk-style peanut butter
¼ cup solid shortening
1 cup firmly packed dark brown sugar
1 teaspoon vanilla extract
½ cup boiling water
2 cups commercial biscuit mix

Combine peanut butter, shortening, sugar, vanilla, and water, in that order, beating on medium speed of mixer. Stir in biscuit mix. Drop by small teaspoonfuls on lightly greased cookie sheet. Flatten with bottom of a glass dipped in milk. (Especially attractive if bottom of glass has a design on it.) Bake for 8 minutes at 400°. Yield: about 6 dozen cookies.

CRISSCROSS COOKIES

1 cup smooth or crunchy peanut butter
½ cup butter or margarine
½ cup sugar
½ cup firmly packed brown sugar
½ teaspoon vanilla extract
1 egg
1½ cups all-purpose flour
¾ teaspoon soda
½ teaspoon baking powder
¼ teaspoon salt

Cream peanut butter and butter. Add sugars gradually; cream until light and fluffy. Add vanilla and egg, beating well. Combine flour, soda, baking powder, and salt; blend into creamed mixture. Chill.

Shape dough into 1-inch balls, and place about 2 inches apart on ungreased cookie sheets. Flatten in crisscross pattern with a fork. Bake at 375° for 10 to 12 minutes. Yield: 5 dozen cookies.

CRESCENT COOKIES

1 cup butter or margarine, softened
½ cup sugar
½ teaspoon almond extract
1 tablespoon water
2¼ cups all-purpose flour
1 cup chopped almonds
Sugar

Combine butter, sugar, almond extract, water, and flour; blend well. Add nuts. Chill for several hours. Pinch off tablespoon-sized pieces, roll between palms, and shape into crescents. Place on greased cookie sheets, and bake at 300° for 20 to 25 minutes. Do not let cookies brown. Roll in white or colored sugar. Yield: about 3½ dozen cookies.

WALNUT-FRUIT COOKIES

2 cups all-purpose flour
2 teaspoons baking powder
½ teaspoon salt
½ cup butter or margarine, softened
1 cup firmly packed light brown sugar
1 egg, beaten
¼ cup orange juice
1 small banana, mashed
¾ cup English walnuts, chopped
1 teaspoon grated orange rind
⅓ cup candied orange peel, finely
    chopped

Sift or stir together the flour, baking powder, and salt. In mixer bowl, combine butter and sugar, and beat until light. Beat in egg. Add flour mixture alternately with orange juice and banana. Fold in nuts, orange rind, and candied peel. Drop by teaspoonfuls on greased cookie sheet. Bake at 350° for 15 minutes. Yield: about 4½ dozen cookies.

ALMOND COOKIES

½ cup butter or margarine, softened
⅓ cup firmly packed dark brown sugar
½ teaspoon vanilla extract
1¼ cups self-rising flour
½ cup finely chopped almonds

Combine butter and sugar; beat until light. Beat in vanilla. Add flour and almonds, blending well. Drop by teaspoonfuls on ungreased baking sheet, and bake at 400° for 8 to 10 minutes. Yield: 2 dozen or more cookies.

ALMOND SHORTBREAD COOKIES

1 cup all-purpose flour
½ cup cornstarch
½ cup powdered sugar
1 cup finely chopped
    almonds
¾ cup butter, softened

Combine flour, cornstarch, and powdered sugar; stir in almonds. Add butter; blend with a wooden spoon until a soft dough forms.

Shape dough into small balls. Place on ungreased cookie sheet; flatten each ball with lightly floured fork. Bake at 300° for 20 to 25 minutes or until edges are only lightly browned. Cool before storing. Yield: about 3 dozen cookies.

ALMOND ANGELS

4 egg whites
¼ teaspoon cream of tartar
¼ teaspoon salt
1½ cups sugar
½ teaspoon vanilla extract
½ teaspoon almond extract
    almonds
1 cup blanched slivered

Combine egg whites, cream of tartar, and salt; beat until mixture holds soft peaks. Gradually beat in sugar, then flavorings; fold in almonds.

Grease cookie sheets well. Line with unglazed brown paper, and grease paper well. Drop mixture by teaspoonfuls onto greased paper. Bake at 250° for 50 minutes. Remove from cookie sheets immediately, and cool on wire racks. Yield: 3½ to 4 dozen cookies.

SPICED PUMPKIN COOKIES

½ cup solid shortening
1 cup firmly packed light brown sugar
1 egg
1¾ cups all-purpose flour
½ teaspoon salt
1 teaspoon ground cinnamon
½ teaspoon pumpkin pie spice
¼ teaspoon ground nutmeg
1 cup pureed pumpkin
1 cup all-bran cereal
½ cup chopped nutmeats
½ cup chopped dates

In a large bowl of mixer, combine shortening with sugar, and beat until light. Add egg and blend. Sift or stir together the flour, salt, cinnamon, pie spice, and nutmeg. Add flour mixture alternately with pumpkin to creamed mixture. Add remaining ingredients, stirring sufficiently to blend. Drop from teaspoon onto greased cookie sheet. Bake 15 minutes at 375°. Yield: about 4 dozen 1½-inch cookies.

Note: The dates are easily cut into bits with wet scissors. And they are easier to add to dough if first hand-mixed with the nuts and cereal.

SALTED CASHEW COOKIES

½ cup butter
1 cup firmly packed light brown sugar
1 egg
1 teaspoon vanilla extract
2 cups all-purpose flour
¾ teaspoon baking powder
¼ teaspoon soda
  Dash salt
⅓ cup commercial sour cream
1¾ cups salted cashews
  Butter Icing

Combine butter and sugar in large bowl of mixer. Beat until creamy. Beat in egg and vanilla. Sift or stir dry ingredients together, and add, alternately with sour cream, beginning and ending with flour. Fold in salted whole cashews. Drop by teaspoonfuls onto greased cookie sheet. Bake 10 minutes at 400°. Cool on racks. When cool, frost them with Butter Icing. Yield: about 4½ dozen cookies.

Butter Icing:

2 cups powdered sugar, sifted
¼ cup butter, melted
2 to 3 tablespoons hot milk
½ teaspoon vanilla extract

Stir sugar into butter; add enough hot milk to make a nice spreading consistency. Add vanilla, mixing well. Spread thinly on cookies.

BUTTERSCOTCH DROP COOKIES

⅓ cup sugar
½ cup butter or margarine, softened
1 (3¾-ounce) package butterscotch
    pudding and pie filling
1 egg
1 cup all-purpose flour
  Dash salt
½ teaspoon soda
½ teaspoon cream of tartar
1 cup quick-cooking oats

Cream sugar and butter thoroughly; add pudding and egg, and beat well. Add flour, salt, soda, and cream of tartar. Add oats, stirring well. Dough will be rather stiff.

Drop by teaspoonfuls onto greased cookie sheets. Bake at 375° for 12 to 15 minutes. Yield: about 3 dozen cookies.

CHEWY POTATO WHITES

⅓ cup butter or margarine
1 cup sugar
1 egg
1 teaspoon coconut or vanilla extract
1⅓ cups commercial biscuit mix (or 1
    5½-ounce packet)
1 cup instant potatoes

Combine butter and sugar in bowl, and beat until creamy. Add egg and flavoring, and beat well. Blend in biscuit mix and potato. Chill, covered, 1 hour. Shape dough into small balls, and place about 2 inches apart on ungreased cookie sheet. Bake at 350° about 12 minutes. Cookie should not brown; do not overbake. Yield: 2 to 3 dozen cookies.

COCONUT-PINEAPPLE COOKIES

1 cup butter or margarine, softened
1½ cups sugar
½ cup firmly packed brown sugar
2 eggs
2¼ cups all-purpose flour
1 teaspoon soda
½ teaspoon salt
1 cup candied pineapple, chopped
2 cups uncooked rolled oats (regular or
    quick-cooking)
2 (3½-ounce) cans flaked coconut

Beat butter and sugars together until creamy. Add eggs and beat well. Combine flour, soda, and salt; add to creamed mixture, and beat well. Stir in pineapple and oats.

Shape dough to form 1-inch balls. Roll in coconut, and place on ungreased cookie sheets. Bake at 375° for 12 to 15 minutes. Yield: 6 dozen cookies.

SCOOTER DATE COOKIES

1 cup sugar
1 cup firmly packed brown sugar
1 cup shortening or margarine
3 eggs, well beaten
3 cups all-purpose flour
1 teaspoon salt
1 teaspoon soda
1 teaspoon baking powder
2 cups chopped dates
2 cups chopped nuts

Cream sugars and shortening until light and fluffy; add eggs, beating well. Combine flour, salt, soda, and baking powder; add to creamed mixture, mixing well. Stir in dates and nuts.

Roll dough into walnut-size balls; flatten. Place on greased cookie sheets. Bake at 300° about 15 minutes or until lightly browned. Yield: about 4 dozen cookies.

DANISH SUGAR COOKIES

½ cup butter
1 cup sugar
1 egg
2 cups all-purpose flour
1 teaspoon vanilla extract
Colored sugar or icing

Combine butter and sugar, and beat until light. Beat in egg, then flour and vanilla. Drop by teaspoonfuls on greased cookie sheet, allowing about 3 inches between cookies. Place a clean, wet cloth over bottom of a tumbler. Flatten cookies, continuing to wet cloth to keep dough from sticking. Bake 12 to 15 minutes at 325°. Remove cookies immediately from pan, or they will stick and break up. For Christmas, these cookies may be sprinkled with colored sugar or frosted with tinted icing. Yield: about 5 dozen cookies.

SOUR CREAM-CHOCOLATE SNAPPERS

  2 eggs
⅔ cup shortening
  1 (18.5-ounce) package sour cream
      chocolate fudge cake mix
    Pecan halves
  1 (14.3-ounce) package sour cream
      chocolate fudge frosting mix

Combine eggs and shortening; beat well. Add about half of cake mix, and beat at medium speed of electric mixer until light and fluffy. Add remaining cake mix, beating at low speed and scraping bowl often.

On greased cookie sheets, place groups of 3 pecan halves in a cluster so that ends touch in center.

Shape dough into 1-inch balls, and place in center of each group of nuts.

Bake at 375° for 8 to 10 minutes. Cool slightly before removing from cookie sheet; cool on rack.

Prepare frosting mix according to package directions; frost cookies. Yield: about 5 dozen cookies.

ORANGE-GINGER COOKIES

  1 cup butter or margarine, softened
1½ cups sugar
  1 egg
  2 tablespoons light corn syrup
  3 cups all-purpose flour
  2 teaspoons soda
  2 teaspoons ground ginger
½ teaspoon ground cloves
  1 tablespoon grated orange rind

Cream butter and sugar until light and fluffy; add egg and corn syrup, beating well. Combine dry ingredients; add to creamed mixture, and mix well. Stir in orange rind.

Shape into two rolls about 9 inches long and 2 inches in diameter. Wrap in waxed paper; chill several hours or overnight.

Slice about ⅛ inch thick, and place 2 inches apart on greased cookie sheets. Bake at 400° for 5 to 6 minutes or until done. Yield: 8 dozen cookies.

SOFT OATMEAL COOKIES

  1 cup sugar
  1 cup solid shortening
  2 eggs
  2 cups all-purpose flour
¾ teaspoon ground cinnamon
¾ teaspoon ground cloves
¼ teaspoon salt
¾ teaspoon soda
¼ cup milk
  2 cups quick-cooking oats
  1 cup seedless raisins
½ cup chopped nuts (optional)

In large bowl of mixer, combine sugar with shortening, and beat until fluffy. Beat in eggs, one at a time. Sift or stir the flour with cinnamon, cloves, and salt. Combine soda with milk. Beat flour mixture into the batter, mixing thoroughly. Add milk mixture. Remove mixing bowl from machine, and work oats, raisins, and nuts into dough with wooden spoon or your hands. Drop by teaspoonfuls, 2 inches apart, on greased cookie sheet. Bake at 350° for 12 to 15 minutes. Yield: about 4 dozen cookies.

Note: Soft cookies stay moist when stored tightly covered; crisp ones keep best in a jar with a loose-fitting lid.

Fruits

Fruits, one of our most important vitamin sources, should be enjoyed in season when they are most reasonably priced. Shipping from afar pumps up the price, and every hour involved in the process subtracts from freshness. Fruit juices are wonderfully refreshing, and we adore them. But the machines on the market, which will reduce a 5-pound bag of apples or several pounds of carrots to two helpings of juice, are guilty of a crime: they squander our money and rob us of the roughage we need.

Practice segmenting oranges and grapefruit. An entire bagful can be cut for serving and stored in the refrigerator in very little time. Remember to use fruit often, simply dressed as salad or with a bit of cheese for dessert.

ORANGES PORTUGUESE

  4 seedless oranges
  1 cup sugar
  1 cup water
  2 tablespoons port

Peel oranges with potato parer, taking off only the rind (outer). Cut rind into thin strips. Peel off and discard white inner peel. With a sharp knife, cut between segments, almost but not quite through to center, so segments remain in place. Place in deep bowl only large enough to contain them. Combine sugar and water, add slivered rind, and boil 5 minutes; add wine. Pour over oranges, and refrigerate overnight, turning once if only partially covered by syrup. Serve cold in individual dessert dishes, with their liquid. Yield: 4 servings.

LIVELY DESSERT COMPOTE

  2 grapefruits
  4 oranges
  ¼ cup lime marmalade
  ⅓ cup orange marmalade
  1 tablespoon lemon juice
  2 tablespoons orange juice
  2 bananas

Section grapefruits and oranges; combine, and refrigerate. In small saucepan, combine the marmalades and fruit juices. Heat and stir for a few minutes to make a sauce. Chill. To serve, slice bananas, and arrange with citrus segments in dessert dishes. Distribute sauce over each serving. Yield: 8 to 10 servings.

PEARS BAKED IN PORT

  4 firm pears
  ½ cup sugar
  ½ cup port
  3 whole cloves
    Dash salt
  1 tablespoon lemon juice
  4 tablespoons whipping cream or cream
    cheese, whipped

Remove cores from pears with an apple corer, and peel them. Combine remaining ingredients, except cream, in saucepan, and boil 10 minutes. Stand pears upright in small, deep baking dish, and pour syrup over them. Bake, covered, at 350° for 30 minutes. Uncover, and bake 30 minutes longer or until tender, basting or gently turning the fruit for uniform color and flavor. Serve warm or cold, with syrup. Garnish with cream. Yield: 4 servings.

CURRIED FRUIT

1 (16-ounce) can peach halves
1 (16-ounce) can pear halves
1 (8-ounce) can pineapple slices, halved
1 cup dried apricot halves
½ stick (¼ cup) butter
2 or 3 teaspoons curry powder
1¼ cups firmly packed light brown sugar
8 maraschino cherries (optional)

Drain juice from canned fruit into a saucepan. Put dried apricots in juice, and simmer 10 minutes. Drain, reserving juice for another purpose such as a gelatin dessert. Arrange drained fruits in buttered baking dish. Dot with butter. Stir curry powder into sugar, and sift or sprinkle over top of fruit to cover completely. Bake at 350° for 35 minutes. Garnish with cherries, and serve hot. Yield: 8 servings.

BROILED CURRANT PEACH HALVES

4 large peach halves, canned or fresh
2 tablespoons currant jelly
2 tablespoons sweet sherry
4 dashes cinnamon

Place peaches in small pan for broiling. If fresh peaches are used, poach them for 5 minutes in a little water before broiling. Put ½ tablespoon of jelly and ½ tablespoon sherry in center of each. Top each with a dash cinnamon. Place under broiler until bubbly and hot. Use for garnish on meat platter, or top with vanilla ice cream and serve as dessert. Yield: 4 servings.

PEACHES WITH CINNAMON SAUCE

1 (29-ounce) can peach halves
1 (3⅜-ounce) package cinnamon candies
Sugar cookies (optional)

Combine 1 cup of the liquid from the peaches with the cinnamon drops in small saucepan. Stir over medium heat until candies are dissolved. Place drained peach halves, 3 or 4 at a time, in syrup just until heated. Stack peaches in 1½-pint jar and pour remaining syrup over them. Cover tightly. If syrup does not quite cover peaches, make sure container is leakproof, and turn jar over occasionally. Refrigerate at least overnight before using, or use within a week. To serve as dessert, place peach halves in individual serving dishes. If desired, pass a plate of plain sugar cookies. Yield: 7 or 8 servings.

Note: You can also use the peaches as garnish for a meat platter.

LUNCHEON COOLER

1 medium-size honeydew melon,
   quartered
2 medium-size peaches, peeled and
   sliced
2 bananas, sliced
½ cup halved strawberries
½ cup seedless grapes
3 tablespoons honey
   Lime sherbet (optional)
   Mint leaves

Cut ½ cup melon balls from the quartered honeydew, and combine with peaches, bananas, strawberries, grapes, and honey; toss gently. Spoon into melon quarters. Top with sherbet, if desired; garnish with mint. Yield: 4 servings.

GLAZED CRAB APPLES

**About 20 crab apples
Syrup**

Arrange in single layer in baking dish. Pour Syrup over crab apples, and bake at 350° for 1 hour or until apples are tender; baste occasionally during baking. Use as garnish for holiday turkey or roast pork. Yield: 20 crab apples.

Syrup:

**1 cup sugar
1 cup water
Juice of 1 lemon
Juice and grated rind of 1 orange
Few drops red food coloring, optional**

Combine ingredients, and cook until mixture spins a light thread or registers 225° on candy thermometer.

APRICOT POLONAISE

**1 stick piecrust mix or pastry for 1
   (9-inch) pie shell
¼ cup finely chopped candied orange
   peel
1 (29-ounce) can apricot halves
1 (8- or 10-ounce) jar apricot preserves
¼ cup macaroon crumbs
   Ice cream (optional)**

Prepare pastry stick according to package directions or make homemade pastry. Roll into a rectangle to fit bottom only of an 8- x 12-inch baking dish. Sprinkle orange peel over crust, pressing down slightly to imbed pieces in pastry. Drain apricots, reserving liquid. Arrange apricot halves, cut side up, evenly on pastry. Dilute preserves with 2 tablespoons of reserved liquid, and spread over fruit. Add 2 tablespoons of the liquid to the macaroon crumbs, and distribute evenly over fruit, making sure some of the mixture falls into centers of apricots. Bake at 375° about 20 minutes or until nicely browned. Cool. May be served à la mode, if desired. Yield: 6 or 8 servings.

BLACKBERRY CUP

**1 (16-ounce) can blackberries
2 fresh oranges, segmented
1 cup fresh pineapple chunks
¼ cup toasted coconut
   Mint sprigs, optional**

Chill all fruit. Partially drain blackberries, and distribute berries in 4 dessert dishes with a little of their juice. Add oranges and pineapple. Top with coconut. Garnish each serving with a sprig of mint. Use as first course or as light dessert. Yield: 4 servings.

COCONUT FLAN HAVANA

**1¼ cups sugar, divided
½ cup flaked coconut
5 eggs
2 cups milk
½ teaspoon vanilla extract
   Dash salt**

Place ¾ cup sugar in small skillet, which has been rinsed but not dried, over low heat, and stir until it melts. (Use wooden spoon.) Working quickly, protecting the hands with pot holders, pour melted sugar into 1-quart ring mold, tilting mold to coat bottom and as much of the sides as possible. Sprinkle coconut over caramelized sugar.

Beat eggs with remaining ½ cup sugar; add milk, vanilla, and salt. Pour into mold. Set mold in pan of water so that water is halfway up sides of mold. Bake at 400° until top browns. Reduce heat to 325°, and bake until knife inserted into the center of custard comes out clean, about 30 to 40 minutes. Cool to lukewarm. To unmold, run knife around edges, place serving plate over mold, and turn the whole assembly over. The custard will be bathed in a caramel-coconut sauce, so serving dish should have ½-inch sides. Yield: 5 to 6 servings.

FROZEN BANANA SURPRISE

2 large ripe bananas
2 tablespoons powdered sugar
½ cup whipping cream
4 large fresh strawberries

Peel bananas, and wrap separately in foil or plastic wrap, twisting ends to seal. Freeze. Place 4 flat dessert plates in refrigerator or freezer to chill. Moments before serving, unwrap bananas and slice, diagonally, ⅔ inch thick directly onto dessert plates. Spoon sugar into sifter, and sprinkle over slices. Spoon cream (not whipped) over each sliced. Cream will freeze to the bananas. Garnish each serving with a strawberry, washed, stem on. It is necessary to work quickly in order to serve before bananas thaw, but if everything is in readiness, it takes only minutes to prepare the dessert. Yield: 4 servings.

Variation: Use only ¼ cup cream and ¼ cup chocolate syrup, spooning alternately on banana slices for an interesting and delicious effect.

FRESH STRAWBERRIES EUGENIE

1 pint fresh strawberries
2 tablespoons maraschino liqueur
2 tablespoons curaçao or other orange
**   liqueur**
¼ cup sugar
½ cup commercial sour cream
¼ cup firmly packed light brown
**   sugar**

Wash and stem berries; drain well, and place in bowl. Pour liqueurs over them, sprinkle with the sugar, and refrigerate several hours. At serving time, spoon berries and liquid into 4 dessert dishes. Top each with sour cream. Place brown sugar in sifter and, stirring sugar through sifter with a spoon, cover the sour cream. Yield: 4 servings.

PINEAPPLE FRITTERS

1 cup all-purpose flour
**   Pinch salt**
1 tablespoon sugar
2 teaspoons baking powder
1 egg, slightly beaten
¾ cup crushed pineapple, drained
**   Oil**
**   Powdered sugar**

Mix all dry ingredients by sifting or stirring. Add egg and pineapple, beating until well blended. Heat oil to 375°. Drop batter by rounded teaspoonfuls into oil for frying, and fry until lightly browned and done in the center. To test, cut into the first one; it should not be doughy in the center. Drain on absorbent paper, and dredge with powdered sugar while still warm. Yield: about 2 dozen small fritters.

BLUEBERRY BUCKLE

¾ cup sugar
¼ cup shortening
1 egg
2 cups all-purpose flour
2 teaspoons baking powder
½ teaspoon salt
½ cup milk
2 cups fresh blueberries, washed and
     drained
  Topping

Combine sugar, shortening, and egg; beat until smooth. Combine dry ingredients, and add to creamed mixture; stir in milk. Gently fold in blueberries. Spoon into a greased 9-inch square pan; sprinkle with Topping. Bake at 375° about 45 minutes or until brown. Yield: 8 servings.

Topping:

½ cup sugar
⅓ cup all-purpose flour
½ teaspoon ground cinnamon
¼ cup butter or margarine, softened

Combine dry ingredients; add butter, and cut in with pastry blender or 2 knives until mixture is consistency of cornmeal.

BLUEBERRY FLUMMERY

4 cups milk
1¼ cups sugar, divided
¾ cup uncooked regular rice
1 teaspoon vanilla extract
4 cups fresh or frozen blueberries
2 cups water
1 tablespoon lemon juice
1 cup whipping cream, whipped

Combine milk and ¼ cup sugar in top part of double boiler; place on burner, and bring to a boil. Stir in rice. Then place over hot water, and cook for 45 minutes or until rice is very soft. Stir in vanilla; cool, and pour into a bowl.

Wash blueberries, and drain thoroughly. Combine water, lemon juice, and remaining 1 cup sugar in a saucepan; bring to a boil, and cook over high heat for 5 minutes. Add berries, and cook 2 minutes.

Cool; then pour over rice mixture. Chill thoroughly; serve with whipped cream. Yield: 6 servings.

Sandwiches

Take two slices of good bread, preferably whole grain and homemade, spread them with real mayonnaise (butter if you're a bit of a Yankee), and it hardly matters what you put between them: the sandwich is one of the pleasanter facts of life. It works for us from breakfast, when bacon and egg slip neatly between the slices for a rib-sticking breakfast, to a casseroled luncheon or dinner entrée made of layered bread and meats with a custard poured over and baked.

Open-faced, almost anything can become a sandwich. A slice of bread, lavished with bacon, tomato, and cheese, briefly broiled, comes out a hearty lunch. Top bread with an elegant salad of crabmeat or chicken, garnish it for cosmetic effect, and you have a ladies' luncheon par excellence.

Consider the lowly peanut butter and jelly sandwich. Have you tried using crunchy peanut butter and cherry preserves, then grilling it in butter? That's a specialty at my house, as is a sharp cheese-tuna mixture, either grilled on bread or piled on rye buns, wrapped in foil, and baked.

Sandwiches also make excellent party fare, whether they provide the main course at a tailgate picnic during football season or dainty finger-food at an afternoon tea. The Pumpernickel Strata listed in the Summertime Luncheon for 6 or 8 menu is a fresh and filling main-dish sandwich, and the Party Foods chapter in Part II illustrates a variety of party sandwich techniques.

If you are freezing sandwiches ahead for a party, always use butter instead of mayonnaise for spreading the bread, as it insulates the bread against the moisture of the filling. Never use hard-cooked egg or celery in the filling; egg toughens, celery "waters out" on thawing.

BEAN SANDWICHES

1 (15-ounce) can red kidney beans
   Mayonnaise
4 slices bread, toasted
2 cups saukerkraut, rinsed and drained
8 strips bacon, cooked
1 tomato, sliced (optional)

Heat beans. Spread mayonnaise on each slice of bread; top with sauerkraut, beans, and 2 slices bacon. Garnish with tomato slices, if desired. Yield: 4 open-face sandwiches.

VIKING LEMON-EGG SANDWICH

1 medium-size lemon
¼ cup olive oil
2 tablespoons white wine vinegar
¼ teaspoon dry mustard
   Pinch cayenne pepper
½ teaspoon salt
   Freshly ground pepper
1 (1-pound) loaf white bread, unsliced
¼ cup mayonnaise
   Lettuce
4 hard-cooked eggs, sliced
2 green onions, chopped
1 (3¾-ounce) can sardines, drained

Boil whole lemon in salty water for 15 minutes or until tender; cool. Cut lemon in half; pull out and discard the pulp and white pith. Mince the peel.

Make a dressing by combining lemon peel, oil, vinegar, dry mustard, cayenne, salt, and pepper.

Split bread in half lengthwise, and spread with mayonnaise. Arrange lettuce, eggs, and onion on bottom half; top with sardines. Pour lemon dressing over all. Cover with top half of bread; slice into sandwiches. Yield: 4 servings.

MINI-SLIM SANDWICHES

    Butter or margarine, softened
  6 onion rolls, split
  1 (8-ounce) package cream cheese
  1 teaspoon dried chives
  ¼ teaspoon dillweed
  3 hard-cooked eggs, chopped
  6 lettuce leaves
  6 slices smoked salmon

Butter onion rolls. Blend cream cheese, chives, and dillweed; mix well. Fold in chopped eggs. Spread bottom half of each roll with cream cheese mixture; cover with lettuce leaf and salmon slice and top of roll. Yield: 6 sandwiches.

FIX AHEAD CHEESE-TUNA SANDWICH

  1 cup (¼-pound) sharp cheese cubes
  1 (7-ounce) can flaked tuna fish
  2 tablespoons chopped onion
  2 tablespoons chopped sweet pickle
  3 hard-cooked eggs, chopped
  2 teaspoons diced green pepper
  2 teaspoons diced stuffed olives
  ½ cup mayonnaise
  6 hot dog buns

Combine all ingredients for filling, and spread on bottom slice of bun. Add top and place each sandwich on a large square of heavy-duty aluminum foil. Wrap securely and keep chilled until ready to cook.

  To cook, place sandwiches on grill over a medium-hot fire and cook about 30 minutes, turning only once. Yield: 6 servings.

BAKED TUNA BUNS

  1 (9-ounce) can tuna fish
  ½ cup mayonnaise
  3 or 4 dashes hot pepper sauce
    Juice of ½ lemon, strained
  1 teaspoon prepared mustard
  ½ pound shredded sharp cheddar cheese
  8 medium-size hamburger buns

Put tuna in mixing bowl, and break it into flakes. Add mayonnaise. Without stirring in mayonnaise, add pepper sauce, lemon juice, and mustard; then stir into mayonnaise, and then, into tuna. Add mustard and cheese. Blend well, and divide mixture among the 8 buns, making sandwiches. Wrap buns either separately or 2 at a time in pieces of aluminum foil, and seal well. Place on baking sheet, and bake at 325° for 20 minutes. Yield: 8 sandwiches.

FRENCH-TOASTED SEAFOOD SANDWICH

  1 cup cooked or canned shrimp, chopped
  1 cup cooked or canned crabmeat, chopped
  ¼ cup chopped ripe olives
  ¼ cup finely chopped celery
  2 hard-cooked eggs, chopped
  ½ cup shredded sharp cheddar cheese
  2 teaspoons grated onion
  2 teaspoons lemon juice
    About ½ cup mayonnaise
    Salt and pepper to taste
  1 long loaf French bread, sliced ½ inch thick
    Butter for sautéing
    Batter

Combine shrimp, crabmeat, olives, celery, eggs, cheese, onion, and lemon juice. Mix well. Add just enough mayonnaise to bind, remembering that the cheese will liquify when heated. Add seasonings.

Make sandwiches; the number depends on length and diameter of bread. Heat butter in large skillet or on griddle. Dip each sandwich into Batter, and sauté on both sides until lightly browned. Yield: 10 or more sandwiches.

Batter:

3 eggs
1 cup milk
¼ teaspoon salt

Beat eggs with milk and salt. Dip sandwiches.

GOLDEN DELIGHT SANDWICHES

12 slices white bread
    Butter or margarine, softened
3 cups shredded cheddar cheese
1 cup chopped cooked shrimp
¾ cup mayonnaise
1 tablespoon lemon juice
1 teaspoon Worcestershire sauce
½ teaspoon curry powder
    Paprika

Trim crusts from bread; spread slices with butter. Combine remaining ingredients except paprika. Spread mixture on each slice of bread; sprinkle with paprika.

Cut 6 slices of bread in half. Broil whole and half slices until cheese bubbles. Arrange 1 whole and 2 half slices of bread on plate, open faced. Serve hot. Yield: 6 servings.

HAWAIIAN SANDWICHES

12 round buns, split
¾ cup mayonnaise
¾ pound sliced ham
12 pineapple slices, drained
¼ cup firmly packed brown sugar
12 slices pasteurized process American
    cheese
    Paprika

Spread buns with mayonnaise. Place a slice of ham and a slice of pineapple on bottom of each bun; sprinkle with brown sugar. On the top half of each bun place a slice of cheese and a dash of paprika.

Broil the sandwich, open faced, until cheese is just melted and brown sugar bubbles. Close buns, and serve hot. Yield: 12 sandwiches.

PIMIENTO CHEESE SANDWICH FILLING

⅔ to ¾ pound mild cheddar cheese
1 (4-ounce) jar whole pimiento
3 whole sweet pickles
1 teaspoon sugar
½ teaspoon salt
¼ teaspoon pepper
½ cup mayonnaise

Put cheese, pimiento, and pickles through fine blade of food grinder, letting food fall into large bowl of mixer. With mixer on medium speed, beat cheese mixture while adding remaining ingredients, and scrape down sides with rubber spatula. If necessary, a little more mayonnaise may be added for desired consistency. Yield: about 3 cups.

PIMIENTO CHEESE SPREAD

½ pound pasteurized process American
   cheese, shredded
1 (5⅓-ounce) can evaporated milk
1 (2-ounce) jar pimientos, chopped
2 tablespoons mayonnaise
⅛ teaspoon garlic salt (optional)

Combine cheese and evaporated milk in top
of double boiler; heat until cheese is melted.
Add remaining ingredients, mixing well.
Cool, and use as a sandwich spread. Yield:
1 cup.

CHEESY SARDINE CIRCLES

2 (3¾-ounce) cans sardines in mustard
   sauce
½ pound sharp cheddar cheese, finely
   shredded
1 cup chopped celery
¼ cup chopped black olives
2 pimientos, chopped
1 tablespoon minced onion
8 hamburger buns

Put sardines in bowl, and break up with
fork. Add next 5 ingredients, and mix well.
Fill buns with mixture, and place on baking
sheet. Cover with foil, and heat at 300°
about 30 minutes. Yield: 8 sandwiches.

OLIVE-CHEDDAR SANDWICH
SPREAD

1 pound mild cheddar cheese, shredded
¾ cup mayonnaise
1 (8-ounce) jar pimiento-stuffed olives,
   drained and chopped (1½ cups)
   Bread or toast
   Lettuce

Combine cheese, mayonnaise, and olives;
stir until well blended. Spread cheese mixture on bread or toast slices. Top with lettuce and additional slices of bread to make
sandwiches. Yield: about 4 cups sandwich
spread.

AVOCADO-SLAW SANDWICHES

4 cups finely shredded cabbage
12 stuffed olives, sliced
1 cup mayonnaise or a favorite thick
   dressing for slaw
   Salt and pepper to taste
12 slices whole wheat bread
   About ½ cup melted butter, divided
2 medium-size ripe avocados
   Juice of 1 lemon
2 large tomatoes, thinly sliced

To make slaw, combine cabbage, olives,
and mayonnaise; add salt and pepper. Let
stand for 30 minutes; then drain well.
Lightly brush one side of bread with part
of butter; spread slaw on 6 slices. (Slaw
should be about ½ inch thick.)

Peel avocados, and slice in lengthwise
strips; dip in lemon juice and place in a
layer over slaw. Arrange 3 tomato slices
over avocado; top with a second slice of
buttered bread. Tie each sandwich together
with a string. Brush both sides with
remaining butter. Wrap in waxed paper or
foil and refrigerate, if desired.

Before serving, unwrap and place on a
cookie sheet; bake at 375° about 20 minutes, turning to brown both sides. Cut
strings and serve immediately. Yield: 6
servings.

GRILLED TURKEY OR CHICKEN SANDWICHES

1½ cups finely chopped cooked turkey or
    chicken
½ cup chopped stuffed olives
1 teaspoon prepared mustard
⅓ cup mayonnaise
8 slices sandwich bread
¼ cup butter, melted

Mix turkey, olives, mustard, and mayonnaise. Make 4 sandwiches, and grill in hot butter, lightly browning both sides. Yield: 4 servings.

TURKEY-ZUCCHINI CHEESEWICH

½ cup butter
¼ teaspoon dillweed
    Dash thyme
3 small zucchini, thinly sliced
6 sliced Vienna or white bread,
    toasted
12 slices cooked turkey
12 slices tomato
    Cheese Sauce

Melt butter in a large skillet; stir in seasonings. Sauté zucchini in butter mixture until tender. Remove zucchini; brush toast with butter. Set skillet aside, reserving the butter in it.

Place 2 turkey slices on each slice of bread. Arrange 2 turkey slices on each slice of bread. Arrange 2 tomato slices and zucchini slices over turkey.

Place sandwiches on baking sheet; cover with foil. Bake at 400° for 10 to 15 minutes or until heated thoroughly. Scoop Cheese Sauce over sandwiches. Yield: 6 servings.

Cheese Sauce:

¼ cup all-purpose flour
½ teaspoon salt
    Dash pepper
    Reserved seasoned butter
2 cups milk
2 cups shredded pasteurized process
    American cheese

Combine flour, salt, and pepper with reserved seasoned butter in skillet. Gradually stir in milk. Cook over medium heat, stirring constantly, until thickened. Add cheese; stir until melted. Yield: sauce for 6 sandwiches.

Sauces

The French first discovered that sauces are one of the most versatile of foods, and sauces have since become one of the most international. White Sauce, whose preparation is discussed in Part II, provides an ideal binder for a casserole, a tasty accent for a vegetable dish, and is itself the basis for the inimitable soufflé; remoulade sauce adds Creole cachet to all types of seafood; tomato sauce supplies a spicy footnote for fish, meat, vegetables, and, of course, Italian-style spaghetti; and let's not forget that delicious, all-American contribution to the picnic scene, barbecue sauce.

Others find their favorites among the myriad of dessert sauces — fresh fruit sauces, candy sauces, nut sauces — which can be used to top all manner of desserts from ice cream to cake to fruit. Easily and quickly made, a sweet sauce can turn an ordinary dessert into spur-of-the-moment party fare. But whether you prefer them spicy or sweet, sauces add a memorable fillip to any dish they accompany.

FRESH BLUEBERRY SAUCE

 2 cups fresh blueberries
⅓ cup sugar
 1 tablespoon freshly squeezed lemon
   juice
¼ teaspoon salt
½ teaspoon vanilla extract

Wash and crush blueberries. Combine blueberries, sugar, lemon juice, and salt in saucepan. Bring to boiling point, and boil for 1 minute. Add vanilla; chill. Serve over pudding, cake, or ice cream. Yield: 1½ cups.

TAFFY-PEANUT BUTTER SAUCE

¾ cup peanut butter, creamy or crunchy
1 cup evaporated milk
½ cup unsulfured molasses

To peanut butter add the evaporated milk; blend until smooth. Then stir in molasses. Serve over vanilla ice cream. Yield: 2½ cups.

APPLE ICE CREAM SAUCE

½ cup firmly packed brown sugar
1 tablespoon cornstarch
½ teaspoon ground cinnamon
¼ teaspoon ground nutmeg
½ teaspoon grated lemon rind
¾ cup water
1 (20-ounce) can pie-sliced apples,
   undrained
1 quart vanilla ice cream

Combine brown sugar, cornstarch, cinnamon, nutmeg, lemon rind, and water; blend well. Stir in apple slices; cook over medium heat, stirring constantly, until thickened. Serve hot over ice cream. Yield: 6 servings.

TRIPLE ORANGE DESSERT SAUCE

¼ cup frozen orange juice concentrate
¼ cup Grand Marnier or other orange
   liqueur
1 (11-ounce) can mandarin oranges,
   drained
Vanilla ice cream

Combine first 3 ingredients; chill. Serve over vanilla ice cream. Yield: 6 servings.

TENNESSEE BORDER SAUCE

2 cups firmly packed light brown sugar
1 cup water
1 cup chopped pecans
1 cup strawberry preserves
1 orange
1 lemon
1 cup bourbon

Combine sugar and water in saucepan, and stir until it boils. Cook until it spins a fine thread or registers 240° on candy thermometer. (Do not stir after mixture reaches a boil.) Remove from heat, and add pecans and preserves.

With potato parer, peel rind from orange and lemon; finely chop the rind, and add to sauce. With sharp knife, peel off white membrane; discard. Remove sections of fruit, and cut up rather small. Add to sauce. Add bourbon last. Mix, and store in jars in refrigerator to ripen. Keeps indefinitely. Yield: a little over a quart.

Note: Use on vanilla, strawberry, caramel, or pecan ice cream.

PRALINE ICE CREAM SAUCE

1 cup firmly packed light brown sugar
¼ cup light corn syrup
½ cup half-and-half
2 tablespoons butter or margarine
1 teaspoon vanilla extract
⅛ teaspoon salt
1 cup pecan halves
Vanilla ice cream

Combine all ingredients except ice cream in a saucepan. Cook over medium heat, stirring constantly for 10 minutes or until sauce is thickened and smooth. Cool slightly; serve over vanilla ice cream. Yield: 1½ cups.

Note: This sauce may be stored in a covered container in the refrigerator for several days. Before serving, add a small amount of cream; then heat, stirring until smooth.

CHOCOLATE SAUCE

¼ cup butter
1 cup sugar
1 teaspoon all-purpose flour
4 squares unsweetened chocolate, finely chopped
¾ cup whipping cream

Melt butter over low heat; add remaining ingredients. Stir, and cook gently 5 minutes. Yield: about 2 cups.

EASY BARBECUE SAUCE

1 (8-ounce) can tomato sauce
⅓ cup catsup
1½ teaspoons vinegar
Dash salt and pepper
½ teaspoon Italian seasoning
1 teaspoon prepared mustard
2 teaspoons commercial French dressing
2 teaspoons firmly packed brown sugar
1 tablespoon butter or margarine
¼ cup chopped onion

Combine all ingredients, mixing well. Simmer 15 to 20 minutes. Use on chicken, pork chops, ribs, or hamburgers. Yield: 1⅓ cups.

TANGY SAUCE FOR PARTY MEATBALLS

1 (10½-ounce) jar orange or lime
    marmalade
6 tablespoons prepared mustard
2 or 3 tablespoons water

Melt marmalade over low heat. Add mustard. If necessary add a little water for good consistency. Bring to boiling point, and pour over hot meatballs in chafing dish. Yield: about 1⅔ cups sauce.

REMOULADE SAUCE FOR SEAFOOD

1 cup mayonnaise
1 tablespoon chopped onion
1 tablespoon chopped parsley
1 tablespoon chopped celery
2 tablespoons Dijon mustard
1 tablespoon prepared horseradish
1 teaspoon paprika
½ teaspoon salt
    Dash hot sauce
¼ cup salad oil
1 tablespoon vinegar
½ teaspoon Worcestershire sauce

Combine all ingredients in a small bowl; mix until well blended. Refrigerate several hours or overnight. Yield: 1½ cups.

TOMATO SAUCE FOR FISH

2 cups tomato sauce
1 teaspoon Worcestershire sauce
2 tablespoons chopped fresh parsley
¼ cup chopped stuffed olives
½ cup cooked or canned shrimp
½ cup canned sliced mushrooms
¼ cup diced celery

Combine all ingredients in saucepan, and heat to the boiling point. Taste, and add more seasoning, if desired. Serve this sauce with baked or broiled fish. It is best served with a platter that can be placed under the broiler for just a few minutes. Yield: 3½ cups.

GRAPE SAUCE FOR PARTY BEEF FRANKS

1 (10½-ounce) jar grape jelly
1½ cups commercial Italian spaghetti
    sauce
2 or 3 tablespoons water

Melt jelly in small saucepan. Add spaghetti sauce, and thin with a little water as necessary for consistency. Heat to boiling, and pour over hot party beef franks in chafing dish. Yield: about 3 cups.

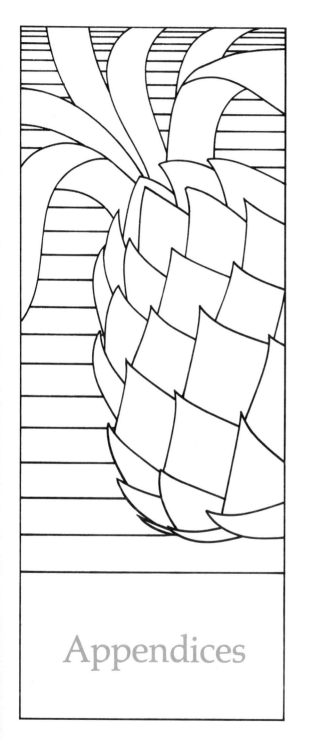

Appendices

Building a Cookbook Library

All of us know cooks who pride themselves on their cookbook collections, the very immensity of which is calculated to impress us with their expertise. And there are cooks who will boast that they do not own a single cookbook, which comes over as, "I'm a great natural cook, tribal knowledge, bred-in-the-bone."

A food writer of several years experience will soon be exposed for the jaded cynic he or she has become. Before that happens, let me confess that I no longer collect cookbooks by the numbers. I limit my collection to some 12 feet of shelving, which happens to be all the space I could devote to bookshelves the last time my kitchen was remodeled. It was a valuable experience, weeding out and fitting in, very much like going from a large garden plot to a small city patio, transplanting the best-loved ones and regretfully leaving others behind.

Every year I weed that patch of books, keeping sacred my hardy perennials, giving this or that laggard one more year to produce something I need, pitching out the books so limited in scope that their content can be found in a good general work. In the space gained by weeding, I plant such new cookbooks as have come to my attention during the year that I believe deserving of reference status. My system works; I recommend it.

RECOMMENDED COOKBOOKS

The foundation of any cooking library is a fine general purpose cookbook. The Rombauer-Becker *Joy of Cooking* has yet to be bested as an encyclopedic basic recipe and good reference work. There are others, on a more modest scale, well suited to basic status. To mention a few, there are the Fanny Farmer *Boston Cooking School Cookbook, The Betty Crocker Cookbook, The Good House-keeping Cookbook, House & Garden's New Cook-book,* and *America Cooks,* edited by Ann Seranne.

Special Interest Books

Special interest books are another matter. Again, take time to study the market, learn what is available. If you want a book on chicken or hamburger, there are dozens of them. Desserts, too. Look them over, peruse the indices; open a book at random and read a recipe. Does it seem complete, sound as though it is worth trying?

As you gain cooking experience, you may well develop an overriding fascination with one or more specialties. You can then begin to weight your collection toward those spe-cial categories. Without the least idea of suggesting anything beyond the bare bones of a cooking library in this small space, here are a few suggestions.

Southern

By far the most definitive contemporary cookbooks on Southern cookery are those published by *Southern Living: For the Love of Cooking* and *Our Best Recipes* by Lena Sturges; *Southern Country Cookbook* by the Editors of the *Progressive Farmer* magazine; *Southern Hospitality Cookbook* by Winifred Green Cheney; and *Party Cookbook* by Celia Marks.

French

If French cooking is your passion, then eventually you should own Henri Pella-prat's *Modern French Culinary Art.* It is beau-tifully illustrated with color photographs showing dishes professionally prepared and

garnished, and it includes black-and-white how-to photographs demonstrating rather advanced techniques. *The Escoffier Cook Book* is useful to the cook who is already profi-cient enough to benefit from its telegraphic style.

While I have had reservations about Julia Child's earlier books, I have nothing but praise and admiration for her recent *From Julia Child's Kitchen.* With her usual passion for detail and her tutorial style, she has widened her scope, broken out of the classic French and into other kinds of food. It is a book to be coveted and put high on one's Christmas list.

Chinese

Chinese food is a mania with many of us. The Chinese invented meat stretching and heat conservation, and their low-fat cookery and crisp steamed vegetables give us valuable lessons on how to cook in defense of our health. One of the hand-somest and certainly the largest Chinese cookbook I know is the *Thousand Recipe Cookbook,* by Gloria Bley Miller. But Helen Lang, who teaches Chinese cooking in the Louisville area, recommends to her students as most authentic these two books for starters: Johnny Kan's *Eat Immortal Flowers* for Cantonese-style cooking, and *The Joyce Chen Cookbook* for the spicier Northern Chinese cuisine. Kan is a San Francisco restauranteur and Ms. Chen is known for her television cook shows.

Italian

Italian cookbooks comprise a rather crowded field. You must spend time look-ing and be very selective. There are as many regional differences in Italy's food as there are in our U.S. food. Ada Boni's *Italian Cooking* is a fine book; it covers 14 recog-nizably different regional styles. The recipes in the book originally appeared in the Italian magazine *Arianna.* It sometimes seems to me that everyone who has eaten a plate of spaghetti has written an Italian cookbook.

By all means, experiment with the cuisines of other cultures; you'll find good books on German, Hungarian, Indonesian, Japanese food—good and bad. But study them before you buy. The libraries and bookstores are vast supermarkets for your cookbook shopping.

Breads

The Complete Book of Breads, by Bernard Clayton, Jr., is a must for the cook who specializes (or wants to) in baking bread. Its worldwide selection of breads will take you all the way from back home in Indiana to Portugal, India, Ireland, and so on. The only criticism the author received on his bread book was from a man in Ecuador who bought it to learn how to make bagels, and there isn't a bagel in it.

Except for the Clayton bread book, I have reservations about any book whose title starts with *The Complete Book of*— as in beans, tea, avocado—just because none of them is or can be "complete." But if an off-beat one takes your fancy, by all means buy it.

Cheese and Wine

For the cheese lover, *A Salute To Cheese,* by Betty Wasson, is a good investment. The would-be wine afficionado would want a heavy reference, such as Alexis Lichine's *Encyclopedia of Wines and Spirits.* Frank Schoonmaker's *Encyclopedia of Wine* is also a fine reference work and is not so technical as to put off the amateur.

Vegetable Protein

Diet for a Small Planet, by Frances Moore Lappe, probably should be required reading for us all in the light of the present world food crisis. The subtitle tells why: "How to Enjoy a Protein Harvest by Getting Off the Top of the Food Chain."

Convenience Cooking

Usually the booklet you get with any appliance is amply filled with recipes to show its versatility. Certainly the literature supplied by the pressure cooker and the crock cooker, for example, told me all I needed to know about them. An exception is the electric blender, without which I think I could not cook at all. Its uses seem limitless, and the number one book on the blender is still *Mary Meade's Magic Recipes* by Ruth Ellen Church.

Dictionaries

A cookbook shelf must be considered incomplete if it does not include a good dictionary of cooking terms. For the serious student of cooking, the glossaries included in most cookbooks are necessarily incomplete. Among the better cooking dictionaries are *The Wise Encyclopedia of Cookery* by David B. Wise; Myra Waldo's *International Encyclopedia of Cooking,* which is Volume II of a set (Volume I is a very good cookbook); *A Dictionary of Cooking* compiled by Ralph and Dorothy De Sola; and *The Grammar of Cooking* by Carol Braider.

Special Diets

If you or a member of your family suffers from a medical disability requiring a specialized diet over an extended period of time, you should invest in a book of recipes and methods for that particular disorder. Allergies, diabetes, heart disease, low-fat, low-sodium—all of these are conditions that are serious enough to warrant special cookbooks. After working with the material for a time, you will be able to adapt some of your favorite recipes to fit the new regimen. The best book I know for diabetics is *Cooking for Diabetics at Home and Away* by Winnie Balfour Rhodes.

Collectors' Items

Among the modest jewels in my collection are the homegrown cookbooks put out by women's clubs, Junior Leagues, and church women's groups. True, sometimes their indices are not too good, and their recipes will occasionally omit a baking temperature. Yet, there is an implicit promise in such books that every recipe is somebody's best.

For pure fun, anyone who loves cooking and food should pick up whenever possible a very old cookbook or two just for reading pleasure. It is nice to know how to make lye soap from wood ash, how to stiffen your veil, and how to make a poultice for a sore throat. My favorite oldie is *Miss Leslie's Cookery Book,* published in Philadelphia in 1859. Miss Leslie commanded that vegetables be cooked in vast amounts of water and the water discarded as "unwholesome." The pride of the South, beaten biscuits, were called Maryland biscuits and dismissed as "unwholesome," allowing that, while unpalatable, they were good enough for people who could afford nothing better. Her directions for the preparation of turtle and calves' heads read like a novel of crime and violence.

It would be nice if the book you are reading now could find a place on your shelf, at least until you have outgrown it and are ready to pass it along to another aspiring cook. It is hoped that before you part with it, it will have taught you some things you will want to keep among your mental furnishings.

Substitution of Ingredients

It is always best to follow a recipe closely, using the ingredients called for. However, if you are out of one ingredient, you may be able to substitute something else. A good rule of thumb is if you must make more than 1 substitution, select another recipe.

If you don't have:	Use:	If you don't have:	Use:
1 cup sweet milk	½ cup evaporated milk and ½ cup water or 1 cup reconstituted dry skim milk plus 2 teaspoons butter	1 square unsweetened chocolate	3 tablespoons cocoa plus 1 tablespoon butter or margarine
1 tablespoon cornstarch (for thickening)	2 tablespoons flour or 4 teaspoons quick-cooking tapioca	1 small onion, chopped	1 tablespoon instant minced onion
1 cup sour milk or buttermilk	1 cup sweet milk (whole *or* skim) plus 1 tablespoon vinegar or lemon juice (Let stand 5 minutes.)	1 teaspoon dry mustard	1 tablespoon prepared mustard
		1 teaspoon baking powder	¼ teaspoon soda plus ½ teaspoon cream of tartar or use ¼ teaspoon soda and replace ½ cup of the liquid called for in recipe with sour milk
1 egg (for custard or pie)	2 egg yolks		
1 cup cake flour	1 cup less 2 tablespoons regular flour, sifted 2 or 3 times	1 cup catsup or chili sauce (for cooking)	1 cup tomato sauce plus ½ cup sugar and 2 tablespoons vinegar
		1 teaspoon fresh herb	⅓ teaspoon crushed dry herb
½ cup butter or margarine	½ cup shortening plus ¼ teaspoon salt (It will work but flavor will differ.)	¼ cup chopped fresh parsley	1 tablespoon freeze-dried parsley

Timetable for Roasting Stuffed Chilled Poultry

Kind of Poultry	Ready-To-Cook Weight	Approximate Amount of Stuffing	Approximate Roasting Time at 325°F.
	pounds	quarts	hours
Chicken			
Broilers or fryers	1½ to 2½	¼ to ½	1¼ to 2*
Roasters	2½ to 4½	½ to 1¼	2 to 3½†
Capons and caponettes	4 to 8	1¼ to 1¾	3 to 5
Duck	3 to 5	½ to 1	2½ to 3
Goose	4 to 8	¾ to 1½	2¾ to 3½
	8 to 14	1½ to 2½	3½ to 5
Turkey			
Fryers or roasters (very young birds)	4 to 8	1 to 2	3 to 4½
Roasters (fully grown young birds)	6 to 12	1½ to 3	3½ to 5
	12 to 16	3 to 4	5 to 6
	16 to 20	4 to 5	6 to 7½
	20 to 24	5 to 6	7½ to 9
Halves, quarters, and half breasts	3½ to 5	1 to 1½	3 to 3½
	5 to 8	1½ to 2	3½ to 4
	8 to 12	2 to 3	4 to 5

*Or roast unstuffed at 400°F. for ¾ to 1½ hours
†Or roast unstuffed at 400°F. for 1½ to 2¾ hours

Timetable for Roasting Smoked Pork

Cut	Approximate Weight	Internal Temperature	Approximate Roasting Time
	pounds		hours
Fully Cooked Ham, Bone-in	6 to 8	130°F.	2¼
	10 to 12	130°F.	2½ to 3
	15 to 18	130°F.	3½ to 4
Fully Cooked Picnic Shoulder, Bone-in	3 to 5	130°F.	1½ to 2
	7 to 9	130°F.	2½ to 3
Cook-Before-Eating Hams, Bone-in	6 to 8	160°F.	3¼
	10 to 12	160°F.	3½ to 4
	12 to 15	160°F.	4 to 4½
	18 to 22	160°F.	5 to 6
Cook-Before-Eating Picnic Shoulders, Bone-in..	4 to 6	170°F.	2½ to 3
	8 to 10	170°F.	4 to 4½
Cook-Before-Eating Boneless Shoulder Butt*	2 to 3	170°F.	2 to 3

*Boneless shoulder butt also may be covered with water and simmered over low heat about 45 minutes per pound.

Timetable for Roasting Fresh Pork

Cut	Approximate Weight	Internal Temperature	Approximate Roasting Time
	pounds		*hours*
Leg (Fresh Ham) — Whole	8	185°F.	4½
	10	185°F.	5½
	14	185°F.	6½
Leg (Fresh Ham) butt or shank portion	4 to 6	185°F.	3 to 3½
Loin, center	3 to 5	170°F.	2¼ to 2¾
Loin, half	4 to 6	170°F.	2¾ to 3½
Loin, end	3 to 4	170°F.	2¼ to 2¾
Boston butt (shoulder), bone-in	4 to 6	185°F.	3¾ to 4¼
Boston butt (shoulder), boneless	4 to 6	185°F.	3 to 4¾
Fresh picnic (shoulder), bone-in	4 to 6	185°F.	3 to 4¾

*Fresh pork roasts are excellent for rotisserie cooking. Usually about one-third less time is required than that given for oven roasting.

Timetable for Roasting Beef and Lamb

Kind and Cut	Approximate Weight	Internal Temperature	Approximate Total Cooking Time at 325°F.
	pounds		*hours*
Beef			
Standing ribs* (10-inch ribs)	4	140°F. (rare)	1¾
		160°F. (medium)	2
		170°F. (well done)	2½
	6	140°F. (rare)	2
		160°F. (medium)	2½
		170°F. (well done)	3⅓
	8	140°F. (rare)	2½
		160°F. (medium)	3
		170°F. (well done)	4½
Rolled ribs	4	140°F. (rare)	2
		160°F. (medium)	2½
		170°F. (well done)	3
	6	140°F. (rare)	3
		160°F. (medium)	3¼
		170°F. (well done)	4
Rolled rump	5	140°F. (rare)	2¼
		160°F. (medium)	3
		170°F. (well done)	3¼
Sirloin tip	3	140°F. (rare)	1½
		160°F. (medium)	2
		170°F. (well done)	2¼
Lamb			
Leg	6 to 7	180°F. (well done)	3¾
Leg (half)	3 to 4	180°F. (well done)	2½ to 3
Cushion shoulder	5	180°F. (well done)	3
Rolled shoulder	3	180°F. (well done)	2½
	5	180°F. (well done)	3

*Standing ribs, 8-inch ribs, allow 30 minutes longer.

Timetable for Cooking Fish and Shellfish					
Method of Cooking	*Product*	*Market Form*	*Approximate Weight or Thickness*	*Cooking Temperature*	*Approximate Total Cooking Time*
Baking	Fish	Dressed	3 to 4 lb.	350°F.	40 to 60 min.
		Pan-dressed	½ to 1 lb.	350°F.	25 to 30 min.
		Steaks	½ to 1 in.	350°F.	25 to 35 min.
		Filets		350°F.	25 to 35 min.
	Clams	Live		450°F.	15 min.
	Lobster	Live	¾ to 1 lb.	400°F.	15 to 20 min.
			1 to 1½ lb.	400°F.	20 to 25 min.
	Oysters	Live		450°F.	15 min.
		Shucked		400°F.	10 min.
	Scallops	Shucked		350°F.	25 to 30 min.
	Shrimp	Headless		350°F.	20 to 25 min.
	Spiny lobster	Headless	4 oz.	450°F.	20 to 25 min.
	tails		8 oz.	450°F.	25 to 30 min.
Broiling	Fish	Pan-dressed	½ to 1 lb.		10 to 15 min.
		Steaks	½ to 1 in.		10 to 15 min.
		Filets			10 to 15 min.
	Clams	Live			5 to 8 min.
	Lobster	Live	¾ to 1 lb.		10 to 12 min.
			1 to 1½ lb.		12 to 15 min.
	Oysters	Live			5 min.
		Shucked			5 min.
	Scallops	Shucked			8 to 10 min.
	Shrimp	Headless			8 to 10 min.
	Spiny lobster	Headless	4 oz.		8 to 10 min.
	tails		8 oz.		10 to 12 min.
Cooking in water	Fish	Pan-dressed	½ to 1 lb.	Simmer	10 min.
		Steaks	½ to 1 in.	Simmer	10 min.
		Filets		Simmer	10 min.
	Crabs	Live		Simmer	15 min.
	Lobster	Live	¾ to 1 lb.	Simmer	10 to 15 min.
			1 to 1½ lb.	Simmer	15 to 20 min.
	Scallops	Shucked		Simmer	4 to 5 min.
	Shrimp	Headless		Simmer	5 min.
	Spiny lobster	Headless	4 oz.	Simmer	10 min.
	tails		8 oz.	Simmer	15 min.
Deep-fat frying	Fish	Pan-dressed	½ to 1 lb.	375°F.	2 to 4 min.
		Steaks	½ to 1 in.	375°F.	2 to 4 min.
		Filets		375°F.	1 to 4 min.
	Clams	Shucked		375°F.	2 to 3 min.
	Crabs	Soft-shell	¼ lb.	375°F.	3 to 4 min.
	Lobster	Live	¾ to 1 lb.	350°F.	3 to 4 min.
			1 to 1½ lb.	350°F.	4 to 5 min.
	Oysters	Shucked		375°F.	2 min.
	Scallops	Shucked		350°F.	3 to 4 min.
	Shrimp	Headless		350°F.	2 to 3 min.
	Spiny lobster	Headless	4 oz.	350°F.	3 to 4 min.
	tails		8 oz.	350°F.	4 to 5 min.

HERB CHART

For:	Appetizers & Garnishes	Soups	Fish	Eggs or Cheese	Meats	Poultry & Game	Vegetables	Salads	Sauces
Use:									
Basil	Tomato Juice Seafood Cocktail	Tomato Chowders Spinach Minestrone	Shrimps Broiled Fish	Scrambled Eggs Cream Cheese Welsh Rabbit	Liver Lamb Sausage	Venison Duck	Eggplant Squash Tomatoes Onions	Tomato Seafood Chicken	Tomato Spaghetti Orange (for Game) Butter (for Fish)
Bay Leaves	Tomato Juice Aspic	Stock Bean	Court Bouillon Poached Halibut Salmon		Stews Pot Roast Shish Kebab Tripe	Chicken Fricassee Stews	Tomatoes	Aspic Marinades for Beet Onion	All Marinades Espagnole Champagne
Dillweed	Cheese Dips Seafood Spreads Pickles	Borscht Tomato Chicken	Halibut Shrimp Sole	Omelet Cottage Cheese	Beef Sweetbreads Veal Lamb	Chicken Pie Creamed Chicken	Cabbage Beets Beans Celery	Coleslaw Cucumber Potato	Cream (for Fish) Tartare
Fines Herbs			Baked or Broiled Cod or Halibut Stuffings	Omelet Scrambled Eggs Cheese Sauce Soufflés	Broiled Liver and Kidneys Roast Pork Pot Roast, Stews Meat Loaf Hamburgers	Stuffings Broiled Chicken	Peas Mushrooms Tomatoes		
Marjoram	Liver Pâté Stuffed Mushrooms Butters	Spinach Clam Mock Turtle Onion	Crab, Tuna Clams Halibut Salmon	Omelet Scrambled Eggs	Pot Roast Pork Beef Veal	Creamed Chicken Stuffings Goose	Carrots Zucchini Peas	Chicken Mixed Green	Cream Brown Sour Cream
Oregano	Guacamole Tomato	Tomato Bean Minestrone	Shrimp Clams Lobster	Huevos Rancheros	Sausage Lamb Meat Loaf	Marinades Stuffings Pheasant Guinea Hen	Tomatoes Cabbage Lentils Broccoli	Vegetable Bean Tomato	Spaghetti Tomato

Continued on next page

HERB CHART — Continued

For:	Appetizers & Garnishes	Soups	Fish	Eggs or Cheese	Meats	Poultry & Game	Vegetables	Salads	Sauces
Peppermint*	Fruit Cup Melon Balls Cranberry Juice	Pea	Garnish for Broiled Shrimps Prawns	Cream Cheese	Lamb Veal		Carrots New Potatoes Spinach Zucchini	Fruit Coleslaw Orange Pear	Mint
Rosemary	Fruit Cup	Turtle, Pea Spinach Chicken	Salmon Halibut	Omelet Scrambled Eggs	Lamb, Veal Beef Ham Loaf	Partridge Capon, Duck Rabbit	Peas Spinach Potatoes	Fruit	Cream Barbecue Tomato
Saffron		Bouillabaisse Chicken, Turkey	Halibut Sole	Cream Cheese Scrambled Eggs	Veal	Chicken Rabbit	Risotto Rice	Seafood Chicken	Fish Sauce
Sage	Sharp Cheese Spreads	Chicken Chowders	Halibut Salmon	Cheddar Cottage	Stews Pork Sausage	Goose Turkey Rabbit Stuffings	Lima Beans Eggplant Onions Tomatoes		
Salad Herbs	Fruit Cup Vegetable and Tomato Juices Seafood Cocktail Sauce		All Fish		Meat Loaf			All Salads	
Savory	Vegetable Juice Cocktail	Lentil Bean Vegetable	Crab Salmon	Scrambled or Deviled Eggs	Pork Veal	Chicken Stuffings	Beans, Rice Lentils Sauerkraut	Mixed Green String Bean Potato	Horseradish Fish Sauce
Tarragon	Tomato Juice Cheese Spreads Liver Pâtés	Chicken Mushroom Tomato Pea	All Fish	All Egg Dishes	Veal Sweetbreads Yorkshire Pudding	Chicken Squab Duck	Salsify Celery Root Mushrooms	Mixed Green Chicken Fruit Seafood	Bearnaise Tartare Verte Mustard
Thyme	Tomato Juice Fish Spreads Cocktails	Borscht Gumbo, Pea Clam Chowder Vegetable	Tuna Scallops Crab Sole	Shirred Eggs Cottage Cheese	Mutton Meat Loaf Veal Liver	Stuffings Venison Fricassee Pheasant	Onions Carrots Beets	Beet Tomato Aspics	Creole Espagnole Herb Bouquets

*Use 1/2 teaspoon for 6 servings

Courtesy of Spice Islands

SPICE CHART

For:	Appetizers & Garnishes	Fish	Eggs or Cheese	Meats	Poultry & Game	Vegetables	Sauces	Desserts & Beverages
Use: **Allspice**		*Marinades		Pot Roast Stew Braised Veal Pork, Lamb	*Marinades (for Game)	*Pickling liquids for all vegetables	Chili, Catsup Barbecue Spaghetti Brown	Fruit and Spice Cakes Mincemeat Apple Pie Pumpkin Pie
Beau Monde Seasoning	Dips Spreads	Broiled Baked	All Egg Dishes	Steaks Chops Roasts	Chicken Duck Turkey		Cream Tomato Barbecue	
Cardamom				Spareribs Ham Pork			Barbecue	Coffee Cakes Breads Fruitcake Cookies Hot Fruit Punches *Mulled Wines
Chili Con Carne Seasoning	Cheese Dips Spreads		Rabbits Soufflés Baked or Scrambled Eggs	Marinades for Pork Lamb Beef	Marinades for Chicken	Corn Rice Kidney Pink or Lima Beans	Barbecue Cheese	
Cinnamon	Cranberry Sauce Pickled or Spiced Fruits Broiled Grapefruit *Pickles *Chutney Catsup	*Court Bouillon for all Fish and Shellfish		Ham Lamb Pork Chops Beef Stews *Stock for Pickled or Smoked Meats	Stuffing for Goose			All Milk Drinks Custard, Fruit or Rice Puddings Pumpkin, Apple, Peach, Cream or Custard Pies *Mulled Wine *Hot Tea *Coffee *Chocolate *Spiced and Pickled Fruits
Cloves		*Court Bouillon Baked Fish	Scrambled or Creamed Eggs	*Marinades for Beef, Pork Lamb, Veal *Stock for Boiling Meat Loaf	*Marinades for Game *Stock for Boiling Poultry	Harvard Beets Sweet Potatoes Tomatoes	Spaghetti Chili Wine Barbecue	*Hot or Cold Fruit Punches *Mulled Wines All spice cakes, cookies, and puddings
Curry Powder	Dips	Broiled Baked	Deviled Eggs Egg Salad Cheese Spreads	Lamb Pork Beef	Chicken	Cooked Vegetables	Curry Marinades for Lamb, Beef Chicken Fish, Game Cream Sauce	
Ginger	*Pickled or Spiced Fruits *Preserves Jams Jellies	Broiled Baked		Pot Roast Steak Lamb *Marinades for Beef, Lamb	Stuffing for Poultry *Marinades for Chicken, Turkey	Candied Sweet Potatoes Glazed Carrots or Onions Winter Squash	For Pork Veal Fish	Canned Fruit Gingerbread Gingersnaps Ginger Cookies Steamed Puddings Bread or Rice Puddings

442

For: Use:	Appetizers & Garnishes	Fish	Eggs or Cheese	Meats	Poultry & Game	Vegetables	Sauces	Desserts & Beverages
Mace	Pickles Fruit Preserves Jellies	Trout Scalloped Fish	Rabbit	Lamb Chops Sausage		Buttered Carrots Cauliflower Squash Swiss Chard Spinach Mashed or Creamed Potatoes	Fish Veal Chicken	Cooked Apples Cherries Prunes Apricots Pancakes Chocolate Pudding / Fruit Cottage or Custard Puddings
Mustard (Hot)	Butter for Vegetables Seafood Cocktail	Crab		Stew Pot Roast Ham Pork	Fried Chicken	Creamed Asparagus Broccoli Brussels Sprouts Cabbage Celery Green Beans Pickled Beets	French Dressing Mustard Sauce Gravies Cream Cheese and Newburg Sauces	
Mustard (Mild)		Fried Broiled	Rabbit	Beef Stew Swiss Steak		Scalloped & Au Gratin Potatoes Steamed Cabbage Brussels Sprouts Asparagus Broccoli	French Dressing Cooked Salad Dressing Mayonnaise Raisin, Cream Sauces	
Nutmeg	Garnish for milk, chocolate, and spiced drinks	Baked Croquettes Broiled	Rabbit	Swedish Meat Balls Meat Loaf Meat Pie	Chicken	Glazed Carrots Cauliflower Squash Swiss Chard Spinach	Cream Sauce for Chicken Seafood Veal	Ice Cream Cakes / Cookies Puddings
Paprika	Pâtés Canapes Hors d'oeuvres		All Cheese Mixtures	Ground Beef Dipping Mixture for Pork Chops Veal Cutlets	Dipping Mixture for Fried Chicken	Baked Potatoes	Cooked French Sour Cream Salad Dressings Cream Sauce	
Tumeric		Marinades for Broiled Salmon, Lobster, or Shrimp	Scrambled or Creamed Eggs	Curried Beef or Lamb	Marinades for Chicken		Cream Mustard	
Vanilla Beans							Fruit	Ice Cream Cakes / Custards Puddings

Note: All spices are ground except those indicated by an asterisk (*), which indicates whole spice

Courtesy of Spice Islands

443

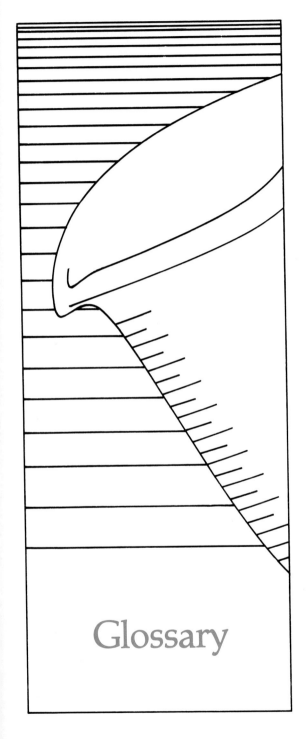

Glossary

à la Mode   Food served with ice cream

à la Mode, Boeuf   Beef prepared as an elegant pot roast

Al dente   The point in the cooking of pasta at which it is still fairly firm to the tooth; that is, very slightly undercooked

Aspic   A jellied meat juice or a liquid held together with gelatin

Baste   To spoon pan liquid over meats while they are roasting

Béchamel   White sauce of butter, flour, cream rather than milk, and seasonings

Biscuit   A small, leavened, unsweetened bread, usually served hot

Bisque   A thick, creamy soup usually of shellfish, but sometimes made of pureed vegetables

Blanch   To dip briefly into boiling water

Blend   To stir 2 or more ingredients together until well mixed

Blintz   A cooked crêpe stuffed with cheese or other filling

Borscht   Soup containing beets and other vegetables, usually with a meat stock base

Bouillon   Clear soup made by boiling meat in water

Bouquet Garni   Herbs tied in cheesecloth which are cooked in a mixture and removed before serving

Bourguignon (French for Burgundian)   Any food containing Burgundy may be so named

Braise   A 2-step method of cooking involving first searing, then steaming a food

Bread, to   To cover with crumbs, usually in combination with egg or other binder

Broil   To cook over live coals or under gas or electric heat source

Broth   Liquid in which any food is cooked

Capers   Buds from a Mediterranean plant, usually packed in brine and used as a condiment in dressings or sauces

Capon   Castrated male chicken

Caramel   Melted sugar or food flavored with melted sugar

Casserole   An ovenproof baking dish, usually with a cover; also the food cooked in it

Charlotte   A molded dessert containing gelatin, usually formed in a dish or a pan lined with ladyfingers or cake

Chiffonade (French for something shredded)   A dressing containing shreds of vegetables

Chill   To cool by placing on ice or in a refrigerator

Chop   A cut of meat usually attached to a rib

Chop, to   To cut into pieces by using sharp downward strokes

Coat   To cover completely, as in "coat with flour"

Compote   Mixed fruit, raw or cooked, usually served in "compote" dishes

Condiments   Seasonings that enhance the flavor of foods with which they are served

Consommé   A clarified meat stock

Court Bouillon (French for short broth)   An aromatic broth made with water and meat, fish or vegetables, and seasonings

Crackling Bread   Corn bread baked with chopped cracklings added

Cracklings   The crunchy, crisp bits of pork left after the fat is rendered for lard

Cream, Chantilly   Cream that has been whipped and flavored with powdered sugar and vanilla extract and is usually softer than "whipped cream"

Cream, to   To blend together, as sugar and butter, until mixture takes on a smooth creamlike texture

Cream, whipped   Cream that has been whipped until it is stiff

Crème de Cacao   A chocolate-flavored liqueur

Crème de Café   A coffee-flavored liqueur

Crêpes   Very thin pancakes

Croquette   Minced food, shaped like a ball, patty, cone, or log, bound with a heavy sauce, breaded, and fried

Crouton   Bread that has been diced and baked or fried until crisp

Cube, to   To cut into cube-shaped pieces

Curaçao   Orange-flavored liqueur

Cut in, to   To incorporate by cutting or chopping motions, as in cutting shortening into flour for pastry

Deglaze   To dilute and wash down pan juices by adding liquid

Demitasse   A small cup of coffee served after dinner

Devil, to   To prepare with hot seasoning or sauce

Dice   To cut into small cubes

Dot   To scatter small bits of butter over top of a food

Dredge   To coat with something, usually flour or sugar

Filé   A powder made of sassafras leaves and used for seasoning and thickening foods

Filet   Boneless piece of meat or fish

Flambé   To flame, as in Crêpes Suzette or in some meat cookery, using alcohol as the burning agent; flame causes some caramelization, enhancing flavor

Flan   In France, a filled pastry; in Spain, a custard

Florentine   A food containing, or placed upon, spinach

Fold   To add a whipped ingredient, such as cream or egg white to another ingredient by gentle over and under movement

Frappé   A drink whipped with ice to make a thick, frosty consistency

Fricassee   A stew, usually of poultry or veal

Fritter   Vegetable or fruit dipped into, or combined with, batter and fried

Fry   To cook in hot shortening

Garnish A decoration for a food or drink, for example a sprig of parsley

Glaze (To make a shiny surface) In meat preparation, a jelled broth applied to meat surface; in breads and pastries, a wash of egg or syrup; for doughnuts and cakes, a coating with a sugar preparation

Gratin, au A food served crusted with bread crumbs or shredded cheese

Grill To broil under or over a source of direct heat, such as charcoal

Grits Coarsely ground dried corn, served either boiled or boiled, then fried

Gumbo Soup or stew made with okra

Hollandaise A sauce made of butter, egg, and lemon juice or vinegar

Hominy Whole corn grains from which hull and germ have been removed

Jardiniere Vegetables in a savory sauce or soup

Julienne Vegetables cut into long thin strips or a soup containing such vegetables

Jus, au Meat served in its own juice

Kahlua A coffee-flavored liqueur

King, à la Food prepared in a creamy white sauce containing mushrooms and red and/or green peppers

Kirsch (or Kirschwasser) A cherry-flavored liqueur

Knead To fold, press, and stretch dough with hands

Maître d'hotel Style Plainly cooked food, usually meat, served in parsley-flavored butter sauce

Marinade A seasoned liquid in which food is soaked

Marinate, to To soak food in a seasoned liquid

Mayonnaise A rich sauce made of egg, oil, and lemon juice or vinegar

Meringue A whole family of egg white-sugar preparations including pie topping, poached meringue used to top custard, crisp "egg kiss" cookies, crisp meringue dessert shells, Italian meringue (such as 7-minute frosting), and divinity candy

Mince To chop as finely as possible

Mornay White sauce with egg, cream, and cheese added

Mousse A molded dish based on meat or sweet whipped cream stiffened with egg white and/or gelatin (if mousse contains ice cream, it is called bombe)

Mousseline Sauce A sauce made of 1 part whipped cream to 2 parts hollandaise

Naturel, au To serve natural style, that is raw and unseasoned

Panbroil To cook over direct heat in an uncovered skillet containing little or no shortening

Panfry To cook in an uncovered skillet in a shallow amount of shortening

Parboil To partially cook in boiling water before proceeding with final cooking

Pasta Any of a large family of flour paste products, such as spaghetti, macaroni, and noodles

Pâté (French for paste) A paste made of liver or meat

Paupiette Thin slice of meat stuffed and rolled; a meat roll

Petit Four A small cake, which has been frosted and decorated

Pilau (pilaf in French) A dish of the Middle East consisting of rice and meat or vegetables in a seasoned stock

Poach To cook in liquid held below the boiling point

Pot liquor Vegetable stock

Praline A confection of boiled sugar and nuts, which is sometimes finely crushed and used to flavor dessert preparations

Puree A thick sauce or paste made by forcing cooked food through a sieve

Reduce To boil down, evaporating liquid from a cooked dish

Remoulade A rich mayonnaise-based sauce containing anchovy paste, capers, herbs, and mustard

Render To melt fat away from surrounding meat

Rind Outer shell or peel of melon or fruit

Roulade A thin slice of meat, stuffed and rolled, which is also called a meat roll or paupiette

Roux A mixture of butter and flour used to thicken gravies and sauces; the color may be brown (if mixture is browned before liquid is added) or white

Sangría A beverage based on dry red wine and flavored with various fruit juices (and sometimes brandy) and served cold

Sauté To fry food lightly over fairly high heat in a small amount of fat in a shallow, open pan

Scald To heat liquid, such as milk, not quite to boiling point, or to dip food into boiling water to help loosen skins, as for tomatoes or peaches

Scallop A bivalve mollusk of which only the muscle hinge is eaten; also to bake a food in a sauce topped with crumbs

Score To cut shallow gashes on surface of food, as in scoring fat on ham before glazing

Sear To brown surface of meat over high heat to seal in juices

Set Term used to describe gelatin when it has jelled enough to unmold

Shred To reduce a food to small pieces by rubbing it on a metal plate with sharp-edged perforations

Simmer To cook gently at a temperature below boiling point

Singe To touch lightly with flame

Sliver A fine thin slice, as in slivered almonds

Soak To immerse in water for a period of time

Soufflé A savory main dish or a sweet dessert made light and spongy by adding egg white

Steam To cook food with steam either in a pressure cooker, on a platform in a covered pan, or in a special steamer

Steep To let a food stand in not quite boiling water until flavor is extracted

Stew A mixture of meat or fish and vegetables cooked by simmering in its own juices and liquid, such as water and/or wine

Stir To mix with a steady, circular motion with a spoon, whisk, or beater

Stir-fry To cook quickly in oil over high heat, using light tossing and stirring motions to preserve shape of food

Stock The broth in which meat, poultry, fish, or vegetables has been cooked

Syrupy Thickened to about the consistency of egg white

Toast To brown by direct heat, as in a toaster or under broiler

Torte A round cake, sometimes made with bread crumbs instead of flour, which may contain dried fruits and nuts

Tortilla A Mexican flat bread made of corn or wheat flour

Toss To mix together with light tossing motions, in order not to bruise delicate food, such as salad greens

Tournedo Choice filet of beef

Triple Sec An orange-flavored liqueur

Veal Flesh of a milk-fed calf up to 14 weeks of age

Velouté White sauce made of flour, butter, and a chicken or veal stock, instead of milk

Vinaigrette A cold sauce of oil and vinegar flavored with parsley, finely chopped onions and other seasonings and served with cold meats or vegetables

Wok A round bowl-shaped metal cooking utensil of Chinese origin used for stir-frying and steaming (with rack inserted) of foods

Zest The paper-thin, colored outer peel of citrus fruit

Index